University of Plymouth
Charles Seale Hayne Library
Subject to status this item may be renewed
via your Primo account

http:/primo.plymouth.ac.uk
Tel: (01752) 588588

Dyadic Decision Making

David Brinberg   James Jaccard
Editors

Dyadic Decision Making

With 17 Illustrations

Springer-Verlag
New York Berlin Heidelberg
London Paris Tokyo

David Brinberg
Marketing Department
School of Business
State University of New York at Albany
Albany, NY 12222
USA

James Jaccard
Department of Psychology
State University of New York at Albany
Albany, NY 12222
USA

Library of Congress Cataloging-in-Publication Data
Dyadic decision making/edited by David Brinberg, James Jaccard.
    p. cm.
    Bibliography: p.
    Includes indexes.
    ISBN-13: 978-1-4612-8136-8
    1. Marriage—United States—Decision making. 2. Decision-making—United States.
I. Brinberg, David. II. Jaccard, James.
HQ728.D93 1988
302.3—dc19   88-15989

Printed on acid-free paper

© 1989 by Springer-Verlag New York Inc.
Softcover reprint of the hardcover 1st edition 1989

Typeset by Asco Trade Typesetting Ltd., Hong Kong.

9 8 7 6 5 4 3 2 1

ISBN-13: 978-1-4612-8136-8   e-ISBN-13:978-1-4612-3516-3
DOI: 10.1007/978-1-4612-3516-3

Preface

The study of dyadic decision making requires a multidisciplinary perspective. The chapters we have drawn together in this volume each address different components of the dyadic decision process. Four disciplines are represented in this volume—psychology, consumer behavior, communication, and sociology. We have selected these areas of research because they provide information concerning both individual and dyadic level factors.

Within each of these four substantive areas, we have included at least one chapter that focuses on conceptual issues and at least one chapter that addresses procedural (or analytic) issues. The specific theories and methods used to examine dyadic decision making vary from area to area. For instance, communication researchers have focused on process variables (e.g., patterns of interaction) to describe a dyadic decision. Psychological researchers, on the other hand, have used theories and methods such as information integration technology to examine dyadic decisions.

In the section on psychological perspectives, Anderson and Armstrong present a detailed discussion on the application of information integration theory to dyadic decision making. The set of empirical studies described in their chapter provides an insightful illustration on the use of this theory for assessing the decision processes of married couples. Kenny and Acitelli present a brief review of group decision making, interpersonal perception, and an application of the round robin analytic technique to marital satisfaction and couple agreement. The third chapter in this section (Beach and Morrison) discusses the application of image theory to decisions about childbearing. That theory describes four images (or decision schema) that determine the decision process: self-image, which are the values, beliefs, and ethics of the individual; trajectory image, which are the immediate and remote goals of the individual; action image, which are the plans the individual implements to attain the goals; and projected image, which are the consequences the individual anticipates from his or her plans.

In the section on consumer behavior perspectives, Jaccard, Brinberg, and Dittus present an integration of the behavioral alternatives model with observational methods to examine dyadic decision processes. The thesis of that chapter is the need to assess, in depth, the perceptions and preferences of each individual in the dyad prior to the interaction, and then to evaluate the dyadic interaction by using a coding scheme that incorporates measures of preferences and perceptions. Kumar and Dillon summarize a variety of techniques currently available for the analysis of interaction data (e.g., the analysis of conditional probabilities, the use of log-linear and logit models). These authors conclude their chapter with a brief presentation of a general probabilistic model for the analysis of dyadic interaction. The next chapter in this section (Troutman and Shanteau) applies information integration theory toward husband-wife decision making about health care services. Several experiments are described that make use of integration theory on either experimenter-generated or individual-generated information in the analysis of decisions to select pediatricians.

In the section on communication perspectives, Fitzpatrick describes the use of the Relational Dimensions Inventory and a verbal interaction compliance-gaining coding system in the analysis of influence attempts in married couples. She found that the three couple types (i.e., independent, traditionals, and separates) used different compliance-gaining strategies in their interaction patterns. Sillars and Kalbflesch present a detailed discussion of the influence of decision styles (i.e., either implicit or explicit) on dyadic processes. External factors such as expertise, time, or energy are described as constraints or boundaries that influence the decision process. Poole and Billingsley discuss a theory of structuration to describe the dyadic decision process. That theory incorporates factors internal to the dyad (e.g., the individual's actions) and factors external to the dyad (e.g., social roles, nature of the decision task) in assessing the decision process.

In the section on sociological perspectives, Scanzoni presents a broad portrait of factors that influence joint decision making. In his view, joint decision making is influenced by context, process, and outcomes. Within context, numerous factors are postulated to influence the joint decision (e.g., economic, occupation, social class). Thomson describes the use of logit models for the estimation of decision rules used by married couples. She specified interaction models to represent decision rules of husbands and wives and tested for the effect of potential differences on a joint decision. In the final chapter of this section, Szinovacz focuses on the joint decision to retire. Within that context, she proposes a model of decision making that incorporates the perspective of each individual in the dyad.

Our major goal in this volume is to present to the reader a selection of theories and methods that provide some insight into the decision process of dyads. Our hope is that the set of chapters will stimulate researchers in this field to integrate, reshape, synthesize, or reformulate these theories and methods to create a new, more complex and sophisticated perspective on dyadic decision making.

David Brinberg
James Jaccard

Contents

Part 2   Consumer Behavior Perspectives

Chapter 4
Couple Decision Making: Individual- and Dyadic-Level Analysis
James Jaccard, David Brinberg, and Patricia Dittus

Chapter 5
Analyzing Sequential Categorical Data on Dyadic Interaction
Ajith Kumar and William R. Dillon

Chapter 6
Information Integration in Husband-Wife Decision Making
About Health-Care Services
C. Michael Troutman and James Shanteau

Chapter 12
Decision-Making on Retirement Timing
Maximiliane Szinovacz 286

Part 5   A Reprise

Chapter 13
Multiple Perspectives on Dyadic Decision Making
David Brinberg and James Jaccard 313

Contributors

Linda K. Acitelli Center for Research on Learning and Teaching, University of Michigan, Ann Arbor, MI 48109, USA

Norman H. Anderson Department of Psychology, University of California, San Diego, La Jolla, CA 92093, USA

Margaret A. Armstrong Department of Psychology, University of California, San Diego, La Jolla, CA 92093, USA

Lee Roy Beach Department of Psychology, University of Washington, Seattle, WA 98195, USA

Julie Billingsley Department of Speech Communication, University of Minnesota, Minneapolis, MN 55455, USA

David Brinberg Department of Marketing, SUNY-Albany, Albany, NY 12222, USA

William R. Dillon Department of Marketing, University of South Carolina, Columbia, SC 29208, USA

Patricia Dittus Department of Psychology, SUNY-Albany, Albany, NY 12222, USA

Mary Anne Fitzpatrick Center for Communication Research, University of Wisconsin, Madison, WI 53706, USA

James Jaccard Department of Psychology, SUNY-Albany, Albany, NY 12222, USA

Pam J. Kalbflesch Department of Speech Communication, California State University Northridge, Northridge, CA 91330, USA

David A. Kenny   Department of Psychology, University of Connecticut, Storrs, CT 06268, USA

Ajith Kumar   Department of Marketing, SUNY-Albany, Albany, NY 12222, USA

Diane Morrison   Department of Psychology, University of Washington, Seattle, WA 98195, USA

Marshall Scott Poole   Department of Speech Communication, University of Minnesota, Minneapolis, MN 55455, USA

John Scanzoni   Department of Sociology, University of Florida, Gainesville, FL 32611, USA

James Shanteau   Department of Psychology, Kansas State University, Manhattan, KS 66506–7095, USA

Alan L. Sillars   Department of Interpersonal Communication, University of Montana, Missoulu, MT 59812, USA

Maximiliane Szinovacz   Division of Human Development and Family Ecology, University of Illinois, Urbana IL 61801, USA

Elizabeth Thomson   Department of Sociology, University of Wisconsin, Madison, WI 53706, USA

C. Michael Troutman   Charles, Charles and Associates Inc., 8676 West 96 Street, Suite 200, Overland Park, KS 66212, USA

Part 1
Psychological Perspectives

CHAPTER 1

Cognitive Theory and Methodology for Studying Marital Interaction

Norman H. Anderson and Margaret A. Armstrong

This chapter approaches dyadic interaction in terms of a unified theory of social cognition. Dyadic interaction is considered communication of information and is conceptualized within the framework of the theory of information integration (Anderson, 1981a, 1982). This theory, IIT for short, studies how people evaluate and integrate diverse pieces of information in arriving at judgments and decisions. Within social psychology, IIT has been applied in nearly every area, including person cognition, attitudes, attribution, moral judgment, and social development. Applications to dyadic interaction are reviewed in this chapter, with primary concern for marital interaction.

Information integration theory is a cognitive theory, as indicated by its analysis of information processing. It differs from mainstream cognitive theory, however, by its focus on goals and experiences of everyday life. In particular, IIT has central concern with affect and emotion, which have largely been ignored in mainstream cognitive theory.

Everyday life has been a primary domain of IIT. This is the domain of everyday motivations and actions, of liking and affection, of desire and jealousy, of striving, excuses, and blame, and of heartfelt love and shared quiet happiness. For this domain of everyday psychodynamics, IIT provides a theoretical foundation that has had substantial empirical success.

In this chapter, a key theme is *personal design*. Personal design aims to apply experimental methods at the level of the individual, by personalizing an experimental task to the individual's own experience and knowledge. Personal design seems useful, sometimes essential, to allow for particular contexts and situations. Personal design thus seems suited to the study of married life, which is the main concern of this chapter.

Personal design is in the initial stages of development, and the experiments reported here are exploratory applications. It is hoped that they will bring out something of the uses and limitations of personal design, especially of its potential for studying marriage and family life.

Theoretical Overview

Dyadic interaction is considered here as social communication of information. Social communication involves sending and receiving of information signals in pursuit of goals. The sender constructs signals that communicate attraction, threat, distress, and so on, often relying heavily on nonverbal components such as dress, tone of voice, facial expression, posture, and gesture. This complex of signal information must then be integrated by the receiver.

Nearly always there are multiple information signals. How to react to criticism from a spouse depends not only on the manifest content of the criticism, but also on other information, such as cues to intentions. Quarreling and making up, similarly, involve a temporal sequence of information signals. Judgment and action thus depend on integration of information—a basic problem for cognitive theory.

This problem of information integration is the theoretical focus of IIT. Information integration follows certain rules whose structure can be determined using concepts and methods of IIT. This section presents a brief overview of basic concepts (see also Anderson, 1981a,b, 1986, 1988, in press).

Knowledge Systems

Knowledge systems are organized complexes similar to schemas. Knowledge systems, however, contain affect and value, which are excluded from most schema concepts. Knowledge systems are also dynamic, for they include operators for processing affective and semantic knowledge in relation to goals.

Within IIT, attitudes are considered a prototypical class of knowledge systems. This differs qualitatively from the modal view in social psychology, which defines attitudes as one-dimensional evaluative reactions. Such evaluative reactions are here considered only one class of attitudinal responses, which are qualitatively different from the underlying attitude, considered as a knowledge system. This distinction between attitudes as knowledge systems and attitudinal responses has general importance, as in helping to clear up prevailing confusion over attitude-behavior relations. A final section gives a more detailed comparison of IIT with other attitude theories.

Dyadic interaction relies heavily on attitudes and related knowledge systems. Family interaction is special, however, in that it is itself a basic determinant of attitudes. This aspect of family life is explored in the first several experimental studies of the later empirical section.

Motivation and Affect

Information integration theory treats motivation and affect as integral aspects of cognition. Since this view differs from predominant conceptions in both cognitive and social psychology, not to mention sociology, it deserves justification. One argument for the present view is that in human society biological motivations are so heavily overlaid with social learning as to be cognitive in structure as well as in content. A more basic argument is that motivation and affect *are* biosocial information; they provide signals whose biosocial function is to guide judgment and action (Anderson, 1988, in press).

Nowhere are motivation and affect more important than in dyadic interaction. The family, in particular, is a primary center of affective life and a basic source of values. In work and play, moreover, self-esteem is a primary motivational factor as is goal-attainment itself. Any complete theory of cognition must recognize and incorporate such basic affective forces.

This informational view of motivation and affect seems so simple and necessary that it is worth considering what led to the predominance of other views. The historical reasons are different for the three cited fields. Sociology, of course, finds it awkward to deal with psychological concepts such as motivation and affect. Mainstream cognitive psychology was largely conceived in terms of perceptual problems such as letter-word recognition, on one hand, and a serial computer metaphor, on the other hand, neither of which had any natural representation for motivation and affect. Social psychology itself clung to the classic armchair trichotomy of affect-cognition-volition, and later to arousal theory, in which verbal, "cognitive" labels were necessary to define the quality of emotion. In IIT, by contrast, affective and nonaffective information have equivalent status.

Assemblage and Action

Action in any particular situation involves activation of selected memory information. This includes components of relevant attitudes as well as pragmatic information for dealing with the situation. Action thus depends on cognitive construction, or *assemblage,* that is controlled by operative motivations and goals. Two forms of assemblage will be described briefly here to illustrate some of the conceptual issues.

One form of assemblage may be represented as a sequence, for example, a sequence of actions to attain a goal. The assemblage involves construction of some mental representation of the sequence. This form of assemblage is related to current concepts of plans (e.g., Miller, Galanter, & Pribram, 1960), mental models (e.g., Johnson-Laird, 1983), as well as to the image theory of Beach and Morrison (this volume). Goal-oriented assemblage is ubiquitous in marital interaction, as with resolving conflict among goals of wife and husband. Role behavior, a dominant concern of much sociological theory, may also be considered assemblage, in which role prototypes are integrated with one another and with situational determinants to produce an operating role. This form of assemblage is basic to social thought and action.

A second form of assemblage may be represented as multiple determination, in which multiple factors determine some judgment or action. In the later experimental studies, for example, blame depends on the three determinants of damage, intention, and extenuation. Marriage satisfaction and decisions depend similarly on multiple determinants.

Multiple determination is a central problem for cognitive theory and it is the primary focus of IIT, as indicated in the following discussion of the information integration diagram. A key advantage of IIT is the associated functional measurement methodology, which can, under certain conditions, fractionate the observed judgment or action into otherwise unobservable determinants.

This measurement capability opens up a new way of thinking. Most actions depend on integration of both affective and nonaffective determinants. The traditional affective-nonaffective dichotomy loses its meaning when functional measurement can measure the separate contributions of affective and nonaffective determinants on a common scale of measurement. Similarly, traditional views of emotion as conscious experience become untenable when functional measurement can measure and validate the separate contributions of conscious and unconscious emotion (Anderson, in press). How this is possible is indicated in the next three subsections.

Information Integration Diagram

Three kinds of processing are basic to IIT, namely, *valuation, integration,* and *action,* as depicted in the simplified diagram of Figure 1.1. The person is

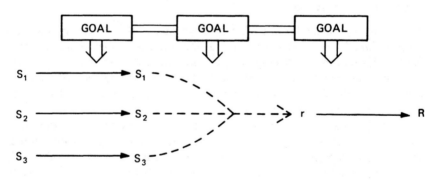

INTEGRATION DIAGRAM

VALUATION	INTEGRATION	RESPONSE
V-FUNCTION	I-FUNCTION	A-FUNCTION
(PSYCHOPHYSICAL LAW)	(PSYCHOLOGICAL LAW)	(PSYCHOMOTOR LAW)

Figure 1.1. Information integration diagram. Chain of three linked operators, V, I, and A, leads from field of observable stimuli, {S_i}, to observable response, R. Valuation operator, V, transforms observable stimuli, S_i, into subjective representations, s_i. Integration operator, I, transforms subjective stimulus field, {s_i}, into implicit response, r. Action operator, A, transforms implicit response, r, into observable response, R. (After N. H. Anderson, 1981a. *Foundations of Information Integration Theory,* New York: Academic Press, 1981.)

considered to reside in a field of information. Observable stimuli, uppercase S_i, are integrated by the cognitive machinery to produce some observable response, uppercase R. The three processing operators lead from the information field to the observable response.

The first operator is *valuation*, denoted by V, which gives stimuli their meaning and value. Primary concern is not with the physical stimuli, therefore, but with their subjective counterparts, denoted by lowercase s_i. Valuation is goal-directed, as the diagram indicates, for it is axiomatic that the same physical stimulus may have different values and implications relative to different goals. Valuation is also personal, for two persons may interpret the same physical stimulus in different ways.

The *integration* operator, I, combines the several separate stimuli into a unified response, denoted by lowercase r. This internal response is then made overt through the *action* operator, A. Both I and A depend on the goal, as indicated in the diagram (see also Anderson, 1981a, in press).

This distinction between V, I, and A is essential for any theory that attempts to handle multiple determination. Information integration theory provides an effective analysis of all three operators. This analysis is based on the cognitive algebra of integration, as illustrated in the following subsection.

Cognitive Algebra: The Parallelism Theorem

Work in IIT has demonstrated the existence of a fairly general *cognitive algebra*. Simple algebraic rules have been found to govern judgment in virtually every area of psychology, from psychophysics to person cognition. Cognitive algebra appears to be a natural capability of the mind, for it appears in children as young as 3 + years of age.

The power and simplicity of cognitive algebra may be illustrated with the parallelism theorem, which provides an analysis of adding-type models. Consider two stimulus variables, A and B, manipulated in a standard row × column factorial design. Let the subjective value of stimulus S_{Ai} in row i of the design be s_{Ai} and similarly let the subjective value of stimulus S_{Bj} in column j be s_{Bj}. The integrated subjective response to the pair of stimuli (S_{Ai}, S_{Bj}) is denoted by r_{ij}, and the corresponding observed response is denoted by R_{ij}. This notation follows the foregoing integration diagram.

The primary hypothesis of additivity must be written in terms of subjective values:

$$r_{ij} = s_{Ai} + s_{Bj}. \tag{1}$$

This hypothesis has long eluded test. The obvious step is to measure the three terms of the equation to check if they add up. But this will not work unless all three terms are measured on true psychological scales with comparable units and zero points. Such measurement scales have not been available. From the psychophysics of Fechner to the paired comparisons of Thurstone, linear (equal interval) scales of subjective value have been a matter of controversy. Without such scales, the additive model, although widely popular, has perforce remained conjectural.

The parallelism theorem employed in IIT provides a simple test for the hypothesis of additivity that simultaneously solves the problems of measurement. The hypothesis of additivity is supplemented by an assumption of response linearity, specifically, that

$$R_{ij} = c_0 + c_1 r_{ij}, \qquad (2)$$

where c_0 and c_1 are inessential zero and unit constants. Under this linearity assumption, the observable response, R_{ij}, is a linear function of the unobservable response, r_{ij}. The parallelism theorem may then be stated as follows.

Parallelism Theorem

Suppose that the adding rule of Equation (1) *holds and that the response scale is linear, as in Equation* (2). *Then the factorial graph will form a set of parallel curves. Also, the row means of the factorial design will estimate the subjective values of the row stimuli on linear scales, and similarly for the column means.*

The parallelism theorem thus provides an objective test of additivity, based on the observable property of parallelism. An empirical illustration of a *factorial graph* is shown later in the initial experiment of Figure 1.2, which also illustrates the parallelism property. Such observed parallelism provides strong support for the primary hypothesis of additivity. The logic and ramifications of the parallelism theorem are discussed more extensively in the cited references, but two aspects deserve mention here.

Prior knowledge of the subjective stimulus values is not required by the parallelism theorem. Whereas previous attempts at psychological measurement have taken stimulus measurement as primary, functional measurement succeeded because it finessed the problem of stimulus measurement. Indeed, the stimulus values may be derived once the key property of parallelism has been established: the second conclusion of the theorem implies that the stimulus values are just the marginal means of the factorial data table.

Observed parallelism thus accomplishes three simultaneous goals:

1. It supports the adding rule of integration.
2. It supports the linearity of the observable response measure.
3. It provides linear (equal interval) scales of the stimulus variables.

The power of the theorem may be shown by noting that *non*parallelism will generally be obtained if just one of the two assumptions is incorrect. There is, of course, a logical possibility that nonlinearity in the response will just offset nonadditivity in the integration rule to yield net parallelism. This logical possibility becomes empirically relevant in certain situations, but need not be considered further here.

The success of the parallelism theorem has depended on two conditions. First, nature has endowed the mind with adding-type rules. Without this, the parallelism theorem would be barren formalism. Second, practical procedures have been developed that eliminate various measurement biases to obtain true linear scales for the response measure (Anderson, 1981a, Chapter 1; see also Chapter 5).

Cognitive Algebra: General Considerations

Other algebraic rules may be studied in similar manner. Multiplication rules, ratio rules, and, most important, averaging rules, have been found in many areas. This cognitive algebra has provided a foundation for psychological measurement, especially of social concepts, such as likableness and fairness, and of affective reactions, such as hope and blame. This *functional measurement* solves a longstanding problem in psychology, for it can provide validated linear (equal interval) and ratio scales of psychological entities at the level of the individual person and within the particular context and situation.

Cognitive algebra has provided a new beachhead for cognitive analysis. That cognition often follows algebraic rules is interesting in itself. Not less important, the algebraic rules provide a base for analysis of nonalgebraic rules and processes. Of special interest is that cognitive algebra can analyze unconscious determinants of conscious experience, thus providing a validational base for phenomenology.

Personal Experimental Design

A primary concern of this chapter is with personal experimental design. Experimental control is the most effective and perhaps the only truly satisfactory tool for probing complex systems. Although experimental manipulation has severe limitations of practicability, as experimentalists are aware, it can provide analytical power not otherwise available.

Information integration theory conjoins experimental control with quantitative model analysis, as indicted in the foregoing overview. Personal design aims to set the experiment within the experiential framework of the individual. A complete experiment may thus be constructed around the individual. Although relatively undeveloped, personal design seems attractive for the study of attitudes, judgments, and actions of everyday life.

Personal Design

Personal design has two main characteristics: it applies experimental analysis at the level of the individual and it employs personalized stimulus manipulation. In one ideal form, the design would be constructed around some life event of the individual's past, present, or future. The event might be a reliving of a husband-wife quarrel, for example, a current decision about medical regimen, or a plan for having children. The design would present various combinations of information about the event, chosen to be meaningful to the individual and to constitute a factorial-type design. Processes of valuation and integration could then be studied using concepts and methods of IIT already outlined.

Construction of a personal design depends on the question being studied by the investigator. In the study of marriage satisfaction of Figure 1.6, for example, the informational stimuli were remembered incidents from the woman's own marriage. In a reliving of a quarrel, the informational stimuli could be alternative versions of what each person said or "should have said," and the judgment could be how much each was to blame in each variant quarrel. In a prospective decision, the informational stimuli could define the properties of ideal and real choice alternatives, and the judgment could be of the preference value of each alternative, much as in the study of contraceptive use cited later. Values, integration rules, and various cognitive processes could then be studied using the concepts and methods already outlined.

Personal experimental design has not received much systematic attention, although many investigators have employed the essential ideas to greater or lesser degree. Design considerations will differ for husband-wife or dating-couple decisions (Armstrong, 1984; Armstrong & Anderson, 1983; Jaccard & Becker, 1985), for dyadic bargaining (Graesser, 1977, Figure 1.8 following), for studies of phobic reactions or chronic pain (Anderson, in press), and for case law (Hommers & Anderson, in press). The experimental examples of the later empirical section illustrate a number of applications. The following subsections consider uses and limitations of personal experimental design in relation to other approaches.

Phenomenology

Phenomenology plays a basic role in IIT because of mutual concern with everyday life. Phenomenology is a basis for personalization of design as well as a source of theoretical hypotheses. Conversations, interviews, observations, and other everyday experiences can provide priceless clues about psychological structure and process. To this extent, IIT is in harmony with the various phenomenologically based approaches, ranging from Piaget's (1932/1965) studies of moral judgment to the sociological schools of symbolic interaction (see Stryker & Statham, 1985).

Phenomenology, however, is fundamentally inadequate as a base for knowledge inquiry. Phenomenology has been obstinately erroneous, as illustrated by the meaning-constancy investigations (Anderson, 1981a, Chapter 3), because it lacks a validity criterion to correct itself. Everday explanations are sometimes no more than post hoc rationalizations or cognitive illusions. Phenomenology takes these at face value because it takes itself at face value.

Phenomenology is inherently inadequate. It cannot, even in principle, be made adequate; some aspects of psychological process are inaccessible to introspection. In emotion theory, for example, functional measurement leads to definition and measurement of emotion at both conscious and unconscious levels (Anderson, in press). Both are essential. In this case, as in general, everyday explanations cannot be understood without capability for analysis of processes not accessible to consciousness.

Personal design can help place phenomenology on a solid foundation. Although phenomenology can provide priceless clues, it also provides clues that are worthless or misleading. The problem is to utilize the information in phenomenological report without going astray on the misinformation. Phenomenology is inadequate because it lacks a validational base. With personal design, IIT aims to provide a validational base for better utilization of phenomenological report.

Observational Approaches

Personal experimental design seems a useful complement to the observational approaches to marriage. These approaches have emphasized systematic observation of wife-husband interaction and coding of this interaction in terms of objective, observable categories of behavior (see, e.g., Bakeman & Gottman, 1986; Filsinger & Lewis, 1981; Gottman, 1979). Such observational data can help diagnose distressed and nondistressed couples (e.g., Olson & Ryder, 1970; Birchler, 1979), which has been the most popular issue. More generally, observational data can reveal important information about interaction dynamics, including information that would not be available from phenomenological report.

Personal design agrees with the observational approaches in concern with systematic assessment of married life, but personal design also places central emphasis on experimental manipulation, as illustrated in the later discussion of the Inventory of Marital Conflict (Olson & Ryder, 1970). Observation data alone, without such experimental manipulation, cannot answer basic theoretical questions about attitudes towards obligation, responsibility, attribution, blame, and other issues of social cognition. Systematic design is essential for progress in social cognition, especially psychodynamics of everyday life.

From the perspective of social cognition, the observational aproaches appear narrow and bleak. Attitudes, attributions, and roles receive little attention. Aspirations, motivations, and goals, which are surely essential to understanding marriage, are similarly ignored. Even simple affective reactions, such as feelings of affection and resentment, have received only limited recognition (Lowman, 1981).

This neglect of social cognition arises in part because the usual coding categories are too narrow to describe the psychodynamics of everyday life. This narrowness is understandable. Much work is needed to develop an observational procedure, so it seems natural to begin with objective, observable behaviors that allow unambiguous coding categories. The danger is that failure to incorporate social cognition at an early stage will lead to methods that cannot be broadened at later stages. This danger is well illustrated in Conger and Smith's (1981) study of equity, which runs afoul of virtually every concept of psychological equity theory (Anderson, 1976a; Farkas & Anderson, 1979; Farkas, in press; Walster, Walster, & Berscheid, 1978), especially in its failure to recognize that equity must be defined in subjective terms.

This same danger appears in Gottman's (1979, pp. 289–292) claim that the behavioral sciences have suffered from premature theorizing and that the essential first phase of investigation is discovery and description of the phenomena. This claim has some justification, and Gottman's own investigations are impressive in thoroughness and dedication. But Gottman's structural model is tied to its observational categories and has minimal relation to any of the concepts of social cognition just cited.

As an inductive theory, IIT is sympathetic with the emphasis on phenomena that appears in the observational approaches. But phenomena are not merely observables; they depend in part on theory for their definition. Observational data are not enough. The observational method is not enough. Observation, experiment, and theory need to advance hand in hand.

Group Design

Personal design aims to construct a complete experiment around single individuals. This differs from common group design, in which different subjects are randomly assigned to different experimental conditions. Both kinds of design have advantages and limitations, many of which revolve around the distinction between outcome generality and process generality (Anderson, 1981a, pp. 91–92).

Group design is appropriate for studies concerned with outcome generality, as in assessing instructional programs for marriage and parenting, for example, or therapeutic treatments for marital difficulties. The large individual differences in response to such treatments make it necessary to use fairly large numbers of individuals to assess and establish generality of the outcomes.

Personal design is typically concerned with analysis of psychological process rather than outcomes. Analysis of integration rules, for example, is generally most satisfactory using individual-subject design. Group design is far less powerful than within-subject, repeated-measurements design (Anderson, 1981a, Section 1.3.2), and even within-subject design can average out real individual differences (e.g., Anderson, 1981a, Section 1.3.4).

Personal design still seeks generality across individuals, of course, which makes it necessary to run a number of individuals. Communication of the results, however, usually precludes presentation of all individual analyses and entails some kind of summary statistics. When most individuals follow similar rules, a group mean graph may suffice, as in the marital attitude studies of Figures 1.2–1.5. In other cases, it is necessary to cluster subjects into subgroups, as in Leon's (1984) study of mother-son similarity, which found three different integration rules. And in some cases, it may be most useful to present graphs for selected subjects, as in Shanteau and Nagy's (1979) study of date preferences (see Anderson, 1981a, Figure 1.24).

Choice of design thus depends both on the kinds of questions being asked by the investigator and on the nature and extent of individual differences. However, one general rule seems warranted: outcome generality and process generality are typically incompatible, so it is advisable to be clear about which is desired and to design the experiment accordingly.

Extensions of Personal Design

Personal design can be simplified in various ways and made more flexible than is indicated in the foregoing parallelism theorem, which requires a factorial design. The main reason for using factorial design is to maximize power in assessment of integration rules. For other questions, factorial design may be unnecessarily demanding.

One such extension is illustrated in the single story method of Study 3 of marital attitudes presented later. This method allowed test of a change manipulation with a single story and before-after measurement. With a number of such stories, it was possible to compare wife and husband influences, to obtain generality, and to provide a proper statistical test.

A different kind of extension involves *self-estimation methodology*, in which subjects are asked directly for their personal scale values and weights. Self-estimation methods have been suspect because they are subject to various biases, as illustrated in the controversy between ratings and magnitude estimation. Progress was blocked because no validity criterion was available for determining the true values and weights. This difficulty was resolved by cognitive algebra, which was able to determine true values, as illustrated in the parallelism theorem. With such criteria, methods of self-estimation can be validated and used more generally. Progress has been promising (Anderson, 1982, Chapter 6; Anderson & Zalinski, in press), as illustrated later in the study of attitudes in dyadic discussions of Figure 1.7.

Empirical Analysis

Seven applications of IIT to dyadic interactions are presented in this section. The first four deal with marriage and the last with contraceptive behavior by college students. The remaining two deal with casual dyads but are included because of their methodological importance for studying marital interaction. Aside from their substantive interest, all involve some degree of personal experimental design, and serve to bring out prospects and problems of this approach.

Marital Attitudes: Study 1

This experiment was the first of a sequence that studied marital influence in attitudes (Armstrong & Anderson, 1983). A primary issue in this first study concerned the operation of cognitive algebra in wife-husband interaction. Disciplinary judgments about children's misdeeds were chosen for study here, in part because of their relevance to family life, in part because cognitive algebra of moral judgment had been studied extensively in developmental psychology. Following customary usage, the term *attitude* is used here and in the following experiments for what are strictly attitudinal responses as defined earlier.

Method and Procedure

Method and procedure are described in some detail, as they were much the same for the present and two following studies (Armstrong, 1984). Couples received stories about children who had misbehaved and judged how much discipline they deserved. Additional information was then given, but this was different for wife and husband. They exchanged information with each other and then revised their own judgments in light of their own and their partner's added information. This method of information exchange allowed separate assessments of the influence of husband on wife and of wife on husband.

The following story illustrates the nature of the integration task.

Danny's best friend was his dog Chips. One day, Chips bit Stevie, a new boy in the neighorhood. Stevie's parents had Chips taken away to the city pound.

Danny was really mad at Stevie, so he deliberately tried to hit Stevie with a rock.

The rock hit Stevie and broke his nose. Stevie had to have splints on his nose for a month.

As in this example, each story had three parts. The first part gave *background* information about the situation. The second part gave information about the *intent* of the misbehaving child, and the third part specified the *damage* caused by the child's action.

Stories were given in sets of 12, all with the same background information, but with different intent and damage information. Within each story set, damage varied from none to serious in four levels. Intent varied over three levels, namely, carelessness, intent to scare, and intent to harm. For each background situation, the 12 stories thus formed a 3 × 4, Intent × Damage factorial design (see Figure 1.2).

For generality, four sets of 12 stories were used, each with a different background situation and, of course, corresponding specifications of damage and intent. Extensive pilot work was performed to develop stories that would be realistic and meaningful, similar to child-rearing situations that arose in everyday life.

Initial judgments were made on the basis of the given story information, including background, intent, and damage. Additional information was then given, with one spouse receiving one piece of slightly negative information and the other spouse receiving three pieces of quite positive, extenuating information. Information was personalized through a *discussion procedure*, in which both spouses, on presenting the added information, discussed its relevance to the stimulus stories and how it had changed their own attitude. Following this information exchange, both members of the couple revised their judgments about deserved discipline.

The foregoing discussion procedure of information exchange had several purposes. The initial information provides a baseline from which changes in attitude can be measured; each subject's final attitude can thus be adjusted for initial attitude, thereby increasing power. The added information gives experimental control over the attitude change. The added information was split disproportionately between spouses so that the direction of change could be attributed to a particular spouse. Both spouses present some information, which preserves an atmosphere of mutuality that would be lost by giving all the added information to one spouse. Most important, the discussion procedure allows subjects to bring their own thoughts and experiences into the experimental situation.

The experiment was performed in each couple's home. A sample story was given to read, after which the judgment scale was explained. This was a 1 to 20 rating scale, employed with functional measurement methodology to obtain a linear response (Anderson, 1982, Chapter 1). This response scale was defined in terms of "how much discipline" the child deserved. Type of discipline was deliberately left unspecified since different subjects might have different ideas about spanking, for example, or scolding. A practice set of 12 stories was then given, followed by the first experimental set of 12 stories. Each spouse made separate independent judgments for each of the 12 stories.

The next step involved the information exchange. Each member of the couple was given different additional information, as already noted, and each in turn read aloud their information and commented on how it had changed their own attitude. Following this information exchange, the 12 stories were rerated as before. Altogether, four experimental sets of 12 stories were presented in this way. Each set involved the three steps just described. Stimulus materials were completely balanced across serial position and wife-husband.

Subjects were 20 married couples, age 19 to 36 years, in student housing at the University of California, San Diego. Each couple was paid $10 per hour for the experiment, which lasted about 2.5 hours.

Integration of Information

Two successive integrations are involved in this experiment: first, for the information about intent and damage given by the experimenter; second, for the additional information presented by the spouse. Both integrations appear to follow an adding-type process.

This integration process is revealed in the four factorial graphs of Figure 1.2. All four graphs have similar pattern, which can be explained with the upper-left graph. These 12 data points represent the wives' initial judgments, before the information exchange. The three curves represent the three given levels of intent, labeled beside each curve; the four points on each curve represent the four levels of damage, listed on the horizontal axis.

The trends in this graph exhibit the expected effects of each moral variable. The vertical spacing among the curves shows that stronger discipline is assigned when the child acts with more intent to harm. Similarly, the upward slope of each curve shows that stronger discipline is assigned when the child's action leads to greater damage.

Theoretical interest focuses on the pattern of near-parallelism in this graph. This pattern points to an adding-type rule, according to the parallelism the-

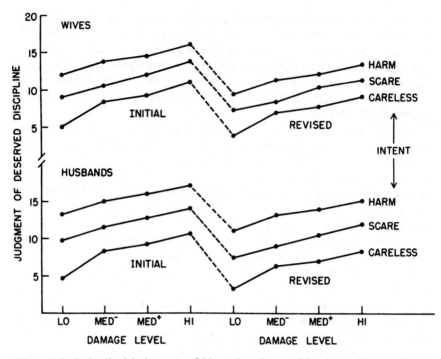

Figure 1.2. Attitudinal judgments of blame by wives and husband, Study 1. Initial judgments based on information about intent (curve parameter) and damage (horizontal axis). Revised judgments based on additional extenuating information presented by spouse. (Lo, Med⁻, Med⁺, and Hi represent four graded levels of damage.)

orem given previously. Husbands show a similar pattern of near-parallelism, as seen in the lower-left graph. The results of Figure 1.2 are thus consistent with previous developmental studies of moral judgment (e.g., Grueneich, 1982; Hommers & Anderson, 1985; Leon, 1980, 1984; Surber, 1977).

The second integration is of greater interest, for it involves new information transmitted by the spouse. The initial judgments, already seen in the left of Figure 1.2, must be revised to incorporate the spouse's information. These revised judgments are shown in the two right-hand graphs, for wives above and for husbands below. The revised judgments show a pattern of near-parallelism, similar to that in the initial judgments.

Strictly speaking, the adding-type rule exhibited in Figure 1.2 is actually an averaging rule. This averaging-adding distinction was one of the cruxes in the development of cognitive algebra, and it has extensive ramifications in theoretical interpretation and in experimental design. The averaging rule implies that the curves for the revised judgments will remain parallel but will have flatter slope and lie closer together than for the initial judgments. This prediction is supported for the wives in Figure 1.2, although not for the husbands. The subsequent experiments, however, show uniform support for the averaging rule for both wives and husbands.

One minor but consistent deviation from parallelism appears in the lower left-most data point of each graph. This data point represents a careless action that results in no damage and may be interpreted in terms of the accident-configural rule reported by Leon (1980). Some subjects discount carelessness when no damage occurs but not when there is damage. Except for this point, however, the parallelism patterns point to an adding-type rule for both integrations. It is a true cognitive equation, therefore, to say that

$$\text{Blame} = \text{Intent} + \text{Damage} - \text{Extenuation}.$$

Spouse Similarity in Moral Value

Wife and husband showed substantial similarity in moral value. Each subject was given two scores, Damage and Intent, to represent the main effects of the two moral variables, damage and intent. The Intent score may be envisaged as the vertical distance between the upper and lower curves in the left part of Figure 1.2. The Damage score, similarly, may be envisaged as the net vertical rise of a single curve. The moral ratio, Damage/(Damage + Intent), exhibited wide individual differences, from .06 to .90 for wives and from .03 to 1.00 for husbands.

These moral ratios were significantly correlated across couples, $r(19) = .56$, $p < .01$. The ratio score adjusts for individual differences in usage of the rating scale. Different subjects are thus directly comparable even though they differ in their zero points and units for the response scale.

A more illuminating view of this moral similarity is shown in Figure 1.3. The top-left panel shows the seven husbands with moral ratios greater than .5; these curves are close together, reflecting a relatively small effect of intent. The bottom-left panel shows the 13 husbands with moral ratios less than .5; these curves are far apart, reflecting a relatively large effect of intent. This difference in pattern between the top and bottom graphs merely reflects individual differences among the husbands.

The central point of Figure 1.3 is that the wives, graphed in the right panels, show the same patterns as their husbands. The curves are close together in the two top graphs for wives as well as husbands. These seven wives, therefore, show small effect of intent, like their husbands. Similarly, the curves are far apart in the two bottom graphs for wives as well as husbands. These 13 wives, therefore, show large effects of intent, like their husbands. This correlation of response pattern is similar to but more revealing than the foregoing correlation of moral ratios.

Spouse Influence

To assess the effect of each spouse on the other involves more complex analysis. The usual comparisons of wife-husband influence require wife and hus-

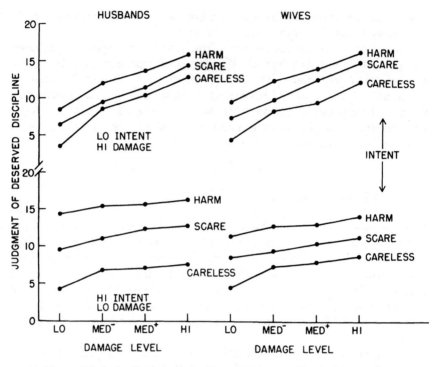

Figure 1.3. Attitudinal similarity between wives and husbands, Study 1.

band to reach a single, common judgment. The present method, in contrast, obtains private, separate judgments from both spouses and hence studies a nonforced influence process.

Relevant data are shown in Table 1.1, which presents mean attitudes before and after the information exchange, together with the change scores. The two change scores for wives, 1.96 and 1.98, are virtually identical, which implies that wives rely as much on their own information as on their husband's information. The wives are integrating the same added information in both cases, in effect, because of the story balancing in the design, but the information source is different. In the 75% case, the wives have the major information, whereas in the 25% case, their husbands have the major information. Attitude research implies that the major information will have greater effect when presented by more influential source (Anderson, 1981b; Eagly, 1983). Comparison of the two change scores is thus a comparison of the relative influence of the two sources, wife and husband, on the wife's judgment. Design and data thus show an egalitarian relation, in which wife and husband have equal influence on the wife's attitudinal judgment.

For the husbands, an exactly similar argument applies. Here again, the two change scores are almost identical, 2.17 versus 2.15. Both tests, for wives and

Table 1.1. Attitude change by wives and husbands: Study 1.

	Wives		Husbands	
	25%	75%	25%	75%
Initial attitude	11.52	11.14	11.93	11.98
Revised attitude	9.56	9.16	9.76	9.83
Change	1.96	1.98	2.17	2.15

Note: 25% and 75% denote percentages of added information presented by each spouse.

for husbands, thus show an egalitarian pattern of influence. This egalitarian outcome is not an artifact of group averaging, for it appeared in most of the individual couples as well. More important, this egalitarian outcome does not reflect a social demand of the experimental situation, such as politeness, for it appears in the private attitudes of both spouses.

Discussion

The foregoing results support the working hypothesis that marital interaction and influence follow simple cognitive processes, for information presented by the spouse was integrated by a simple adding-type rule. Indeed, the same adding-type rule was found for integration of information presented by the spouse as for information presented by the experimenter. This suggests that the cognitive algebra established in previous experimental work will generalize to marital interaction.

Cognitive algebra has been useful in studying other interpersonal processes, including social attribution, judgments of fairness and unfairness, and general person cognition. It provides a depth and precision of analysis not available with other methods. It seems reasonable to expect similar results in marital interaction, although the present experiment is only one step in this direction. Additional support is given in later experiments but two objections to the present interpretation must be considered here.

It has been objected that there is no essential difference between the information presented by the spouse and the information presented by the experimenter, for each spouse knows that the information presented by their partner originates from information supplied by the experimenter. This objection misses the main point. The operative stimulus in a spouse presentation has many elements not in the information supplied by the experimenter. These include oral and nonverbal factors of delivery as well as the spouse's own evaluation of the supplied information. The personal subjective value of this operative stimulus must be allowed for in order to determine the integration rule. That is what functional measurement does. Functional measurement makes complete and exact allowance for each and all elements of the operative stimulus, whether or not they can be independently observed and measured. This reflects the property of *molar unitization* discussed further in connection with Figure 1.7.

This issue is central to analysis of dyadic interaction. Without the present method, or some equivalent, the integration rule could not be determined. That each spouse will be substantially influenced by the information presented by their partner may be taken for granted; that is deliberately built into the experiment. But what is at issue is how this information is evaluated and how it is integrated. These questions cannot be resolved with customary methods. These questions can be resolved with functional measurement methodology.

The second objection, voiced by Filsinger (1983) and Hooper (1983), is that individual couple analysis will yield as many different descriptions as there are couples. But the fact is that all the couples followed the *same* integration rule. This commonality of process was demonstrated by the individual analyses.

Far from being a disadvantage, the present focus on response pattern provides a new tool for cognitive analysis. The present finding of a single common integration rule should not be expected in general. In some studies, different subgroups may appear, reflected in different response patterns (see, e.g., Leon, 1984). Once such individual differences have been established, it may be of interest to see how they correlate with external variables such as personality test scores or socioeconomic status. Such correlations are typically too weak, however, to be of much help in cognitive analysis.

Individual couples will certainly differ widely in their *values*. This was demonstrated by the individual variation in moral ratios. Even here, however, functional measurement methodology was able to provide a meaningful index, as shown by the spouse similarity of Figure 1.3.

Further Work: Spouse Similarity

Cognitive algebra provides new methods for studying similarity between spouses, as illustrated by the foregoing moral ratio score. The pattern of parallelism in Figure 1.2 indicates that the response scale is linear (equal interval), by virtue of the parallelism theorem. The moral ratio, Damage/(Damage + Intent), makes sense, therefore, because both numerator and denominator have common zero and common unit for each subject. Similar measurement logic underlies the comparison of wife-husband response patterns in Figure 1.3. The ratio score may be more useful than typical test scores, which do not adjust for individual differences in scale zero and unit.

For more extensive assessment of spouse similarity, it would seem desirable to obtain similar ratio scores from a battery of social judgment situations. Simpler design would also be desirable. In fact, ratio scores can be obtained from only a three-cell design (Anderson, 1982, Section 6.1.2). The larger factorial design used in the present experiment was important for establishing the model and the response scale. Once that is done, the simpler three-cell design is sufficient for measuring effect ratios.

Further Work: Marital Conflict

The present method may be used in conjunction with the Inventory of Marital Conflict (IMC) of Olson and Ryder (1970) to study wife-husband conflict. The IMC presents vignettes that represent common conflict situations, for example, a hypothetical husband's party behavior, and each spouse judges who is more to blame, first, on the basis of their own given information, and then after discussion with partner. Some vignettes give wife and husband different information to induce conflict.

The IMC vignettes are like the stories used in the present study and could be treated similarly. This would entail more systematic manipulation of the information given to each spouse to ensure initial differences of opinion. To attempt to hide this manipulation completely seems unnecessary and undesirable, for it could be rationalized in various ways without losing the intended conflict of opinion. An essential change would be to use a rating response of how much each spouse is to blame. The IMC choice response, which spouse is more to blame, loses quantitative information that is vital for cognitive analysis.

With these adaptations, the IMC vignettes could be used to study cognitive algebra of marital conflict and compromise, to measure spouse similarity, and to assess wife-husband influence and power relations. Judgment of blame, which is the focus of the vignettes, should follow the foregoing blame equation. Measurement of spouse similarity could use the simpler three-cell design of the preceding subsection. Assessment of influence and power could follow the method of Table 1.1 or use the simpler method described later in Study 3. In this way, functional measurement methodology could be personalized to study cognitive processes as they function in individual marriages.

Marital Attitudes: Study 2

One limitation of the previous experiment was that the information exchanged between spouses was given by the experimenter. A more personalized procedure was used in this experiment by having wife and husband themselves compose the information they presented their partner. The theoretical hypothesis was that self-composed information would exhibit the same processes already found for given information (Armstrong, 1984, 1985).

Procedure

General procedure was very similar to that of the previous experiment. Couples first judged two sets of Intent-Damage stories, as in Study 1, and then one set was assigned to each spouse. For their assigned story set, each spouse composed two pieces of extenuating information and also chose one of three pieces of extenuating information given by the experimenter. The spouse then read and discussed these three pieces of extenuating information with the partner, following which both revised their judgments. This procedure was repeated five times for a total of 10 story sets, half with additional information composed by the wife, half by the husband. The stories were given in sets of six, according to the 2 × 3, Intent × Damage design indicated in Figure 1.4. Subjects were 10 married couples living in university housing who received $50 for participating in two sessions of 2.5 to 3 hours.

Results and Discussion

The theoretical hypothesis was fully supported: information composed by the subjects is integrated by the same rule as information given by the experimenter. The data are shown in Figure 1.4, which follows the same format as Figure 1.2 from the previous experiment. The near-parallelism in the left panels shows the recurrence of the rule, Blame = Intent + Damage, for the initial judgments based on the experimenter-given information. The revised judgments in the right panels reflect the integration of the spouse-composed

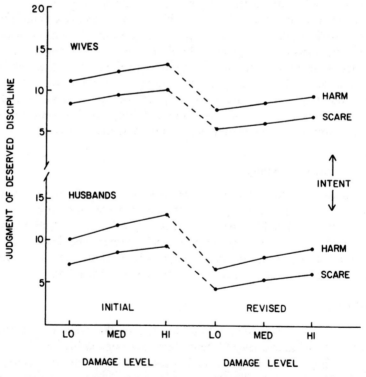

Figure 1.4. Attitudinal judgments of blame by wives and husbands, Study 2. Initial judgments based on information about intent (curve parameter) and damage (horizontal axis). Revised judgments based on additional extenuating information composed and presented by the spouse. (After Armstrong, 1984.)

extenuating information. This spouse-composed information caused substantial and highly significant attitude change, $F(1,18) = 54.41$.

The critical aspect of the data is the pattern of revised judgments in the right panels. Each pair of curves is parallel, which supports an adding-type rule, either averaging or summation. Compared with the corresponding left panel, however, each right-hand pair of curves is closer together and flatter in slope. Both differences are significant, as shown by the corresponding interaction terms, $F(1,18) = 7.00$ and $F(2,36) = 8.17$. This is just as predicted by the averaging rule but sharply contrary to a summation rule (see Armstrong, 1984). It is a true cognitive equation, therefore, to say

$$\text{Blame} = \text{Intent} + \text{Damage} - \text{Extenuation},$$

as long as this is understood to represent an averaging process.

This experiment extends the method of personal design to incorporate information composed by the subjects themselves. This allows more realistic information exchange, of a kind that not infrequently appears in everyday life. By formalizing this within the experimental design, experimenter-given and spouse-given information were shown to obey the same rule of integration.

Thompson (1985) has criticized the present method for neglecting processes involved in the information exchange and the attitude change. But the basic process is informational, following a chain of communication, evaluation, and integration. Information is communicated between spouses; this information is evaluated and integrated with prior information, resulting in changed attitudes. The present results show that this information processing follows exact quantitative rules.

Other methods of studying marital interaction (e.g., Bakeman & Gottman, 1986; Filsinger & Lewis, 1981) would be unable to determine the integration process. One reason is that they deal only with part of the information exchange, for much of the social interaction is unobservable. Information integration theory, in contrast, takes account of *all* the social communication. By virtue of the principle of molar unitization, discussed in the later study of attitudes in group discussion, functional measurement yields a complete and exact summary of each and every detail. In this respect, paradoxical though it may seem, a method that does not attempt detailed delineation of communication is superior to methods that do.

This point deserves reflection. There is no doubt of the usefulness of the cited observational approaches nor of the importance of detailed analysis of marital interaction. But the observational approaches have strong limitations, already discussed, that need recognition in any attempt to develop general theory of social cognition.

Further Work: Marital Conflict

The present procedure of self-composed information is attractive because it yields greater personalization than in the previous study, which relied on experimenter-given information. Although replication of the present study is needed, it indicates that the same integration processes operate in either case. Hence this procedure may be used to study moral algebra, spouse influence, and spouse similarity, in the manner previously outlined in the discussion of further work for Study 1.

Also attractive is the possibility of incorporating the present procedure within an observational framework, especially in marital therapy. The observational and experimental aproaches both have advantages that can be combined in a joint attack. This agrees with the aim of personal design to embed experimental manipulations within natural settings. Experimental control is still needed. This may be obtained by specifying the general tone of the to-be-composed information, as here, or with similar specifications.

Self-composed information will reflect each spouse's own values and conflicts. Indeed, self-composed information may be considered a projective test. With this kind of personalization, it should be possible to embed the study of social cognition within the dynamics of ongoing therapy.

Marital Attitudes: Study 3

The goal of this experiment was more extensive analysis of influence processes within individual couples. Although the factorial design used previously is appropriate for analysis of integration rules, it provides less data on influence than is desirable. The present experiment, accordingly, included a new procedure to obtain influence scores from single stories, thus allowing a substantial number of influence scores for each couple. Two more content areas, family finance and social obligation, were added to the moral judgment task used previously (Armstrong, 1984).

Procedure

Three judgment domains were studied: child rearing, family finance, and social obligation. Two different designs were used for each domain: a factorial design and a single-story design. The factorial design for *child rearing* was essentially the same as the Intent-Damage design of the previous experiments. Similar designs were constructed for family finance and for social obligation. In *family finance*, each factorial set of stories was based on an unforeseen financial dilemma faced by a couple, with wife's need and husband's need each manipulated over four graded levels. Subjects judged how serious the situation was for the couple. In *social obligation*, each story set was based on an unreturned loan or broken promise. The two factors were the strength of the original obligation and the extenuating need of the actor. Subjects judged moral seriousness of the action. Following initial judgments based on the factorial stories, additional information was given using the discussion procedure of the first experiment and both spouses then revised their judgments.

The single-story design employed 40 single stories for each of the three domains. Each story described a difficulty or dilemma, which each subject judged on seriousness. Next a random half of the stories was presented to each spouse, each accompanied by a list of four possible solutions, and each subject chose which solution seemed best to ameliorate the difficulty. The 40 stories were then presented a second time, one half accompanied by solutions chosen by the subject, the other half accompanied by solutions chosen by the subject's spouse. Subjects then judged the seriousness of the situation on the assumption that the given solution had been put into effect. Here is one of the 40 stories about social obligation, together with the four given solutions.

Jim found out that his friend's girlfriend was seeing another man.
Possible solutions:

1. Jim should confront his friend's girlfriend with his knowledge and give her the option to tell his friend before Jim does.
2. Jim should send his friend an anonymous note informing him that his girlfriend is seeing another man.
3. Jim should tell his friend in as tactful a manner as possible that his girlfriend is seeing another man.
4. Jim should mind his own business and not say anything to his friend.

A complete list of the factorial stories and the single stories, together with other information and analyses, is given in Armstrong (1984).

Subjects were 19 married couples, aged 22 to 47 years, living in student housing. They received $100 for serving in three 3-hour sessions, one for each judgment domain. This experiment was run in a university research room, which was found to be much more expeditious than in the couples' homes, as in the previous experiments, which were subject to interruption from telephone calls, unexpected visitors, cranky children, and so forth.

Results and Discussion

The single-story data revealed different patterns of influence for each content area: greater influence of the wife for family finance; greater influence of each spouse on the other for child rearing; and equal influence of spouse and self for social obligation. Wife influence is measured by the change in judged seriousness for the 20 stories accompanied by solutions chosen by the wife; husband influence is measured similarly. These change scores are listed in Table 1.2.

To understand the influence patterns in Table 1.2, look at the left subtable for family finances. The wives change 5.42 points when reacting to their own

Table 1.2. Attitude change by wives and husbands: Study 3.

	Family finance		Child rearing		Social obligation	
Source	Spouse	Own	Spouse	Own	Spouse	Own
Wives	4.79	5.42	5.55	4.98	5.11	5.43
Husbands	5.00	3.89	4.62	4.05	4.82	4.91

chosen solutions, but only 4.79 points when reacting to their husband's solutions. The husbands, on the other hand, change 3.89 points when reacting to their own solutions, but 5.00 points when reacting to their wive's solutions. Both differences were statistically significant and, since the sets of stories were counterbalanced, represent a real effect of sex. This greater wife influence in money matters runs counter to social stereotypes. It is consistent, however, with the fact that a good two-thirds of the wives were the main wage earners in these student couples and suggests an unexpected docility of social stereotypes.

For child rearing, wives and husbands both show significantly more change for their spouse's information than for their own. For social obligation, there are only small differences of any kind. Overall, therefore, these within-person comparisons show that influence in marriage is not unitary but depends on context.

A notable advantage of the present method of single stories is that it allows analysis of influence within each couple. These individual analyses were generally consistent with the group means of Table 1.2. A natural concern with group means is that they may conceal important individual differences. The egalitarian pattern for social obligation, in particular, might be an artifact of averaging over couples, half of whom showed greater wife influence, half greater husband influence. The individual analyses revealed a number of mixed influence patterns, in which one spouse was egalitarian and the other was not. On the whole, however, they required little qualification of the mean trends already shown in Table 1.2.

For the factorial stories, the Intent-Damage judgments showed the same pattern already seen in Figures 1.3–1.4. So did the Need-Obligation judgments, shown in Figure 1.5. The family finance data, however, yielded a strong convergence pattern: if one's spouse's need was high, the other's need had little effect. This pattern of nonparallelism agrees with the averaging model under the assumption that higher levels of need have greater weight. This is the common negativity weighting (Anderson, 1981a, Section 4.4.2).

Finally, substantial spouse similarity in values was observed for child rearing and for social obligation. Moral ratios for child rearing, Damage/ (Damage + Intent), were calculated as defined previously and again showed significant correlation between wife and husband, $r(18) = .49$. A similar moral ratio, Need/(Need + Obligation), for social obligation showed a similar correlation of .45. The corresponding correlation for family finance was negligible, but this was presumably caused by the very limited range of individual differences for the corresponding ratio, Wife's Need/(Wife's Need + Husband's Need).

The present results confirm and extend the first two experiments. All three concur that a uniform averaging rule governs integration of information given by the experimenter as well as information transmitted or supplied by the spouse. This finding is as important as the methodology that was able to reveal it. No less important is the single story method, which has potential for extensive analysis of individual couples.

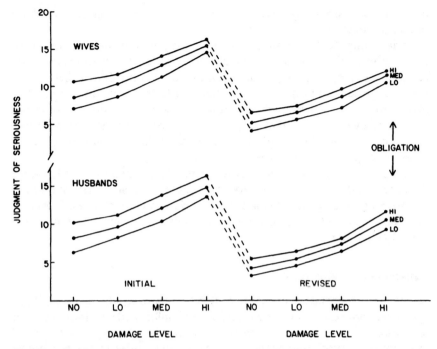

Figure 1.5. Judgments of seriousness of broken social obligations by wives and husbands, Study 3. Initial judgments in left panel based on strength of obligation (curve parameter) and extenuating need of actor who broke the obligation. Right panel shows revised judgments after additional extenuating information was presented by the spouse. (After Armstrong, 1984.)

Further Work: Marital Influence

Further work on marital influence must address the question of measuring both directions of spouse influence, wife on husband and husband on wife, across a variety of content areas. The present method of single stories provides a reasonably flexible assessment procedure that can be applied with personal design at the individual level.

A few methodological aspects of the single-story technique deserve mention. In a simple form, the procedure begins with a pool of stories, all of which may be judged by each spouse initially. Half the stories are assigned randomly to each spouse, who adds certain information to the assigned stories. Following this, both spouses again judge all the stories, this time taking account of the added information. The response measure may be the final judgment by itself or the change between the two judgments (Anderson, 1982, Note 7.7b).

On the null hypothesis of equal spouse influence, the two spouse means will be equal except for sampling variability. With stories assigned randomly to each spouse, variability among responses for each spouse includes the between-story variability. Hence ordinary analysis of variance provides a proper test of the null hypothesis.

Various amplifications and extensions of this procedure deserve consideration. For example, some stories could have no added information and might not even be judged initially. These stories would control for effects of the initial judgment and for practice–adaptation effects. Again, the added information for some stories could be attributed to another source, for example, the wife or husband of another couple. Comparison of these stories with those in which the added information is attributed to the spouse would yield a measure of spouse influence per se.

This procedure allows substantially simpler design than was employed for the influence data reported in Table 1.1. The main cost is that involved in constructing initial pools of stories for a variety of content areas. However, the procedure may be used to study many kinds of influence manipulation at the individual level.

Satisfaction in Marriage

Satisfaction is a primary indicator of functioning in dyadic relations. Each person has individual needs and goals, whose fulfillment depends on the other person and on their interaction. Satisfaction is a global concept, an integrated resultant of diverse components, with many similarities to the concept of likableness in person cognition. A natural hypothesis, accordingly, is that the theory developed so extensively in person cognition (Anderson, 1978, 1981a) will generalize to marriage satisfaction.

An ethical problem arises in applying personal design to satisfaction in marriage. Focusing attention on unsatisfactory aspects of an ongoing marriage could exacerbate them with consequent harm to the marriage. This exploratory experiment, therefore, studied retrospective judgments by divorced women. The goal was to study the foregoing parallel between satisfaction in marriage and likableness in person cognition using personalized design.

Procedure

The subjects, 16 divorced women, first recalled specific incidents from their marriages in which their husbands had shown various degrees, positive and negative, of appreciation, affection, and respect. These incidents were then rated by the women and categorized as H, M^+, M^-, and L, denoting very satisfactory, mildly satisfactory, mildly unsatisfactory, and very unsatisfactory, respectively. Illustrative incidents in the four respective categories for Subject M. R. were: Husband took her to dinner for her birthday; Husband very helpful when she had leg problems; Husband tore down the wallpaper she had put up; Husband made joke about her looking like the living dead.

Two of these three dimensions were used to construct a 4 × 4, row × column design for each woman. She was instructed to imagine that each pair of incidents had occurred close together in her marriage and to judge how satisfied she would have been with her marriage at that time. In addition to the 16 pairs, some single incidents and some sets of three incidents were judged in the same way; these judgments provided critical tests between adding and averaging rules of integration.

Results

The results supported the averaging rule. The four solid curves in Figure 1.6 represent the mean judgments for the 4 × 4 design. The near-parallelism of these four solid curves points to an averaging process, and a critical test is given by the greater slope of the dashed curve. The dashed curve represents judgments based on only one incident (the column incident listed on the horizontal axis), and its slope is markedly greater than the slopes of the solid curves. This slope comparison eliminates any kind of adding rule and supports the averaging rule by a standard logic (see Anderson, 1981a, Section 2.3). Similar tests based on the sets of three incidents provided similar support for the averaging rule (see Anderson, 1981a, p. 319, Figure 4.21).

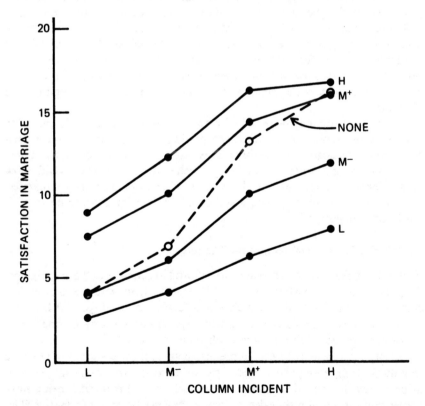

Figure 1.6. Divorced women follow averaging model in judgments of marriage satisfaction based on actual incidents from their marriage. (After N. H. Anderson, 1981a. *Foundations of Information Integration Theory*, Academic Press, 1981.)

Closer study of Figure 1.6 shows small but systematic deviations from parallelism: the four solid curves are closer together at the left. This pattern of nonparallelism represents the negativity effect (Anderson, 1981a, Section 4.4.2), in which less favorable information has greater importance or weight. Summation rules cannot account for this negativity effect, whereas the averaging rule can.

Discussion

The foregoing results point to the operation of a general averaging process for marriage satisfaction. This is not surprising, for marriage satisfaction has many similarities to the much-studied concept of likableness in person cognition. Other results from person cognition may be expected to generalize similarly. This would provide a useful tool for deeper analysis of cognitive processes in marriage.

The potential of personal design also appears in these results. The stimuli for each woman represented actual incidents from her own marriage. The same basic design was personalized for each individual woman. Cognitive processes can thus be studied within the context of each woman's experience.

Similar processes may be expected to hold in ongoing marital interaction. The present judgments were retrospective, so the values of the remembered incidents would differ from their original values. Present concern is with process generality, however, and it seems reasonable to expect the process of integration to remain the same even though the values being integrated are different.

This expectation may be tested with an extension of personal design. With participating couples, positive incidents could be injected into ongoing marriages with some degree of experimental control, each spouse being instructed to do something positive for the other at scheduled times. This would allow tests of the serial averaging model as well as information on marital dynamics. The present experiment provides some justification for proceeding to such more costly investigations.

Further Work: Factorial Graphs for Therapy

Factorial graphs may be as revealing to wife and husband as to the investigator. People may be only partially aware of their underlying values and how they determine overall evaluations, such as satisfaction in marriage. The factorial graph provides a visible representation. Systematic scrutiny of one's own factorial graph could thus facilitate self-understanding.

Factorial graphs may be even more instructive for the spouse. For effective communication, both positive and negative reactions from one's spouse need to be related to their determinants. But such overall reactions, being integrated resultants of multiple determinants, may not be very informative. The factorial graph can thus be a useful communication device between spouses, shedding light on the perpetual question, "Why does s/he act that way?"

Requiring each spouse to predict the other's factorial graphs could provide an instructive confrontation with marital reality.

With personal computers, the factorial graph approach could be readily implemented in marital therapy sessions. Indeed, simple representations of wife and husband personalities could be stored to allow immediate reaction, as with feedback about correctness of predictions about spouse's factorial graph.

Further Work: Affect and Emotion in Marriage

No listing is needed to show the diverse pervasiveness of affect and emotion in married life. Berscheid (1983) made a similar point, but concluded that "the affective mathematics people use to review and combine their affective experiences within a relationship are not known" (p. 168). Actually, something substantial is known about this affective mathematics, as shown in Figure 1.6. More can be learned in similar manner. Indeed, the body of work on cognitive algebra may be expected to have reasonable generality for affective components of marriage. Further work with personal design is needed to study affective mathematics in its most natural setting.

Attitude Change in Group Discussion

Formation and change of attitudes in interpersonal interaction is difficult to study because the flow of information is complex and largely uncontrolled. As Anderson and Graesser (1976) put it:

The impact of any group member on the others is spread out in time, conditioned by his(her) motivations to influence and to conform, interlinked with others' comments and silences, dependent on prior knowledge and on expressive factors from clarity of thought to eye contact and personal attractiveness. Thus, the attitude of each group member reflects an ongoing, time-dependent process in which the information components seem close to unknowable [p. 210].

Information integration theory can provide exact analyses of such complex interactions by defining units at a molar level. In this particular experiment, each group member was treated as a molar unit. Even though the molecular detail of the influence processes is unknown, the integration analysis obtains an exact molar summary of this unknown processing. The present experiment involved casual dyads, but is included here because it illustrates the concepts of *molar unitization* and *self-estimated parameters*, both of which are important for the study of marital interaction.

Procedure

Each subject in groups of two or three first received different paragraphs of information about some U. S. president and judged the president on statesmanship. Subjects then exchanged and discussed their information with one another and revised their judgment of the president. Different configurations of paragraph information were used in different groups in order to provide a strong test of the integration rule.

This experiment used a method of self-estimated parameters to test the integration rule with a nonfactorial design. Besides their attitudinal judgments of the president, each subject also made self-estimates of the weight and value of their own given information and of the attitudes expressed by the other group member. The model hypothesis implies that their attitudinal judgment will be the weighted average calculated from these self-estimated parameters.

Results and Discussion

One illustrative result is shown in Figure 1.7, in which the open circles represent postdiscussion attitudes towards the presidents. The solid and

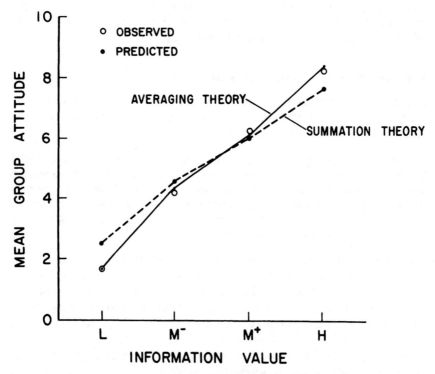

Figure 1.7. Tests of two theories of attitude change in group discussion. Open circles represent mean attitudes of group members for information configurations of varied value. Visual inspection indicates that averaging theory does well (dotted line), whereas summation theory does ill (solid line). (After Anderson & Graesser, 1976.) An information integration analysis of attitude change in group discussion, *Journal of Personality and Social Psychology, 34,* 210– 222. Copyright 1976 by American Psychological Association.)

dashed lines represent theoretical predictions from the averaging and summation models, respectively. The summation model shows large systematic deviations, whereas the averaging model does very well. Results from the other experimental conditions also supported averaging theory and infirmed the summation model.

This experiment is notable because it provided a valid statistical test of goodness of fit of the theoretical models. Discrepancies from the averaging model were small and about the size expected by chance. Other theories of group attitudes seem inadequate to resolve even the basic question of testing goodness of fit (Anderson & Graesser, 1976).

Tests of summation models have relied almost completely on inadequate correlation-regression statistics. In Figure 1.7, for example, the summation model correlates .99 with the observed data—even though the deviations from the summation model are large and highly significant. Such correlation-regression methods, which remain frequent in attitude theory and group dynamics, have been called *weak inference* methods (Anderson, 1981a, Section 1.2.8; 1982, Sections 4.1 and 7.9) because they seem to test the model but do not really do so. Functional measurement methodology, by contrast, can provide valid tests of theoretical models that allow for individual differences in value. This facilitates cognitive analysis in realistic dyadic interaction.

Further Work: Self-Estimated Parameters

Simpler and more flexible experimental design is possible with self-estimated parameters. The main problem, as noted earlier, is to develop methods that can eliminate the biases to which self-estimation is subject. One approach is illustrated in the present experiment, in which the success of the averaging model simultaneously supports the validity of the self-estimation procedure (see also Anderson, 1982, Chapter 6). Further work is desirable to develop self-estimation as a means to extend personal experimental design (Anderson & Zalinski, in press).

Further Work: Molar Unitization

The present approach to dyadic interaction relies on molar unitization (Anderson, 1981a, Section 1.1.5, 1982, Section 7.15). Much of what goes on in interpersonal interaction is unknowable in detail, as the foregoing quote indicates. Theory must employ molar concepts, therefore, that are summaries of more molecular processing, beginning at the neural level, continuing through levels of words and meanings, and culminating in the dyadic interaction process itself. The danger, of course, is that such molar summary concepts may misrepresent or omit some of the molecular processing. Information integration theory can avoid this danger because functional measurement provides complete and exact summaries of all molecular processing. In the blame equation of the first experiment, for example, the *Intent* term is an exact, complete summary of all cognitive processing entailed in the valuation operation.

Molar unitization cannot be accomplished by fiat. In the present experiment, the group members were provisionally treated as molar units, but the model analysis must justify this assumption. This justification rests on cognitive algebra. Functional measurement methodology makes such justification possible, whereas standard correlation-regression methodology does not. The empirical success of the averaging model provides empirical justification for the present application of molar unitization.

Study of marital interaction requires more systematic investigation of molar units. Everyday perception suggests that the mind has a natural and flexible capability for unitization. Marital interaction, although a continuous stream, appears to have natural boundaries that constitute discrete events, actions, and time periods. But this intuitive feeling may reside merely in the surface words, not in the underlying cognitive processes. Cognitive algebra provides a tool for cognitive analysis of unitization.

Social Decision: Tests of Two Theories

Two theories have attempted to provide detailed quantitative analysis of group decisions. One is the social averaging theory of IIT, the other is the theory of social decision schemes by Davis (1973) and his associates (e.g., Davis, Cohen, Hornik, & Rissman, 1973). As Davis has emphasized, most theories of group decision have been too vague and general to permit serious tests. Davis presented a precise testable theory, and it was compared with IIT by Graesser (1977, in press) as illustrated in the result noted here.

Social Averaging Theorem

Consider a dyadic decision that requires a compromise over distribution of some good, such as time or money, say, or sex or appreciation. Person i prefers some ideal point on the good dimension, denoted by x_i, and exerts a bargaining power, w_i, which is a molar unit that includes diverse bargaining tactics and personal persuasiveness. For any proposed decision, X, the effective force exerted by i equals i's power times the distance from the ideal point:

$$F_i(X) = w_i(X_i - X).$$

The social decision, denoted by X^*, is that X for which the forces balance, or sum to zero net force:

$$\sum F_i(X^*) = \sum w_i(X_i - X^*) = 0.$$

Solving yields the social decision as the average of the individual ideal points, each weighted by the individual's social power:

$$X^* = \sum w_i X_i / \sum w_i.$$

Implications for social power, conformity, and group cohesiveness are discussed by Anderson (1976b) and an extensive empirical analysis is given by Graesser (1977, in press).

Social Decision Schemes

Social decision schemes may be illustrated with the equal-distance compromise model, which was the most successful scheme in the experimental study by Davis et al. (1973). In this experiment, each subject was instructed to role-play a local politician and represent the interests of his/her constituency, whose preferences were represented by a frequency histogram defined over a given preference dimension (e.g., percentage control students should have in the university). Each subject in a dyad received a different histogram and the pair arrived at a common decision in any way they wished.

The decision process for the equal-distance compromise model had two simple steps: first, each subject was assumed to select a single point on the preference dimension at random, according to the probabilities indicated by the given histogram; second, the two subjects compromised midway between their selected points. This model is remarkable in that it makes predictions completely a priori, based only on the shapes of the given histograms. No individual difference parameters are included.

Procedure and Results

Graesser (1977, Exp. 3) followed essentially the same experimental procedure just outlined for Davis et al. (1973). A visual comparison between the two theories is given in Figure 1.8, presented in the same form as used by Davis et al. The solid curve represents the cumulative frequency of observed decisions. The long-dash curve represents predictions by the social averaging theorem, which fit the data quite well. The short-dash curve represents predictions by the social decision scheme, which are not even close to the data.

Nine such tests were included in Graesser's experiment. All agreed with social averaging theory. All disagreed sharply with the social decision scheme. Indeed, the test shown in Figure 1.8 was actually the one most favorable to the decision scheme. A second experimental study by Graesser yielded similar results: the social averaging theorem did very well, whereas the social decision schemes failed badly.

Discussion

Why did Davis's decision schemes, which had seemed to show promise in extensive empirical tests by Davis and his students, fail so badly in Graesser's study? The main answer lies in the power of the respective methods. Proponents of the social decision schemes used a method that was too weak to provide worthwhile tests of their theory. The stronger methodology of IIT immediately revealed the severe shortcomings of the social decision schemes.

It is to the credit of Davis and his students that they developed a theory that could be disconfirmed through precise predictions. They have rightly criticized the common use of informal theories that do not provide precise, disconfirmable predictions. Their method, unfortunately, did not match this ideal. They relied on a simplifying assumption of no individual differences

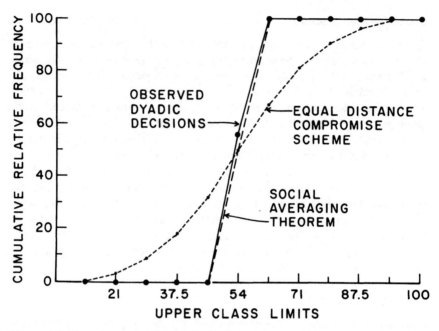

Figure 1.8. Test of two theories of dyadic bargaining. Solid curve gives cumulative frequency of empirical dyadic decisions as a function of preference continuum on horizontal axis. Theoretical predictions from social averaging theory indicated by long-dash curve. Theoretical predictions from social decision scheme indicated by short-dash curve.

that was shown seriously incorrect by Graesser and that mathematically vitiates all their empirical applications (Anderson, 1976b, Note 7.5.3c). Given the reality of individual differences, the only definite conclusion from all these studies is that a scheme that seems to fit the data is almost certainly wrong.

The hypothesis that group compromise can be represented as some kind of average is plausible, but Graesser's study was the first to provide serious evidence. Her work provides strong evidence for averaging as an exact rule for group decision making. This outcome fits well with the general theory of averaging processes developed in IIT. The social averaging theorem thus provides a base for analysis of dyadic interactions within a general theory of social cognition.

Further Work: Social Power

The concept of social weight, or social power, is central to social averaging theory of dyadic interaction. Graesser's work showed large individual differences in social power, but dyadic interaction depends not only on the individuals but also on their interpersonal relations. The same individual might have high social power in one dyad, low social power in another, as may often be seen in family relations. Within a marital dyad, moreover, the foregoing work by Armstrong implies that power will depend on the situation or context. Understanding dyadic interaction thus requires a capability for analyzing possibly complex networks of power relations. Functional measurement of social power thus becomes a tool for more extensive study of dyadic interactions.

Conceptually, social weight is a proper measure of social power (Anderson, 1976b, Section 7.5.5). The actual force exerted on each person is not a proper measure of social power, for force depends also on the difference between the person's ideal and the advocated action, as shown in the first of the foregoing force equations. A person with lower power might exert greater force and have greater influence by advocating a greater change. Standard treatments of social power do not adequately distinguish the concepts of force and power (see Huston, 1983; Scanzoni 1979). Establishing social averaging theory begins the process of transforming the intuitive concept of power into a concept that is theoretically grounded.

For measuring social power, simpler design is possible. Indeed, only a single decision would be required to estimate w_i under the conditions of the foregoing experiment. The factorial design used by Graesser was important to secure adequate sensitivity for worthwhile tests of the two theoretical models. Once established, however, the model provides a base for measurement with simpler design. This simplifies the more detailed analysis of the network of dyadic power relations.

Attitudes and Behavior

The most completely realized personal design to date is that developed by Jaccard and Becker (1985), who studied attitudes and contraceptive behavior. This thoughtful, innovative study extended integration theory to analysis of ongoing behavior. Personal design made possible the determination of both values and integration rules for individual subjects, thereby allowing analysis of attitude-behavior relations with greater power than available from other theories.

Procedure

Subjects were sexually active college students, 20 male and 20 female. They rated each of seven methods of birth control on each of seven attributes (e.g., little negative impact on sexual pleasure, convenient to use) with an A-B-C scale (above average, average, below average). Each subject also selected the three personally most important attributes and these were quantified at the three cited levels, A, B, and C, to form a $3 \times 3 \times 3$ design. This design yielded 27 hypothetical methods of birth control, each of which was rated on a -10 to $+10$ scale in each of four separate sessions, thereby providing four replications for individual analyses.

Results

The results showed large discrepancies from the additive model employed by Ajzen and Fishbein (1980) for nearly every individual subject. On the other hand, the results supported the averaging model with differential weighting from IIT. The relevant data were the factorial graphs, which showed a general tendency to converge at lower levels of the attributes. This reflects the negativity effect, discussed previously, stemming from greater importance weighting of more negative stimuli.

Prediction of the actual contraceptive method used by the subjects employed an interesting innovation. Since each of the seven methods had been rated A-B-C on each attribute, each method could be identified with one cell of the factorial design. Predicted responses for these seven cells were generated using theoretical measurement analyses. Correlations of the seven predicted and seven obtained attitudinal responses were greater than .90 for half the individuals, with an overall mean of .84. This high attitude–behavior relation suggests the potential of IIT and personal design in practical behavior prediction.

Discussion

The study by Jaccard and Becker (1985) shows a clear superiority of integration theory of attitudes over the theory of Fishbein and Ajzen (1975; Ajzen & Fishbein, 1980). This is no surprise, for the Fishbein-Ajzen theory rests on a summation rule that has been clearly erroneous in many tests in attitude research (see, e.g., Figures 1.6 and 1.7 above). Jaccard and Becker extend previous work to prediction of everyday sexual behavior.

Personal design takes an important step forward in the thoughtful study of Jaccard and Becker. The design factors themselves were personalized for each subject, thereby making the same abstract design meaningful within each individual's everyday life. The clever use of quantified attribute levels allowed a simple approach to the measurement problems. These personalization procedures provided an effective way to use judgments of hypothetical stimulus combinations in prediction of actual contraceptive behavior.

Further Work: Survey Research

Jaccard and Becker discuss extensions of IIT to survey research, especially in prediction of choice decisions. Their approach utilizes a multiattribute representation of the alternative choices, but personalizes a small set of basic attributes to the individual decision maker. With their procedures, factorial-type design becomes feasible in survey situations, including marital surveys.

The discussion of Jaccard and Becker emphasizes the need and value of crossing boundaries to combine attitude theory and judgment-decision theory. Their emphasis agrees with the present view, as well as with the emphasis on goals and motivations by Beach and Morrison (this volume). Understanding marital interaction requires a combined attitude-decision theory, for attitudes are sources of values and values determine decisions. Such extensions of personalized design to survey studies promises to be an important direction of further work.

Attitude Theory

Attitudes are the foundation of social thought and action. Negotiation and allocation of rights and responsibilities between wife and husband depend on attitudes about obligation and duty in marriage, especially in relation to sex roles. Disciplining of children depends similarly on attitudes about right and wrong, obedience, and social approval. Outside the family, attitudes are also important in dyadic interactions in the work place and in social life.

Personal design should be useful in studying the operation and function of attitudes in everyday life. Some exploratory steps have been illustrated in the foregoing experiments. This section presents a few more general comments, especially in relation to other approaches to attitude theory.

Attitudes as Knowledge Systems

Attitudes and *attitudinal responses* are conceptualized differently in IIT. Attitudes are considered knowledge systems, as discussed earlier, that function in the construction of attitudinal responses in particular situations. These attitudinal responses, being directed towards particular goals, often have a one-dimensional, approach-avoidance character. The underlying knowledge system, in contrast, generally has a more complex, nondimensional structure. This qualitative distinction seems essential, both for cognitive theory and for social application.

Cognitive algebra provides a cutting edge to this distinction between attitudes and attitudinal responses. The foregoing experiments, together with other integration studies, have shown that evaluative responses, popularly identified with attitudes proper, often follow algebraic rules. This cognitive algebra has provided a new framework for studying attitudes. It allows exact analysis of a major class of attitudinal responses, including the evaluative reactions that are commonly studied. Furthermore, it also yields information about structure of underlying attitudes as knowledge systems. Two such results, the *functional memory representation* and the *basal-surface representation*, will illustrate the potential for structural analysis.

Two hypotheses have been proposed for the memory structure of attitudes. According to the traditional verbal memory hypothesis, attitudinal responses are based directly on the verbal materials retained in memory. This view was attractive because it promised to develop attitude theory on the mass of data and concepts from verbal learning. The integration studies, however, discovered that attitudes involved a memory distinct from the memory for the verbal materials from which the attitude originally developed. This two-memory hypothesis now seems generally accepted (see Anderson, 1981a, Section 4.2, 1987, 1988; Hastie, 1981) and has been incorporated within a more general conception of functional memory.

The basal-surface structure of attitudes was discovered in studies of the long-standing question of primacy-recency (see Anderson, 1981a, Sections 2.5 and 3.3). In this representation, the basal component may be considered primacy, for once formed it is resistant to change. The surface component, in contrast, may be considered recency, for it is sensitive to each new piece of information but decays rapidly. Both basal and surface components make biosocial sense. Much environmental information is redundant, so a small brain generally does well to settle on an attitudinal response from the first few pieces of information, thereby freeing attentional capacity for other signals. The surface component provides a needed supplement to alert the organism to possible shifts in the environment. This basal-surface representation also illustrates the biosocial heuristic (Anderson, 1986) that human thought may be appreciated in terms of its biological foundation and its social development.

Both of these findings bear on the functional structure of attitudes. The problem of functional structure is related to the problem of functional memory (Anderson, 1988) and is more complex than can be pursued here. These results illustrate one way in which IIT can analyze the attitude structures that underlie one-dimensional attitudinal responses.

Fishbein-Ajzen Summation Theory

Three fundamental flaws in the attitude theory proposed by Fishbein and Ajzen (1975; Ajzen & Fishbein, 1980) appear when it is compared with integration theory of attitudes. The first flaw concerns the definition of attitudes, which are taken as one-dimensional evaluative reactions by Fishbein and Ajzen. Their definition misses the distinction between attitudes as knowledge systems and attitudinal responses. Hence their definition is too narrow to understand attitude structure. It is also too narrow to understand behavior, which depends not only on attitudes, but also on integration of other, nonattitudinal factors that operate in particular situations.

The second flaw in the Fishbein-Ajzen approach is that their algebraic model is erroneous and invalid. Information integration theory and the Fishbein-Ajzen approach are sometimes considered similar because both use an algebraic model, but this similarity is superficial. Cognitive algebra is truly cognitive, whereas the Fishbein-Ajzen formula is a largely arbitrary regression equation. This difference is illustrated in the averaging-adding controversy. Fishbein's initial studies (Fishbein, 1967) claimed to support a summation model and to infirm an averaging model. The evidence, however, was only a form of the set-size effect, that more information of equal value produces a more polarized response. This set-size effect does infirm a simple averaging model, but it was successfully predicted, both qualitatively and quantitatively, by the averaging model of IIT (see Anderson, 1981a, Section 2.3.5 and 2.4).

Further integration studies presented critical tests that disproved virtually any form of summation theory. These tests were subsequently confirmed by one of Fishbein's own students (Kaplan, 1972; see Anderson 1981a, pp. 123– 124). Fishbein and Ajzen have continued to use the same basic model even though it has repeatedly been proven erroneous and invalid.

The third flaw in the Fishbein-Ajzen approach is the lack of a base in psychological measurement theory. This flaw has been highlighted by Jaccard and Becker (1985, pp. 460–462), who point out that the Fishbein-Ajzen formula treats subjective norms as a statistical variable that necessitates group analysis and bars individual analysis. Such crude regression analysis may correlate with behavior but it can hardly be considered psychological theory. Psychological attitude theory requires individual analysis; group norms must be conceptualized so as to allow for individual minds. Jaccard and Becker do just that by treating subjective norms as one form of information in the valuation processes of IIT.

Judgment-Decision Theory

Judgment-decision theory virtually ignores the concept of attitude. Values are essential to judgment and decision, however, and values are derived from attitude knowledge systems. To be viable, a cognitive theory of judgment-decision must become helpmates with social psychology of attitudes.

With few exceptions, workers in judgment-decision have taken values for granted. The judgment-decision field has lacked grounded theory of psychological measurement. This lack is not critical of certain purposes. In the dyadic bargaining study of Figure 1.8, for example, the values were defined objectively and numerically in the stimulus materials. But even in this experiment, cognitive algebra was needed to measure the social decision weights.

The neglect of value theory in the judgment-decision field stems from its predominantly normative orientation, which aims to prescribe optimal decision. Values are generally extranormative, however, so normative theory is incomplete. Normative theory is often seriously misleading, moreover, because it interprets behavior by reference to normative prescription, which is often cognitively irrelevant. Examples of the hindering effects of normative thinking are found in the weak inference tests of linear models (Anderson & Shanteau, 1977), the confusion over the concept of weight (Anderson, 1982, Chapter 6; Anderson & Zalinski, in press), and the treatment of heuristics and biases (Anderson, 1986).

The judgment-decision field requires a cognitive foundation, as emphasized here, in the related theoretical approach of Troutman and Shanteau (this volume), and in the image theory of Beach and Morrison (this volume). These cognitive approaches have common interests and concerns, especially with goals and values. Indeed, the function of attitudes in the valuation operation of IIT seems comparable with the compatibility criterion of image theory. Beach and Mitchell (1987) note that image theory departs from conventional thinking about decisions in major ways, all of which revolve around concepts of goal and attitude. Such changes in direction of thinking are essential for a cognitive theory of judgment-decision.

Symbolic Interactionism

There is much similarity of spirit between IIT and the sociological perspective known as symbolic interactionism (see Burr, Leigh, Day, & Constantine, 1979; Stryker & Statham, 1985). Both emphasize the importance of social context; both emphasize the need to allow for personal, individual meanings and values; both emphasize concepts of social attitudes and roles. Information integration theory is more immediately concerned with cognitive process, motivation, and values, but these concerns do not seem alien to symbolic interactionism.

There is, however, one basic difference: Information integration theory has developed a methodology for quantitative analysis at the level of individual and situation. This difference may be illustrated by comparing the interactionist theory of marriage satisfaction presented by Burr et al. (1979) with the integrationist theory discussed in relation to Figure 1.6. Their propositions about factors that affect marriage satisfaction are readily amenable to IIT. For example, the valuation operation of the information integration diagram (Figure 1.1) yields higher weights for more important role expectations about spouses (their Proposition 2) and higher scale values for greater congruence between such expectations and actual behavior (their Proposition 1).

Burr et al. (1979) make the further claim that the cited value relation is linear. This claim, however, is not justifiable within any school of symbolic interaction. Linearity requires scaled variables. Symbolic interaction, because it insists on individual meaning and value, requires that the variables be measured on subjective scales—but provides no measurement theory for this purpose. Without subjective scales, even this simple claim of linearity has no meaning within symbolic interactionism. Information integration theory does provide such a theory of measurement, as illustrated in the model analysis of Figure 1.6. Information integration theory goes farther, to address the integration question of how satisfaction depends on two or more factors operating together.

No school of symbolic interaction has developed a comparable methodology. Some schools categorically deny that such methodology is possible and assert that phenomenology is sufficient (e.g., Blumer, 1969; Mehan & Wood, 1975). But phenomenology is not sufficient, as discussed earlier, and the methodology exists in actual fact. It is no cure-all, but its implementation with personal design can provide exact quantitative analysis of individual meanings and values that are the concern of symbolic interactionism.

Functional Theory of Attitudes

Information integration theory is at home with the functional approaches to attitudes (Katz, 1960; Kelman, 1974), which consider how attitudes operate in everyday thought and action. Four such functions are discussed by McGuire (1969, pp. 157–161, 270f), all of which relate to the present treatment of attitudes as knowledge systems.

The utilitarian and knowledge functions both relate to the valuation operator of the integration diagram (Figure 1.1). A primary function of attitudes as knowledge systems is to assign values to goal-relevant stimuli. Values are thus considered knowledge, that is, guides to action in relation to goals. The valuation operator mediates between the knowledge system and the attitudinal response.

Attitudes also serve motivational functions, including the self-realizing and ego-defensive functions discussed by McGuire (1969). In IIT, motivation is considered biosocial knowledge (Anderson, in press). Social motivations and values are integral components of attitudes considered as knowledge systems. This conception of attitude as a system that incorporates both fact and value is central to the present concern with goal-oriented thought and action. This motivational emphasis is developed further in related discussions of psychodynamics of everyday life (Anderson, 1983).

Previous advocates of the functional approach have stressed the need to consider attitudes in relation to everyday life, but they have not developed systematic theory. Information integration theory gives theoretical body to the functional approach. The representation of attitudes as knowledge systems incorporates motivation as an integral component of cognition, and cognitive algebra provides effective tools for analysis. Progress is thus possible that does not deny or ignore the complexity of goal-oriented thought and action.

Everyday Life

Everyday life is a primary domain of IIT. This appears in the foregoing experiments, which studied such everyday judgments as satisfaction and blame. These judgments are not only clues to underlying process, but stand as psychological entities of interest in their own right. One aim of IIT is to help develop a general cognitive theory that can treat everyday life in something like its own terms.

Cognitive Theory of Everyday Life

Information integration theory begins at a higher level than mainstream cognitive psychology. Whereas mainstream cognitive psychology is much concerned with letter and word recognition, IIT is concerned with higher level processing for values and implications. Whereas mainstream cognitive psychology is dominated by reproductive memory, IIT is concerned with functional memory (Anderson, 1981a, 1986, 1988). And whereas mainstream cognitive psychology largely ignores or even shuns concepts of affect and motivation, IIT considers affect and motivation integral to everyday cognition.

Many other approaches also focus on everyday life and they show the richness and importance of this domain. These include personality theories, especially those with socioanalytic orientation (e.g., Benjamin, 1984; Hogan, 1983), for the psychoanalytic theories say surprisingly little about psychodynamics of everyday life (Anderson, 1983). Also included are the symbolic interactionist schools of sociology, especially those that deal with role theory. The field of social psychology itself might almost be recharacterized as psychology of everyday life, for that is the level of its main concepts and response measures.

In the present view, a general theory of everyday life must satisfy three conditions. It must possess a capability for measurement of individual values and motivations, for these are the bases of goal-oriented behavior. It must provide a validational criterion for definition and measurement of unconscious processes, for these are necessary to understanding everyday phenomenology. And it must solve the assemblage problems of multiple determination and of action sequences, which are central to judgment and action.

Information integration theory aims to satisfy these three conditions. Although it has only begun the study of action sequences, it has provided a fairly general treatment of multiple determination in terms of cognitive algebra. Cognitive algebra has provided a base and frame for functional measurement of individual values and motivations, including certain unconscious processes. Information integration theory is, accordingly, the only theory in psychology that has dealt with the twin problems of valuation and integration in any general and successful way. Within the field of social psychology, IIT has been applied to virtually every area, including attitudes, attribution, person cognition, justice theory, group dynamics, and social development. Outside social psychology, applications have been made in judgment-decision theory, developmental psychology, and psychophysics. All these applications rest on the same theoretical foundation. It seems fair to say, therefore, that IIT provides a unified base of concepts and methods for the study of everyday cognition.

Marriage and Family

Marriage and family constitute a rich, important, and much-neglected domain for studying dyadic interaction of everyday life. These interactions range over all aspects of everyday life, from household chores and the dinner table to the most sensitive parts of the self. No other social domain offers the investigator so much of so much importance.

Marriage and family also bring out an important dimension of depth: Interpersonal interaction depends on underlying knowledge systems. These knowledge systems incorporate the biosocial motivations essential to understanding the goals that drive interactions. These knowledge systems represent the cognitive structures that are utilized in goal-oriented thought and action.

Even a brief listing illustrates the diversity and pervasiveness of everyday experience: caring, appreciation, sex, kinship obligations, fairness, and sociability, not to mention such heavily socialized issues as health, sickness, food, work, and play. Not only do such knowledge systems govern everyday interaction, but they originate in large part in family socialization. No other domain can compare in all these respects with marriage and family as a crucible for the study of interpersonal interaction.

One other advantage is notable: Marriage and family provide a pristine field for psychological research. Workers from other disciplines, mainly sociology and family studies, have made many contributions. Psychologists, however, have strangely neglected the domain that seems most central to understanding the human condition. As noted previously (Anderson, 1979):

Marriage, whose social importance would be expected to place it foremost among areas of psychological research, has been strangely passed by. Clinical psychology is still dominated by the psychoanalytic tradition of reworking the past, a technique that may not be inappropriate for individuals, but is a swift path to blame and recrimination in couples. Social psychologists have stressed the need for realism and relevance, but this has rarely reached to marriage and family. A survey of the 145 articles published in 1978 in *Journal of Personality and Social Psychology* found only one that dealt with married couples and one or two on sex that were relevant. The same pattern can be seen in a best-selling introductory text, by comparing index entries for *marriage* with, for example, *hallucinations, hearing,* and *hypnosis.*

Yet marriage offers a rich field for psychological research. Its social importance is clear, but its advantages as an investigational setting deserve consideration.

• Virtually every area of social psychology comes together in marriage. Person cognition, attitude change, group dynamics, justice theory, and causal attribution all consider phenomena and processes that are basic in marriage. Marriage thus constitutes a central issue, with the potential of unifying social psychological inquiry.

• Marriage is an arena for human motivation. Love, sex, companionship, parenting, among others, provide a more human face to motivation than the biological perspectives of experimental psychology or the typological preconceptions of personality theory.

• Marriage is similarly an area for psychodynamics of everyday life. Jealousy, resentment, blame, and a cluster of self-esteem qualities are all prominent in marriage.

• Marriage is of interest to other disciplines, especially sociology and anthropology, but not excluding economics and education. Marriage thus provides a common ground that is essential to meaningful cross-cultural interdisciplinary study.

• Marriage involves various areas outside of social psychology. Through family life, it relates to developmental psychology. Judgment and decision making are central activities of family life. Behavior modification finds an ideal setting in the family, especially as support for the individual.

• Married life involves well-learned perceptual and motor skills. Experiments within the marriage setting can tap into these skills, thereby obtaining access to cognitive process and structure to greater depth than in casual tasks typical of standard experiments.

• Marriage provides an open social laboratory.

• Marriage is truly an "endless frontier."

Exploration of this frontier depends on experimental control. Experimental control is essential for clarification of cognitive units. Experimental control is necessary for elucidation of cognitive processes. Without experimental control, phenomenology and observation cannot make much progress.

Personal design aims to bring experimental control into everyday marriage and family life. Everyday life is a life of motivations, values, and goals. Personalizing the design makes it meaningful within the individual's system of motivations, values, and goals. Cognitive analysis depends on capability for measurement of individual motivations and values. Most behavior, however, depends on joint action of more than one motivation and value. Hence the understanding and prediction of behavior also require capability for determining rules of integration. Both capabilities, measurement and integration, are available with the concepts and methods of the theory of information integration. This theory provides a useful base for development of personal design in the study of everyday life. Personal design is still in the early stages of development. The experiments reported here are only a beginning. It is hoped, however, that they will illustrate the promise and the challenge of the method of personal design.

Acknowledgments. This work was supported by National Science Foundation grants BNS79-04675, BNS80-04845, and BNS82-12461 to the first author. The second author's graduate studies at the Department of Psychology, University of California, San Diego, 1980–1984, were supported by the Danforth Foundation. Her postgraduate studies at the Laboratory of Comparative Human Cognition, Center for Human Information Processing, University of California, San Diego, were supported by PHS grants MH 14268-10 and MH 14268-11, as well as by a Carnegie Corporation grant, DC15-06/86-COLE. Support was also received by grants from the National Institutes of Mental Health to the Center for Human Information Processing, University of California, San Diego.

References

Ajzen, I., & Fishbein, M. (1980). *Understanding attitudes and predicting social behavior.* Englewood Cliffs, NJ: Prentice-Hall.

Anderson, N. H. (1976a). Equity judgments as information integration. *Journal of Personality and Social Psychology, 33,* 291–299.

Anderson, N. H. (1976b). *Social perception and cognition* (Tech. Rep. CHIP 62). La Jolla, CA: Center for Human Information Processing, University of California, San Diego.

Anderson, N. H. (1978). Progress in cognitive algebra. In L. Berkowitz (Ed.), *Cognitive theories in social psychology* (pp. 1–126). New York: Academic Press.

Anderson, N. H. (1979). *Person perception in marriage* (grant proposal submitted to National Science Foundation). La Jolla, CA: University of California, San Diego.

Anderson, N. H. (1981a). *Foundations of information integration theory.* New York: Academic Press.

Anderson, N. H. (1981b). Integration theory applied to cognitive responses and attitudes. In R. E. Petty, T. M. Ostrom, & T. C. Brock (Eds.), *Cognitive responses in persuasion* (pp. 361–397). Hillsdale, NJ: Erlbaum.

Anderson, N. H. (1982). *Methods of information integration theory*. New York: Academic Press.

Anderson, N. H. (1983). *Psychodynamics of everyday life: Blaming and avoiding blame* (Tech. Rep. CHIP 120). La Jolla, CA: Center for Human Information Processing, University of California, San Diego. In N. H. Anderson (Ed.), *Contributions to information integration theory* (in press).

Anderson, N. H. (1986). A cognitive theory of judgment and decision. In B. Brehmer, H. Jungermann, P. Lourens, & G. Sevón (Eds.), *New directions in research on decision making* (pp. 63–108). Amsterdam: Elsevier North-Holland.

Anderson, N. H. (1987). [Review of Lau, R. R. & Sears, D. O. (Eds.): *Political cognition*]. *American Journal of Psychology. 100*, 295–298.

Anderson, N. H. (1988). A functional approach to person cognition. In R. S. Wyer, Jr., & T. K. Srull (Eds.), *Advances in social cognition* (pp. 37–51). Hillsdale, NJ: Erlbaum.

Anderson, N. H. (in press). Information integration approach to emotions and their measurement. In R. Plutchik & H. Kellerman (Eds.), *Emotion: Theory, research, and experience* (Vol. 4). New York: Academic Press.

Anderson, N. H., & Graesser, C. C. (1976). An information integration analysis of attitude change in group discussion. *Journal of Personality and Social Psychology, 34*, 210–222.

Anderson, N. H., & Shanteau, J. (1977). Weak inference with linear models. *Psychological Bulletin, 84*, 1155–1170.

Anderson, N. H., & Zalinski, J. (in press). Functional measurement approach to self-estimation in multiattribute evaluation. *Journal of Behavioral Decision Making*.

Armstrong, M. A. (1984). *Attitudes and attitude change in marriage, studied with information integration theory*. Unpublished doctoral dissertation, University of California, San Diego.

Armstrong, M. A. (1985). *Synthesizing theory and methods of symbolic interaction and cognitive psychology: An inductive research strategy*. Paper presented at Theory Construction and Research Methodology Workshop, annual meeting of the National Council on Family Relations, Dallas, TX.

Armstrong, M. A., & Anderson, N. H. (1983). *Influence in marriage, studied through information exchange*. Paper presented at Theory Construction and Research Methodology Workshop, annual meeting of the National Council on Family Relations, St. Paul, MN.

Bakeman, R., & Gottman, J. M. (1986). *Observing interaction: An introduction to sequential analysis* . London and New York: Cambridge University Press.

Beach, L. R., & Mitchell, T. R. (1987). Image theory: Principles, goals, and plans in decision making. *Acta Psychologica. 66*, 201–220.

Beach, L. R., & Morrison, D. (this volume). Expectancy theory and image theory in the description of decisions about childbearing. In D. Brinberg & J. Jaccard (Eds), *Dyadic decision making*. New York: Springer.

Benjamin, L. S. (1984). Principles of prediction using structural analysis of social behavior. In R. F. Zucker, J. Aronoff, & A. I. Rabin (Eds.), *Personality and the prediction of behavior* (pp. 121–174). New York: Academic Press.

Berscheid, E. (1983). Emotion. In H. H. Kelley, et al. (Eds.), *Close relationships* (pp. 110–168). San Francisco: Freeman.

Birchler, G. (1979). Communication skills in married couples. In A. S. Bellak & M. Hersen (Eds.), *Research and practice in social skills training* (pp. 273–315). New York: Plenum.

Blumer, H. (1969). *Symbolic interactionism: Perspective and method.* Englewood Cliffs, NJ: Prentice-Hall.

Burr, W. R., Leigh, G. K., Day R. D., & Constantine, J. (1979). Symbolic interaction and the family. In W. R. Burr, R. Hill, F. I. Nye, & I. L. Reiss (Eds.), *Contemporary theories about the family* (Vol. 2, pp. 42–111). New York: Free Press.

Conger, R. D., & Smith, S. S. (1981). Equity in dyadic and family interactions: Is there any justice? In E. E. Filsinger & R. A. Lewis (Eds.), *Assessing marriage* (pp. 217–231). Beverly Hills, CA: Sage.

Davis, J. H. (1973). Group decision and social interaction: A theory of social decision schemes. *Psychological Review, 80,* 97–125.

Davis, J. H., Cohen, J. L., Hornik, J., & Rissman, A. K. (1973). Dyadic decision as a function of the frequency distributions describing the preferences of members' constituencies. *Journal of Personality and Social Psychology, 26,* 178–195.

Eagly, A. (1983). Gender and social influence: A social psychological analysis. *American Psychologist, 38,* 971–981.

Farkas, A. J. (in press). *Cognitive algebra of interpersonal unfairness.* In N. H. Anderson (Ed.), *Contributions to information integration theory.*

Farkas, A. J., & Anderson, N. H. (1979). Multidimensional input in equity theory. *Journal of Personality and Social Psychology, 37,* 879–896.

Filsinger, E. E. (1983, October). [Comments on *Influence in Marriage* by Armstrong and Anderson.] Paper presented at Theory Construction and Research Methodology Workshop, annual meeting of the National Council on Family Relations, St. Paul, MN.

Filsinger, E. E., & Lewis, R. A. (Eds.) (1981). *Assessing marriage: New behavioral approaches.* Beverly Hills, CA: Sage.

Fishbein, M. (1976). A behavior theory approach to the relations between beliefs about an object and the attitude toward the object. In M. Fishbein (Ed.), *Readings in attitude theory and measurement.* New York: Wiley.

Fishbein, M., & Ajzen, I. (1975). *Belief, attitude, intention and behavior.* Reading, MA: Addison-Wesley.

Gottman, J. M. (1979). *Marital interaction: Experimental investigations.* New York: Academic Press.

Graesser, C. C. (1977). *A social averaging theorem for group decision making.* Unpublished doctoral dissertation, University of California, San Diego.

Graesser, C. C. (in press). *A social averaging theorem for group decision making.* In N. H. Anderson (Ed.), *Contributions to information integration theory.*

Grueneich, R. (1982). The development of children's integration rules for making moral judgments. *Child Development, 53,* 887–894.

Hastie, R. (1981). Schematic principles in human memory. In E. T. Higgins, C. P. Herman, & M. P. Zanna (Eds.), *Social cognition* (pp. 39–88). Hillsdale, NJ: Erlbaum.

Hogan, R. (1983). A socioanalytic theory of personality. In R. A. Dienstbier & M. M. Page (Eds.), *Nebraska Symposium on Motivation 1982* (pp. 55–89). Lincoln, NE: University of Nebraska Press.

Hommers, W., & Anderson, N. H. (1985). Recompense as a factor in assigned punishment. *British Journal of Developmental Psychology, 3,* 75–86.

Hommers, W., & Anderson, N. H. (in press). Algebraic schemes in legal thought and in everyday morality. In F. Lösel, H. Wegener, H. J. Haisch (Eds.), *Psychology and the criminal justice system*. Berlin: Springer.

Hooper, J. O. (1983, October). [Comments on Armstrong & Anderson: *Influence in marriage, studied through information exchange*.] Paper presented at Theory Construction and Research Methodology Workshop, annual meeting of the National Council on Family Relations, St. Paul, MN.

Huston, T. L. (1983). Power. In H. H. Kelley, et al. (Eds.), *Close relationships* (pp. 169–219). San Francisco: Freeman.

Jaccard, J., & Becker, M. A. (1985). Attitudes and behavior: An information integration perspective. *Journal of Experimental Social Psychology, 21*, 440–465.

Johnson-Laird, P. N. (1983). *Mental models*. Cambridge, MA: Harvard University Press.

Kaplan, K. J. (1972). From attitude formation to attitude change: Acceptance and impact as cognitive mediators. *Sociometry, 35*, 448–467.

Katz, D. (1960). The functional approach to the study of attitudes. *Public Opinion Quarterly, 24*, 163–204.

Kelman, H. C. (1974). Attitudes are alive and well and gainfully employed in the sphere of action. *American Psychologist, 29*, 310–324.

Leon, M. (1980). Integration of intent and consequence information in children's moral judgments. In F. Wilkening, J. Becker, & T. Trabasso (Eds.), *Information integration by children* (pp. 71–97). Hillsdale, NJ: Erlbaum.

Leon, M. (1984). Rules mothers and sons use to integrate intent and damage information in their moral judgments. *Child Development, 55*, 2106–2113.

Lowman, J. (1981). Love, hate, and the family: Measures of emotion. In E. E. Filsinger & R. A. Lewis (Eds.), *Assessing Marriage* (pp. 55–73). Beverly Hills, CA: Sage.

Mehan, H., & Wood, H. (1975). *The reality of ethnomethodology*. New York: Wiley.

McGuire, W. J. (1969). The nature of attitudes and attitude change. In G. Lindzey & E. Aronson (Eds.), *The handbook of social psychology* (2nd ed., Vol. 3, pp. 136–314). Reading MA: Addison-Wesley.

Miller, G. A., Galanter, E., & Pribram, K. (1960). *Plans and the structure of behavior*. New York: Holt, Rinehart and Winston.

Olson, D. H., & Ryder, R. G. (1970). Inventory of marital conflicts (IMC): An experimental interaction procedure. *Journal of Marriage and the Family, 32*, 443–448.

Piaget, J. (1965). *The moral judgment of the child* (M. Gabain, Trans.). New York: Free Press. (Originally published, 1932).

Scanzoni, J. (1979). Social processes and power in families. In W. R. Burr, R. Hill, F. I. Nye, & I. L. Reiss (Eds.), *Contemporary theories about the family* (Vol. 1, pp. 295–316). New York: Free Press.

Shanteau, J., & Nagy. G. F. (1979). Probability of acceptance in dating choice. *Journal of Personality and Social Psychology, 37*, 522–533.

Stryker, S., & Statham, A. (1985). Symbolic interaction and role theory. In G. Lindzey & E. Aronson (Eds.), *Handbook of social psychology* (3rd ed., Vol. 1, pp. 311–378).

Surber, C. F. (1977). Developmental processes in social inference: Averaging of intentions and consequences in moral judgment. *Developmental Psychology, 13*, 654–665.

Thompson, L. (1985, November). [Comments on Armstrong: *Synthesizing theory and methods of symbolic interaction and cognitive psychology: An inductive research strategy*.] Paper presented at Theory Construction and Research Methodology

Workshop, annual meeting of the National Council on Family Relations, Dallas, TX.

Troutman, C. M. & Shanteau, J. (this volume). Consumer information integration in husband-wife decision making. In D. Brinberg & J. Jaccard (Eds.), *Dyadic decision making*. New York: Springer-Verlag.

Walster, E., Walster, G. W., & Berscheid, E. (1978). *Equity: Theory and research*. Boston: Allyn and Bacon.

CHAPTER 2

The Role of the Relationship in Marital Decision Making

David A. Kenny and Linda K. Acitelli

Social behavior can be construed as relational in the sense that it is manifested by people in relation to other people. Ironically, the study of dyadic relationships has typically been individual-centered rather than relationship-centered. Often studies examine a single individual's views of, reactions to, and behavior toward another. Many times the other is an imaginary person or is a confederate who has been instructed to behave in a prespecified way. Sometimes the other is a real person like the subject, but the two persons are strangers who have no relational history. Even when persons are studied who have a relationship, all too often only one person is studied. Studying relationships with these procedures cannot possibly result in a complete understanding of relational processes. Much of supposedly dyadic research is really the study of individual processes.

Just because the two interacting persons are both observed does not mean the results are necessarily relational. Sometimes supposedly dyadic processes are actually individual ones. The critique of accuracy research in the mid 1950s hinged on this point. Accurate interpersonal perception, presumably a dyadic phenomenon, was shown to be in part an individual-level phenomenon in that it was influenced by response set, that is, how one generally viewed others. To study truly relational phenomena, we need to remove individual effects. The essential difficulty in dyadic research is the unconfounding of relational and individual phenomena.

In this chapter we will examine marital decision making from a relational point of view. Our concern is not what persons bring to a relationship but rather what is unique about their interaction. We will attempt to show that it is necessary to account for relational aspects to understand marital decision making. Where possible we will point to methodologies that have a relational component and are not exclusively individualistic.

In this chapter we will consider three different topics. First, we will discuss marital decision making from the point of view of the group productivity literature. Second, we will focus on the role of interpersonal perception in decision making. Finally, we will discuss the topic of decisions about the relationship.

Group Decision Making

Historically, an important topic in small group research has been the effects of group size on the quality of group decisions. The most critical group size comparison is that between groups and individuals: When do groups perform better than individuals? One very influential model in this area is Steiner's (1972) model of productivity. He argues that a group's productivity equals its potential productivity minus process loss. The potential productivity is determined by member resources and the type of task. Member resources are the knowledge and the skills that individuals bring to the task. Process refers to how a decision is reached as opposed to what the decision is, that is, the outcome. According to Steiner, process results in only decreased productivity, a view that we will question.

One type of Steiner task is an optimizing, discretionary task. An example of this type of task is to have people guess the room's temperature or have them estimate the population of Washington D.C. Steiner calls this a discretionary task because he assumes the group's decision is a weighted average of the individual members' opinions; what is discretionary is how the individuals' opinions are weighted. It is called an optimizing task because the correct answer is some optimum value. Optimizing is contrasted with maximizing, arriving at the correct answer as opposed to obtaining as many points as possible.

Couples frequently make discretionary decisions. They have to decide how much money to spend on a car, how long a vacation to take, how many years to wait to have children, and how many persons to invite to a party. These decisions differ from those in laboratory research because the correct answers are not known and often cannot be known, but the process of arriving at decisions may be the same.

In a discretionary task, the couple's decision is presumed to be a weighted average of the two persons' positions. If the decision is the number of children to have and he wants two and she wants four, and they decide to have three, then the weights are .5 for each person. More formally, if we denote one person's judgment as a, the other's as b, and the dyadic decision as c, then the weight for the first person is $(c - b)/(a - b)$. (If $a = b$ then the weight is .5.). The weight for the second person is one minus the weight of the first person.

Actually it is almost certainly never the case that the couple's decision is exactly a weighted average of their individual opinions. First, people often do not state exactly their own opinion. As will be discussed in the next section, people will sometimes state as their opinion the presumed opinion of their partner. People tell their partners what they think their partners want to hear. Second, the couple may in the course of their discussion create new information and this information may well influence their joint decision. Third, the weighted average model ignores the fact that in some dyadic decisions the joint decision is more extreme than either person's opinion. Such a result, which is called *polarization*, implies that the weight for one of the persons is negative, an anomalous result. Thus, the couple's decision is more than a weighted average of their individual opinions.

Because in laboratory studies the correct answers are known, the quality of group decisions can be determined. Research generally shows for optimizing, discretionary tasks that groups make better decisions than a random individual does (Steiner, 1972). The reason for this is found in the logic of statistics: An average is less variable than a single score. If the population mean of members' scores tends to be closer to the truth than a single randomly chosen person, then virtually any weighting of individual scores (even a random weighting) tends to be closer to the truth on average than a random score.

Although groups outperform individuals, they do not usually outperform a statistical average of scores from a pseudo-group of the same size (Hastie, 1986). So groups of size five are further away from the truth than the average of five randomly chosen scores of individuals. One explanation for this result is that groups are unequally weighting individual members' opinions, and those individuals with more influence are no more accurate than others. For instance, it is likely that a person who participates more is given greater weight. This variable weighting scheme tends to lower the quality of decisions. It follows then that the more heavily weighted persons do not necessarily have the better opinions.

Weights in marital decisions may not be equal for two reasons: power and impact. *Power* means that one person has more influence because of expertise, authority, or interpersonal skills. *Impact* means that one has more influence because the decision affects him or her more. That is, one person has more influence because the consequences of the decision alter that person's life more. For instance, consider the decision of whether or not to move to another part of the country. The decision might have more impact on the spouse who is moving to further his or her career. On the other hand, the impact may be greater for the other spouse who has to give up an already established position. While power has been studied, we know of no research on impact.

If in a given marriage the woman has more power than the man, it would be interesting to know whether she exerted more power in all of her relationships or only with her husband. That is, is her power individual-based or relationship-based? One could use the Social Relations Model (Kenny & La Voie, 1984; Malloy & Kenny, 1986) to determine the relative role of individual and dyadic effects in determining power. To use the model each person interacts with multiple partners. For instance, in a round robin design, all persons interact with each other. One important determinant of power is talk time (Dabbs & Ruback, 1987; Strodtbeck, 1951). Warner, Kenny, and Stoto (1979) using college students in pairs, Dindia (1987) using married couples in pairs, and Dabbs and Ruback (1987) using college students in groups have documented individual differences in talk time with the round robin design. That is, they were able to show that some persons talked proportionately more with all of their interaction partners. However, dyadic effects were also evident in that some persons talked consistently more to some partners

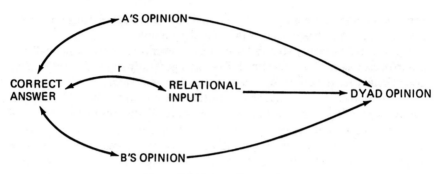

Figure 2.1. Process loss and gain.

than others. It thus appears that talk time is both individual-based and relationship-based. In addition to talk time, other variables that are related to power (unequal weighting of members' opinions) can also be studied by using the Social Relations Model.

As was stated earlier, the couple's final decision is not just a function of their prior positions. The interaction between the partners produces a relational input to decision making. Recall that Steiner claimed that process results only in productivity loss. As Shaw (1971) has suggested, communication can lead to a gain in the quality of group decisions, something Shaw calls *process gain*.

We propose a measure of process loss and gain. First, there must be a series of decisions that each couple makes. Then, for each decision we need to know both individuals' preferences and the group decision. As in Figure 2.1, we treat the group decision as the criterion and the two individuals' opinions as the predictor variables in a regression equation. Note that the units in this regression analysis are the series of decisions. Each of the couple's decisions will be influenced by other factors which are called relational input.

For each decision, there is an optimal response, which is labeled the *correct answer* in Figure 2.1. Process gain is indexed by the extent the relational input correlates with the correct answer. This correlation is denoted as r in Figure 2.1. If the correlation is positive there is evidence for process gain. The correlation r can be measured for each dyad and then be correlated with couple-level variables such as satisfaction or process variables. For instance, we might find that equal levels of participation lead to process gain.

The Role of Interpersonal Perception

In two-person relationships, interpersonal perception plays a central role (Sillars & Scott, 1983). Each person continually thinks about how his or her partner perceives the world and especially how his or her partner perceives him or her. This section is divided into three parts. In the first we define self and other perception and the three types of associations between them. In the second part, we discuss the sometimes paradoxical effects of assumed agreement in interpersonal communication. Finally, new approaches to studying interpersonal perception are presented.

Definitions

There are two major types of interpersonal perceptions. First, there is the perception of one's own opinion concerning a topic. We will call this the *self-perception*. Then there is the perception of what one thinks one partner's opinion is. We will call this the *other-perception*.

There are three important types of association between interpersonal perceptions: agreement, assumed agreement, and understanding. Consider a couple, John and Martha, who has a decision to make—whether to buy a Volvo or a Mercedes. (John and Martha are yuppies.) They would be in agreement if they both want to buy a Volvo. If John wants a Mercedes and Martha a Volvo, they would be in disagreement. There would be assumed agreement for John if he wants a Volvo and he thinks that Martha also wants a Volvo. There would be assumed disagreement if Martha wants a Volvo but she thinks that John wants a Mercedes. If Martha thinks that John wants a Volvo and he actually does want a Volvo, Martha understands John's position on this issue. Understanding concerns the extent to which a person knows how his or her partner feels about the topic. To define more formally these three types of association: Agreement is correspondence between his and her self-perceptions. Assumed agreement is the correspondence between one person's self-perception and that person's other-perception. Understanding is the correspondence between one person's self-perception and his or her partner's other-perception.

These three types of associations, while conceptually distinct, are related. If the couple agrees and they assume agreement, there must be understanding. More interestingly, if they actually agree but they assume that they disagree, then there must be no understanding.

Alternative terms for agreement are mutuality, similarity, and reciprocity. Terms for assumed agreement are perceived reciprocity, perceived similarity, and congruence. The term projection is sometimes used for assumed similarity. However, projection is usually viewed as an unconscious process whereas assumed similarity is, at least in part, a conscious process. Moreover, projection has psychoanalytic connotations that are not usually intended. Other terms for understanding are accuracy and empathy.

Assumed Agreement

A key aspect in close relationships is assumed agreement. As has been well documented, married couples tend to think that they agree more than they actually do (Levinger & Breedlove, 1966). However, distressed couples show less of a tendency to assume agreement than do happy couples. While assumed agreement maintains a semblance of harmony, it can lead to misunderstanding.

There are two different ways in which spouses can misunderstand one another. First, a couple can assume that they agree when they actually do not. Second, a couple can assume that they disagree when they actually agree. Let us consider each of these cases.

To exemplify the first case, consider a man who thinks that he and his future wife agree on whether or not to have children and so he does not discuss it with her. After they get married, he finds out that she does not want children. Ironically, this failure to communicate because the couple thinks that they agree is more likely to occur if the couple is satisfied. Underlying such a failure to communicate may be a person's fear of finding out that his or her spouse does not agree with him or her. Thus, to avoid conflict and to maintain harmony, spouses who assume they agree may prefer not to communicate their actual opinions to one another. Perhaps assumed agreement has been associated with marital satisfaction because those couples who assume agreement without communication are also those couples who wish to avoid conflict and to appear to be happy in their self-reports.

At the extreme, partners who always assume agreement may find it difficult to see their partners as persons who are different from themselves or different from their expectations of them. Without this ability to see one's partner as a separate individual, a spouse may believe communication is unnecessary. Furthermore, the rigid maintenance of partner expectations would render communication powerless in resolving conflict. Such expectations can also include the second type of misunderstanding, assumed disagreement.

In the second case, Laing (see especially Laing, Phillipson, & Lee, 1966) has suggested that in distressed couples, if partners assume disagreement, seemingly paradoxical decisions can result. Couples can do what neither wants to do, even though they each truly want to do the same thing. Say that Mary and Sam want to go to the movie "Godzilla Eats Tokyo," but they each think the other wants to stay home. Mary says to Sam, "You do not want to see that movie, do you?" Sam says, "I would be willing to go if you want to." Mary responds, "Let's just stay home. You do not want to go." Note that neither person lies nor distorts their opinions. They communicate not their opinions but rather their mistaken perceptions of the other's opinion. It also happens that persons communicate the perceptions of their partner as their own perception. She might say, "I don't want to go to the movie, do you ?" when she actually wants to go to the movie, but thinks that he does not.

However, each partner may or may not match his or her spouse on assumed agreement. One partner may assume agreement while the other does not. Let us presume that the man assumes agreement and the wife does not. Further, since it is known that assumed agreement is correlated with satisfaction, let us assume that he is satisfied with the relationship and she is not. Consider now what happens if they actually agree, for instance, they both want to go to the movie. She will think that they do not agree, and she may communicate what she thinks her husband feels as her own feeling. She might say, "I don't want to go the movie, do you?" He then thinks that she does not want to go to the movie. He may then hostilely respond to her: "I don't think we should always do what you want to do." So even though they agree, they may get into an argument.

What happens if they actually disagree? For instance, he wants to go to the movie and she does not. He thinks that they agree, and he thinks she wants to do what he wants to do. She thinks that they disagree, and she may state that she wants to go to the movie because she thinks he wants to even though she does not want to. He says, "Fine, let's go." Interestingly, it may happen that they will do the opposite of the dissatisfied member, which could in turn lead to further dissatisfaction.

To summarize, if one member assumes agreement and the other does not and if they actually agree, they may end up in an argument. If they actually disagree, they may end up doing what the person who assumes agreement wants to do. In both cases, the person who assumes disagreement may falsely communicate his or her perception of the other's opinion as his or her opinion.

Most investigations of interpersonal perception do not determine the ease with which spouses make assumptions about one another. Studies of agreement between spouses do not usually ask respondents to state how confident they are in judging their partners' views. Nor do these studies allow the respondent to choose "I don't know" as an alternative response. Typically, partners complete their questionnaires, and they are then asked to complete them as they think their spouses would complete them. We do not know how much couples typically vary in terms of their confidence in completing the task, nor do we know how the confident couples might differ in their decision making than the less confident couples.

Confidence in responding to an item might, in part, be a function of item content. Some items require more inference on the part of the respondent than others. Most investigators do not make the distinction between responses that require a great deal of inference and those that are derived from subject's perceptions of or experiences with his or her partner. The topics of items about which spouses already have shared knowledge (have discussed or observed) would be more likely to result in accurate predictions than items requiring spouses to make inferences. For example, "Which planet would you like to visit?" would require more inference and may be less likely to result in an accurate prediction than "What is your favorite food?" Therefore, studies of interpersonal perception would need further modification before incorporating them into decision-making research. Investigators would need to distinguish between responses based on inference and those based on perception. This would also help clarify the distinction between spouses who are comfortable assuming they know what their partner thinks about a particular topic and spouses who do not assume knowledge of their partners' thoughts.

New Methodological Approaches

We will discuss two different methodological ideas. One is a new and different approach to the topic of interpersonal perception—computer simulation. The other is a new analysis strategy for the data that are traditionally gathered.

Because it may be very difficult to gather data about interpersonal perception as well as observe communication patterns, computer simulation might prove an interesting way to study these processes. We can build on the work of Kelley (1985). He used a computer simulation to study the bargaining process. He showed that accurate interpersonal perception (what we have called understanding) improves dyadic outcomes. If persons know their partners' interaction matrix (the outcomes for the partner given different contingencies), they can improve their outcomes. Kelley's simulations assume perfect understanding. It would be interesting to study the effect of misperception.

We are currently developing an analysis modification of the existing research paradigm. Traditionally agreement, assumed agreement, and understanding are measured by associating two sets of perceptions. That is, agreement between two persons is measured across a set of topics. There are typically three types of measures: correlation, sum of squared differences, and sum of absolute discrepancies. (The term discrepancy should be preferred over difference because difference implies that the signs are preserved.) Whatever the measure used, we believe in the following type of adjustment.

Our approach (Kenny & Acitelli, 1987) is as follows. Let us consider agreement. First, agreement is measured by some index for each couple. Then each person is paired with someone else's spouse to form a pseudo-couple. From this pair a measure of "agreement" is computed and this serves as a measure of an individual's tendency to agree with a randomly paired spouse. For each person an agreement score can be taken for all pseudo-couples. The resulting data structure of agreement scores of pseudo-couples is a round robin data structure.

The rows of the round robin data respresent wives and the columns represent husbands. The couple's actual agreement score would be on the diagonal and all of the off-diagonal scores would be the agreement of the pseudo-couples.

We can view the agreement between a particular pseudo-couple as due to the tendency for the husband to have opinions that are typical of other wives and the wife to have opinions that are typical of other husbands. Thus, an agreement score is assumed to depend on the wife's and husband's typicality.

It is possible to remove these typicality effects to obtain a truly dyadic measure of agreement. We can estimate a component that measures each member's tendency to agree with persons of the opposite sex, the typicality score. (Typicality is closely approximated by the person's mean agreement with pseudo-partners.) We can then subtract the husband's and the wife's typicality score from the couple-agreement score. This will result in a dyadic measure of agreement. That is, there are two ways in which couples can appear to agree. First, their responses may be typical, and so they will agree with many people and not just their own spouse. This is an individual measure of agreement. Second, there can be unique dyadic agreement.

We applied this method in a study of 42 Midwest couples (Acitelli, 1986). We found that marital satisfaction is correlated with couple agreement. Couples who tended to agree with one another were more satisfied. But the reason for the correlation is that wives' tendencies to be agreeable correlate with satisfaction. There is little or no correlation between the purely relational measure of agreement with satisfaction. That is, women who have data that "agrees" with other men tend to have more satisfaction in their marriages, but if a woman uniquely agrees with her husband, there is not a greater level of satisfaction.

Thus, the role of interpersonal perception in marital decision making is likely to be complex. Not only must we consider spouses' tendencies to agree and assume they agree with each other, we need also to determine whether spouses' tendencies to agree occur across all spouses or only within the context of the marital relationship. Therefore, if researchers find an association between partner agreement and marital decision making, investigators should determine whether such agreement is unique to the marital relationship or due to the individual tendencies of the partners.

Decisions About the Relationship

So far we have discussed how agreement and assumptions of agreement might influence marital decision making. Studies of agreement typically focus on partners' perceptions of each other or of something external to themselves. Moreover, studies of decision making typically involve decisions about something other than the persons making the decisions, for example, what car to buy or how much to spend on food (Szinovacz, 1981).

It seems likely that these decisions differ from those decisions that couples make about their own relationship. Researchers studying such a question must address several issues. We do not intend to resolve all of them here, but rather point to the areas that researchers must clarify before embarking upon such a study.

Most importantly, the question of what constitutes a decision about the relationship must be answered. When partners decide to get married they have made an overt decision regarding their commitment to one another. The decision that they will be related to one another is obviously a decision about their relationship. But beyond that, couples can decide in more detail just what their relationship will entail. They can decide what being married means to them and what behaviors are appropriate within the context of their marriage. In short, partners can decide how they expect to relate to one another.

One very practical difficulty inherent in the study of such decision-making processes is that they rarely occur once a couple is married. Rosenblatt (1977) notes that "making a high commitment seems to be freedom from having to make decisions" (p. 83). On the other hand, Rosenblatt also notes that this freedom might also prevent discussions that might help resolve marital problems. Such discussions could reduce the aforementioned problem of assumed agreement or disagreement and could increase understanding between spouses. Thus, although decisions about the relationship may be important to its success, couples who make them may be difficult to find.

A related issue involves the distinction between individual and dyadic decision making. One partner can make decisions that can drastically change the nature of the relationship. John may decide to distance himself from Martha. Martha may decide to have an affair. Each partner, without consulting the other, has made a decision that affects their relationship. Could these individual decisions be considered decisions about the relationship? Or should investigators only include joint decisions (made by both partners)? These questions should be answered before researchers study this type of decision making.

The argument can be made, however, that John and Martha have made an implicit agreement about the nature of their relationship. Thus, a distinction must also be made between the unspoken creation of relational standards (see Montgomery, 1988), and the deliberate dyadic decision-making process. Couples often create the nature of their relationship without making explicit, joint decisions about it. Therefore, researchers need to make the distinctions between (1) implicit agreements and explicit decisions, and (2) individual and dyadic decisions about the relationship.

Another problem with studying decisions about relationships is the determination of success or failure. What constitutes a good decision about a relationship? Should the partners themselves decide or can there be more objective criteria? What is good for the relationship may or may not be seen as good for each partner, depending on how goodness is determined. Kelley (1983) has made the distinction between making a commitment to a partner and making a commitment to the relationship. Decision making could presumably be influenced by which type of commitment spouses have made. Partners with a relationship orientation may bring different agenda to the decision-making process than those with an individual orientation. What constitutes a good decision may be different between persons with these distinct orientations.

Matters become even more complicated with the consideration that decisions about the relationship influence the decision-making process itself. For example, the couple may have decided that the wife is the expert when it comes to the relationship and that she should be given more power in such decisions. Or a pair may have decided to be egalitarian in all types of decisions. Not only may the outcomes of such decisions differ, but the process of making the decisions about relationships may not be easily studied by traditional methods.

Investigations of such decisions might best involve the questions of how, when, and in what contexts they are made. These findings could then be related to each partner's perception of their own and the other's satisfaction with not only the outcome, but also with the process of making such decisions.

Conclusion

We have discussed three different questions. First, we have applied the group productivity literature to couple decisions and have shown ways in which partners are afforded unequal weights. Impact as well as power can contribute to their relative weighting. We also developed a method of measuring process loss and gain. Second, we have demonstrated that what spouses think about one another (interpersonal perception) should not be ignored when studying marital decision making. We discussed the various complicating influences that assumed agreement can have on couples' decisions. We also presented a way of assessing overlapping interpersonal perceptions that distinguishes the contributions of each partner from the contributions of their unique interaction. Finally, we have discussed decisions about the relationship. Various conceptual and methodological issues must be addressed before researching this type of decision.

Overall, we have shown that the role of the relationship in marital decision making can differ from the role of the individual. Methodological issues and conceptual concerns regarding the study of dyads were outlined. We have not so much summarized previous literature, but rather we have suggested new lines of research. We hope that these new lines of research will be pursued.

Acknowledgments. Supported in part by a grant to the first author from the National Institute of Mental Health, R01 MH4029501.

References

Acitelli, L. K. (1986). The influence of relationship awareness on perceived marital satisfaction and stability, Doctoral dissertation, The University of Michigan, Ann Arbor.

Dabbs, Jr., J. M., & Ruback, R. B. (1987). Dimensions of group processes: Amount and structure of vocal interaction. In L. Berkowitz (Ed.), *Advances in experimental social psychology* (Vol. 21). Orlando, FL: Academic Press.

Dindia, K. (1987). Communication with spouses and strangers. In P. Noller & M. A. Fitzpatrick (Ed.), *Perspectives on marital interaction*. San Diego: College Hill Press.

Hastie, R. (1986). Review essay: Empirical research on accuracy of group judgment. In B. Grotman & G. Owen (Eds.), *Information pooling and group decision making*. Westport, CT: JAI Press.

Kelley, H. H. (1983). Love and commitment. In H. H. Kelley, E. Berscheid, A. Christensen, J. H. Harvey, T. L. Huston, G. Levinger, E. McClintock, L. A. Peplau, & D. R. Peterson (Eds.), *Close relationships*. New York: Freeman.

Kelley, H. H. (1985). A theoretical analysis by means of computer robots, of single interactions in 2 × 2 games. *Electronic Social Psychology, 1*, Article #8501013.

Kenny, D. A., & Acitelli, L. K. (1987). How marital pairs view their relationships: A round robin analysis. Unpublished manuscript, University of Connecticut.

Kenny, D. A., & La Voie, L. (1984). The social relations model. In L. Berkowitz (Ed.), *Advances in experimental social psychology* (Vol. 18). Orlando: Academic Press.

Laing, R. D., Phillipson, H., & Lee, A. R. (1966). *Interpersonal perception: A theory and a method of research.* New York: Harper & Row.

Levinger, G., & Breedlove. J. (1966). Interpersonal attraction and agreement: A study of marriage partners. *Journal of Personality and Social Psychology, 4*, 367–372.

Malloy, T. E., & Kenny, D. A. (1986). The Social Relations Model: An integrative method for personality research. *Journal of Personality, 54*, 199–225.

Montgomery, B. (1988). Quality communication in personal relationships. In S. Duck (Ed.), *Handbook of personal relationships.* London: Wiley.

Rosenblatt, P. C. (1977). Needed research on commitment in marriage. In G. Levinger & H. L. Raush (Eds.), *Close relationships: Perspectives on the meaning of intimacy.* Amherst: University of Massachusetts Press.

Shaw, M. E. (1971). *Group dynamics: The psychology of small group behavior.* New York: McGraw Hill.

Sillars, A. L., & Scott, M. D. (1983). Interpersonal perception between intimates: An integrative review. *Human Communication Research, 10*, 153–176.

Steiner, I. D. (1972). *Group process and productivity.* New York: Academic Press.

Strodtbeck, F. L. (1951). Husband-wife interaction over revealed differences. *American Sociological Review, 16*, 468–473.

Szinovacz, M. E. (1981). Relationship among marital power measures: A critical review and an empirical test. *Journal of Comparative Family Studies, 12*, 151–169.

Warner, R., Kenny, D. A., & Stoto, M. (1979). Round robin analysis of variance for social interaction data. *Journal of Personality and Social Psychology, 37*, 1742–1757.

CHAPTER 3

Expectancy Theory and Image Theory in the Description of Decisions About Childbearing

Lee Roy Beach and Diane Morrison

In 1973, Hoffman and Hoffman issued a call for the study of the psychological costs and benefits that influence decisions about childbearing. This call prescribed an alternative to the then dominant demographic viewpoint that featured the social correlates of childbearing. The alternative featured the assumption that the positive (benefits) and negative (costs) consequences of childbearing for individual couples dictated the decisions that they made (see Newman & Thompson (1976) for examples of this line of research.)

The first purpose of this chapter is to examine critically the adequacy of the cost-benefit assumption for childbearing decisions in particular, and for personal decisions in general. The second purpose is to introduce an alternative logic and to outline some of its implications for the study of childbearing decisions.

The Benefits and Costs of Cost-Benefit

The various responses to Hoffman and Hoffman's (1973) call interpreted cost-benefit rather loosely. Indeed, most investigations were couched in one or another of the family of models that make up "expectancy theory," (e.g., Beach, Townes, Campbell, & Keating, 1976; Davidson & Jaccard, 1975, 1979; Fried, Hofferth, & Udry, 1980; Fried & Udry, 1979; Loken & Fishbein, 1978; Werner, Middlestadt-Carter, & Crawford, 1975; Vinokur-Kaplan, 1978).

All of these variations on the expectancy theme are linear models in that they are of the form $y = a + b_1x_1 + b_2x_2 + \cdots + b_nx_n$. In general, y is an indicant of the overall attractiveness of a course of action (having a baby), each x_i is an indicant of the attractiveness of a specific consequence of the action, i = 1 to n, and each b_i is an indicant of the impact that its x_i has on the final product sum, y. In each variation on the expectancy theme the components of this linear form are interpreted in a slightly different way, hence the variation, but because they all use it, they are all more alike than different (Mitchell & Beach, 1977).

The linear model is a mainstay in psychology because of its benefits—it is simple and familiar (if only from our basic statistics courses) and it predicts behavior. Its simplicity and familiarity are a benefit because they free theorists from having to explain the math, which allows them to concentrate on the content (the x_i) of interest. The linear model's predictiveness is a benefit only if predictiveness is all that is required, otherwise it is a cost. That is, the model is exceptionally robust (Dawes, 1979; Dawes & Corrigan, 1974); unless the process the model proports to describe is grossly nonlinear, the model usually will do a creditable job of predicting its output (Fischhoff, Goitein, & Shapira, 1983). Because researchers tend to rely upon predictiveness as the major test of their theories' validity, the robustness of the underlying linear model biases in favor of apparent validity. Thus, if by validity one merely means predictiveness, then the robustness of the linear model might be thought of as beneficial. On the other hand, this criterion is distressingly similar to the interpretations of demographic data that motivated the Hoffman and Hoffman (1973) call in the first place. The demographic studies could predict childbearing, but they failed to illuminate the nature of the childbearing decision itself. Predictiveness in expectancy investigations, capitalizing as it does on the robustness of the linear model, similarly fails to illuminate. In this sense robustness is a cost because it may lead to an inflated belief in how well we understand childbearing decisions.

Another questionable benefit of cost-benefit logic is its focus upon the possible consequences of performing a specific act and the attractiveness of those consequences to the decision maker. The overall attractiveness of the act is a function of the net balance between the potentially good consequences and the potentially bad consequences. Some variants view the propensity to perform the act as an increasing function of the size of the net balance in the positive direction or of the net difference among a set of options (e.g., Fishbein's model). Other variants view the decision as all-or-none; when the balance is unequal the decision is determined solely by the direction of the imbalance, not by its magnitude. The latter commonly is called "maximization." In either case the decision follows the net payoff. In essence, the decision maker is motivated by something akin to a profit motive. The questionableness of cost-benefit logic lies in the fact that although a profit motive interpretation of choice motivation has intuitive and theoretical appeal (a benefit), decision makers often strongly disavow its role in personal decisions such as those about childbearing. The strength of these disavowals suggests that a model incorporating a concept like profit motivation may not be descriptively accurate (a cost).

Some Lessons Learned

Now we turn to what our own and others' data have to teach about the adequacy of cost-benefit logic in describing decisions. We will begin by refering to data from a childbearing decision study done in our own laboratory (Beach, Campbell, & Townes, 1979). Then we will review the conclusions drawn by investigators who have studied decision making in other contexts.

The Childbearing Decision Study

The results of the Beach et al. (1979) study appear to support the descriptive validity of a cost-benefit approach to investigating couples' childbearing decisions. However, closer examination reveals several serious flaws:

1. Although the model apparently described the decisions made by couples who had not yet attained their desired family sizes (DFS), it could not do so for those who had not. This was because very few (5) of the 68 couples who had attained their DFS decided to have yet another child. This was true even for the couples in this group (2 out of 19) for whom the perceived benefits associated with having another child exceeded the perceived costs. It was as though having achieved the prior goal of a specific number of children made considering another child an empty, irrelevant exercise, even though the other considerations favored having the child.
2. Even in the case of the 97 couples who had not yet attained their DFS, the errors in prediction were systematic and could not be accounted for solely in terms of cost-benefit. Negative decisions were correctly predicted but positive decisions were not, an error pattern found in other expectancy theory studies (Davidson & Beach, 1981). That is, of the 21 couples who were predicted to decide *not* to have a child, 18 (86%) decided not to and only 3 (14%) decided to do so. In contrast, of the 76 couples who were predicted to decide to have a child, only 53 (70%) did so while 23 (30%) did not. As discussed by Davidson and Beach (1981) and Beach, Hope, Townes, and Campbell (1982), this result reflects an unwillingness to leave the status quo unless the attractiveness of the alternative (having the child) is extremely attractive (the latter article reports similar results for sterilization decisions). These decisions are called *optional change* decisions, because the decision maker has the option of remaining with the status quo, in contrast to *nonoptional change* decisions, in which the status quo ceases to be an option and the question is what to do next. Deciding what to do after graduating from college or after losing one's job are examples of nonoptional change decisions.
3. Examination of the consequences that had a large effect on couples' childbearing decisions showed that they were different from those that had a small effect. In general, the decision turned on consequences such as the possible impact of a (another) child on the parents' achievement of educational or career goals, their growth and maturity, their relationship, or on the well-being of the family (Townes, Campbell, Wood & Beach, 1980). These consequences can be cast as profit or loss, costs or benefits, but doing so requires considerable contortion. A more straightforward interpretation is that the contributing consequences were those involving the child's compatibility with a couple's existing values, goals, and plans. Thus, com-

patibility, or "fit," of a (another) child with the rest of a couple's life and their vision of their future, rather than maximization of return, appeared to most heavily influence the childbearing decision.

Observations in Other Settings

The descriptive inadequacy of expectancy versions of cost-benefit has been noted for other than childbearing decisions. For example, Mintzberg (1973) observed managers while they made a variety of decisions and found that most of the decisions were about optional change and that few involved explicit balancing of costs and benefits. Peters (1979) confirmed these findings and, in addition, observed that ". . . managers seldom deal with problems in isolation. They deal with a 'flow'" (p. 167). The flow is the ongoing execution of plans in pursuit of communally recognized goals. Moreover, Peters found that managers' decisions seldom diverted that flow by much; the decisions usually nudged it in the proper direction. In fact, the criterion for decisions seldom was whether or not the change offered a maximal payoff. Rather it was, "Does this option contain the thrust we want to see?" (p. 166). Peters agrees with Selznick's (1957) conclusion that the decision-making manager primarily acts as a promoter and protector of the organization's values.

These and similar studies have led to conclusions such as, ". . . The problem may well be . . . that subjects just do not follow expectation models" (Hershey & Shoemaker, 1980, p. 417), or ". . . there is a nagging suspicion that expectancy theory overintellectualizes the cognitive processes people go through when choosing alternative actions" (Schwab, Olian-Gottlieb, & Heneman, 1979, p. 146), or "The story of behavioral decision theory has been the growing realization that [the model] often does not describe the decision-making process . . . The dramatic tension has been provided by [the model's] remarkable ability to hang on despite mounting doubts about its descriptive competence" (Fischhoff et al., 1983, p. 185).

In summary, the costs of using expectancy versions of cost-benefit logic seem to outweigh the benefits. Their robust linear form may be responsible for a fair portion of the observed predictive accuracy. The failure of the logic to account for the fine grain of the data from the Beach et al. (1979) study, one of the few studies that explicitly used cost-benefit in a straightforward manner, are inconsistent with cost-benefit logic. Observations of ongoing decisions in other settings have led many investigators to severely question the descriptive adequacy of expectancy theory. Clearly an alternative description is needed, an alternative that differs from the characterization provided by expectancy theory, but that still accounts for those infrequent decisions for which decision makers actually attempt to balance costs and benefits. Most important, to account for the majority of decisions the alternative description must be of an almost nondeliberative process that is motivated less by maximization of gain and loss than by the desire to keep life on an even keel and to maintain progress toward the many goals that make up the decision maker's vision of the future.

Image Theory

Image theory is a schema theory. There are many kinds of schema theories, each specific to some particular behavioral area, for example, script theory, stereotype theory, prototype theory, etc.—and image theory. Images (Miller, Galanter, & Pribram, 1960) are schemata that are specific to decision behavior and that represent the decision maker's ideals or principles relevant to some sphere of decision making, his or her goals in that sphere, what he or she is doing to reach those goals, and his or her view of how those efforts are faring. Image theory is described in detail in a number of places (e.g., Beach & Mitchell, 1985, 1987; Mitchell, Rediker, & Beach, 1986); a brief outline of its salient points will serve the present purpose.

The Images

Image theory holds that decisions are the result of the decision maker's management of the following four informational representations, called images, that constitute his or her decision schema.

Self Image

The constituents of the self-image are the decision maker's basic values, morals, ethics, principles, etc., which are unquestioningly regarded as self-evidently and imperatively desirable. Examples are religious principles, requisites of good manners and standards for social intercourse, and fundamental personal beliefs.

Trajectory Image

The constituents of the trajectory image are the decision maker's immediate and remote goals, temporally ordered to form an agenda for the future. Examples are landmark goals such as getting a Ph.D. degree or more humble goals such as finishing a project on time. Candidates for adoption as new goals for this image are evaluated in terms of the constituents of the self image and in terms of the existing constituents of the trajectory image. The decision rule is that candidates that are insufficiently compatible with the constituents of these two images are not adopted for the trajectory image.

Action Image

The constituents of the action image are the various plans that the decision maker implements to attain the goals on the trajectory image. Examples are taking specific courses, scheduling generals, writing a proposal, gathering data, writing the dissertation, all in the service of attaining the Ph.D. goal. When a new goal is adopted or when progress toward goal attainment is insufficient, a new plan must be adopted for the action image. The decision rule is that to be adopted, the evaluation of a candidate to become this new plan must show it to be both compatible with the self image (i.e., it must not seriously violate the decision maker's principles), and to offer promise for goal attainment by increasing the projected image's compatibility with the trajectory image.

Projected Image

The constituents of the projected image are the events and states that the decision maker anticipates will eventuate if he or she does what he or she plans to do in an attempt to achieve the goals on the trajectory image. For example, in implementing the plan to achieve the Ph. D., the decision maker may realize that the necessary course work will not be offered at the times that were assumed in the original plan, thereby threatening goal attainment. When evaluation of the correspondence between the projected image and the trajectory image shows that the two do not match, that they are insufficiently compatible, the decision rule requires reevaluation of the plans and either replacement by more promising plans or, if no plan seems promising, rejection of the related goals as unattainable.

Types of Decisions and Decision Rules

Image theory requires one to view decisions in a slightly different way than is customary. Rather than solely being about alternative courses of action, decisions primarily are about adopting or rejecting goals and plans of action, and secondarily about whether those plans are making sufficient progress toward achieving those goals to warrant continuing with their implementation. These are called *adoption decisions* and *progress decisions*, respectively.

Decisions are evaluated in terms either of a *compatibility criterion* or a *profitability criterion*, or a combination of the two. Compatibility is a simple, easily evaluated criterion for the acceptability for adoption of a goal or plan, or of the "fit" between the trajectory and projected images. It is defined as whether or not a candidate goal or plan is sufficiently congruent with the self image (principles), trajectory image (existing goals), or the action image (existing plans) to warrant its adoption. When a candidate goal or plan is being considered for adoption, the decision maker simply tallies the number of constituents of each image that the candidate "violates." When this sum exceeds threshold, the candidate is rejected, otherwise it is accepted. Compatibility also is the criterion for acceptable congruity between the trajectory and projected images. In this case the decision rule is that when the number of violations exceeds some threshold, reassessment of the plans and goals is instigated. However, the decision maker seldom explicitly is aware of these violations per se. That is, violations may not be monitored consciously. Rather, violations generate an emotional state of discomfort about the candidate goal or plan, or about the progress being made toward a goal. This emotional state is revealed in statements such as, "Somehow that just doesn't seem like the right thing to do," or "I would feel bad about doing that," or "I don't feel like I'm getting anywhere on this."

The congruity criterion is conservative. It is noncompensatory in that good "fit" with some constituents will not compensate for bad "fit" with others. This means that sufficient compatibility is rather difficult to attain and it therefore serves to maintain the status quo and avoid abrupt and profound changes in the ongoing course of the decision maker's life. Decisions based upon the compatibility criterion ordinarily are referred to as "intuitive" decision because sufficient compatibility is simple to ascertain and usually is emotionally mediated; the decision maker is unaware of the specifics of the process—he or she merely knows whether things "feel okay" or not.

Profitability is defined as the *degree to which* a candidate goal or plan conforms to the existing set of images (it is only for adoption decisions, not for progress decisions). Here the decision criterion is not merely sufficient compatibility, it also includes maximization. That is, when deciding among multiple alternatives, the subset of alternatives that are sufficiently compatible with the decision maker's images are passed on for evaluation in terms of their relative profitability. The alternative with the maximal *combined* compatibility and profitability is selected. This combination is compensatory and the process that uses it is described to one degree or other by expectancy versions of cost-benefit. Degree of profitability is conceptually similar to degree of utility: It is negative, neutral, or positive. The negative degrees and positive degrees (costs and benefits) compensate for (balance) each other, and the maximization rule dictates that the candidate with the larger net degree should be selected.

Finally, decision situations are either optional or nonoptional. Optional decisions, in which it is possible to remain with the status quo, constitute the majority of decisions that are encountered. Childbearing decisions ordinarily are of this kind. These decisions almost always are made on the basis of sufficiency of compatibility between the alternative to the status quo, a potential new goal or plan, and the principles that constitute the self image as well as the existing goals and plans that constitute the trajectory and action images. Nonoptional decisions are those in which it is not an option to remain with the status quo. They almost always involve multiple alternatives, each of which is a potential replacement for the terminating status quo. Childbearing decisions *may* become nonoptional for women as they approach their perceived biological deadline for having children (or for men as they approach their perceived energy and stamina limits for being fathers). Nonoptional decisions are made using maximization of profitability and the process approximates the descriptions provided by expectancy versions of cost-benefit analysis.

It should be noted in passing that image theory, which began as a theory of individual decision making (Beach & Mitchell, 1987), has been generalized to decision making by individuals working in groups (Mitchell et al., 1986). This will become relevant later on when we discuss the implications of the theory for couples' childbearing decisions, viewing couples as two-member groups.

Clearly, image theory does not refute or even conflict with expectancy theory. Instead, it provides an alternative, broader conceptual framework that goes beyond expectancy theory to address the descriptive inadequacy of the very analytic, compensatory decision process implied by expectancy theory but so seldom observed in practice. That is, introspection as well as observation of others' decisions (e.g., Mintzberg, 1973; Peters, 1979) makes it difficult to believe that the decisions we all attribute to intuition and muddling through are aptly described by a process that presumes careful balancing and maximizing or some version thereof. Indeed, it is this lack of belief that makes clinical workers resist attempts to dress up reproductive decision making in the logical, rational trappings of expectancy theory. In contrast, by advancing the concept of sufficiency of compatibility between candidates and images as the criterion for most personal decisions, image theory provides a more palatable description of intuitive decision processes. At the same time, by retaining the concept of maximization of profitability for decisions for which decision makers actually attempt to be logical, rational, and careful, image theory retains and encompasses the attractive aspects of the expectancy variants of cost-benefit.

Implications for Research

The first research implication of image theory for childbearing decisions is that before a study begins it is necessary to understand whether the decision makers view the decision as optional or nonoptional. For decisions viewed as optional, sufficiency of compatibility is the focus. The research interest will be in which of the decision maker's principles, goals, and plans play dominant roles in determining the decision.

However, if the decision makers view the decision as nonoptional, the focus is different and the investigation becomes more complicated. Recall the subtle but important theoretical assumption that nonoptional decisions usually involve the relative profitability of multiple alternatives, each of which is sufficiently compatible with the decision maker's images to make it acceptable in its own right were it the sole alternative under consideration. This means that nonoptional decisions are three-stage, requiring (1) assessment of compatibility, (2) evaluation of profitability, and (3) combining assessed compatibility and evaluated profitability in order to apply the maximization rule.

For example, suppose a working married woman loses her job (the status quo ceases). Suppose she finds that she has four alternatives to which she can turn. She can move on to a similar job; she can go back for an MBA degree; she can become a mother; she can collect unemployment while concentrating on her tennis game. She regards these four candidate goals as mutually exclusive and exhaustive, at least in the short run. Moreover, while the first three are compatible with her principles and her other goals and plans, tennis supported by unemployment insurance is not. She therefore rejects the fourth candidate and retains the first three. However, this does not mean that she feels indifferent among the remaining three even though they all are compatible with her images. It merely means that while she may feel that one of them "fits" better than the others (i.e., fewer violations), she would not be displeased by any of them (i.e., they all have sufficiently few violations).

To decide among the three acceptable goal candidates it is necessary for the woman to consider their relative merits more closely. Because all of the information provided by compatibility already has been used to get this far in the decision, getting further requires new information. The new information is in the form of conjectures about each candidate goal's potential consequences and the perceived costs and benefits, and losses and profits, represented by these consequences. The final decision is made by selecting the candidate for which the expected profits most heavily outweigh the losses. Note, however, that a condidate's total profitability includes the woman's feelings about how compatible it is with her other images.

This example shows that even though nonoptional decisions resemble expectancy variants of cost-benefit, they apparently are more complicated than those variants suggest. The process suggested by image theory is three-stage; the final set of candidates all must pass muster on compatibility before profitability is considered, and compatibility and profitability must be combined before the maximization rule is applied. However reasonable all of this may seem, the fact remains that the existence of and the working of this three-step process must be investigated experimentally.

The second research implication of image theory involves the design of counseling methods to aid decisions about childbearing. This was one purpose of the Beach et al. (1979) study. The product was the Optional Parenthood Questionnaire (OPQ; Beach et al., 1978), which was a "decision aid" for helping people think through and evaluate the consequences of having a (another) child. The OPQ was used primarily in family planning counseling, and over 2,000 copies were distributed. However, a follow-up survey of counselors revealed that they did not use it in the way intended by the researchers who created it. They seldom had their clients numerically evaluate the probabilities and utilities of the various consequences. Even when they did, they seldom performed the cumbersome calculations that are necessary to precisely weight and balance the evaluations. On the rare occasions that they did the calculations, they did not use the results to prescribe the "correct"decision to the clients. Instead, they used the OPQ as a consciousness-raising device. That is, they used it to lead their clients through a thorough but informal survey of their own feelings about the implications of having the child. In short, they used the OPQ to educate intuition rather than to help their clients perform a precise analytical examination of the costs and benefits of having the child.

Instead of berating the counselors or bemoaning their lack of appreciation of cost-benefit-based prescriptive decision aids, we must recognize that the education of intuition is a quite legitimate enterprise. Certainly from the point of view of image theory it is fundamental. Educated intuition is better able to assess compatibility. Because childbearing decisions usually are optional decisions, assessment of compatibility is the sole basis for decision making, and anything that facilitates its assessment will be of value.

Facilitation of compatibility assessment raises an interesting research question that must be part of the research on decision aids. It has become axiomatic in psychology that the human mind is a limited information processor. However, the data that demonstrate this refer almost exclusively to conscious capacity. We have little or no idea about nonconscious or unconscious capacity, especially when the process in question involves something as simple as merely tallying violations. Thus, an important prior question for decision aiding and the education of intuition involves finding out just what such aids are in aid of. That is, if there are cognitive limits on the thoroughness of compatibility assessment, how severe are they and what are their ramifications for decision making? Until this has been addressed in childbearing decisions and elsewhere, attempts to design decision aids may be premature.

The third research implication of image theory involves couples making decisions together. In our research on childbearing decisions (Beach et al., 1979) and our related work on voluntary sterilization (Beach et al., 1982), we found that couples' decide to stay with the status quo unless the alternative was extremely attractive. In the course of examining these data further we found that there were two ways in which a couple could end up staying with the status quo. One way was for neither partner to strongly favor the alternative (having a child or sterilization). The other way was for one partner to favor the alternative and the other not favor it, thus leaving them stalemated (although for both childbearing and sterilization the woman's view counted for more than the man's). Stalemated couples were labeled "conflict couples" (Beach et al., 1979). Of the 97 couples in the childbearing study who had not already attained their desired family size, 25 were conflict couples. Of the 150 couples in the sterilization study, another 25 were conflict couples.

Examination of the individual conflict couples' results showed that there were major differences in what was determining the two partners' disparate viewpoints, and that these differences often were about consequences that, in image theory terms, could be described as principles and goals. Indeed, the overall impression was that these conflicting partners held distinctly different views and that they often did not recognize how much their views differed from their respective partner's. In related work, Wood, Campbell, Townes, and Beach (1977) describe cases in which such differences were encountered in the course of family-planning counseling using the OPQ. They suggest that these differences could be used as a way of diagnosing the stability of the couples' relationships. Subsequent anecdotal reports by other counselors who have used the OPQ in their practices indicate that such differences frequently are encountered and that counseling often revolves around them.

While conflict couples constituted a minority of the couples in these two studies, they still were a sizable minority ($50/247 = 20\%$). Moreover, as pointed out by Wood et al. (1977), conflict in an area as basic to a relationship as family building may be symptomatic of a relationship that is unstable and in danger of dissolution. It is this issue that constitutes the third research area, and we turn now to its image theory interpretation.

It is easy to assert that conflict implies that a relationship is in difficulty. However, beyond the inherent reasonableness of such an assertion, image theory provides a framework for understanding it. A digression is necessary in order to make the reasoning clear. We begin by describing a study by Beach, Smith, Lundell, and Mitchell (1988), a study that arose in the course of attempts to extend image theory to individuals working in groups (Mitchell et al., 1986).

As a background, assume first that the decision maker's decision schema (the four images and the related decision mechanisms) in the reproductive decision sphere has counterparts in other spheres of his or her life. Second, assume that one of these other spheres is the decision maker's job, and that the images comprising his or her job decision schema share principles, goals, and plans with the job decision schema of fellow employees. Third, assume that decision makers can differentiate between their own individual job decision schemata and that of the employing organization, that is, they can differentiate between their own images and those of "the company."

The rationale for these assumptions lies in observations about how employees become acculturated to an employing organization. Acculturation requires that each employee learn about the guiding principles, the "culture" of the organization (Peters & Waterman, 1982). Moreover, in order to function effectively in the organization, each employee must adopt (accept, buy into) the major points of the organization's culture. When this happens, the company's principles to some degree become part of each employee's job decision schema. Of course, the decision maker can differentiate between his or her own private images, the "I" part of his or her schema, and those of the organizational culture to which he or she now belongs, the "we" part of his or her schema. The result is that different employees who may have very different images for other spheres of their lives may have very similar images for their job decision schemata because they share images for the organization as an entity separate from, but including, themselves—"What we do at Company X, what we believe, what we strive for."

From a research viewpoint this acculturation process provides a natural laboratory for examining the role of the self image in adoption of goals or of plans. Capitalizing on this, the Beach et al. (1988) study examined the shared "we" job decision schemata of executives in two large, nationally known, historically successful commercial firms. Although it was not anticipated, one firm was untroubled throughout the period of the research project, while the other firm was greatly troubled and came near to failing. The results showed that in the untroubled firm the executives had highly shared "we" schema that clearly influenced their decisions about the firm's activities. In contrast, the troubled firm's executives disagreed about the "we" schema and disagreed in their decisions about what the firm should do.

At first glance this line of thought may seem far removed from the issue of conflict couples making decisions about childbearing. However, if couples are thought of as two-partner organizations that each have their own culture ("what we do, believe, strive for"), the results of the Beach et al. (1988) study have very important implications. Just as the untroubled firm's stability was reflected in highly shared views about what it valued and how it ought to behave, the partners in a stable relationship might be expected to exhibit similarly shared views. Just as the troubled firm's instability was reflected in the absence of unanimity among its employees about values and behavior, so too might couples in an unstable relationship lack unanimity, especially about something as central to a relationship as childbearing.

To go even further, it may well be that the partners in stable couples share a "we" schema to which their respective "I" schemata are to a large degree similar. In contrast, the partners in an unstable relationship, conflict couples, may not have similar "we" schemata, and this dissimilarity may result from their incorrect assumptions that "we" are more like "I" than is justified.

There are several lines of research in the literature on marital conflict and interpersonal attribution that, to one degree or other, support what is being suggested here. One such line has focused on the congruence between individuals' self-concepts and their partners' concepts of them. People tend to form relationships with individuals who see them as they see themselves (Swann, 1983) and are happier in such relationships (Laing, Phillipson, & Lee, 1966; Swann & Predmore, 1985). Research on self-disclosure and perspective taking in close relationships has focused on individuals' attempts to explain their points of view to their partners and to understand conflicts from their partners' viewpoints. Higher rates of self-disclosure are associated with greater happiness in close relationships (Burke, Weir, & Harrison, 1976). Franzoi, Davis, and Young (1985) found that greater perspective taking skill was related to greater relationship satisfaction, over and above the effects of self-disclosure.

Attribution theory also has been extended to the study of close relationships. Sillars (1985) distinguishes between attributions (naive constructions of the partner's intentions and feelings) and metaperspectives (understanding from the partner's perspective). He notes that familiarity, though generally assumed to lead to greater understanding, also may be misleading and cause people to overestimate how much they know about their partners. This can result in entrenchment of existing impressions such that partners fail to notice, acknowledge, or adapt to changes in the other person.

Knudson (1985) comes closest to the concept of a "we" schema. In his view, marital compatibility is a function of "the degree to which, at any given point in time, the parties . . . have achieved and can sustain a shared construction of reality" (p. 233). The concept of a shared construction of reality emphasizes the partners' shared views of themselves as opposed to their views of themselves as separate units. In the same vein, Berger and Kellner (1984) suggest that couples are motivated to construct a joint reality through both their relationship generally and through conversation with each other, resulting in a strengthened relationship and a stable "common objectivated reality" (p. 10).

In short, ideas similar to those being advanced here already exist in the literature—which is comforting. However, while the research resulting from them may bear on the issue, they do not speak directly to the question of childbearing decisions and the stability of couples' relationships. Moreover, they do not have a common theoretical core, such as image theory, to hold them together.

Concluding Remarks

Expectancy theory responses to the Hoffman and Hoffman (1973) call have proved to be valuable. They identified many of the factors, the "costs and benefits," that predict decisions about childbearing, even though there are systematic prediction errors. On the other hand, although predictive ability is necessary for affirming a theory's descriptive ability, it is not sufficient. There are compelling reasons to doubt that expectancy theory describes the processes by which childbearing decisions usually are made.

Image theory is an alternative process description. Its key feature is the primacy of the compatibility criterion for optional decisions, and most childbearing decisions are optional decisions. Compatibility favors the status quo and it assures that changes from the status quo are not radically disruptive of the ongoing flow of the decision maker's life (his or her images). It also is "intuitive," in that assessment of compatibility usually is emotionally mediated rather than consciously calculated.

In large part, image theory grew out of research on decisions about childbearing. Now it is time to go back and empirically test the theory's descriptive adequacy for decision making about childbearing and related matters, perhaps along the lines suggested herein.

References

Beach, L. R., Campbell, F. L., & Townes, B. D. (1979). Subjective expected utility and the prediction of birth-planning decisions. *Organizational Behavior and Human Performance, 24,* 18–28.

Beach, L. R., Hope, A., Townes, B. D., & Campbell, F. L. (1982). The Expectation-Threshold Model of reproductive decision making. *Population and Environment, 5,* 95–108.

Beach, L. R., & Mitchell, T. R. (1985). *Emotional concomitants of decision making.* Paper presented at the annual meetings of the Society for Organizational Behavior, Pittsburgh, PA.

Beach, L. R., & Mitchell, T. R. (1987). Image theory: Principles, goals and plans in decision making. *Acta Psychologica, 66,* 201–220.

Beach, L. R., Smith, B., Lundell, J., & Mitchell, T. R. (1988). Image theory:

Descriptive sufficiency of a simple rule for the compatibility test. *Journal of Behavioral Decision Making, 1,* 17–28.

Beach, L. R., Townes, B. D., & Campbell, F. L. (1978). *The optional parenthood questionnaire.* Baltimore: National Alliance for Optional Parenthood.

Beach, L. R., Townes, B. D., Campbell, F. L., & Keating, G. W. (1976). Developing and testing a decision aid for birth planning decisions. *Organizational Behavior and Human Performance, 15,* 99–116.

Berger, P., & Kellner, H. (1984). Marriage and the construction of reality. *Diogenes, 46,* 1–24.

Burke, R. J., Weir, T., & Harrison, D. (1976). Disclosure of problems and tensions experienced by marital partners. *Psychological Reports, 38,* 531–542.

Davidson, A. R., & Beach, L. R. (1981). Error patterns in the prediction of fertility behavior. *Journal of Applied Social Psychology, 11,* 475–488.

Davidson, A. R., & Jaccard, J. (1975). Population psychology: A new look at an old problem. *Journal of Personality and Social Psychology, 31,* 1073–1082.

Davidson, A. R., & Jaccard, J. (1979). Variables that moderate the attitude behavior relation. *Journal of Personality and Social Psychology, 37,* 1364–1376.

Dawes, R. M. (1979). The robust beauty of improper linear models in decision making. *American Psychologist, 34,* 571–582.

Dawes, R. M., & Corrigan, B. (1974). Linear models in decision making. *Psychological Bulletin, 81,* 95–106.

Fischhoff, B., Goitein, B., & Shapira, Z. (1983). Subjective expected utility: A model of decision making. In R. W. Scholz (Ed.), *Decision making under uncertainty.* Amsterdam: Elsevier North Holland.

Franzoi, S. L., Davis, M. H., & Young, R. D. (1985). The effects of private self-consciousness and perspective taking on satisfaction in close relationships. *Journal of Personality and Social Psychology, 48,* 1584–1594.

Fried, E., Hofferth, S., & Udry, J. (1980). Parity-specific and two-sex utility models of reproductive intentions. *Demography, 17,* 1–12.

Fried, E., & Udry, J. (1979). Wives' and husbands' expected costs and benefits of childbearing as predictors of pregnancy. *Social Biology, 26,* 265–274.

Hershey, J. C., & Shoemaker, P.J.H. (1980). Prospect Theory's reflection hypothesis: A critical examination. *Organizational Behavior and Human Performance, 25,* 395–418.

Hoffman, L. W., & Hoffman, M. L. (1973). The value of children to parents. In J. T. Fawcett (Ed.), *Psychological perspectives on population.* New York: Basic Books.

Knudson, R. M. (1985). Marital compatibility and mutual identity confirmation. In. W. Ickes (Ed.), *Compatible and incompatible relationships.* New York: Springer-Verlag.

Laing, R. D., Phillipson, H., & Lee, A. R. (1966). *Interpersonal perception: A theory and a method of research.* New York: Springer-Verlag.

Loken, B., & Fishbein, M. (1978). The relationship between occupational variables and child-bearing intentions: Fact or artifact? [Unpublished manuscript cited] In I. Ajzen & M. Fishbein (1980). *Understanding attitudes and predicting social behavior.* Englewood Cliffs, NJ: Prentice-Hall.

Miller, G. A., Galanter, E., & Pribram, K. H. (1960). *Plans and the structure of behavior.* New York: Holt, Rinehart, & Winston.

Mintzberg, H. (1973). *The nature of managerial work.* New York: Harper & Row.

Mitchell, T. R., & Beach, L. R. (1977). Expectancy theory, decision theory, and occupational preference and choice. In M. F. Kaplan & S. Schwartz (Eds.), *Human judgment and decision making: Applied aspects*. New York: Academic Press.

Mitchell, T. R., Rediker, K. J., & Beach, L. R. (1986). Image theory and its implications for organizational decision making. In H. P. Sims & D. A. Gioia (Eds.), *The thinking organization*. San Francisco: Jossey-Bass.

Newman, S. H., & Thompson, V. D. (Eds.). (1976). *Population psychology: Research and educational issues* (DHEW Publication No. 76–574). Bethesda, MD: National Institute of Health.

Peters, T. (1979). Leadership: Sad facts and silver linings. *Harvard Business Review*, November/December, 164–172.

Peters, T. J. & Waterman, R. H. (1982). *In search of excellence*. New York: Harper & Row.

Schwab, D. P., Olian-Gottlieb, J. D., & Heneman, H. G. (1979). Between-subjects expectancy theory research: A statistical review of studies predicting effort and performance. *Psychological Bulletin, 86*, 139–147.

Selznick, P. (1957). *Leadership in administration*. Evanston, IL: Row, Peterson.

Sillars, A. L. (1985). Interpersonal perception in relationships. In W. Ickes (Ed.), *Compatible and incompatible relationships*. New York: Springer-Verlag.

Swann, W. B., Jr. (1983). Self-verification: Bringing social reality into harmony with the self. In G. S. Saunders & J. Suls (Eds.), *Social psychology in health and illness*. Hillsdale, NJ: Erlbaum.

Swann, W. B., Jr., & Predmore, S. C. (1985). Intimates as agents of social support: Sources of consolation or despair? *Journal of Personality and Social Psychology, 49*, 1609–1617.

Townes, B. D., Campbell, F. L., Wood, R. J., & Beach, L. R. (1980). A social psychological study of fertility decisions. *Population and Environment, 3*, 210–220.

Vinokur-Kaplan, D. (1978). To have—or not to have—another child: Family planning attitudes, intentions, and behavior. *Journal of Applied Social Psychology, 8*, 29–46.

Werner, P. D., Middlestadt-Carter, S. E., & Crawford, T. J. (1975). Having a third child: Predicting behavioral intentions. *Journal of Marriage and the Family, 37*, 348–358.

Wood, R. J., Campbell, F. L., Townes, B. D., & Beach, L. R. (1977). Birth planning decisions. *American Journal of Public Health, 67*, 563–565.

Part 2
Consumer Behavior
Perspectives

CHAPTER 4

Couple Decision Making: Individual- and Dyadic-Level Analysis

James Jaccard, David Brinberg, and Patricia Dittus

Research on dyadic decision making has tended to emphasize the analysis of role relationships between couple members and/or the patterns that emerge as individuals interact. In addition, research has been conducted on how the beliefs, values, and traits that the individuals bring to the decision situation influence the decision outcome. In this chapter, we will integrate two perspectives for the analysis of dyadic decision making— an individual-level analysis that examines the perceptions, preferences, and orientations that each individual brings to the interaction, and a dyadic-level analysis that examines the process by which these individual perspectives are expressed, comprehended, and acted on by the dyad to reach a decision. The first section of the chapter outlines an approach for conceptualizing and measuring key individual-level variables. The framework is grounded in research on individual decision making, drawing heavily from a framework developed by Jaccard and Wood (1986). The second section outlines an observational approach for studying the interaction process between individuals, as they discuss different aspects of the decision problem. In the final section, we consider the integration of the two approaches, focusing on the advantages of the framework relative to current systems, as well as the general implications of the approach for studying dyadic decision making.

Couples make hundreds of decisions each day of their lives. The framework that we are proposing is not applicable to the analysis of all decisions. Decision theorists typically distinguish between three types of decisions. *Impulsive* decisions are those which are determined by impulsive or emotional reactions of the individual, without reflection. *Routine* decisions concern familiar situations in which decisions are made with little reflection and in accord with habits, customs, or moral/social rules. *Thoughtful* decisions are made after giving thought to such factors as the problem situation, the alternative courses of action available, and the probable consequences of each course of action. When making a decision in a familiar situation, individuals typically accept the suggestion of impulse, habit, custom, or rule without serious reflection. Most behavioral decisions in everyday life are of this character. However, when the decision is perceived as being important or when impulse, habit, or custom are questioned, then the individual will reflect on the matter, considering one or more courses of action. The present framework is concerned with such thoughtful decisions.

Individual-Level Analysis

When a couple makes a joint decision, each individual brings to the interaction process a set of beliefs and attitudes about the decision topic. For example, when making a birth control decision, each member of the couple may have a preferred method of birth control and a set of reasons underlying that preference. Members of the couple may be in agreement about the preferred method, and the interaction process between them serves to reveal this agreement. In these instances, the choice from the set of decision options is relatively straightforward. In contrast, each individual in the couple may differ in the preferred option. In this case, the interaction process focuses on the resolution of differences (sometimes unsuccessfully), so that a joint decision can be reached. In this section, we describe a theoretical framework for analyzing the beliefs and attitudes that an individual brings to the interaction situation.

Jaccard (Jaccard & Wood, 1986; Jaccard, Wan, & Wood, 1987) discusses decision making in terms of two types of structural analyses: (1) perceptual-structure analysis, and (2) preference-structure analysis. These will be discussed, in turn.

Perceptual-Structure Analysis

For a given decision topic (e.g., choice of a birth control method), the individual will be aware of a set of options from which to choose (e.g., birth control pills, condoms, diaphragm). These options are typically elicited by asking the individual to list all of the options he/she can think of (e.g., name all of the methods of birth control that you can think of). Each option varies on one or more informational dimensions (e.g., effectiveness in preventing pregnancy, health risks, costs, convenience in using). The content of these dimensions is determined by asking individuals to name all of the factors they would consider when evaluating the different options. The dimensions vary in their importance to the individual (e.g., being effective in preventing pregnancy may be more important to the individual than the cost of the method). Measures of the subjective importance of each dimension in evaluating options also are obtained routinely. Finally, *a perceptual-structure matrix* characterizes the individual's perceptions of each option on each dimension, as illustrated in Table 4.1. The cell entries refer to the extent to which the individual believes the option is "good" or "bad" (typically measured on a +5 to −5 rating scale) on the dimension in question. For example, the pill might be perceived as being "very good" in terms of its

Table 4.1. Perceptual-structure matrix.

	Option 1	Option 2	Option 3	....	Option p
Dimension 1	R_{11}	R_{12}	R_{13}	....	R_{1p}
Dimension 2	R_{21}	R_{22}	R_{23}	....	R_{2p}
Dimension 3	R_{31}	R_{32}	R_{33}	....	R_{3p}
.	.	.	.	....	.
.	.	.	.	....	.
.	.	.	.	....	.
Dimension m	R_{m1}	R_{m2}	R_{m3}	....	R_{mp}

effectiveness in preventing pregnancy, but "bad" in terms of its associated health risks.

Given an individual's data from a perceptual-structure matrix, numerous insights into beliefs about the decision topic can be gained. For example, for any given pair of options (e.g., the diaphragm and the condom), the degree to which the individual perceives the options as being similar across the dimensions can be calculated. This would take the form of a Euclidean distance score in which the difference between ratings of the options on each dimension is computed (e.g., the rating for the diaphragm on the dimension of effectiveness is subtracted from the rating for condoms on the dimension of effectiveness). The differences are then squared and summed across all dimensions, yielding a distance score. A score of zero indicates that the ratings of the two options were identical. Larger scores imply greater differences in the ratings. Given p options, a $p \times p$ matrix of dissimilarity scores can be computed and subjected to cluster analysis (or, alternatively, multidimensional scaling analysis). The cluster analysis will identify groups of options that are perceived as similar yet distinct from other clusters of options. In our research, we have found considerable individual differences in the number of clusters of options that result from a cluster analysis. Some individuals exhibit a small number of clusters, indicating that they do not perceive many differences among the various options. Other individuals exhibit a large number of clusters, indicating that the different options are viewed as distinct.

A similar analysis can be conducted for dimensions. A distance score between any given pair of dimensions can be computed by calculating the difference between ratings of the two dimensions on each option (e.g., the rating for the diaphragm on the dimension of effectiveness is subtracted from the rating for the diaphragm on cost). The differences are then squared and summed across all options, yielding a distance score. A score of zero indicates that the ratings of the two dimensions across the options were identical. For example, when effectiveness was perceived as "good," cost also was seen as being "good." When effectiveness was perceived as being "bad," cost also was seen as being "bad." Larger distance scores imply greater differences in the ratings, indicating that the dimensions are distinct. Given m dimensions, an

Table 4.2. Relative-score matrix.

	Option 1	Option 2	Option 3	....	Option p	Mean sd
Dimension 1	Z_{11}	Z_{12}	Z_{13}	....	Z_{1p}	
Dimension 2	Z_{21}	Z_{22}	Z_{23}	....	Z_{2p}	
Dimension 3	Z_{31}	Z_{32}	Z_{33}	....	Z_{3p}	
.	.	.	.	....	.	
.	.	.	.	....	.	
.	.	.	.	....	.	
Dimension m	Z_{m1}	Z_{m2}	Z_{m3}	....	Z_{mp}	

$m X m$ matrix of dissimilarity scores can be computed and subjected to a cluster (or MDS) analysis. This analysis would indicate clusters of dimensions that tend to covary in the same fashion and at the same level as one shifts from one option to another. In this way, the extent to which an individual perceives certain dimensions as being related can be isolated. Again, we have observed considerable individual differences in the number of clusters of dimensions. Some individuals exhibit a relatively small number of dimensions, indicating that variations in any one dimension are tied to variations in other dimensions. Other individuals exhibit a relatively large number of dimensions, indicating perceptions of dimension independence.

For a given individual, the perceptual-structure matrix also can be transformed to a *relative-score matrix*. This involves calculating the mean rating and standard deviation for each dimension across options (see Table 4.2). The scores within a row are then standardized relative to the mean and standard deviation for that row. The mean score for a given row indicates the tendency for the individual to view the options, on the average, as positive (large scores) or negative (low scores). The standard deviation reflects variability in options across the dimension. A small standard deviation would indicate that options tend to be perceived as being the same on the dimension. In general, dimensions with small standard deviations will be unimportant in determining the choice of one option over another, because all options are perceived as being the same on that dimension. Finally, the within-cell standard scores indicate how "unique" an option is on the dimension (relative to the mean and standard deviation).

The major components of the perceptual-structure matrix suggest features of the decision topic that a couple may discuss when interacting to reach a joint decision. First, the individuals may discuss the different options that are available to them. Second, they may discuss what dimensions should be considered when evaluating the options. Third, they might discuss the relative importance of different dimensions for each member of the dyad. Finally, they might discuss the "standings" of particular options on particular dimensions.

Couples will vary in the extent to which they agree and complement each other on the above four facets. At the level of complete couple similarity, each member would bring to the situation an awareness of the same number and content of options, they would evaluate the options on the identical dimensions, and they would be in complete agreement about the relative importance of the dimensions and the standing of each option on each dimension in the same way. Such levels of similarity will be rare.

The extent of couple similarity can be quantified in different ways, depending on the facet under consideration. For awareness of decision options, each couple member can be asked (separate from each other) to list all of the decision options that they are aware of. The number of options named by both members can be calculated (Nc) and this can serve as one index of couple similarity. Alternatively, Nc can be divided by the total number of distinct options mentioned by both members, to indicate the proportion of common options relative to all options. Although numerous other indices could be derived, we have found these two to be the most useful. Similar indices can be computed for the content of dimensions used to evaluate the options.

Overall agreement in the subjective importance of different dimensions in evaluating options can be obtained vis-a-vis Euclidean distance scores. Both members of the couple might be asked to rate the importance of each informational dimension on an 11-point scale ranging from "not at all important" to "extremely important" (see Jaccard & Wood, 1986). A distance score can be calculated by computing the difference between the two couple members on each dimension (e.g., the importance rating by the husband for the dimension of health risks minus the importance rating for the wife for the dimension of health risks). The difference scores are squared and then summed across all dimensions. A score of zero indicates complete agreement, whereas larger scores indicate greater levels of disagreement.

A useful property of Euclidean distance scores is that they can be decomposed into component parts to indicate different sources of disagreement (Jaccard & Wood, 1986). More specifically, the distance score between the couple members can be conceptualized as being a function of three components: (1) elevation, (2) scatter, and (3) shape. *Elevation* refers to the mean difference between importance ratings, collapsing across dimensions. Table 4.3 illustrates a couple whose members differ in elevation (see couple A). Note that the couple members have identical patterning of scores across dimensions, with the only difference being that the male member consistently rates

Tabel 4.3. Examples of elevation, scatter, and shape.

Belief	Couple A		Couple B	
	Male	Female	Male	Female
1	7	5	7	5
2	6	4	6	5
3	7	5	5	5
4	3	1	4	5
5	4	2	3	5

the dimensions as being 2 units higher than the female member. In this case, the nonzero distance score is due to differences in elevation. *Scatter* refers to the standard deviation of ratings for a given individual. Table 4.3 presents a couple whose members differ in scatter (see couple B). In this case, the nonzero distance score is due, in part, to differences in the standard deviations of importance ratings. *Shape* refers to the correlation between ratings of the couple members across dimensions. It focuses on common patternings of rating across dimensions. Table 4.3 presents a couple whose ratings are correlated 1.00 (see couple A), indicating an identical "shape" (patterning of ratings).

A Euclidean distance score (as defined above) can be expressed in terms of these components as follows:

$$d_{ij} = (M_i - M_j)^2 + (s_i - s_j)^2 + 2s_i s_j(1 - r) \tag{1}$$

where M = the mean rating for a given couple member across dimensions, s = the standard deviation for a given couple member across dimensions, and r = the correlation between ratings across dimensions for the two couple members. The first component of the right-hand side of equation 1 reflects elevation, the second component reflects scatter, and the third reflects a scatter by shape interaction. The relative contributions of these three components to any given distance score can be computed as follows:

$$Ce = (M_i - M_j)^2/d_{ij} \tag{2}$$

$$Csc = (s_i - s_j)^2/d_{ij} \tag{3}$$

$$Csh.sc = (2s_i s_j(1 - r))/d_{ij} \tag{4}$$

where Ce is the contribution of elevation, Csc is the contribution of scatter, and Csh.sc is the contribution of the shape by scatter interaction. The three contribution indices will sum to one, and when multiplied by 100 can be interpreted as percents.

Couple agreement in the perceptions of the "standing" of each option on each dimension can be indexed by Euclidean distance scores, based on the difference between member ratings in each cell of the perceptual structure matrix. Decomposition of the scores into the three components identified above can be effected by execution of equations 2 through 4. Alternatively, one can use the decomposition procedures discussed by Cronbach (1955) to obtain more precise information about the contributions of differences due to options, dimensions, and elevation. Analyses can be conducted on either the perceptual-score matrix or the relative-score matrix.

Couple similarity on higher order statistics also can be derived from perceptual-structure analysis. For example, similarity indices can be calculated for the standard deviations of dimensions in the relative-score matrix. Or the difference in the number of option clusters between couple members can be calculated. And so on. We will discuss hypotheses about the impact of these various similarity indices on couple interaction and joint decision making shortly.

Preference-Structure Analysis

Given p options, an individual may be said to have an attitude toward choosing each option. An attitude is conceptualized in very restricted terms in our framework. It refers to the extent to which an individual feels favorable or unfavorable toward enacting a given behavioral option. A preference structure is measured by asking the individual to rate each decision option on a -10 to $+10$ unfavorable-favorable rating scale (e.g., how favorable or unfavorable would you feel about using the pill?). The preference structure refers to the set of p attitudes. Consistent with subjective-expected-utility (SEU) theory, it can be argued that an individual will choose to perform that option toward which the most positive attitude is held (although there may be some exceptions to this). Thus, the attitude measures are analogous to global measures of SEU, without requiring the measurement of specific probabilities and utilities (see Jaccard, 1981).

The patterning of attitude scores across the decision options has implications for the individual's decision behavior. For example, one possible pattern would be where the most positive option is evaluated very positively (e.g., $+9$) and the next most positively evaluated option is considerably lower (e.g., $+1$). Given a large discrepancy between the individual's two most positively evaluated options suggests that the individual's choice of an option will be straightforward and stable over time. In contrast, an individual whose attitudes towards the two most positively evaluated options are similar (e.g., $+9$ and $+8$) will be more conflicted in his/her choice and the decision may be relatively unstable. Viewed from another perspective, the first individual (with scores of $+9$ and $+1$) may not be agreeable to choosing an option other than the most favorable one, whereas the second individual (with scores of $+9$ and $+8$) may be agreeable to either of the two options.

An individual's attitude toward a given option will, in part, be influenced by the individual's perceptions of the option vis-a-vis the perceptual-structure matrix. An option perceived as good on all dimensions will, everything else being equal, be evaluated more positively (in attitudinal terms) than an option perceived as bad on all dimensions. The relationship between perceptions on an informational dimension and the preference structure can be explored by means of correlational statistics (for an alternative approach, see Jaccard & Wood, 1986). This involves correlating the ratings of the options on a given dimension from the perceptual-structure matrix with the attitudinal ratings of the individual across the options. Note that this analysis is conducted on the idiographic level, that is, given p options, the correlation will be based on a sample size of p. A high correlation would indicate that as perceptions of the options on the dimension change, so do the attitude ratings (or preferences). A low correlation would indicate that variations in perceptions on a given dimension are independent of variations in the attitudes. We have found it interesting to compare these correlations with the subjective importance ratings of dimensions obtained in the perceptual structure task. We have observed considerable individual differences in the convergence of these two sets of indices of "dimension importance." The relationship of multiple beliefs to the attitude ratings can be analyzed using multiple regression. Standard significance tests are not valid in this case, and the resulting statistics must be used descriptively. To reduce the number of dimensions employed in such an analysis, one can use the cluster analysis of the perceptual-structure matrix (discussed earlier) to select a single "prototypical" dimension from each dimension cluster. These dimensions then can be screened further by using simple correlations with the attitude ratings (e.g., eliminate any dimension that does not account for at least 5% of the variance in attitude ratings). More complex interactive and nonlinear models between multiple dimensions and their impact on attitudes can be explored using polynomial/interactive regression analyses.

Couple members may differ on either the patterning of their preference structures or on the way in which informational dimensions map onto the attitudes comprising the preference structure. For example, two members of a couple may have identical preference structures, but the first member's preference structure may be determined primarily by dimensions A and B, whereas the second member's preference structure may be determined primarily by dimensions C and D. Alternatively, the two individuals may have radically different preference structures, yet have a common underlying model for the way in which perceptual dimensions map onto the preference structures.

The agreement between patterning of preference structures for couple members can be indexed by a Euclidean distance score, as discussed above. This score also can be decomposed into component parts of elevation, shape, and scatter. Also of interest will be whether the couples are in agreement about the most positively evaluated (MPE) option (i.e., the same option is the most positively evaluated one by each member), as well as the discrepancy in attitude ratings between these options. Another useful index is the rank order value of one person's MPE option within the other individual's preference structure. Similarities in the ways that perceptual dimensions map onto preference structures can be indexed in numerous ways and will depend in large part on the results of the correlational analyses. For example, one could compute the number of dimensions that are common to both members that achieve a squared zero-order correlation of at least 0.05. Or one could convert this index to a proportion by dividing it by the total number of distinct dimensions that achieve squared correlations of 0.05 or greater. Or, given a common target dimension for both members, one could calculate the differences in slopes between the couple members.

Implications of Member Differences on Perceptual and Preference Structures

When making a joint decision, members of a couple potentially will have differences on any of the above factors. One of the most crucial determinants of how readily and easily a joint decision is made derives from the individuals' preference structures: If the individuals are in agreement about the content of the MPE option, then the joint choice is straightforward. Given discrepancies in the MPE options, a joint solution can become complicated. At this point, a series of interactions may be enacted to explore the reasons underlying the different orientations, with pursuant attempts to alter aspects of the other individual's perceptual structure. Several different strategies might be used in this regard. First, one might suggest an option that the target member had not thought of and will be positively evaluated by the target member. Second, one can explore the target person's perception of the standing of the MPE option on each of the informational dimensions. The strategy would be to identify "misperceptions" that the target individual might have. The most effective approach would be to identify misperceptions on informational dimensions that are important in influencing the preference structure of the target individual. Third, given no misperceptions, one can attempt to change the criteria that the target individual uses in forming attitudes toward the different options. Thus, dimension A might be relatively unimportant in influencing the preference structure of the target person, and an attempt might be made to alter the importance of the dimension.

In our opinion, joint decision making, including both its process and product, cannot be well understood without a thorough documentation of the preference structures and perceptual structures that each individual brings to the situation. These structures will shape the resulting interactions and decisions in a dramatic fashion. Observational schemes of the interaction process have tended to ignore such variables in their observational codes. By contrast, the framework that we suggest will explicitly incorporate codes for documenting the influence strategies that participants use and the resolution of discrepancies vis-a-vis perceptual and preference structure analysis.

More General Individual Variables and Relational Variables

In addition to perceptual- and preference-structure analysis, there are several general variables that directly affect the decision-making process of an individual. These include personality orientations of the individual (e.g., impulsiveness, risk taking), intelligence/cognitive skills, and emotional states (such as anger). A comprehensive analysis of the biases and orientations that individuals bring to the joint decision-making situation should include assessment of these variables.

Dittus and Jaccard (1987) have conducted an extensive analysis of personality variables and how they are related to the decision-making process. The analysis focuses on eight types of decision activities that individuals might perform when making decisions, and identifies personality-like variables that influence or characterize how individuals might approach these decision activities. The eight activities are summarized in Appendix 4.A. Dittus and Jaccard (1987) have developed a battery of 20 scales from major personality inventories [e.g., Jackson's Personal Research Form (PRF), Gough's California Psychological Inventory (CPI)] that represent relevant "personality" dimensions. These are summarized in Appendix 4.B. The list of variables is intended to be representative but not exhaustive. Many other personality variables could have been included. However, the intent was to identify variables that would be most relevant to one or more of the eight decision activities listed in Appendix 4.A, and that focused on individual decision making (as opposed to joint decision making).

A short version (200 items) of the battery is currently being developed. Once administered, the battery can be used to profile an individual's general decision-making tendencies. An individual's score on any given scale can be contrasted with national norms, to indicate orientations that are unusually high or unusually low, and that may be problematic. The rationale for the approach is described in more detail by Dittus and Jaccard (1987).

Emotional states of the individual also may impact on decision making. These states tend to be transitory and will impact on decision making to the extent that they occur during or just prior to a given decision activity. A useful conceptualization of emotional states is presented in Masculo and Mancuso (1988). The role of emotional states in couple decision making is discussed in later sections.

Couples also approach joint-decision activities within the context of role relationships that have emerged and solidified over the history of the dyad. A substantial body of research has been generated on the effect of role relations on variables such as marital conflict, dyadic adjustment, communication styles, and power. Fitzpatrick (1984; this volume) provides a detailed description of couple types (i.e., traditionals, independents, and separates) and the relationship of these types to a wide range of variables. The Relational Dimensions Inventory (RDI; Fitzpatrick, 1984) provides a typology of couples on three dimensions—interdependence, ideology, and conflict—and a strong empirical basis for using the instrument in the analysis of dyadic interaction. Interdependence refers to the connectedness of partners physically, temporally, and psychologically. Ideology refers to the beliefs, standards, and values that individuals hold concerning relationships. Conflict refers to the willingness of the partners to engage in conflict and the general level of assertiveness. These role dimensions and the measurement of them are discussed in more detail by Fitzpatrick (this volume). We have found the RDI to be useful for assessing relatively stable role relationships that are active in joint decision-making activities.

The Decision Context

Each member of the couple brings to the decision situation a set of beliefs and attitudes about the decision topic, as well as more generalized decision-making orientations and role relationships. The manner in which these variables affect couple interaction and the ultimate joint choice will be influenced, in part, by the task-related and contextual demands of the decision. For example, couple members may differ in their decision-making and problem-solving skills. One individual might be adept at executing one type of decision activity (e.g., problem recognition) but poor with respect to another activity (e.g., information gathering). In some situations, decision skills will be *compensatory*, such that one members's weaknesses can be offset by another member's strengths. In other situations, a couple's ability to cope with a problem will be *noncompensatory*, and performance will be either a function of the level of the "best" decision maker or the "worst" decision maker. Thus, decision making is influenced not only by the independent decision-making orientations of individual members, but also by such variables as who has primary responsibility for making decisions related to particular goals, who monitors the consequences of particular decisions, and so on. The decision-making process also will be influenced by situation-specific or environmental factors that help to define the decision context, such as time constraints.

Interaction Processes

Although individual members of a couple have initial beliefs and attitudes about the decision topic, at some point, interaction will take place between the couple members. During these interactions is when that information is exchanged and interpersonal dynamics reveal themselves. The present section describes the observational coding scheme that we have developed for purposes of characterizing dyadic interaction.

A desired goal of a coding system is the ability to reproduce the patterns of interaction (both the tone and content) based on the coded information. The more specific the coding system, the better able the researcher is to reproduce the interaction from the coded information. Such specificity, however, may restrict the researcher's ability to apply the coding system to a range of problems and decision topics. Our coding system uses specific content information derived from the individual-level analysis of perceptions and preferences as well as (adapted) codes from Gottman's (1979) Couple Interaction Scoring System (CISS). The specific content codes, however, maintain generality because our focus is on psychological categories of decision making defined by Jaccard and Wood (1986). These categories focus on the concepts of options, dimensions, and standings on dimensions, rather than the content of the options and dimensions per se. As will be discussed shortly, it is possible to incorporate even more specific codes, depending on the purposes of the research.

The Coding System

When making a dyadic decision, one important component of the interaction is the communication and interpretation of the individual perceptions and preferences. Our basic unit of analysis uses the concept of a "thought unit," as developed by Gottman (1979). A thought unit is a sentence (or phrase) grammatically separated by commas, ands, buts, and/or periods. Each thought unit expressed in the conversation (by either member of the dyad) receives a code.

The categories in our coding system are designed to be mutually exclusive and exhaustive. No unit should receive a double code (i.e., be coded in more than one category). The coding system has at least three levels of specificity. At the most general level, we use (adapted) codes developed by Gottman (1979). Specifically, we propose eight general categories into which each thought unit is classified. They are:

1. Agreement—which includes direct agreement, accepting responsibility for a past or present problem, accepting modification and compliance with a preceding request or command and assent.
2. Disagreement—which includes direct disagreement, denial of responsibility, disagreement with rationale or justification applied.
3. Communication Talk—which is a comment on the process of communication, directing the conversation back to a given topic or toward a resolution of a problem, an evaluation of a conversation, or a request for clarification. In addition to this definition, we suggest that agenda setting be included, namely the attempt to structure the conversation.
4 Mind Reading—which is an inference about feelings, opinions, or motives of the spouse or couple, or which makes attributions about the past, present, or future behavior of the other person.
5. Summarize Other—which is a review or summary of the previous statements made by the partner.
6. Summarize Self—which is a review or summary of the previous statements made by oneself.
7. Expressing Feelings about the Decision—a statement of feelings expressed by the speaker. These feelings may be coded in terms of intensity and direction (positive or negative).
8. Information Exchange—a statement that suggests a specific solution to a problem or that presents information or behavioral facts related to the decision stated in either past, present, or future tense.

In our system, each thought unit is assigned three codes. The first code is a number from 1 to 8 and represents the relevant category from the above list. Within each category, a thought unit can be further classified into one of at least three subcategories corresponding to the major components of individual-decision analysis. These are:

1. Option analysis—statements concerning the options identified in the individual analysis. Thus, if the thought refers to an option within Jaccard's option/dimension framework, it receives a code of 1. The focus of this category is on thought units that consider what options are available to the couple or on statements of preference for one or more options. For a decision about what method of birth control to use, an example would be

a person indicating that he/she "likes the pill." Or a person might suggest that the couple consider using a diaphragm.

2. Dimension Analysis—statements concerning the dimensions identified in the individual analysis. Thus, if the thought unit refers to a dimension within Jaccard's option/dimension framework, then it receives a code of 2. The focus of this category is on thought units that consider what dimension should be examined as well as the relative importance of dimensions. For a decision about what method of birth control to use, an example would be a statement like "we should consider the health risks that are involved" or "preventing an unwanted pregnancy is very important to me."

3. Option Standing on Dimension—statements concerning the "standing" of an option on a dimension. Thus, if the thought unit refers to how an option performs on a dimension, it receives a code of 3. For a decision about what method of birth control to use, an example would be a statement like "the pill has serious side effects" or "condoms interfere with the spontaneity of the sex act." Note that although these statements refer to an option and a dimension, they are not assigned codes of 1 or 2, because their focus is on the standing of an option on a dimension. A code of 1 is reserved for statements about options that should be considered and statements of attitudes towards options. A code of 2 is reserved for statements about what dimensions should be considered and the relative importance of dimensions.

Thus, the second code of the three-code "thought unit" would be assigned a 1, 2, or 3, if it pertained to one of the above three categories. The placement of a thought unit into one of these categories may require consideration of the thought units that precede or follow it. For example, a husband might say, "I prefer the condom" and the wife then might say, "So do I." These represent two thought units. The first thought unit would receive a code of 81, because it represents information exchange about a preference or attitude toward an option. The second thought unit would receive a code of 11, because it represents agreement about an attitude toward an option.

In practice, a large proportion of the conversation will not fall into one of the above three subcategories. How these aspects of the conversation are coded will depend, in part, on the purposes of the researcher. In his early use of the CISS, Gottman (1979) distinguished subcategories and assigned individual codes to them. For example, within the category of agreement, separate codes were assigned to "direct agreement," "accepting modification," and "compliance with a preceding request." In his later research, these distinctions were dropped and focus was on coding only the general categories. If one were to adopt this more general orientation within our framework, then a fourth category would be added to the above three-code subclassification. This category would represent any statement within the general category that did not focus on an option, a dimension, or the standing of an option on a dimension. The code would then only differ from Gottman's general analysis in that three additional distinctions have been made (corresponding to the codes 1–3 above). Alternatively, the investigator might want to impose more structure, and make finer discriminations within the fourth subcategory. In sum, the second code of the three-code system will start with a number from 1 to (at least) 4.

The third code in our coding scheme focuses on affect, independent of content. Gottman (1979) incorporates affective coding into the CISS, using voice tone as an index of emotional content. This approach treats the voice as the vehicle for setting the "climate" of the conversation. Three categories are used: positive, neutral, and negative, and are assigned values of 1, 2, and 3, respectively. The primary cues used to determine direction are loudness, pitch, timbre, rate, inflection, rhythm, and enunciation. Gottman (1979) provides a detailed discussion of the specific levels of each cue that reflect positive and negative emotional "climates." We have reproduced portions of the criteria used by Gottman in Table 4.4.

In sum, any given interaction can be broken down into thought units. Each thought unit can be characterized in terms of three codes. The first code refers to a general category of purpose and the second code indicates the focus of the thought unit. The third code indicates the affective "climate" within which the thought unit occurs.

Additional levels of specificity can be imposed, if desired. For example, the content of the options and dimensions discussed within a thought unit can be coded. These more specific codes would become part of the second set of codes. For instance, prior to coding, each potential option receives a numerical code (e.g., 01 = the pill, 02 = condom), as does each potential dimension (e.g., 01 = health risks, 02 = cost). The specific option and/or dimension being referred to is then indicated with these codes. For instance, suppose the wife states that she agrees with her husband concerning their preference for the pill. That unit would receive a code of 1(agree), then 101 (where the first 1 refers to an option and the second value—01—refers to the pill). A similar approach would be used for coding dimensions. When coding both options and dimensions (e.g., the wife states, "I agree with you that the pill may be unsafe"), both specific codes should be used. In this example, the thought unit would receive the following code: 1(agree) 30101 (where the three refers to the category "option standing on the dimension", the first 01 refers to the specific option (pill), and the second 01 refers to the specific dimension (health risks). We suggest that the second set of codes always include option and dimension codes, thus making the second code consist of five digits. If a *dimension* code is not applicable (because the thought unit pertains to an attitude toward an *option*, such as a code of 81), then a 00 is coded in the relevant digits. The same would be true for codes where an option is not applicable. One difficulty that arises with such content coding is that some thought units may involve multiple options or dimensions. For example, the thought unit "I prefer the pill to the condom" refers to two options, not one. The method of coding such statements will depend on the purposes of the research.

Table 4.4. Cues for detecting emotion in voice tone.

Feeling	Loudness	Pitch	Timbre	Rate	Inflection	Rhythm	Enunciation
Positive voice							
Affection	Soft	Low	Resonant	Slow	Steady and slightly upward	Regular	Slurred
Satisfaction	Normal	Normal	Somewhat resonant	Normal	Slightly upward	Regular	Somewhat slurred
Cheerfulness	Moderate high	Moderate high	Moderate blaring	Moderate fast	Up and down Overall upward	Regular	
Joy	Loud	High	Moderate blaring	Fast	Upward	Regular	
Negative voice							
Boredom	Moderate to low	Moderate to low	Moderate resonant	Moderate slow	Monotone		Somewhat slurred
Impatience	Normal	Normal to moderate high	Moderate blaring	Moderate fast	Slightly upward		Somewhat clipped
Anger	Loud	High	Blaring	Fast	Irregular Up and down	Irregular	Clipped
Sadness	Soft	Low	Resonant	Slow	Downward	Irregular	Slurred

Adopted from Gottman and Mettetal (1977).

Implementation of Coding System

In our research, couples are invited to our laboratory for purposes of discussing one or more decision topics. Each individual member completes questionnaires designed to assess their individual perceptions, preferences, orientations, and role relationships. In addition (where applicable), we assess the extent to which the couple has discussed the topic in the past. The couple is then seated at a table and asked to discuss the decision topic and reach a joint solution. These interactions are videotaped and then transcribed. We recommend the use of videotaping rather than audiotaping because of the additional information provided by the nonverbal cues. Those cues, in addition to voice tone, can be used to provide information concerning the emotional climate of the interaction. Initial analysis of the interaction, however, should focus primarily on content and voice codes because of the overwhelming complexity in the description of the interaction that would result when including a third concurrent channel of information (i.e., nonverbal cues). We have found that split-screen taping rather than the simultaneous taping of both individuals using one camera provides more useful information in the identification of interaction patterns.

The training of coders requires that the coders first memorize the codes, apply them to specific examples, and then generalize the codes to other examples. The second task is to give each coder a sample transcript, have them divide the transcript into thought units, and then place the appropriate content code next to the thought unit. Reliability estimates may be obtained by contrasting the coders against each other and with the trainer. Typically, training coders to criterion (at least 90% agreement) takes 25 to 30 hours. During the actual coding of transcripts, the trainer should code randomly selected pages to provide reliability checks.

Integration of Individual and Dyadic Decisions

We have argued for the utility of two levels of analysis when studying dyadic decision making. The first is an analysis of individual perceptions, attitudes, orientations, and role relationships that the individual brings to the interaction situation. The second is an analysis of the interaction per se between couple members. We have presented an observational scheme for coding such interactions, merging concepts from individual decision theories with Gottman's CISS. By integrating these frameworks, many new approaches for analyzing joint decision making are possible. We will now discuss some of these possibilities.

The first step in applying our framework involves obtaining a detailed assessment of the beliefs and attitudes of each couple member, separately. This permits the researcher to identify a priori areas in which there are disagreements between the couple members and are most likely to lead to decision difficulties. For example, if the individual couple members disagree on the most preferred option, but agree on the criteria that are most important in evaluating options, then the differences in preferences probably exist because of disagreement about the standing of options on dimensions. A careful analysis of individual preference and perceptual structures should prove to be most useful in counseling contexts. In addition, the nature of individual perceptions and preferences may be predictive of events that occur in the interaction between couple members. It may be possible to develop mathematical (e.g., regression) equations using these measures to make a priori predictions about the nature of couple interaction. We are currently exploring this possibility.

We also believe it is important to document more stable orientations of the individuals involved, including personality variables that are relevant to decision making, as well as role relationships. These variables should also be predictive of the quality of joint decisions and the occurrence of events within couple interaction. For example, couples whose members exhibit relatively "poor" personality profiles (e.g., an external locus of control, high impulsiveness, poor cognitive abilities, low self-acceptance) may be prone to less effective decision strategies and adverse decision outcomes. The implications of different personality variables will vary, depending on the topic area and the interplay of couple strengths and weaknesses on each dimension.

In terms of interaction analysis, our code offers more specificity about the focus of conversation relative to more general coding schemes, such as the CISS. For example, if a disagreement occurs, then the CISS provides little information on what the disagreement is about. It could represent a disagreement about a matter only tangentially relevant to the decision topic or it could represent a disagreement about a major aspect of the decision topic. In contrast, our coding scheme permits a more detailed analysis of the conversation.

Such a detailed analysis is important because one can derive measures that may be predictive of certain outcome variables and that may be useful from a counseling perspective. For example, using the second digit of the coding scheme, one can calculate the proportion of thought units that are directly relevant to the decision topic (i.e., the proportion of units that have codes of 1, 2, or 3). It is possible that couples who spend a large proportion of their time discussing nontopic related issues (as reflected by a code of 4), will have greater difficulty reaching a mutually satisfactory joint decision, everything else being equal. Such couples may be less prone to discuss and explore the issues that really matter to them and for which it is important to obtain a resolution of differences.

Research on individual decision making has documented different decision rules and decision styles that individuals use when making decision. For example, Jacoby, Jaccard, Kuss, Troutman, & Mazursky (1987) have documented two ways in which stockbrokers process information about investment options. Presented with a set of options and information about each option, some stockbrokers will adopt a within-option, across-dimension-processing strategy. This strategy involves considering all of the information on each dimension for a single option. After doing so, all of the information for a second option is considered. This process is repeated until all options have been explored. A choice is then made. A second processing strategy is one based on across-option, within-dimension processing. This strategy involves focusing on a specific informational dimension and comparing all options on that dimension. After doing so, a second dimension is selected, and the options are again compared on that dimension. The process continues until all relevant information is considered. Jacoby et al. (1987) found that this latter strategy led to better decisions (i.e., more successful investment choices) than the former strategy. Using our coding scheme (including specific content codes), the tendencies of couples to consider information by means of either of these two processing strategies can be documented. Jacoby et al. (1987) and others (e.g., Payne, 1976) have elaborated other processing strategies that have implications for decision making and that are directly measurable using our framework.

Another set of measures that may be meaningful are the number of different options that are considered or discussed by the couple and the number of informational dimensions that are considered. It might be argued that couples who explicitly discuss a large number of options and dimensions ultimately will be more satisfied with their decisions and will make better decisions because of the thorough analysis of all the options involved. The analysis of situational variables (such as time constraints) on these measures (as well as on measures of processing strategies) can be studied effectively within this paradigm.

Joint decision-making tendencies such as those discussed above can be documented for a couple and tendencies that are counterproductive can be addressed by means of couple counseling. Such counseling efforts would be based on a complete profile of each individual in isolation (as described in the section on individual-level analyses) as well as the interaction patterns that are observed as couples discuss that target issue.

Concluding Remarks

In this chapter, we have emphasized the importance of studying both the decision orientations that individuals bring to the interaction as well as the interaction process per se when analyzing couple decision making. We have presented a theoretical framework for organizing data in both of these domains, as well as described methodologies that can be used effectively to gather such data. Our belief is that dyadic analysis can benefit greatly by considering the extensive literature on individual decision making. The present chapter was intended to illustrate some of these benefits.

References

Boice, R. (1988). The measurement and conceptualization of procrastination. Unpublished manuscript, University at Albany, State University of New York, Department of Psychology.

Cronbach, L. J., (1955). Processes affecting scores on "understanding of others" and "assumed similarity." *Psychological Bulletin, 52*, 177–193.

Dittus, P., & Jaccard, J. (1987). An analysis of personality dimensions in the context of individual decision making processes. Unpublished manuscript, State University of New York, Albany, Department of Psychology.

Eysenck, S., & Eysenck, H. (1977). The place of impulsiveness in a dimensional system of personality description. *British Journal of Social and Clinical Psychology, 16*, 57–68.

Fitzpatrick, M. A. (1984). Marital interaction: Recent theory and research. In L. Berkowitz (Ed.), *Advances in experimental social psychology.* New York: Academic Press.

Fitzpatrick, M. A. (this volume). After the decision: Compliance-gaining in marital interaction. In D. Brinberg and J. Jaccard (Eds). *Dyadic decision making*, New York: Springer-Verlag.

Gottman, J. M. (1979). *Marital interactions: Experimental investigations.* New York: Academic Press.

Gottman, J. and Mettetal, G. (1977). Couples' interaction scoring system: Voice macro codes. Unpublished manuscript.

Gough, H. (1957). *California psychological inventory manual.* Palo Alto, Ca: Consulting Psychologists Press.

Jaccard, J. (1981). Attitudes and behavior: Implications of attitudes towards behavioral alternatives. *Journal of Experimental Social Psychology, 25*, 41–58.

Jaccard, J., Wan, C., & Wood, G. (1987). Idiothetic methods for the analysis of behavioral decision making: Computer applications. In J. Mancuso & M. Shaw (Eds.), *Cognition and personal structure: Computer access and analysis.* New York: Praeger.

Jaccard, J., & Wood, G. (1986). An idiothetic analysis of behavioral decision making. In D. Brinberg & R. Lutz (Eds.), *Perspectives on Methodology in Consumer Research.* New York: Springer-Verlag.

Jacoby, J., Jaccard, J., Kuss, A., Troutman, T., & Mazursky, D. (1987). New directions in behavioral process research: Implications for social psychology. *Journal of Experimental Social Psychology, 23*, 146–175.

Jackson, D. (1967). *Personality research form manual.* Goshen, NY: Research Psychologists Press.

Jackson, D., Hournay, L., & Vidmar, N. (1972). A four dimensional interpretation of risk. *Journal of Personality, 40*, 483–501.

Levenson, H. (1974). Activism and powerful others: Distinctions within the concept of internal-external locus of control. *Journal of Consulting and Clinical Psychology, 28*, 377–383.

Lubin, B. (1967). *Manual for the depression adjective checklists.* San Diego: Educational and Industrial Testing Service.

Masculo, M., & Mancuso, J. (1988). A prototype analysis of the structure and content of basic level emotion concepts. Unpublished manuscript, University at Albany, State University of New York, Albany, Department of Psychology.

Payne, J. W. (1976). Task complexity and contingent processing in decision making: An information search and protocol analysis. *Organizational Behavior and Human Performance, 16*, 366–387.

Rotter, J. (1954). *Social learning and clinical psychology.* Englewood Cliffs, NJ: Prentice Hall.

Saranson, I. G., Saranson, B. R., Keefe, D. E., Hayes, B. E., and Shearin, E. N. (1986). Cognitive interference: Situational determinants and trait-like characteristics. *Journal of Personality and Social Psychology, 51(1),* 215–226.

Watson, G., & Glaser, E. (1980). *Critical thinking appraisal: Manual.* New York: The Psychological Corporation.

Appendix 4.A.

Activities in Individual Decision Making

Problem Recognition: The individual determines that a problem state exists and that a decision must be considered.

Goal Identification: The individual specifies a priori the purpose of the decision; that is the ideal outcome of the decision.

Option Generation/Identification: The individual thinks of potential alternative solutions to the problem at hand.

Information Search: The individual seeks information, either about what additional options might be available or about properties of one or more of the options under consideration.

Assessment of Option Information: The individual consciously considers the information they have about the different options. Based on this information, the individual forms preferences for some options relative to others.

Choice: The individual selects one of the decision options for purposes of future behavioral enactment.

Behavioral Translation: The individual translates the decision into overt behavior.

Post-decision Evaluation: The individual reflects on the decision after the option has been enacted, then evaluates the decision (and the decision process) in light of the outcomes that have resulted.

Appendix 4.B.

General Personality-Like Variables Related to Decision Making

General

Locus of Control: According to Rotter (1954), there are individual differences in generalized expectancies concerning reinforcement. Those individuals who have an internal locus of control believe that rewards follow from, or are dependent on, their own behavior. They believe that their actions can affect the course of their lives. Individuals who have an external locus of control believe that rewards are controlled by forces outside themselves and that their lives are determined by chance, luck, or fate. Internal locus of control individuals will be more likely to take an active role in decision making. Measure: Levenson's (1974) multidimensional measure.

Impulsivity: People who are implusive tend to act on the spur of the moment without deliberation and may be volatile in emotional expression. When confronted with a problem and decision, those high in impulsivity may act rashly, without careful thought. Measure: PRF or Eysenck and Eysenck (1977).

Endurance: Endurance is defined by Jackson (1967) as characterizing someone who is willing to work long hours, doesn't give up quickly on a problem, is persevering, even in the face of great difficulty, is patient and unrelenting in his/her work habits. Measure: PRF.

Flexibility: Flexibility is the extent to which an individual is able to adapt their thinking and behavior to fit novel or unusual circumstances. The more rigid and inflexible an individual is, the less likely that that person will be receptive to new information regarding choices and may not even consider options that would involve a change from the norm. Measure: CPI.

Responsibility: Responsibility refers to the extent to which an individual is conscientious and dependable. Such an individual may be more likely to carry through with decisions and to be careful in his or her approach to important decisions. Measure: CPI.

Risk Taking: Risk taking refers to the extent to which an individual is willing to choose options or make decisions that do not have a high probability of payoff. That is, high-risk takers are willing to take a chance. Measure: Jackson, Hournay, and Vidmar's (1972) four-dimensional measure of risk taking.

Procrastination: Procrastination is the tendency to delay actions or completion of tasks. Measure: Boice (1988).

Order: Order pertains to neatness, organization, planfulness, and consistency. Individuals who are orderly tend to be interested in developing methods for keeping materials methodically organized; they dislike clutter and confusion. Measure: PRF.

Achievement Orientation and Intellectual Interest

Understanding: Jackson defines this orientation as characterizing individuals who want to understand many areas of knowledge; who value the synthesis of ideas and logical thought, particularly when directed at satisfying intellectual curiosity. Measure: PRF.

Innovation: Generally, innovation can be defined as the introduction of new things or methods. According to the Jackson (1967), an innovator is someone who is "creative and inventive; capable of originality of thought; motivated to develop novel solutions to problems; values new ideas; likes to improvise." Measure: JPI.

Achievement: A high achiever is someone who aspires to accomplish difficult tasks, maintains high standards, and is willing to work toward distant goals. Measure: PRF.

Orientations Towards Others

Conformity: Conformists are those who act in accordance with a standard or norm; they tend to comply, to acquiesce. Such individuals will be susceptible to social influence and group pressures. These individuals will also modify their behavior to be consistent with standards set by others. Conformists may be less likely to consider options that do not meet with group approval. Measure: JPI.

Value Orthodoxy: Individuals with orthodox values tend to value traditional customs and beliefs, and take a conservative view regarding contemporary standards of behavior. Such people are moralistic, conventional, and rigid. Measure: JPI.

Feelings About Self

Self-Acceptance: Self-acceptance refers to feelings of personal worth, self-confidence, and self-assurance. Individuals who have little self-confidence may be less likely to take an active role in decision making and may lack the initiative to carry through on decisions. Measure: CPI.

Anxiety: Anxiety can be generally defined as a state of apprehension. Jackson (1967) describes an anxious person as one who "tends to worry over inconsequential matters, is more easily upset than the average person; and is apprehensive about the future." It would follow that anxious individuals may have trouble making decisions. Measure: JPI.

Depression: Depression can be defined as an emotional dejection greater and more prolonged than that warranted by any objective reason. An individual in a depressed state is morose, despondent, and generally distressed. Depression would serve to reduce one's motivation to pursue active decision making. Measure: Lubin (1967).

Cognitive/Thinking Orientations

Critical Thinking: Watson and Glaser (1980) view critical thinking as a composite of attitudes, knowledge, and skills. This composite includes: (1) attitudes of inquiry that involve an ability to recognize the existence of problems and an acceptance of the general need for evidence in support of what is asserted to be true; (2) knowledge of the nature of valid inferences, abstractions, and generalizations in which the weight or accuracy of different kinds of evidence are logically determined; (3) skills in employing and applying the above attitudes and knowledge. Measure: Watson and Glaser (1980).

Complexity/Cognitive Structure: Complexity, as conceptualized by Jackson (1967) involves seeking intricate solutions to problems and being interested in pursuing topics in depth, as well as being impatient with oversimplification; there is a desire to make decisions based on definite knowledge. Measure: JPI.

Cognitive Interference: Cognitive interference refers to the tendency for one's thinking about a topic to be interrupted by "intrusive," nonrelevant thoughts. Individual's who are subject to cognitive interference may have difficulties considering all of the relevant information when making decisions. Measure: Sarason et al. 1986.

Intellectual Efficiency: Intellectual efficiency characterizes individuals who are clear thinking, capable, intelligent, and who place a high value on cognitive and intellectual matters. Such individuals are likely to be more thorough in their approach to thoughtful decisions. Measure: CPI.

Note. PRF = Jackson's Personal Research Form; CPI = Gough's California Psychological Inventory; JPI = Jackson's personality inventory.

CHAPTER 5

Analyzing Sequential Categorical Data on Dyadic Interaction

Ajith Kumar and William R. Dillon

Recently there has been a change in focus from the study of one organism over time to the study of the social interaction between organisms. This change in focus has brought with it a renewed interest in what is generally referred to as *sequential analysis* (Altman 1965; Blurton-Jones, 1972; Gottman 1980a, 1980b; Gottman & Ringland, 1981; Wilson, 1975). In investigating the influences among interacting organisms, the influence that one organism has on the other members of the interacting system is typically recorded as a sequence of events in which each data entry corresponds to a behavioral state emitted by one or more of the organisms. The data, therefore, are in categorical form and frequently the simple observed frequencies of each behavioral state are used as descriptors of the various populations, for example, distressed and nondistressed marital partners (Gottman, 1979; Margolin & Wampold, 1981).

Early work on the analysis of categorical sequential data on dyadic interactions was preoccupied with determining whether or not behavioral states are independent. Thus, it is not surprising to note the reliance on test statistics based on the binomial and hypergeometric distributions (cf. Gottman, 1979, 1980a, 1980b; Kraemer & Jacklin, 1979), which can determine the unidirectional independence from one state to another. Today, however, researchers appear to be more concerned with the subtle influences that one organism has on the other members of the interacting system; hence, the emphasis is on the use of modeling techniques that can provide the researcher with the ability to test a wide array of common propositions in the study of dynamic social interactions, and that are also admissible to statistical inference testing (cf. Allison & Liker, 1982; Dillon, Madden, & Kumar, 1983).

In this chapter we review statistical methods for the analysis of sequential categorical data that are predicated on a model-building and testing approach. Because the statistical analysis of any given data set is determined by the type of data collected and the constructs of interest, we begin the discussion with a description of the type of data collected and a definition of several key constructs in the study of dyadic interactions. We then discuss a variety of alternative statistical methods that have been used to analyze categorical sequential dyadic data. The treatment is organized according to the kind of data available and the constructs of interest. After finishing the discussion of the conventional approaches to analyzing sequential dyadic interaction data in the penultimate section of this chapter, we exercise our license to venture into new methods that can potentially offer insights into dyadic relationships. There we briefly introduce and sketch a model for analyzing dyadic interaction data under the most general of conditions, namely, observable and unobservable covariates, behavioral states, and multiple time periods.

Background: Data Format and Construct Definition

Data Collection Formats

The type of data collected depends on certain decisions made by the researcher about how and when the observations should be recorded. One decision pertains to whether or not responses of both members of the dyad should be recorded at any given point in time. In this case, the data generated over time is a sequence of ordered pairs of observations. The first element of the ordered pairs is the response of one member, while the second element is the response of the second member at the same point in time.

On the other hand, if the decision is to record the response of only one member of the dyad, then the data consists of a single sequence of observations. A related decision issue when collecting data in this format is whether observations should be recorded at fixed times or when a change of behavior occurs. This has implications for the appropriateness of the statistical technique used to analyze the data (Wampold & Margolin, 1982). Alternative typologies of data collection formats are given by Wampold and Margolin (1982) and Bakeman and Gottman (1986).

Definition of Constructs

Some constructs of interest in social interaction analysis are defined below.

Dominance

Gottman (1980a) defines dominance as follows: "In a dyad, if B's future behavior is more predictable from A's past behavior than conversely, then A is said to be dominant" (p. 71).

Reciprocity

If A's performance of a certain behavior at time t increases the probability of B's performing the same behavior at time $t + k$, then reciprocity is said to exist (Gottman, 1980a). If i denotes the behavioral response of interest then reciprocity is characterized by the inequality

$$P(B_{t+k} = i | A_t = i) > P(B_{t+k} = i). \tag{1}$$

If the behavioral response i is coded as a positive response, then the dependence of B's behavior at time t + k on A's behavior at time t is termed positive reciprocity. Negative reciprocity is defined analogously.

Negative Reactivity

According to Margolin and Wampold (1981) negative reactivity is " ... the likelihood that a positive response given a negative stimulus is less than the unconditional probability of positive behaviors."

Independence of States

A state is defined as the emission of a particular behavioral response by a specific member of the dyad. For example, in a husband-wife dyad with behavioral responses of each member coded as positive, neutral, or negative, "husband-positive" is one of the six possible states. Letting i and j denote two such states, if the probability of observing i at time t + k given that j has been observed at time t is equal to the unconditional probability of observing i at time t + k, then there exists unidirectional independence from j to i. Following Wampold and Margolin (1982) we can write

$$P(i_{t+k}|j_t) = P(i_{t+k}) \tag{2}$$

where, for instance, i denotes "husband-positive" and j denotes "wife-positive." If, in addition to the above,

$$P(j_{t+k}|i_t) = P(j_{t+k}) \tag{3}$$

then the two states i and j are said to be bidirectionally independent.

Bidirectionality

Defined by Gottman and Ringland (1981) as the symmetrical predictability in behavioral states.

Structures of Dominance

Budescu (1984) extends the notion of dominance as defined by Gottman (1980a) and provides a typology of dominance structures, as well as a definition of additional types of dominance. In his framework, Gottman's concept is defined as direct dominance. An alternative type of dominance, indirect dominance, is defined as follows: "If under the appropriate model for predicting the joint behavior of a couple of actors from the past behavior, the nature of their future interaction is more predictable from A's past behavior than from B's, then A is said to be indirectly dominant" (p. 409). In this definition the phrase "appropriate model" implies that the model may contain independent variables other than the ones entering into the definition, for example, controls for autodependence (i.e., the dependence of a member's behavior at time t + k on his/her own behavior at time t).

Except for the concept of independence of states, all constructs impose structures of dependence on the data. However, in all cases, the null hypothesis specifies some type of independence, between subjects or among variables. In our discussion of the null hypotheses and their statistical testing, we examine the correspondence between construct explication and null hypothesis formulation, as well as the interrelationships among the constructs.

Analysis of Sequences of Paired Data

From the definition it is clear that dominance is the asymmetry in the predictability of dyadic behavior and is therefore related to the notion of bidirectionality. Both dominance and bidirectionality are concerned with predictability of one dyad member's future behavior from knowledge of the other member's past behavior. Thus in terms of formulating null hypotheses, the first question to ask is whether the dyadic behavior is characterized by any kind of predictability—symmetric or asymmetric. If there is no predictability, that is, neither member's future behavior can be predicted from the other's past behavior, then there is no dominance or bidirectionality in the dyadic interaction.

In statistical parlance, the null hypothesis of no predictability translates to the hypotheses of independence between variables B_{t+k} and A_t and between the variables A_{t+k}, and B_t in the four-way cross-classification of A_t, B_t, A_{t+k}, and B_{t+k}. An appropriate procedure for testing such hypotheses is provided by the general framework of log-linear models. In the assessment of dominance and bidirectionality we suggest that the researcher start by fitting the following three hierarchical log-linear models:

$$\text{Model 1.} \quad [A_t B_t][A_t A_{t+k}][B_t B_{t+k}][A_{t+k} B_{t+k}]$$

$$\text{Model 2.} \quad [A_t B_t B_{t+k}][A_t A_{t+k} B_{t+k}]$$

$$\text{Model 3.} \quad [A_t B_t A_{t+k}][B_t A_{t+k} B_{t+k}]$$

The notation conforms to the standard convention used to represent log-linear models (cf. Fienberg, 1980). The expressions within each bracket represent the highest order interaction terms included in the model. For example, Model 1 includes the main effects of the four variables, A_t, B_t, A_{t+k}, and B_{t+k}, and four two-way interactions, which are shown in brackets. The excluded two-way interactions are those between A_t and B_{t+k} and between B_t and A_{t+k}. Thus, Model 1 tests the hypothesis that A's behavior at time t + k is independent of B's behavior at time t and B's behavior at time t + k is independent of A's behavior at time t. An acceptable fit of this model to the data indicates that neither member's future behavior can be predicted from the other's past behavior. Model 2 tests the hypothesis that A's behavior at time t + k is independent of B's behavior at time t. Model 3 tests the hypothesis that B's behavior at time t + k is independent of A's behavior at time t. If Model 1 fits the data, then it can be concluded that each member's future behavior is independent of the other's past behavior and that the interaction is characterized neither by dominance nor by bidirectionality. If Models 1 and 3 do not fit the data but Model 2 does, then the conclusion is that A dominates B. Similarly, an acceptable fit for Model 3 coupled with a lack of fit for the other two models indicates the dominance of B over A. The remaining unambiguous scenario is one where none of the three models fits the data. The conclusion in this instance is that each member's future behavior is predictable from, that is, not independent of, the other member's past behavior and that the interaction is characterized either by dominance of one member over another or by bidirectionality.

Although Models 2 and 3 are nonnested relative to each other, Model 1 is nested in both Models 2 and 3 in the sense that the parameters estimated under the former model form a proper subset of each of the parameter sets of the latter models. In this sense Model 1 can be used as a baseline model for fit comparisons.

An alternative approach has been suggested by Allison and Liker (1982). In their approach dominance is assessed by use of a logit model (cf. Fienberg, 1980). Consider a three-way table generated by the cross-classification of A_t, B_t, and A_{t+k}. The logit model is

$$\text{logit}_{ij} = w + w_{At(i)} + w_{Bt(j)} \tag{4}$$

where the subscripts i and j denote the levels of A_t and B_t, respectively. A similar model

$$\text{logit}_{kl} = w + w_{Bt(k)} + w_{At(l)} \tag{5}$$

is fit to the $A_t \times B_t \times B_{t+k}$ table. The terms w_{At} and w_{Bt} are included in the models to partial out (i.e., control for) autodependence of A_{t+k} on A_t and B_{t+k} on B_t, respectively. The assessment of dominance is accomplished by comparing the parameter estimates w_{Bt} and w_{At}. Let s and s* denote the respective standard errors of w-terms. Under the null hypothesis that the two parameters are equal in the population, the test statistic

$$w_{Bt} - w_{At}/\{s^2 + s^{*2}\}^{1/2} \tag{6}$$

is distributed asymptotically as a standard normal random variable. Significant values of the test statistic indicate that the interaction is characterized by dominance. Allison and Liker (1982) note that the test statistic is likely to be biased downwards since w_{Bt} and w_{At} are likely to be positively correlated. Further, each logit model is estimated under the assumption of no three-way interaction. Allison and Liker also provide guidelines for the extension of the analysis as well as the analysis of multiple groups.

Budescu (1984) questions the validity of Allison and Liker's (1982) approach on the grounds that by analyzing each actor separately, a discrepancy arises between the unit of analysis and the unit of randomization (p. 404). As an alternative he presents a logit-linear approach where certain functions of cell probabilities (typically linear or logarithmic) are hypothesized to be generated by a linear model. The parameters of this model include two terms for the effects of each member's past behavior on the other member's future behavior. Dominance is assessed by testing the hypothesis of equality of these two parameters. The parameters of the linear model are estimated by the method of weighted least squares (Grizzle, Starmer, & Koch, 1969). The issue of interpretability of parameters and their correspondence to the concept of dominance warrants further attention. Consequently, we discuss Budescu's (1984) approach in greater detail below.

The linear model is fit to functions of the cell probabilities of the four-way table generated by the cross-classification of dichotomous variables A_t, B_t, A_{t+k}, and B_{t+k}. The saturated model consists of 12 functions, which are divided into three groups. The first two groups of functions are models for actors A and B, respectively. The third group captures "those aspects of the joint behavior of partners that cannot be accounted for by a direct aggregation of their individual responses" (Budescu, 1984, p. 409). The model for A consists of the following four equations:

$$\log[P(A_t=1, B_t=1, A_{t+k}=1)/P(A_t=1, B_t=1, A_{t+k}=0)]$$

$$= \beta_{01} + \beta_{11} + \beta_{21} + \beta_{31} \tag{7}$$

$$\log[P(A_t=1, B_t=0, A_{t+k}=1)/P(A_t=1, B_t=0, A_{t+k}=0)]$$

$$= \beta_{01} + \beta_{11} - \beta_{21} - \beta_{31} \tag{8}$$

$$\log[P(A_t=0, B_t=1, A_{t+k}=1)/P(A_t=0, B_t=1, A_{t+k}=0)]$$

$$= \beta_{01} - \beta_{11} + \beta_{21} - \beta_{31} \tag{9}$$

$$\log[P(A_t=0, B_t=0, A_{t+k}=1)/P(A_t=0, B_t=0, A_{t+k}=0)]$$

$$= \beta_{01} - \beta_{11} - \beta_{21} + \beta_{31} \tag{10}$$

According to Budescu (1984), β_{01} is analogous to a grand mean, β_{11} (β_{21}) represents the effect of A's (B's) past behavior, and β_{31} "the effect of the past interaction of A and B on the present response of A" (p. 408). To see a potential source of ambiguity in this formulation let β_{12} denote the effect of A's past behavior in the equations constituting the model for B. The null hypothesis of no dominance is then equivalent to the hypothesis that $\beta_{21} = \beta_{12}$. However, consider the situation where each actor's future behavior is independent of the other's past behavior—a situation characterized by neither dominance nor by bidirectionality. Then equations (7)–(10) can be rewritten as

$$\log[P(A_{t+k}=1, A_t=1)/P(A_{t+k}=0, A_t=1)]$$

$$= \beta_{01} + \beta_{11} + \beta_{21} + \beta_{31} \tag{11}$$

$$\log[P(A_{t+k}=1, A_t=1)/P(A_{t+k}=0, A_t=1)]$$

$$= \beta_{01} + \beta_{11} - \beta_{21} - \beta_{31} \tag{12}$$

$$\log \left[P(A_{t+k}=1, A_t=0)/P(A_{t+k}=0, A_t=0) \right]$$

$$= \beta_{01} - \beta_{11} + \beta_{21} - \beta_{31} \tag{13}$$

$$\log \left[P(A_{t+k}=1, A_t=0)/P(A_{t+k}=0, A_t=0) \right]$$

$$= \beta_{01} - \beta_{11} - \beta_{21} + \beta_{31} \tag{14}$$

A necessary and sufficient condition for these equations to hold is that $\beta_{21} = \beta_{31} = 0$. Thus the dependence of A's behavior on B's past behavior is not captured solely by the β_{21} parameter. Similarly, it can be shown that the dependence of A's future behavior on his/her past behavior is not accounted for by β_{11} alone. This means that the β_{31} parameter reflects both auto- and cross-dependence, which gives rise to a fundamental problem of lack of correspondence between the concept of dominance and the parameter (β_{21}) that purportedly captures this notion. This ambiguity does not arise in the logit-linear formulation presented by Allison and Liker (1982).

Analysis of Single Sequence Data

Wampold and Margolin (1982) suggest tests for independence of states based on the hypergeometric distribution and the application of the quadratic assignment paradigm (Hubert & Schultz, 1976; Graves & Whinston, 1970). An extension of the same approach to tests of dominance was given by Wampold (1984).

First, with regard to the approach based on the hypergeometric distribution. Let S be the total number of states and the sequence consist of N ($> S$) observations. Let n_i denote the number of occurrences of the ith state in the sequence, and T_{ij} denote the occurrence of the ordered pair (i, j) in the sequence. According to Wampold and Margolin (1982), the probability of observing exactly x (i, j) pairs is given by

$$P(T_{ij}=x) = \frac{\binom{n_i}{x}\binom{n_j}{x}}{\binom{N}{n_i}}$$

where ($\cdot$) denotes the total number of combinations obtained when choosing a subset of x elements from a set of n_i elements. However, this represents an incorrect characterization of the problem, as we demonstrate below with the use of a simple example. Suppose that

$$S = 3$$

$$n_1 = 4$$

$$n_2 = 2$$

$$n_3 = 4$$

$$N = n_1 + n_2 + n_3 = 10.$$

Assume that we are interested in the probability of occurrence of the pair $(1, 2)$ of the sequence. Given the values stated above, T_{12} can only assume the values 0, 1, and 2. Application of Wampold and Maroglin's (1982) formula, however, yields the following:

$$P(T_{12} = 0) = \frac{\binom{4}{0}\binom{2}{0}}{\binom{10}{4}} = \frac{1}{210}$$

$$P(T_{12} = 1) = \frac{\binom{4}{1}\binom{2}{1}}{\binom{10}{4}} = \frac{8}{210}$$

$$P(T_{12} = 2) = \frac{\binom{4}{2}\binom{2}{2}}{\binom{10}{4}} = \frac{6}{210}$$

It is clear that the probabilities do not sum to one. The apparent reason for this is in deriving the expression for the probabilities, Wampold and Margolin use combinatorial arguments involving only the two states of interest and exclude all other states.

The same deficiency is not present, however, in the case of the quadratic assignment paradigm. Under this approach the observed sequence of behavioral states is specified as an N by N data matrix consisting of zeros and ones where N is the number of observations in the sequence. The rows and columns of the matrix are indexed by K ($<$N) behavioral state categories. And each category appears as a row (column) index as frequently as the corresponding behavioral state appears in the data sequence. A one in the matrix indicates a transition from the row category to the column category; a zero indicates no transition. For example, the observed sequence ABCCAAB where A, B, and C denote three behavioral states of interest would yield the matrix

	A	A	A	B	B	C	C
A	0	0	0	1	0	0	0
A	0	0	1	0	0	0	0
A	0	0	0	0	1	0	0
B	0	0	0	0	0	1	0
B	0	0	0	0	0	0	0
C	0	0	0	0	0	0	1
C	0	1	0	0	0	0	0

Note that the data matrix always has $(N - 1)$ ones, equal to the number of transitions in a sequence of N observations. The hypothesis of interest is translated into an N by N structure matrix. A specific function of the elements of the two matrices is used to construct an index. The value of the index changes as the rows and columns of the data matrix are permuted and the structure matrix is kept fixed, or vice versa. If the data support the hypothesized structure, then the value of the index should be large compared with values obtained under random permutations of the data matrix. The rapid increase in the number of permutations possible, as N increases, makes it practically impossible to enumerate the index values for all permutations. Instead expressions are obtained for the expected value and variance of the index across all possible permutations which, in conjunction with the observed value of the index, are used to compute a Z-statistic for testing the hypothesis underlying the structure matrix. Further details and illustrative examples can be found in Wampold and Margolin (1982) and in Wampold (1984).

This finishes our discussion of the conventional approaches to analyzing sequential dyadic interaction data. In the remainder of this chapter we exercise our license to venture into new methods that can potentially offer insights into dyadic relationships. The following section briefly introduces and sketches a model for analyzing dyadic interaction data under the most general of conditions, namely, observable and unobservable covariates, behavioral states, and multiple time periods.

A General Probabilistic Model

In this section we present a new approach to the analysis of dyadic interaction under the most general sets of conditions, namely, both observed and unobserved covariates and multiple time periods. We assume that individuals, perhaps husbands and wives, have been observed with respect to a number of behaviors over multiple occasions where individuals may initially differ with respect to family composition and other psycho-social and background characteristics. The approach to be described is based on a redefinition of the state of the individual in terms of "fuzzy sets," that is, the degree of membership in each of K carrier sets or multivariate profiles that bound the space of observations. Specifically, the general probabilistic model describes the multivariate discrete dyadic data in terms of a fractional bilinear form of dimension K. In the bilinear form, there are incidental parameters that relate individuals to each of the K latent basic dimensions and structural parameters that define those dimensions in terms of the measured variables. Because individuals are observed at multiple time points, cross-temporal dependence can be described as dependency in either the individual or variable space. The parameterization of the general probabilistic model can entertain a variety of discrete-state/ discrete-time processes, for example, simple Markov forms or more general semi-Markov forms.

In the remainder of this section we will define the basic probabilistic model, describe the form of its likelihood, and discuss how various types of stochastic processes can be embedded in the model. The basic general probabilistic model builds on the work of Dillon, et al. (1983), Heckman and Singer (1984a, 1984b), Grover and Dillon (1985), Manton, Stallard, and Vaupel (1986), and Manton, Stallard, Woodbury, and Yashin (1986).

The Model

Let us define the following:

$i = 1, 2, \ldots, N$ index individuals;

$j = 1, 2, \ldots, p$ index the set of multinomial variables;

$l_j = 1, 2, \ldots, L_j$ index the response levels for the jth multinomial variable;

$t = 1, 2, \ldots, T$ index the time periods in which observations are made on each of the variables;

x_{itjl} = an exogenous binary-coded variable indicating the ith individual's response on the l_j^{th} level of the jth variable in the tth time period;

y_{itsu} = an endogenous transition variable defined by $y_{itsu} = y_{its} \times y_{i(t+1)u}$, where y_{its} is the behavioral state of the individual at time period t and $y_{i(t+1)u}$ is the behavioral state of the individual at time period $t+1$.

According to the notation defined above we can describe the situation as follows. Each of N individuals are measured at each of T time periods with respect to a set of exogenous and endogenous variates. The exogenous variables that relate to the individual's condition (i.e., family composition, mental health, distressed versus nondistressed, etc.) are multinomial in nature, each with L_j response levels that can be coded into binary variables. The endogenous variables give the behavioral state of the individual at each time period and interest centers on the transition from state to state and the conditions present when the transition occurs.

The general probabilistic model assumes that each x_{itjl} and y_{itsu} can be described in a K-dimensional space with incidental parameters $\{m_{itk}\}$ and structural parameters $\{\beta_{ktjl}\}$ and $\{\beta_{itsu}\}$. The m_{itk} parameters are linear weights estimated for each individual at each time period according to the constraints that $m_{itk} \geqq 0.0$ and $\sum_k m_{itk} = 1.0$. The β_{ktjl} and β_{itsu} are the probabilities that an individual of the kth pure type (i.e., $m_{itk} = 1.0$) will have l^{th} response to the jth exogenous variable and be in transition from states s to u at time period t. Thus we can write the model as

$$P(x_{itjl} = 1, y_{i(t+1)u}y_{its} = 1) = \sum_k m_{itk}\beta_{ktjl}\beta_{itsu}. \tag{15}$$

The Likelihood

The key statistical assumption underlying the model is local independence of the endogenous and exogenous variables given the scores $\{m_{ikt}\}$. In other words, the m_{itk} parameters describe the state of an individual at a given point in time and all exogenous covariates and endogenous variables describing the transitions are independent conditionally on the state description. The m_{itk}'s represent the multidimensional state description of an individual and can therefore explain the heterogeneity in both covariates and transition variables. Because of the assumption of local independence the expression for the likelihood simplifies to the form

$$L = \prod_{i=1}^{N} \prod_{t=1}^{T_i} \left\{ \prod_{j=1}^{P} \prod_{l=1}^{L_j} P[x_{itjl} = 1 | m_{ikt}]^{x_{itjl}} \right.$$

$$\left. \times \prod_{s=1}^{S} \prod_{u=1}^{S} P[y_{i(t+1)u} = 1 | y_{its} = 1, m_{ikt}]^{y_{itsu}} \right\} \tag{16}$$

where T_i denotes the number of time periods for which measurements have been made on the ith individual (cf. Manton, Stallard, & Woodbury, 1986). The structural parameters can be introduced into (16) by assuming that x_{itjl} and $y_{i(t+1)u} \, y_{its} = 1$ are Poisson distributed and the estimation process can be implemented with a variety of iterative search algorithms.

Stochastic Processes

A variety of stochastic processes can be embedded in the general model (i.e., likelihood) shown above. For example, a simple Markov process implies a homogeneous population and stationarity. Homogeneity can be tested by constraining the transition probabilities across the K types defined using only the exogenous covariates of the process. To test for stationarity we would constrain the transition probability from state s to state u to be the same for each of the K types over all time periods. Both tests can be effected by use of the chi-square difference statistic or with some other suitable goodness-of-fit measure.

By the judicious use of equality constraints across transition states and time periods, first and second order Markov processes can be tested as well semi-Markov processes in which transitions are a function of the time spent within a given state.

Summary

This chapter is a review and critical evaluation of the conventional procedures for analyzing sequential categorical data on dyadic interactions. The discussion has been organized according to the data format used and the constructs of interest. In addition, we introduced a general probabilistic model that can consider covariates, behavioral states, and multiple time periods.

Acknowledgment. This research was supported by a fellowship awarded to the first author by the Research Foundation of the State University of New York under the Faculty Research Assistance Program.

References

Allison, P. D., & Liker, J. K. (1982). Analyzing sequential categorical data on dyadic interaction: A comment on Gottman. *Psychological Bulletin, 91,* 393–403.

Altman, S. A. (1965). Sociobiology of Rhesus monkeys. II: Stochastics of social communication. *Journal of Theoretical Biology, 8,* 490–522.

Bakeman, R., & Gottman, J. M. (1986). *Observing interaction: An introduction to sequential analysis.* New York: Cambridge University Press.

Blurton-Jones, N. (Ed.). (1972). *Ethological studies of child behaviour,* Cambridge, England: Cambridge University Press.

Budescu, D. V. (1984). Test of lagged dominance in sequential dyadic interaction. *Psychological Bulletin, 96,* 402–414.

Dillon, W. R., Madden, T. J., & Kumar, A. (1983). Analyzing sequential categorical data on dyadic interaction: A latent structure approach. *Psychological Bulletin, 94,* 564–583.

Fienberg, S. E. (1980). *The analysis of cross-classified categorical data* (2nd ed.). Cambridge, MA: MIT Press.

Gottman, J. M. (1979). Detecting cyclicity in social interaction. *Psychological Bulletin, 86,* 338–348.

Gottman, J. M. (1980a). Analyzing for sequential connection and assessing inter-observer reliability for the sequential analysis of observational data. *Behavioral Assessment, 2,* 361–368.

Gottman, J. M. (1980b). *Marital interaction: Experimental investigations.* New York: Academic Press.

Gottman, J. M., & Ringland, J. T. (1981). The analysis of dominance and bidirectionality in social development. *Child Development, 52,* 393–412.

Graves, G. W., & Whinston, A. B. (1970). An algorithm for the quadratic assignment problem. *Management Science, 17,* 453–471.

Grizzle, J. E., Starmer, C. F. & Koch, G. G. (1969). Analysis of categorical data by linear models. *Biometrics, 25,* 489–504.

Grover, R., & Dillon, W. R. (1985). A probabilistic model for testing hypothesized hierarchical market structures. *Marketing Science, 4,* 312–335.

Heckman, J. J., & Singer, B. (1984a). The identifiability of the proportional hazards model. *Review of Economic Studies, 51,* 231–41.

Heckman, J. J., & Singer, B. (1984b). A method for minimizing the impact of distributional assumptions in econometric models for duration data. *Econometrica, 52,* 271–320.

Hubert, L., & Schultz, J. (1976). Quadratic assignment as a general data analysis strategy. *British Journal of Mathematical and Statistical Psychology, 29,* 190–241.

Kraemer, H. C., & Jacklin, N. (1979). Statistical analysis of dyadic social behavior. *Psychological Bulletin, 86,* 217–224.

Manton, K. G., Stallard, E., & Vaupel, J. W. (1986). Alternative models for the heterogeneity of mortality risks among the aged. *Journal of the American Statistical Association, 81,* 635–644.

Manton, K. G., Stallard, E., & Woodbury, M. A. (1986). Chronic disease evolution and human aging: A general model for assessing the impact of chronic disease in human populations. *Mathematical Modelling, 7,* 1155–71.

Manton, K. G., Stallard, E., Woodbury, M. A., & Yashin, A. I. (1986). Applications of the grade of membership technique to event history analysis: Extensions to multivariate unobserved heterogeneity. *Mathematical Modelling, 7*, 1375–1391.

Margolin, G., & Wampold, B. E. (1981). Sequential analysis of conflict and accord in distressed and nondistressed marital partners. *Journal of Consulting and Clinical Psychology, 49*, 554–567.

Wampold, B. E., & Margolin, G. (1982). Nonparametric strategies to test the independence of behavioral states in sequential data. *Psychological Bulletin, 92*, 755–765.

Wampold, B. E. (1984). Tests of dominance in sequential categorical data. *Psychological Bulletin, 96*, 424–429.

Wilson, E. O. (1975). *Sociobiology: The new synthesis.* Cambridge, MA: Harvard University Press.

CHAPTER 6

Information Integration in Husband-Wife Decision Making About Health-Care Services

C. Michael Troutman and James Shanteau

The research described in this chapter addresses husband-wife decision making by focusing on the relation between spouses' individual and collective judgments. The purpose is to illustrate a new method for examining how spouses make joint decisions.

The specific research problem involves the selection of medical services by expectant parents. About-to-be parents normally seek services from pediatricians and obstetricians in preparing for childbirth. Even though the mother (and child) are the immediate recipients of medical care, the husband often exerts considerable influence on the decision.

Before turning to empirical research, a methodological review is offered of prior approaches to husband-wife decision making. This review is intended to illustrate the need for an alternative methodological framework. A new method is then suggested to examine how spouses make joint decisions. This method is implemented in three experiments to study couples' collective decisions of pregnancy-related health-care services.

Previous Methods

Research on family decision making has traditionally focused on the influence that each spouse has on consumer choices (Engel, Blackwell, & Miniard, 1986). Although a variety of decision categories have been studied, most decisions concern durable products such as automobiles and furniture. Very few studies have looked at services generally or medical care specifically (for an exception, see Beach, Townes, Campbell, & Keating, 1976). The following review summarizes the methods used to study family decision making and critically evaluates the adequacy of these methods for investigating couples' decisions.

Self-Report Methods

By far the most common method used is direct questioning of one or both spouses (Assael, 1984). Husbands and/or wives are asked through self-report questionnaires to recall how they made past purchasing decisions. These questions are designed to reveal which decisions are made by one spouse exclusively and which are shared. For shared decisions, perceptions of relative influence are assessed.

The results using this method indicate that husbands are often more involved in "women's decisions," for example, grocery items and toiletries, than is commonly believed (Davis, 1976). Analyses of decisions about durable goods (Davis & Rigaux, 1974) and family planning (Dudley & Choldin, 1967) indicate a trend toward shared decision-making responsibilities (Roberts, 1984). Although many decisions are made with input from both spouses, the frequency of shared decisions varies somewhat between and within product categories (Robertson, Zielinski, & Ward, 1984).

Although it is useful to know which spouse makes what decision, most researchers are primarily interested in how much influence each spouse has. Unfortunately, inconsistent results are the rule with self-reported influence. Davis and Rigaux (1974), for instance, reported serious discrepancies between husbands' and wives' responses within families.

Some investigators (e.g., Granbois, 1963) have suggested that these discrepancies are due to a failure to specify different decision stages, such as problem identification and brand selection. In answering questions about relative influence, husbands and wives may recall different stages in the process and so report different degrees of decision influence. Research with questionnaires modified to measure influence at different stages, however, still shows widespread disagreement within families (Davis & Rigaux, 1974; Filiatrault & Ritchie, 1980).

Other researchers have questioned the meaningfulness of self-reported measures of influence. Using four different measures of relative influence, Davis (1971) found only marginal correlations, that is, a lack of convergent validity. Similarly, the results failed to show good discriminant validity. These results tend to cast doubt on direct questioning techniques for measuring relative influence.

Critique

There is little doubt that important contributions toward understanding husband-wife decision making have been made by self-report methods. However, there are a number of problems associated with these methods, which limits their value. Most of these problems have been noted previously (e.g., Davis & Rigaux, 1974) and will be only briefly mentioned here.

First, self-reports are typically assessed well after the decisions have been made. It is well known that recall of past life events is subject to many memory biases (Bartlett, 1932). It may well be that such biases influence spouses' perceptions of past decision activities and so produce the widely reported discrepancies in judged influence (see also Ericsson & Simon, 1980).

Second, self-report measures of relative influence assume that spouses are fully aware of how they influence each other and that they can meaningfully estimate the amount of influence. These assumptions seem questionable, especially since psychologists are unable to reach consensus on what constitutes social influence (Tedeschi, 1972). If psychologists cannot agree, is it any wonder that spouses may disagree?

Third, even when self-reports provide adequate data on decision *outcomes*, they do not necessarily provide insight into the *processes* that accompany decision making. Efforts to define decision stages are helpful, but it has not been made clear whether every purchase proceeds through the same stages (Park, 1982). Thus, direct self-report methods seem to be of limited value for determining how couples go about making collective decisions.

Observational Methods

Instead of relying on self-reports, many investigators have attempted to observe the interaction between spouses while making decisions. Most notable are the pioneering studies by Strodtbeck (1951) and Kenkel (1963). In much of this research, the main thrust has been to observe how much power each spouse has in collective decision making. Kenkel (1963), for instance, observed while spouses decided how they would spend a $300 cash gift. Interestingly, in the majority of families, spouses displayed roughly equivalent power.

In connection with empirical research on social power, several theoretical accounts have been proposed. Pollay's (1968) theory, for example, offers a rigorous account of husband-wife decision making in terms of utility theory. One testable prediction is that a spouse may sacrifice control over a decision that nets little gain in utility in exchange for more control over other decisions that produce a higher utility gain.

Despite the richness of Pollay's and others' theories, researchers have seldom applied the observational methods to the substantive issues raised by these theories. This is due, in part, to a preoccupation with comparing observational methods with self-report methods (e.g, Granbois & Willett, 1970; Turk & Bell, 1972). Most of this research does indeed show that self-reports are inferior. What is needed is more focus on theoretical issues using these methods (Engel et al., 1986).

Critique

Observational methods have enabled researchers to monitor actual husband-wife decision making. These observations have led to a number of useful insights. Nonetheless, the methods are not without criticism.

First, because the spouses' interactions generally are observed under laboratory conditions, there is some question about whether this can be equated with "natural" behavior. Questions about external validity, of course, are hardly unique to this area of research (Ebbesen & Konecni, 1980). To resolve such questions, laboratory-based measures need to be compared with observations in natural environments. So far, there have been few such comparisons.

A second reservation concerns a lack of convergence among different measures of social power. Turk and Bell (1972) compared five measures and observed low intercorrelations. This led Turk and Bell to conclude that "such measures as these are not measuring the phenomenon with enough precision to be useful" (p. 222). These results raise obvious questions about the usefulness of observational methods.

Third, beyond measurement problems, there is a fundamental question about the role of social power in couple decision making. Although relative power is certainly important, there may be other relevant dimensions to marital decision making. In particular, a discussion between husband and wife may involve both power issues and an exchange of information (Park, 1982). The latter more cognitive domain may be just as relevant, but has not been tapped by observational methods. Thus, these methods may have been blind to important cognitive processes in collective decision making.

Experimental Methods

A more recent trend is the use of experimental methods to assess family decision-making processes. These methods can be used to investigate actual decision-making behavior, without a specific concern for social power (Granbois & Summers, 1975). Thus, this approach is not committed to any particular theoretical position or measures (Krishnamurthi, 1983).

To illustrate the approach, Granbois and Summers' (1975) investigation will be described. Husbands and wives were asked separately to make lists of major (over $100) household items that would be purchased in the coming year. The couples then repeated the exercise jointly. The results indicated that although the spouses independently proposed about the same number of items (around 4), they jointly proposed a significantly larger number (over 5).

The differences between joint and separate responses were explained by two types of decision strategies. One was an accommodation strategy in which items selected by one spouse are added to the other spouse's list. The other strategy was to discard the separate lists and to start over. Interestingly, husbands' and wives' responses were more highly correlated with the joint judgments than with each other. This suggests that both spouses were influenced by joint discussion and that neither dominated.

Critique

The advantage of the experimental approach exemplified by Granbois and Summers (1975) is that it provides a means of studying the strategies used by spouses when making joint decisions. Unlike previous approaches that focus on decision *outcomes*, the experimental approach makes an effort to analyze decision *process*. There are, nonetheless, two areas where improvement is possible.

First, instead of having one procedure for separate decisions and a different procedure for joint decisions, greater control can be gained by using the same method for all judgments. This would permit a direct analysis of how husband and wife decisions compare with the joint decisions. It would then be possible to understand better how the joint strategy emerged from the individual strategies.

Second, use of systematic designs, as opposed to ad-hoc stimulus sets, would allow formal assessment of decision strategies. Measurement techniques, such as conjoint measurement (Krantz, Luce, Suppes, & Tversky, 1971; Green & Srinivasan, 1978) or functional measurement (Anderson, 1962, 1981), can then be applied to analyze the results. Such techniques have the advantage of providing quantitative descriptions of both the judgment rules and the measurement values. Wind (1976), for instance, used conjoint analysis to determine that husbands' influence was second only to price on wives' decisions about telephone services.

Of the three methodologies considered, the experimental approach appears most promising for studying joint decision-making processes. In contrast to self-reports, experimental methods enable researchers to look directly at the process of decision making. In contrast to observational methods, experimental methods are useful for studying factors other than influence and power in collective decision making (e.g., cognitive processes). Combined with systematic designs and more rigorous analytic procedures, the experimental approach would appear to have considerable potential. This potential is spelled out in the next section.

Consumer Information Integration

The methods used in the present research were originally developed to analyze individual judgment and decision processes. Although a variety of methods have emerged from this research tradition, the techniques share a common cognitive perspective (Arkes & Hammond, 1986). Decision makers are viewed as selecting information cues, weighting and evaluating the cues, and then combining the cues together to make a decision; in short, decision makers are viewed as information evaluators and processors (Anderson, Deane, Hammond, McClelland, & Shanteau, 1981). Before going into more detail, some comments will be offered on the general approach.

Background

When spouses interact to make a decision, the outcome seems simple—they either agree or disagree. Even a casual analysis of the husband-wife interaction, however, indicates that matters are more complicated than that. Spouses may discover that they have reached the same decision, but for different reasons. Alternatively spouses may have different preferences, but learn that their underlying values are similar. Thus, the process of discussion and interaction is an important part of the decision process.

Whether spouses agree or disagree is not so important in the present view as the sharing of information. Indeed, recognition of agreement or disagreement is only possible after some information has been exchanged. Further if there is disagreement, spouses may exchange information and views in an effort to resolve the conflict. From this analysis, therefore, collective decisions are similar to individual decisions in that both are based on the processing of information.

To understand how collective decisions are made, it is necessary to examine simultaneously the husband's and the wife's individual decision processes as well as the collective decision process. This then allows comparisons both between individuals and between individuals and joint decisions. In this way, it becomes possible to analyze in detail how joint decisions relate to individual decisions.

Decision Task

The purpose of the present research is to investigate husband-wife decision making about health-care services. The task used provided husbands and wives with information about various health services and and asked them to use this information to make judgments about the services. For example, couples were asked about the quality of service expected from a pediatrician based on information about (1) ability of the pediatrician to communicate effectively with children, and (2) manners of the pediatrician's staff (i.e., friendliness and consideration). Spouses must then integrate the two pieces of information into a whole to arrive at their judgment.

By systematically varying the levels of the two factors, a set of alternative pediatric services can be described. For example, a prospective pediatrician might be described as having above-average ability and below-average staff manners. By evaluating the pattern of judgments made under various conditions, the decision strategy can be inferred and quantitatively modeled (Shanteau, 1986). These models are derived for each husband and wife separately, and then for the couple collectively. It then becomes possible to describe each spouse's contribution to the collective decision with some precision.

Information Integration

The methodology that will be used to examine couples' decision processes derives from Anderson's (1981, 1982) information integration theory (IIT). This theory assumes that there are two fundamental processes involved in making decisions. The first is an *evaluation* process by which psychological value is attached to information. A two-parameter representation is assumed, with each piece of information having both a *weight*, or importance value, and a *scale*, or valence value. The "impact" of a piece of information is the product of weight and scale values (Shanteau, 1980).

The second process involves the *integration* of the separate pieces of information into a unitary judgment. Typically, the integration has been found to correspond to simple algebraic rules. The adequacy of these rules, as well as estimates of the weight- and scale-value parameters, is provided by *functional-measurement* (FM) procedures.

In previous applications of this approach to consumer behavior (Lynch, 1985; Shanteau, 1987; Shanteau & Ptacek, 1983; and Troutman & Shanteau, 1976), consistent support has been observed for weighted averaging models of consumer information integration. That is, consumer decisions reflect a compromise or "center of gravity" among various pieces of information.

In mathematical terms, the averaging model can be stated as follows. Let D be the decision for a case specified by a two-factor, row x column factorial design. Various cases are described by level i of the row factor (e.g., Doctor's Ability) and level j of the column (e.g., Staff Manners). Then,

$$D_{ij} = \frac{w_O I_O + w_R s_{Ri} + w_C s_{Cj}}{w_O + w_R + w_C} \tag{1}$$

The w's and s's refer to weights and scale values, respectively; R and C identify the row and column factors. The average includes the initial opinion (subscript 0) consumers bring to decision making. A consumer, for instance, may have a generally positive (or negative) view of doctors and this would be reflected by a high (or low) initial opinion.

The relative weight of each piece of information, k, is

$$w_k / \Sigma\, w_k.$$

By virtue of the denominator, relative weights must sum to one, a necessary condition for an averaging model. Therefore, if weight increases on one factor, then the relative weight of the other factor(s) must necessarily decrease.

One advantage of IIT models is that they can be tested at the level of individual subjects or, in this case, individual couples. Further, weights and scale values can be estimated using FM procedures for each individual subject or couple. For example, the values in collective judgments might resemble those of the wife more than the husband. That would imply that she had more influence on the collective judgment. (Specific procedures for estimating weights and scale values are derived in Appendix 6.A)

Experiment 1

The primary goal of the first experiment was to use information integration techniques to evaluate how expectant parents make decisions about prospective pediatricians. Pediatricians were selected because their services are relevant for expectant parents and, in many cases, these parents had yet to make a final selection. This study also demonstrates the application of functional measurement techniques to test an averaging model and to estimate subjective values.

Method

Subjects

Twenty expectant couples (40 subjects) were recruited from childbirth preparation classes and paid $3.00 per hour for participating. The sample included subjects with a range of occupations (students, military, professionals, and skilled laborers) and educational backgrounds (high school, college, and postgraduate). Mean ages of husbands and wives were 23.7 and 22.1, respectively.

Stimuli

Prospective pediatricians were described by two kinds of information: Doctor's Ability to handle children and Staff Manners. The former was defined as "how well the doctor could communicate with children to relieve their fears about visiting a doctor," and the latter as "how personable the nurses, receptionists, and other staff were."

There were four levels of information associated with each factor: Low, below average, above average, and high. These levels were combined in a 4 × 4 factorial design to produce 16 hypothetical pediatricians (e.g., above-average Doctor's Ability, and below-average Staff Manners.) Additionally, eight other pediatricians were described by just one kind of information (e.g., high Doctor's Ability or low Staff Manners). Two other "filler" pediatricians were described using extreme levels (see below). Thus, 26 different pediatricians were described. All stimuli were presented twice, so that each subject made 52 judgments in all.

Procedure

The information about each pediatrician appeared on an index card. These cards were presented in random shuffled order. Instructions stated that the information had been supplied by a "trusted friend." Subjects were asked to judge the overall quality of service expected based on the information provided.

Decisions were made by sliding a marker on an unmarked 20-cm bar. The left and right boundaries of the bar were labeled "Very Low Quality" and "Very High Quality," respectively. Anchor stimuli with extreme levels (Very Low, Very High) were used to exemplify the boundaries. These were also used as filler stimuli to ensure that the scale was used properly and to prevent floor and ceiling effects. Five practice stimuli were presented at the beginning of the experiment to determine if instructions were understood.

The experiment was conducted in the homes of the couples. It was felt that this would provide a more natural setting for expectant couples. All of the pediatricians were judged first by one spouse, then the other, and finally by the two spouses jointly. For the latter, spouses had to arrive at a decision that was acceptable to both. The entire session typically required 1 1/2 hours to complete.

Results

Figure 6.1 shows plots of the 4 × 4 cells means for husbands, wives, and joint decisions. Overall, these plots appear similar (e.g., the two lines with High and Above-Average Ability are elevated well above the other two lines). There is, however, an S-shape for husbands and wives that does not appear for joint judgments. This suggests that there may be some nontrivial differences between joint and individual decisions.

Differences between individual and joint judgments were examined by an analysis of variance. No main effects were observed. There were inter-actions, however, between husband and joint judgments for Ability ($F = 5.25$; $df = 3,57$) and for Staff Manners ($F = 5.07$; $df = 3,57$)—all with $p < .05$. Similarly, there was an interaction between wives and joint judgments for Ability ($F = 2.70$; $df = 3,57$). These interactions are re-flected, in part, by relative shifts in the lower two curves across the panels in Figure 6.1. Therefore, there were differences between individual and joint judgments.

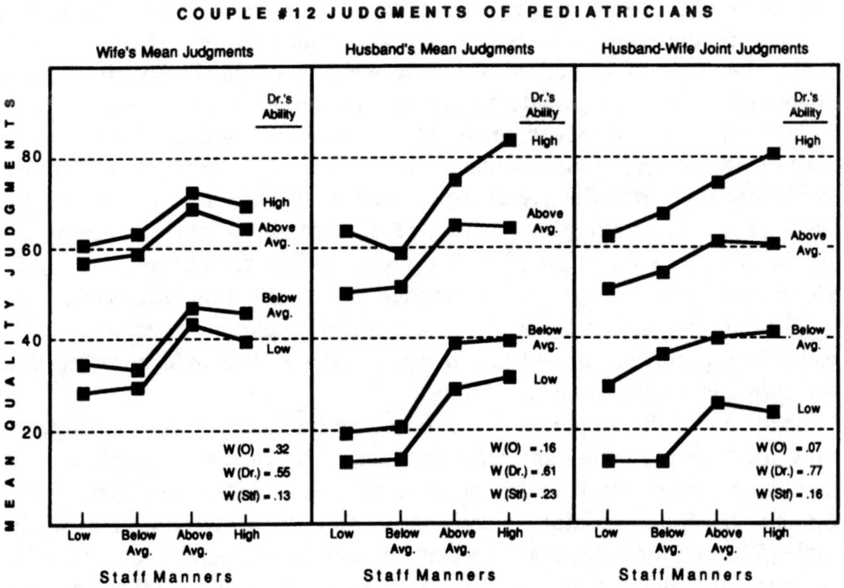

Figure 6.1. Mean judgments of pediatricians by husbands, wives, and joint (collec-tive), Experiment 1. Staff Manners is on the horizontal axis and Doctor's Ability is the curve parameter. Approximately parallel lines support a constant-weight aver-aging model. Weight estimates from the averaging model shown in lower corner.

Functional Measurement Analysis

The FM analysis was carried out in three steps. The first two steps test predictions of an averaging model, and the third step involves estimating the parameters of the averaging model. A constant-weight averaging model (Eq. 1) predicts that the cell means in the 4×4 factorial plot as parallel lines or, equivalently, that there is no interaction in an analysis of variance (Anderson, 1981). In Figure 6.1, there were minor deviations from parallelism that appeared both graphically and statistically in all three panels ($F = 2.01$, 3.30, and 6.45, respectively; $df = 9,171$).

Although these results tend to discredit the constant-weight averaging model, there are two reasons for considering the model further. First, the plots are quite close to parallel, as predicted by constant-weight averaging. In each plot, only the High-High point deviates markedly from parallelism. This suggests that this combination may have become an upper end-anchor. Second, the size of the interaction is not as substantial as would be expected from alternative models. When other models have been tested using FM procedures (e.g., Shanteau & Nagy, 1979), the interaction F-ratios are typically several magnitudes larger than observed here. Therefore, the averaging model appears to provide a first approximation for the couples' decision strategies.

The second step in the FM analysis involves testing for an interaction between decisions based on two pieces of information and decisions based on one piece. In the former case, weight is split among two information sources; in the latter case, weight is concentrated in one source. Accordingly, the slope of the curves (i.e., the weight) should be steeper for the single-information judgments than for the double-information judgments.

This can be tested by comparing the marginal means from the 4×4 factorial with the corresponding means from the single judgments. The results uniformly supported the averaging prediction. In husbands' judgments, for instance, the interaction for Ability and Staff Manners was significant, and in the predicted direction ($F = 27.62$ and 10.68, respectively; $df = 3,57$). Comparable interactions were observed for wives' and joint judgments.

The final FM step is to use the model to derive parameter estimates. The estimation procedure is outlined in Appendix 6.A. It should be noted that the estimates are based on group data.

Estimates of the weights in Table 6.1 show that Ability was more important, for both individual and joint decisions. Also the initial weight is non-zero in each case, implying that prior opinions have a definite impact. Interestingly, the initial opinion value is consistently below the midpoint of the scale (50); this indicates that expectant parents have slightly negative prior opinions of pediatricians. Some scale values are outside the effective range of the response scale (e.g., Low is -7.4 for husbands). Values outside the scale limits represent an asymptotic limit more extreme than the scale endpoints.

Table 6.1. Estimates of weight and scale values for husbands, wives, and joint (collective), experiment 1.

Parameter	Husbands	Wives	Collective
w_O	.29	.18	.20
$w_{\text{Staff manners}}$	.16	.22	.17
$w_{\text{Dr.'s ability}}$	.55	.60	.63
I_O	45.9	40.3	43.2
s_{Low}	−7.4	2.3	−3.9
$s_{\text{Below average}}$	13.5	19.4	18.8
$s_{\text{Above average}}$	81.8	71.3	72.3
s_{High}	103.0	89.2	95.5

Note. The weights are constrained to sum to one. Scale value estimates are averages of the different estimates provided by the solution in Appendix 6.A.

Comparisons reveal that the initial weight is greatest for husbands (.29) and least for wives (.18) and joint (.20). This suggests that husbands depended more on initial opinions when alone, but decreased the weight after talking with their wives. Perhaps husbands felt reluctant to move too far away from their initial views until communicating with their spouse. It is worth observing that the initial weight for wives is less than for husbands. Apparently, wives were more willing to make a decision based on the given information than were husbands.

Table 6.1 shows that the joint weight of Staff Manners (.17) is similar to husbands' weight (.16), but that the joint weight of Ability (.63) is closer to the weight for wives (.60). That suggests a type of compromise strategy for couple decisions based on adjusting weights, rather than on splitting the difference between separate judgments. This was supported by the observation that when spouses disagreed, they tended to discuss the importance of the information dimensions instead of seeking the middle response value.

Table 6.1 also provides the estimates of scale values for individual and joint judgments. Since scale values are interval estimates, it is necessary to examine distance between scale values rather than absolute values. The distance between Low and Below Average, for instance, is greater for joint (22.6) than for individual judgments (20.9 for husbands and 17.1 for wives). Similarly, the distance between High and Above Average for joint (23.1) exceeds the separate values (21.2 and 17.8, respectively). These differences are not consistent with a simple compromise scheme for joint decisions. Instead, disagreements about scale values were apparently resolved by reevaluating the information.

Individual Analyses

Analysis of group results showed that information about Ability increased in importance for joint judgments. This pattern was also found when individual couple data were examined. Figure 6.2 shows the results for one

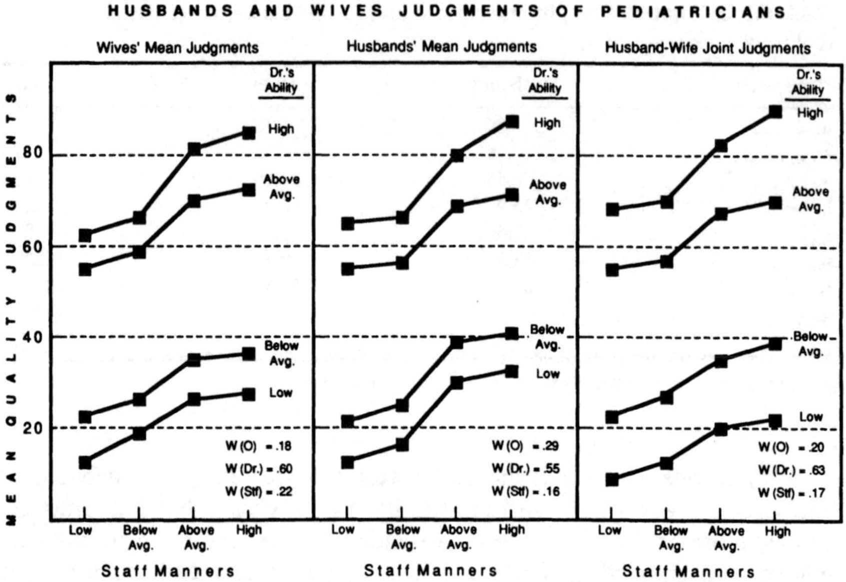

HUSBANDS AND WIVES JUDGMENTS OF PEDIATRICIANS

Figure 6.2. Judgments of pediatricians by one couple, Experiment 1. Staff Manners is on the horizontal and Doctor's Ability is the curve parameter. Weight estimates shown in the lower corner.

couple, with weight estimates given in the lower corner. As can be seen, Ability weight increased from separate to joint judgments while the initial weight decreased. Not all couples, however, showed this pattern. For some couples, one spouse tended to dominate the collective judgments.

Discussion

Experiment 1 demonstrates that the information integration approach to individual decision making can be extended to family decision making. Moreover, IIT provides new insights into the decision strategies used. Previous approaches (e.g., Granbois & Summers, 1975) only compared the observed responses of the spouses. In contrast, the present approach was able to look at weights and scale values as well as the observed responses. By doing so, the increase in importance of Ability was readily apparent.

Joint Decision Processes

Even though the difference between separate and joint judgments is not striking, they are nonetheless surprising given that husbands and wives were quite similar. The only significant difference in the responses between spouses was for judgments based on Staff Manner information alone. Why then should joint judgments differ from separate judgments?

There is a difference in the process of making combined judgments, which may explain these results. When the spouses were together, they frequently exchanged information concerning their feelings about each pediatrician. The spouses, for instance, would discuss how much more important Ability was than Staff Manners. In making joint judgments, therefore, each spouse had information about the other spouse's decision strategy as well as the stimulus information.

In choosing physicians, it may be important for each spouse to know the other's strategy. The criteria for selecting doctors are ambiguous because consumers often feel they lack sufficient technical understanding (Brien, Haverfield, & Shanteau, 1983). If a husband and wife discover that their separate judgments of physicians are similar, they may become more confident that they have made the "right" decision. A common finding in research on interpersonal judgment is that "extra" information often produces more confidence and more extreme responses (e.g., Sloan & Ostrom, 1974). In the present results, some pediatricians were judged more extremely in the joint judgments. As seen in Figures 6.1 and 6.2, for example, pediatricians with low Ability were evaluated more negatively.

The increased confidence interpretation is consistent with IIT if confidence is inversely related to the weight of initial opinion. A decrease in the initial weight would be expected when additional information, such as a spouse's judgments, becomes available. Added information, therefore, decreases the weight of the initial opinion.

Implications

The concept of initial impression was crucial in the present interpretation. Theoretically, the concept seems appealing because consumer decisions are seldom made without prior information or expectations (Shanteau, 1987). It is interesting to note that the scale value of the initial opinion was slightly but consistently negative. This less-than-positive opinion has also been reported in surveys of consumer attitudes toward physicians ("Patients down on doctors," 1976). In subsequent research, it may be worthwhile examining the reasons for consumers' initial opinions about physicians in more depth.

From a practical perspective, the present results have limited applicability for several reasons. First, couples were asked to evaluate single pediatricians. However, the decision typically involves a choice between physicians rather than a judgment of a single physician. This will be examined further in Experiment 2. Second, the stimulus information was arbitrarily selected to contain only two attributes; it would be more realistic to provide consumers with several sources of information (see Experiment 3).

Despite these limitations, the present results suggest that information about the pediatrician is considerably more important than information about the pediatrician's staff. In most pediatric offices, however, nurses perform many (if not most) medical procedures. They frequently give shots, take vital measurements, and answer questions. Clearly poor performance by nursing staff could have serious consequences for a pediatrician. The present expectant parents may have naively underestimated the importance of staff. Indeed, based on comparisons before and after childbirth, new parents have learned to place considerably more importance on staff performance after childbirth (Brien, Haverfield, & Shanteau, 1983).

Experiment 2

In the first study, couples evaluated individual pediatricians. Frequently, consumers consider several physicians before selecting one (Freidson, 1971). Accordingly, the purpose of Experiment 2 was to examine how expectant parents decide between prospective pediatricians.

Subjects were asked to state which of two pediatricians they preferred and by how much. For preference judgments, a subtractive model has been applied in previous IIT research (Birnbaum & Veit, 1974; Shanteau & Anderson, 1969; Shanteau & Nagy, 1979). This model states that preference judgments are the algebraic difference between the values of the two alternatives.

$$P_{ij} = D_i - D_j \qquad (2)$$

Preference, P, is the difference in evaluations for doctors i and j.

The test of Equation 2 is straightforward (Shanteau & Anderson, 1969). Since the value for each doctor is independent of the value of the other doctor, the model predicts that there should be no interaction in the preference judgments. This prediction can be tested directly by analysis of variance.

According to Equation 1, the value for each of the alternative doctors in Equation 2 should be an average of the available information. This prediction was also examined in Experiment 2.

To facilitate comparisons, this experiment was conducted with a subset of the same expectant parents who served in Experiment 1. In addition, prospective pediatricians were described in the same way as the first study. This made it possible to examine the consistency of processing models and subjective values in the two experiments.

Method

Subjects

Thirteen of the couples (26 subjects) from Experiment 1 participated in this study. They were paid as before.

Stimulus Design

A paired-comparison design was used in which pairs of pediatricians from the 4 × 4 factorial in Experiment 1 were compared. To pair every physician with every other would require 256 comparisons, which is excessive. To make the design more reasonable, a fractional factorial design was used to construct 16 choice pairs (Cochran & Cox, 1957). Such designs that allow the evaluation of all main effects and some interactions have been used in prior IIT research (Ettenson, Krogstad, & Shanteau, 1984).

Four other choice stimuli were presented to determine if consumers evaluated the choice alternatives by an averaging rule. These stimuli involved a choice between an alternative described by two pieces of information and an alternative described by one piece (see below).

Procedure

With some exceptions, the procedure was similar to Experiment 1. The alternative pediatricians were presented side-by-side on index cards. Consumers were instructed first to choose one of the two, and then to rate the amount of their preference. The left boundary of the response scale were defined as "no preference" and was exemplified by a case where two doctors were High on both factors and a case where two doctors were Low on both factors, that is, the alternatives were tied. The right boundary was defined as the difference between a pediatrician Very High on both factors and a pediatrician Very Low on both factors. These exemplars were also used as filler stimuli.

Experiment 2 was conducted about a week after the first study. As before, the couples made individual judgments before making joint judgments. These sessions required approximately 2 1/2 hours.

Results

Analysis of variance was used to determine if there was a significant difference between husbands, wives, and joint judgments. Unlike Experiment 1, no differences were found. This apparently reflects a convergence of opinion from having made collective decisions in the first study.

Functional measurement was used (1) to test the subtractive model for preference judgments, (2) to examine the averaging model for evaluation of alternatives, and (3) to estimate subjective values for husbands, wives, and joint judgments.

Subtractive Model

According to a subtractive model, there should be no significant interactions in the fractional factorial design. With the fractional design used, interactions cannot be separately estimated (Addelman, 1962). It is possible, however, to obtain a pooled estimate of various interaction terms and to test it for significance.

The analysis indicated that the pooled interaction term was not significant for wives ($F = 1.74$; $df = 3,400$), but was marginally significant for husbands and joint judgments ($F = 3.06$ and 4.15, respectively). At the individual-couple level, the subtractive model fit reasonably well. Among the 13 couples, there were significant discrepancies for one husband, three wives, and three couples. The magnitude of these discrepancies is comparable with those observed for the subtractive model in Shanteau and Anderson (1969).

Although the subtractive model appears to be marginally acceptable, some doubt remains. The ideal test procedure would be to examine the four two-factor interactions involving one of the two factors from doctor 1 and one from doctor 2. These interactions, however, are confounded with main effects and cannot be tested separately. The test of the pooled residual is less direct and does not allow for localization of significant effects. Thus, the present analyses are only capable of providing tentative tests of the subtractive model.

Averaging

Four pairs of choice stimuli were used to test for averaging. To illustrate, the first pair of choice stimuli are (a) High Ability versus X, and (b) High Ability + Above-Average Staff versus X. In these choices, X represents a common alternative. According to averaging, the preference in (b) should less than the preference in (a). This prediction arises because the addition of Above-Average Staff information should produce a less polarized average impression. To test for averaging, therefore, the preference for (b) is subtracted from the preference for (a); averaging is confirmed by a positive score.

The tests were performed for husbands, wives, and joint judgments. Averaging was supported in half the tests; these were comparisons in which the information about the two alternatives was uniformly negative. For example, the joint judgments for (a) Low Staff versus X were 6.9 scale units more extreme than (b) Low Staff + Below-Average Ability. When the two alternatives were described in positive terms, however, the results were uniformly negative. For example, the joint judgments for (a) High Ability, was 2.6 less extreme than (b) High Ability + Average Staff.

An adding model for information integration predicts in all cases that the (b) stimuli would be more extreme than the (a) stimuli, since the former always contains more polarized information. Therefore, there is no way that an adding model with constant parameters could account for the present results. The mixed results would be compatible with averaging, however, if either the weight of the initial opinion is large or if one dimension dominates the other. Both of these conditions were in fact present in Experiment 1.

To examine this further, the parameters derived from Experiment 1 were used to predict the preferences in Experiment 2. Half of these predicted results produced positive differences and half produced negative results. Thus, the observed pattern of results is consistent with an averaging decision process.

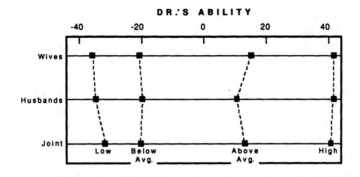

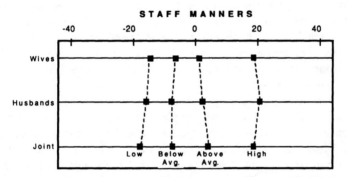

Figure 6.3. Impact values for mean preference judgments for husbands, wives, and joint (collective), experiment 2. Dr.'s Ability presented in top panel and Staff Manners presented in bottom panel. Similarity of spacing reveals lack of disagreement.

Parameter Estimates

The FM procedures outlined in Appendix 6.A cannot be used with fractional designs. Instead, combined weight and scale values or "impact values" can be estimated from the marginal means (Shanteau, 1980). These values are plotted in Figure 6.3.

The first feature to note in Figure 6.3 is the difference in the range of values on the two dimensions. The range for Ability is about twice the range for Staff Manners. This is consistent with the difference in weights observed in Experiment 1.

The second feature is the similarity of results for individual and joint judgments. Apparently, the spouses were using similar choice strategies separately and continued to use these strategies jointly.

Additional Analyses

Three regression analyses were performed to see how well the responses from Experiment 1 predicted the responses in Experiment 2. First, the predicted choices were examined to see if they were in the correct direction. The percentages correct were 93%, 92%, and 95% for husbands, wives, and joint judgments, respectively. Most of the incorrect predictions involved stimuli judged near the center of the scale in Experiment 1; the deviations ranged in size from 1 to 10 scale units.

A second regression analysis used the difference in judgments in Experiment 1 to predict the preferences in Experiment 2. The predicted results correlated .88, .91, and .94, for husbands, wives, and joint judgments, respectively. This suggests that there was a high degree of consistency between the two experiments.

In the final analysis, the joint preferences were regressed on the husbands' and wives' separate preferences. For comparison, a similar analysis was conducted for the evaluations obtained in Experiment 1. The results indicated that the spouses' influence was about equal in both cases. The regression weight coefficients for husbands' and wives' preferences were .47 and .52, respectively. The comparable results for Experiment 1 were .50 and .49 for evaluations. Similar results were obtained when the usefulness index (Darlington, 1968) was examined.

Although these results suggest that each spouse had roughly equal influence, an analysis of separate couples revealed some notable individual differences. In six couples, one spouse tended to dominate in both experiments. Three other couples revealed a pattern where one spouse had more influence in Experiment 1 and the other in Experiment 2. In the remaining four couples, the spouses appeared to have about the same influence throughout. This result suggests that the group data may mask meaningful individual differences.

Discussion

Experiment 2 demonstrates that IIT provides a useful approach for analyzing the health-care choices of expectant parents. Even though the response patterns in the preference task were more complex than in Experiment 1, the subtractive model and the averaging model provided reasonable accounts of the data for husbands and wives separately and jointly. Moreover, the model fit was as good for the joint judgments as it was for the separate judgments.

Comparisons between separate and joint decisions revealed that the strategies were more similar in Experiment 2 than in Experiment 1. Indeed, in the second study there were hardly any differences. This convergence of strategies is probably due to the exchange of views that took place for these couples during the joint-decision phase of Experiment 1. In arriving at a joint judgment, the spouses apparently adopted common strategies that carried over to the preference task.

Support for this convergence hypothesis comes from the analysis of variance. The joint preferences were more closely related to the spouses' individual preferences (Experiment 2) than the joint judgments were to the individual judgments (Experiment 1). Moreover, the joint preferences were highly correlated with the joint judgments.

One reason for this convergence is that husbands became less reluctant to evaluate pediatricians in Experiment 2. The knowledge gained about their wives' views in the first experiment apparently decreased their reliance on the initial opinions. There is also some evidence that the convergence resulted from more unidimensional strategies. Some couples found it easier to resolve disagreements by focusing exclusively on Ability and discounting Staff Manners.

Relative Influence

One question has arisen repeatedly in research on husband-wife decision making (Mowen, 1987): What is the relative influence of each spouse on the final choice? This was examined here by regressing individual responses onto joint responses. For some couples, the relative influence was evenly divided. For the majority of couples, however, one spouse seemed to have more influence. In many cases where one spouse dominated, it was possible to identify contributing factors. In one couple, for example, the husband was a pre-med student and the couple decided that he was more of an authority on how to select a doctor. The wife in another couple was an obstetrical nurse and felt better qualified to judge physicians. In both cases, the regression analyses confirmed the dominant influence.

Although these analyses provided useful information about how much influence each spouse had, they offer little insight into how the spouses influenced each other. This is illustrated by the results for couple 6 in Figure 6.2. The husband's judgments were more extreme than the wife's, but the collective judgments were quite unlike either spouse's responses. The plots and weight values suggest that the spouses influence was mutual and that after their interaction, the Ability dimension became more important. This shift in dimensional importance because of joint interaction is not captured by measures of relative influence. Instead, analyses of decision processes, such as performed here, would appear more useful.

Experiment 3

In the first two studies, only two kinds of arbitrarily selected information were used to describe doctors. Of course, consumers will generally have much more information available in evaluating real physicians. With more information, decision strategies may change. For instance, consumers may find it difficult to focus on all available information (Bettman, 1979). To reduce cognitive load, consumers may discount one or more dimensions of information. This allows for greater differences between individual and joint judgments; with more dimensions of information, there is more room for disagreement.

The purpose of the third study was to extend previous analyses of expectant parents' decision making in three ways. First, the couples evaluated the services offered by obstetricians. Obviously, these services are highly relevant to expectant parents. Second, the options were described by four dimensions of information. Accordingly, the descriptions of obstetricians were more complete than in Experiment 1. Third, the dimensions and their levels were selected on the basis of preliminary work (see below). Thus, the descriptions were more in line with the way that expectant parents typically describe physicians.

Preliminary Work

Questionnaires were constructed to determine which factors are important for evaluating obstetrical care. Through interviews with hospital staff and administrators, instructors of childbirth classes, and expectant couples, a list of 14 factors for obstetricians was constructed. A total of 44 consumers, including those who participated in Experiments 1 and 2, ranked these factors according to importance.

Based on these rankings, four relevant factors were identified. A list of these factors, along with the two levels described for each, is presented in Table 6.2. These factors were constructed by looking at the overall importance rankings and combining dimensions that were conceptually similar. Two levels for each factor were selected to be positive on the one hand, and negative on the other. In describing factors and levels, an effort was made to reflect wording used by consumers when responding to open-ended questions in preliminary work.

Table 6.2. Descriptions of four factors and two levels for each factor used to describe obstetricians, experiment 3.

A. How much time the obstetrician has for the wife during office visit.
  1. Sometimes enough
  2. Usually enough
B. How informative obstetrician is during office visit.
  1. Doesn't discuss much
  2. Explains things well
C. The obstetrician's attitude toward prepared childbirth with the husband participating in the delivery.
  1. Unfavorable
  2. Favorable
D. How the obstetrician feels about your views on the use of drugs and medication during delivery.
  1. Indifferent
  2. Supportive

Method

Eleven new couples (22 subjects) were recruited from childbirth preparation classes. The mean ages of husbands and wives were 25.2 and 24.4, respectively. Couples received $6.00 for participating.

Stimulus Design

Prospective obstetricians were described using a fractional factorial design which yielded eight doctors. There are several important properties of this design which should be noted (Cochran & Cox, 1957, chapter 6A). First, all main effects and four of the two-factor interactions can be estimated. Second, the design assumes that all higher-order (three- and four-factor) interactions are negligible, since their significance cannot be determined.

Procedure

The procedure was basically similar to that of Experiments 1 and 2. For example, the information about options was typed on index cards and presented in random order. The response scale was the same as that used in Experiment 1. The boundaries were exemplified by anchor stimuli with extreme levels.

The stimuli were judged individually and then jointly. There were three replications. In the first replication, consumers were asked to explain each judgment; these constituted practice stimuli and were not included in the final analysis. After the judgment task, couples rank-ordered the obstetricians. While performing the task, couples were asked to explain their rank orders.

Results

Analysis of variance was used to look at overall differences among the separate and joint judgments. The results indicated a difference between husbands and joint judgments ($F = 6.48$; $df = 1,70$; $M = 40.7$ and 29.2) and a suggestive but nonsignificant difference between husbands and wives ($M = 26.5$).

Functional measurement procedures were used to determine what sort of averaging model is most descriptive of the judgments. A constant-weight averaging model (see Eq. 1) predicts that all interactions should be nonsignificant. A more complex differential-weight averaging model predicts that there should be interactions of a specific form (Anderson, 1981). A major purpose of Experiment 3 is to determine which form of averaging is most appropriate.

Analysis of Averaging Models

In tests of the interactions for husbands, there were no significant interactions. For the wives' judgments, there were no significant interactions.

For the wives' judgments, the Time-for-Wife by Attitude-on-Drugs interaction was significant ($F = 4.82$, $df = 1,80$). In the joint judgments, three out of four significant interactions were observed: Time-for-Wife by Attitude-on-Drugs ($F = 7.35$), Time-for-Wife by Informativeness ($F = 4.56$), and Attitude-on-Drugs by Attitude-on-Childbirth ($F = 4.56$). Thus, constant-weight averaging model is acceptable for husbands, questionable for wives, and definitely ruled out for joint judgments.

Figure 6.4 plots three of the interactions for husbands, wives, and joint judgments. A striking aspect of these plots is the uniform tendency for the curves to diverge to the right. In the Time × Drugs interactions (first column), for instance, the difference between top and bottom curves is grea-

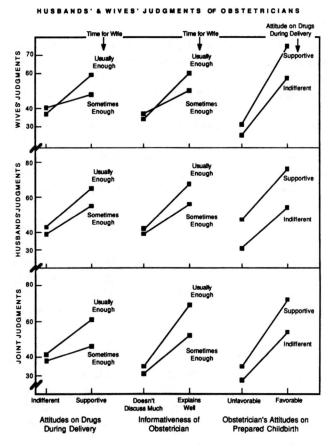

Figure 6.4. Plots of three two-way interactions for mean judgments by wives (top row), husbands (middle row), and joint (collective), Experiment 3. Time × Attitude on Drugs in left column, Time × Informativeness in middle column, and Attitude on Drugs × Attitude on Prepared Childbirth in right column. All plots diverge to the right, supporting a differential-weight averaging model.

ter when the attitude on drugs is Supportive. The other interactions show a
similar trend.

The overall pattern of results indicates that a divergent pattern applies to
wives and joint judgments (and is suggested for husbands). Essentially, the
strategy is interactive in that the evaluation of the obstetrician improves
dramatically when all information is positive. In contrast, negative information on either dimension produces a less favorable evaluation. Apparently,
positive information cannot compensate for negative information (Birnbaum, 1973). Such a noncompensatory strategy, however, is expected from
a differential-weighted averaging model (Oden & Anderson, 1971).

Parameter Estimates

For two reasons, it is not possible to obtain FM estimates of weight and
scale values. First with only two levels, there is no way to disentangle the
combined effect of Weight × Scale values. Second, parameter estimation
for a differential-weighted averaging model is more involved than for the
simpler constant-weight averaging model. Nonetheless, impact values
(weight × scale values) can provide a useful measure of the effect of each
dimension on the judgments (Shanteau, 1980).

Estimation of impact value was obtained by computing the difference in
marginal means for each factor; the effect of two-factor interactions were
estimated from the change in mean judgment across the levels of a pair of
dimensions (Slovic, 1969). Table 6.3 lists the impact values for the four
factors and four interactions.

In both separate and joint judgments, Attitude-on-Childbirth has the
greatest effect. The effect is greater for wives, however, than for husbands of
joint judgments. Perhaps since a wife has more contact with the obstetrician, she is more sensitive to an obstetrician's attitudes. Among the other

Table 6.3. Measures of magnitude of effect (impact value) for main effects and four
two-way interactions, experiment 3.

	Factor		
	Husbands	Wives	Collective
Main Effects			
Informativeness (I)	20.1*	19.7*	28.0*
Time (T)	6.7*	4.6*	8.3*
Attitude on Drugs (AD)	18.3*	12.6*	13.2*
Attitude on Childbirth (AC)	26.5*	36.5*	32.6*
Interactions			
I × AD	2.8	1.9	4.4
T × AD	4.7	11.5*	12.9*
T × I	4.3	10.3	10.1*
AD × AC	4.4	10.2	10.1*

*$p < .05$.

effects, Time-for-Wife had the least effect and, interestingly enough, did not even reach significance in the wives' judgments. The reason why wives are so unconcerned about the time factor needs further investigation.

The magnitude of the interaction effects are comparable with the main effects. The Time × Drug effect for joint judgment, for instance, is nearly as large as the Drug effect alone (12.9 vs. 13.2). Similarly large interaction effects were observed for wives and joint judgments. Therefore, the interactions appear to have played a sizeable role in the evaluation process.

By comparing Table 6.3 and Figure 6.4, a greater understanding of the collective judgment process can be gained. The largest difference between husbands and wives is for Attitude-on-Childbirth. This information has much greater impact on wives than husbands. The impact of Informativeness was similar in separate judgments, but increased in impact for the joint judgments. The size of the interaction effects indicates that wives were closer to the joint judgments than husbands. Even so, the plots show that the combined judgments are a compromise. Thus in joint judgments, both spouses adjusted their strategies in the direction of the other.

Comments of Consumers

When asked to explain their judgments, most consumers gave explanations consistent with the interactive strategies observed in Figure 6.4. For the Time × Informativeness interaction, for instance, several wives said that if an obstetrician did not explain much, the time the obstetrician took was unimportant. Two wives even noted that it would be worse to spend more time with an obstetrician who didn't have much to say. Similarly, several consumers commented that their impression of an obstetrician was favorable only if the Attitudes-on-Drugs and Attitudes-on-Childbirth were *both* positive; if either was negative, their impression was unfavorable. Such comments closely resemble the observed judgment patterns.

The comments made during the joint judgments provided evidence that both spouses were involved in the task. In no case did one spouse withdraw from the process so that the other spouse could make all the judgments. Most couples began by discussing the importance of the various dimensions before judging the first obstetrician. Although spouses often thought they had reached agreement, their judgments differed for the first few stimuli. Instead of compromising their differences, however, most spouses discussed the importance of the information further. The modal strategy, thus, was for couples to exchange information about importance of dimensions, to make some judgments to determine how much disagreement remained, and finally to exchange further information to resolve the remaining conflict.

Discussion

In the selection of obstetricians, several results stand out. The most important attribute in this study was the physician's attitude toward prepared childbirth. It is understandable that this would be critical since the present couples were all enrolled in prepared childbirth classes. This not only validates the present procedure,but it may also represent a trend for future expectant parents (Brien, Haverfield, & Shanteau, 1983).

The obstetrician's attitude on drugs and medication was also important. Many couples viewed medication during delivery as an impediment to the husband's role in childbirth. It it noteworthy that some consumers commented that obstetricians use drugs in childbirth to keep the mother passive and to make the delivery less complicated. This raises the possibility that some consumers mistrust their physician's judgment about drugs.

The amount of time that an obstetrician spent on answering questions turned out to be less important than other dimensions. This was unexpected since the preliminary questionnaire revealed that the most frequent complaint of wives was lack of time to ask questions. This may reflect the relative availability of information. Ordinarily, a consumer cannot evaluate a physician's attitudes unless he/she takes the time to express those attitudes. Therefore, time may be a primary dimension. But, time may decrease in importance once information about other dimensions becomes available, as was the case here.

Overall, the present results suggest that obstetricians might do their patients, and themselves as well, a valuable service by making known their attitudes on childbirth and drugs. This could foster a more open physician-patient relationship than one in which the expectant couple spends time trying to learn about their obstetrician's views. Also, these results indicate that obstetricians should not assume that treatment options are too complex to explain. The present couples expressed great interest in medical options and viewed favorably obstetricians who explained why they did what they did.

Decision Processes

An important finding in Experiment 3 was that the judgment process was interactive. This contrasts with the results obtained in the first two studies that supported a constant-weight averaging model.

There are three possible reasons why interactive strategies may have been observed in this study. First, there were more dimensions of information presented for the consumers to judge. Jacoby, Speller, and Kohn (1974), among others, have suggested that increasing the amount of information alters decision mechanisms. It may be useful in future work, therefore, to determine if health-care judgments become more interactive with increasing amounts of information.

A second reason is that the information presented in this study was chosen to be more realistic, and such information may be inherently interactive. In comparison, the dimensions used in the first two experiments were chosen rather arbitrarily. It should be noted, however, that research in other domains has not found that realistic stimuli are necessarily more interactive

(Ettenson, Krogstad, & Shanteau, 1984). Whether this also applies to consumers' health-care judgments is yet to be determined.

A final factor is that the interactions increased for joint judgments. One possible explanation is that couples adopted a two-process strategy: when both spouses agree on a judgment, the joint judgment follows directly; when there is disagreement, a unique conflict-resolution process is followed.

There have been a number of judgment studies on conflict and its effects on social judgment. Brehmer (1976), for instance, has shown that it is difficult for people to agree on collective judgments when there is inconsistency. It seems plausible that inconsistent strategies for each spouse could have made compromise more difficult and led to interactive joint strategies.

It is worthwhile noting that the family of averaging models was able to account for the compensatory strategies in Experiments 1 and 2, as well as the noncompensatory strategy in Experiment 3. In his categorization of models, Wright (1975, p. 60) states that "compensatory strategies picture a person averaging (or adding) data so that positive and negative data have a balancing impact on his overall product impression." Wright clearly classifies averaging as compensatory. Yet as shown here (also see Anderson, 1972), averaging models can describe either compensatory or noncompensatory strategies.

The difference between constant-weight and differential-weight averaging models is in the relation between weights and scale values. When the weights are a function of the scale values (as in Experiment 3), then an interactive strategy exhibits noncompensatory properties. When the weights are independent of scale values (as in Experiments 1 and 2), then a noninteractive strategy shows compensatory properties. Accordingly, the distinction between compensatory and noncompensatory models may need to be reexamined in the case of averaging.

General Discussion

Implications for Consumer Decision Processes

The primary goal of this research has been to examine the processses that underlie couples' health-care decisions. The research has demonstrated that these processes can be described using methods developed in psychological research on individual judgment and decision making. The first experiment showed that pediatricians were evaluated by a simple averaging strategy. The second experiment indicated that a two-stage process involving both averaging and subtractive strategies was used for making preferences between two pediatricians. The third experiment revealed a more complex averaging strategy for judgments of obstetricians described by more realistic information.

At first glance, this diversity of strategies may seem disconcerting. The question addressed by this research, however, is not whether a single strategy applies for all types of tasks. Rather, the question is whether the underlying processes can be described using IIT. The answer to the latter question is in the affirmative.

Even though consumers may use different processes in different situations, there is considerable value in being able to enumerate these processes. As an example, there are several efforts underway to make information available to consumers about physicians' services (e.g., "A consumer's directory," 1974). As these efforts gain popularity, it will be increasingly important to understand how consumers use this information (also see Bettman, 1975). To design these directories efficiently, it will be necessary to know how consumers process available information. Thus, there may be many situations in which it is important to understand how consumers evaluate medical services.

The present studies demonstrate that information integration and functional measurement procedures can be used to describe consumer healthcare judgments. Not only were specific models identified, but underlying weight and scale values were also estimated. Further, this approach was successful for both individual and joint decisions. Therefore, the usefulness of IIT and FM for couple decision making was amply demonstrated (see Shanteau, 1987).

Of course, the research strategy is not without limitations. The most notable is the relatively small sample size used in the present experiments. In typical consumer studies, large sample sizes are the norm (Churchill, 1983). Moreover, efforts are made to collect data from representative subjects using nonintrusive procedures.

The research strategy employed here was to investigate the psychological processes of a few consumers in great depth. Emphasis was placed on understanding the decision strategies used by individual couples. Moreover, the same couples were tracked (in Experiments 1 and 2) through more than one task to determine the consistency of their decisions. Once the effectiveness of IIT/FM techniques has been demonstrated on a limited sample, it was then possible to extend this approach to larger, more representative subject samples (Louviere & Gaeth, 1987).

Implications for Couple Decision Making

The present results have implications for three aspects of research on couple decision making. These concern methodology, conflict resolution, and theory construction.

In regard to methodology, the approach taken here is to view joint decisions as made by a unit distinguishable from the individuals who make up that unit. In much previous research on husband-wife decision making, the spouses have been studied separately to determine, for example, the roles played by each (Wilkie, 1986). Others have argued that the family itself should be the fundamental unit of analysis (Davis, 1976). The methodology applied here looked at the decisions made at *both* the individual and joint levels.

The application of this methodology led to several insights into the nature of couple decision making. Experiment 1 showed that an important source of information in joint decisions is the information each spouse gains about the other's strategy. This information exchange produced more extreme judgments and a collective strategy characterized by greater confidence. Experiment 2 demonstrated the result of this convergence of opinion in a new context. Although the couples were not aware of the task shift in advance, they were nonetheless able to follow a consensus strategy in making both individual and joint decisions. Experiment 3 revealed that joint decisions do not always reflect the processes used to make individual decisions. The greater interactiveness seen in combined decisions argues against any approach that focuses exclusively on spouses as individual decision-making units (Cox, 1975).

The resolution of conflict has been of continuing interest in analyses of husband-wife decision making (Engel, Blackwell, & Miniard, 1986). Much of this research has focused on categorizing alternative strategies used when spouses disagree. Davis (1976), for instance, discusses the conditions that lead spouses to adopt problem-solving, persuasion, and bargaining strategies. Davis notes that a bargaining strategy might by adopted by a wife who allows her husband to "win" one decision if she is allowed to have her way in a later decision. Thus, the key determinants in strategy selection appear to be motivational (Belch, Belch, & Sciglimpaglia, 1980).

The present results suggest that the Davis (1976) categories are insufficient because they focus on motivational sources of conflict. The approach taken here emphasizes a cognitive approach to determining how conflict is resolved (Brehmer & Hammond, 1977). Several couples, for instance, adopted a "cognitive compromise" strategy of finding middle values for attribute weights. In motivational terms, such a strategy might reflect either bargaining or persuasion (or both). The cognitive approach, in contrast, provided a more direct account of the decision process. Future research on conflict in families will need to focus on cognitive as well as motivational resolution strategies.

These results also raise several questions about theories of husband-wife decision making. Sheth (1974), for example, developed a comprehensive theory that maps the relationships among variables that influence family purchase decisions. The theory encompasses an extensive flowchart with two final branches—autonomous and joint decisions. Sheth's theory attempts to articulate the decision roles of spouses in detail. Although this theory incorporates several cognitive variables, such as each spouse's sensitivity to product information, nothing is said about how the spouses' inputs combine to form a joint decision. Thus, this theory excludes decision mechanisms.

The research described in this chapter appears to contradict Sheth's

(1974) assertion that the area of couple decision making has been researched sufficiently so that a comprehensive theory can be developed. The present findings suggest that the critical cognitive component remains to be understood. Analyses of the effects of information exchange on collective decision making, for instance, seems essential before a comprehensive theory can be developed. Towards that end, the information integration approach of Anderson (1981, 1982) and colleagues (e.g., Anderson & Graesser, 1976) can provide valuable tools in the efforts to understand the cognitive dimensions of husband-wife decision making.

Acknowledgments. The research conducted in this chapter was supported in part by the National Science Foundation (Grant BMS-20504), the National Institute of Child Health and Human Development (Grant HD 11857), and by Kansas State University (BGR Grant).

The authors wish to acknowledge the contributions of Richard Harris, Leon Rappoport, and James Gentry throughout the research project. Additional insights and comments on the manuscript were provided by Norman Anderson.

Correspondence concerning this chapter should be addressed to James Shanteau, Department of Psychology, Bluemont Hall, Kansas State University, Manhattan, Kansas 66506-7095.

References

Addelman, S. (1962). Orthogonal main-effects plans for asymmetrical factorial experiments. *Technometrics, 4*, 21–46.

Anderson, B. F., Deane, D. H., Hammond, K. R., McClelland, G. H., & Shanteau, J. (1981). *Concepts in judgment and decision research: Definitions, sources, interrelations, comments.* New York:

Anderson, N. H. (1962). On the quantification of Miller's conflict theory. *Psychological Review, 69*, 400–414.

Anderson, N. H. (1972). Looking for configurality in clinical judgment. *Psychological Bulletin, 78*, 93–102.

Anderson, N. H. (1981). *Foundations of information integration theory.* New York: Academic Press.

Anderson, N. H. (1982). *Methods of information integration theory.* New York: Academic Press.

Anderson, N. H., & Graesser, C. C. (1976). An integration theory analysis of attitude change in group discussion. *Journal of Personality and Social Psychology, 34*, 210–222.

Arkes, H. R., & Hammond, K.R. (Eds.). (1986). *Judgment and decision making: An interdisciplinary reader.* Cambridge: Cambridge University Press.

Assael, H. (1984). *Consumer behavior and marketing action.* Boston: Kent Publishing.

Bartlett, F. C., (1932). *Remembering: A study in experimental and social psychology.* New York: Cambridge Press.

Beach, L. R., Townes, B. D., Campbell, F. L., & Keating, G. W. (1976). Developing and testing a decision aid for birth planning decisions. *Organizational Behavior and Human Performance.*

Belch, M., Belch, G., & Sciglimpaglia, D. (1980). Conflict in family decision making: An exploratory investigation. In J. Olson (Ed.), *Advances in consumer research VII,* 477–478.

Bettman, J. R. (1975). Issues in designing consumer information environments. *Journal of Consumer Research, 2,* 169–177.

Bettman, J. R. (1979). *An information processing theory of consumer choice.* Reading, MA: Addison-Wesley.

Birnbaum, M. H. (1973). Morality judgment: Test of an averaging model with differential weights. *Journal of Experimental Psychology, 99,* 395–399.

Birnbaum, M. H., & Veit, C. T. (1974). Scale convergence as a criterion for rescaling: Information integration with difference, ratio, and averaging tasks. *Perception & Psychophysics, 15,* 1–9.

Brehmer, B. (1976). Social judgment theory and the analysis of interpersonal conflict. *Psychological Bulletin, 83,* 985–1003.

Brehmer, B., & Hammond, K. R. (1977). Cognitive factors in interpersonal conflict. In D. Druckman (Ed.), *Negotiations: Social-psychological perspectives.* Beverly Hills: Sage Publications.

Brien, M., Haverfield, N., & Shanteau, J. (1983). How Lamaze-prepared expectant parents select obstetricians. *Research in Nursing & Health, 6,* 143–150.

Churchill, G. A. (1983). *Marketing research: Methodological foundations* (3rd ed.). Chicago: Dryden Press.

Cochran, W. G., & Cox, G. M. (1957). *Experimental design.* New York: Wiley.

A consumer's directory of Prince George's County (MD) doctors. (1974). *Consumer Reports, 39,* 685–689.

Cox, E. P. (1975). Family purchase decision making and the process of adjustment. *Journal of Marketing Research, 12,* 189–195.

Darlington, R. B. (1968). Multiple regression in psychological research and practice. *Psychological Bulletin, 69,* 161–182.

Davis, H. L. (1971). Measurement of husband-wife influence in consumer purchase decisions. *Journal of Marketing, 8,* 305–312.

Davis, H. L. (1976). Decision making within the household. *Journal of Consumer Research, 4,* 241–260.

Davis, H. L., & Rigaux, B. P. (1974). Perception of marital roles in decision processes. *Journal of Consumer Research, 1,* 51–62.

Dudley, D. C., & Choldin, H. M. (1967). Communication diffusion of the IUCD: A case study in urban India. *Demography, 4,* 601–614.

Ebbesen, E. B., & Konecni, V. J. (1980). On the external validity of decision-making research: What do we know about decision in the real world? In T. Wallsten (Ed.), *Cognitive processes in choice and decision behavior.* Hillsdale, NJ: Erlbaum.

Engel, J. F., Blackwell, R. D., & Miniard, P. W. (1986). *Consumer behavior* (5th ed.). Chicago: Dryden Press.

Ericsson, K. A., & Simon, H. A. (1980). Verbal reports as data. *Psychological Review, 87,* 215–251.

Ettenson, R., Krogstad, J. L., & Shanteau, J. (1984). Context and experience in auditors' materiality judgments. *Auditing: A Journal of Practice & Theory, 4,* 54–73.

Filiatrault, P., & Ritchie, J. R. B. (1980). Joint purchasing decisions: A comparison of influence structure in family and couple decision-making units. *Journal of Consumer Research, 6,* 131–140.

Freidson, E. (1971). *The profession of medicine: A study of the sociology of applied knowledge.* New York: Dodd, Mead.

Granbois, D. H. (1963) *A study of the family decision-making process in the purchase of major durable household goods.* Unpublished doctoral dissertation, Indiana University.

Granbois, D. H., & Summers, J. O. (1975). Primary and secondary validity of consumer purchase probabilities. *Journal of Consumer Research, 1,* 31–38.

Granbois, D. H., & Willett, R. P. (1970). Equivalence of family role measures based on husband and wife data. *Journal of Marriage and the Family, 32,* 68–72.

Green, P. E., & Srinivasan, V. (1978). Conjoint analysis in consumer research: Issues and outlook. *Journal of Consumer Research, 5,* 103–123.

Jacoby, J., Speller, D. E., & Kohn, C. A. (1974). Brand choice behavior as a function of information load: Replication and extension. *Journal of Consumer Research, 1,* 33–42.

Kenkel, W. F. (1963). Family interaction in decision making on spending. In N. Foote (Ed.), *Household decision making.* New York: University Press.

Krantz, D. H., Luce, D., Suppes, P., & Tversky, A. (1971). *Foundations of measurement* (Vol. 1). New York: Academic Press.

Krishnamurthi, L. (1983).The salience of relevant others and its effect on individual and joint preferences: An experimental investigation. *Journal of Consumer Research, 10,* 62–72.

Louviere, J. and Gaeth, G. J. (1987) Decomposing the determinants of retail facility choice using the method of heirarchical information integration: A supermarket illustration. *Journal of Retailing, 63,* (in press).

Lynch, J. G. (1985). Uniqueness issues in decompositional modeling of multiattribute overall evaluations: An information integration perspective. *Journal of Marketing Research, 22,* 1–19.

Mowen, J. C. (1987). *Consumer behavior.* New York: MacMillan.

Norman, K. L. (1976) A solution for weights and scale values in functional measurement. *Psychological Review, 83,* 80–84.

Oden, G. C., & Anderson, N. H. (1971). Differential weighting in integration theory. *Journal of Experimental Psychology, 89,* 152–161.

Park, C. W. (1982). Joint decisions in home purchasing: A muddling-through process. *Journal of Consumer Research, 9,* 151–162.

Patients down on doctors. (1976, March 10). *Kansas City Star,* 8A.

Pollay, R. W. (1968). A model of family decision-making. *British Journal of Marketing, 3,* 206–216.

Roberts, M. L. (1984). Gender differences and household decision-making: Needed conceptual and methodological developments. In T. C. Kinnear (Ed.), *Advances in consumer research* (Vol. 11) Provo: Association for Consumer Research.

Robertson, T. S., Zielinski, J., Ward, S. (1984). *Consumer behavior.* Glenview, IL: Scott, Foresman.

Shanteau, J. (1980). *The concept of weight in judgment and decision making: A review and some unifying proposals* (Tech. Rep. No. 228). University of Colorado, Center for Research on Judgment and Policy.

Shanteau, J. (1986). Application of information integration theory to methodology of theory development. *Resources in education.* (ERIC Document Reproduction Service No. ED 266 349)

Shanteau, J. (1987). Consumer impression formation: The integration of visual and verbal information. In D. W. Stewart & S. Heckler (Eds.), *Nonverbal communication in advertising.* New York: Heath.

Shanteau, J., & Anderson, N. H. (1969). Test of a conflict model for preference judgment. *Journal of Mathematical Psychology, 6,* 312–325.

Shanteau, J., & Nagy, G. (1979). Probability of acceptance in dating choice. *Journal of Personality and Social Psychology, 37,* 522–533.

Shanteau, J., & Ptacek, C. H. (1983). Role and implications of averaging processes in advertising. In L. Percy & A. Woodside (Eds.), *Advertising and consumer psychology.* Lexington, MA: Lexington.

Sheth, N. J. (1974). A theory of family buying decisions. In J. N. Sheth (Ed.), *Models of buyer behavior: Conceptual, quantitative, and empirical.* New York: Harper & Row.

Sloan, L. R., & Ostrom, T. M. (1974). Amount of information and interpersonal judgment. *Journal of Personality and Social Psychology, 29,* 23–29.

Slovic, P. (1969). Analyzing the expert judge: A descriptive study of a stockbroker's decision processes. *Journal of Applied Psychology, 53,* 255–263.

Strodtbeck, F. L. (1951). Husband-wife interaction over revealed differences. *American Sociological Review, 26,* 460–473.

Tedeschi, J. T. (Ed.), (1972). *The social influence processes.* Chicago: Aldine.

Troutman, C. M., & Shanteau, J. (1976). Do consumers evaluate products by adding or averaging attribute information? *Journal of Consumer Research, 3,* 101–106.

Turk, J. L., & Bell, N. W. (1972). Measuring power in families. *Journal of Marriage and the Family, 34,* 215–222.

Wilkie, W. L. (1986). *Consumer behavior.* New York: Wiley.

Wind, Y. (1976). Preference of relevant others and individual choice models. *Journal of Consumer Research, 3,* 50–57.

Wright, P. (1975). Consumer choice strategies: Simplifying vs. optimizing. *Journal of Marketing Research, 12,* 60–67.

Appendix 6.A. Functional Measurement Procedures for Estimating Weights and Scale Values

Let the stimuli be constructed from a $n \times n$ factorial design where the factors are two dimensions of stimulus information, and the n levels are equivalent on the two factors. A 3×3, Doctor's Ability $\times$ Staff Manners design, where the levels on each factor are Below Average, Average, and Above Average, is an example of such a design. Let there be additional $2n$ stimuli, which result when each level of information is used alone. Below Average Doctor's Ability is an example of such a stimulus. The stimuli with partial information form two one-way designs. Then, a solution for the weights and scale values of Equation 2 is possible if: (1) the simple averaging model is supported by parallelism in the $n \times n$ design; (2) the variance of the cell means from each one-way design is greater than the variance of the corresponding marginal means from the $n \times n$ design; (3) the scale values are equivalent, that is, $s_i = s_j$ for $i, j = 1, 2, \ldots, n$; (4) the parameters are invariant.

For the $n \times n$ design, the following notation is introduced:

$$R_{ij} = w_O I_O + w_R s_i + w_C s_j / w_O + w_R + w_C;$$

$$R_{i.} = w_O I_O + w_R s_i + w_C \bar{S} / w_O + w_R + w_C;$$

$$R_{.j} = w_O I_O + w_R \bar{S} + w_C s_j / w_O + w_R + w_C;$$

$$R_{..} = w_O I_O + w_R \bar{S} + w_C \bar{S} / w_O + w_R + w_C.$$

R_{ij} refers to the cell mean of level i and level j of the row and column factor. $R_{i.}$ and $R_{.j}$ are the marginal means. $R_{..}$ is the grand mean. The following notation is introduced for the one-way designs:

$$R_i = w_O I_O + w_R s_i / w_O + w_R;$$

$$R_{._-} = w_O I_O + w_R \bar{S} / w_O + w_R;$$

$$R_j = w_O I_O + w_C s_j / w_O + w_C;$$

$$R_{\_.} = w_O I_O + w_C \bar{S} / w_O + w_C.$$

R_i and $R_{._-}$ refer, respectively, to the cell mean of level i and the mean of the R_i; R_j and $R_{\_.}$ similarly refer to the mean of level j and the mean of the R_j. In all of the above, $\bar{S}$ refers to the theoretical mean of the scale values.

Solution for the Weights

The weights can be derived from the sums of squares of the marginal means of each design. Note that for the $n \times n$ design

$$\Sigma(R_{i.} - R_{..})^2 = \Sigma(w_R {}^s i - w_R \bar{S} / w_O + w_R + w_C)^2$$

$$= (w_R / w_O + w_R + w_C)^2 \Sigma(s_i - \bar{S})^2.$$

Dividing these terms by the appropriate degrees of freedom gives

$$\sigma^2 = (w_R / w_O + w_R + w_C)^2 \theta^2.$$

where σ^2 is the variance of the marginal means and θ^2 is the variance of the scale values. Thus, the variance of the marginal means is equal to the square of the relative weight times the variance of the scale values. This holds for the other factor of the $n \times n$ design and the one-way designs except that the relative weights differs. There are then four different variance terms that are known from the data:

$$\sigma_1^2 = (w_R / w_O + w_R + w_C)^2 \theta^2$$

$$\sigma_2^2 = (w_C / w_O + w_R + w_C)^2 \theta^2$$

$$\sigma_3^2 = (w_R / w_O + w_R)^2 \theta^2$$

$$\sigma_4^2 = (w_C / w_O + w_C)^2 \theta^2$$

θ^2 is a constant since $s_i = s_j$. By taking standard deviations and forming ratios, the following two equations are obtained:

$$\frac{\sigma_1}{\sigma_3} = \frac{w_O + w_R}{w_O + w_R + w_C}$$

$$\frac{\sigma_2}{\sigma_4} = \frac{w_O + w_C}{w_O + w_R + w_C}$$

These two equations are independent and can be solved simultaneously if it is assumed that $\Sigma w = 1$. Thus,

$$\frac{\sigma_1}{\sigma_3} = 1 - (w_R + w_C) + w_R = 1 - w_C$$

$$\frac{\sigma_2}{\sigma_4} = 1 - (w_R + w_C) + w_C = 1 - w_R$$

$$w_O = 1 - (w_R + w_C).$$

The assumption that the weights sum to one is restrictive, but, nevertheless, still allows the derivation of *interval* estimates. These estimates, therefore, provide information about the order of importance for two stimulus factors and the weight of the initial opinion, and the relative size of the differences in importance.

Solution for the Scale Values

The scale values, including I_O, can be found from the grand means.

$$R_{..} = w_O I_O + w_R \overline{S} + w_C \overline{S}$$

$$R_{._-} = w_O I_O + w_R \overline{S}/w_O + w_R$$

$$R_{-.} = w_O I_O + w_C \overline{S}/w_O + w_C.$$

The weight estimates can be plugged into these equations to solve for I_O and $\overline{S}$; these are necessary to derive scale values.

It will generally be better to derive two estimates of $\overline{S}$ from these three equations; one for the row factor, $\overline{S}_R$, and one for the column factor, $\overline{S}_C$. While it was assumed that $\overline{S}_R = \overline{S}_C$ to derive weight estimates, random error may make $\overline{S}_R$ and $\overline{S}_C$ unequal. This would compound the error in the scale value estimates. The solution obtained then is:

$$\overline{S}_R = \frac{R_{._-}(w_O + w_R) - w_O I_O}{w_R}$$

$$\overline{S}_C = \frac{R_{-.}(w_O + w_C) - w_O I_O}{w_C}$$

$$I_O = \frac{R_{._-}(w_O + w_R) + R_{-.}(w_O + w_C) - R_{..}}{w_O}$$

These values are plugged back into the theoretical equations for $R_{i.}$, $R_{.j}$, R_i, and R_j to derive scale values. Since there are two estimates of $\overline{S}$, it will be possible to derive four sets of scale values by the following:

$$s_i = \frac{R_{i.} - w_O I_O - w_C \overline{S}_C}{w_R}$$

$$s_j = \frac{R_{.j} - w_O I_O - w_R \overline{S}_R}{w_C}$$

$$s_i = \frac{R_i(w_O + w_R) - w_O I_O}{w_R}$$

$$s_j = \frac{R_j(w_O + w_C) - w_O I_O}{w_C}.$$

The scale values may not be equivalent because of either random error, lack of scale value equivalence, or parameter variance. These latter two conditions are serious and would invalidate the solution. Therefore, some statistical test should be performed to determine if there are differences among the four sets of scale values. Analysis of variance can be used for this when the scale values of several subjects are available. If there is a main effect for the "sets," the solution must be considered inadequate.

It should be noted that these developments owe much to a recent paper by Norman (1976). Norman has developed an iterative procedure for deriving weights and scale values when it cannot be assumed that scale value equivalence holds. There are also several statistical tests that can be employed with Norman's procedures to assess the goodness of the estimates. The application of his procedures, however, requires a greater number of stimulus designs and, thereby, many more stimuli for subjects to judge. Thus, the present approach will often be more convenient to implement.

Part 3
Communication Perspectives

CHAPTER 7

After the Decision:
Compliance-Gaining in Marital Interaction

Mary Anne Fitzpatrick

Introduction

Marriage can be conceived of as a continuous confrontation between participants with conflicting—though not always opposing—interests. Within this framework, the focus of attention becomes the ways in which marital dyads negotiate the issues that arise from their joint participation in the institution of marriage and the family (Sprey, 1979). As a communication researcher, I am interested in how these conflicting interests are managed through talk.

Since the needs, desires, and ambitions of people involved in close relationships can not always be synchronized, some form of conflict is inevitable in close relationships like marriage. Conflict is the interaction of interdependent people who perceive incompatible goals and interference from each other in achieving those goals (Folger & Poole, 1984; Frost & Wilmot, 1978). Ideally, couples deal with their conflicting interests with some form of negotiation or problem-solving strategy; one spouse states a position, seeks and obtains validation of the position from the partner, and the two engage in a straightforward problem-solving exchange. In this ideal scenario, communication between spouses is free of distortion, and both parties work toward resolution until some acceptable solution is obtained.

Obviously, all couples do not use this idealized style of negotiation and problem-solving in discussing all the issues that arise between them. Married couples differ in the level of interdependence in the relationship and in how comfortable they are in actively engaging in conflict with their spouses. These dimensions are directly related to the use of a variety of conflict and decision-making strategies. In this chapter, I elaborate on the various verbal tactics that couples use when confronting one another. Of particular interest is how each attempts to gain compliance from the other through verbal means. These competitive, persuasive strategies range from pleading with the spouse for compliance because the issue is important to the partners' relationship, to power plays, or threats demanding a spouse's compliance.

To understand the strategies and tactics that couples use to gain compliance from one another, an understanding of the various types of marriages that individuals evolve with one another is required. In the next section of this chapter, I discuss one approach that differentiates marriages.

A Typological Approach to Marital Interaction

A typological approach to marital interaction presupposes that interaction styles vary in different types of relationships and thus lead to different outcomes (Fitzpatrick, 1976; 1984). Any married couple can be categorized into a specific marital type. The scheme for categorizing couples is based on three underlying conceptual dimensions. The first is *interdependence*, which stresses the connectedness of relational partners physically, temporally, and psychologically. All relationships, by definition, exhibit some form of interdependence. Indeed, the negotiation of an appropriate degree of autonomy and interdependence is an ongoing dialectic between partners (Hess & Handel, 1959). In a marriage, each spouse attempts to define the ways he or she wants to be dependent on the other. The level of interdependence in a marriage is measured by the amount of sharing and companionship as well as by the couple's organization of time and household space. The more interdependent the couple, the higher the level of companionship, the more time they spend together on a regular basis, and the more they organize their space to promote togetherness.

The second dimension is *ideology*, which taps the beliefs, standards, and values that individuals hold concerning relationships. The values that individuals hold concerning marriage and family life are a major factor guiding not only interactions with the spouse but also the judgments individuals make concerning the outcomes of their interactions. Values concerning marriage can range from those stressing the importance of stability and predictability to those emphasizing the excitement of spontaneity and relational uncertainty.

The third dimension is *conflict*. Although it is inevitable that individuals in ongoing relationships experience conflict, people approach the resolution of differences in a variety of ways, ranging from total conflict avoidance to active and open engagement in conflict. This dimension is measured by the willingness of participants to engage in conflict with the spouse and the general level of assertiveness between partners.

In most classical typological approaches, these three major conceptual dimensions would be divided into high and low values and eight possible marital definitions would be hypothesized. Within this polythetic typological scheme, a different approach is taken. A questionnaire, the Relational Dimensions Inventory (RDI), designed to measure the conceptual dimensions of interest, was developed. Appendix 7.A lists some representative statements.

The responses of a number of samples (see Fitzpatrick, 1984, for a description of the sampling procedures utilized) of married individuals have been cluster analyzed. Subsequently, the clusters have been named. Using these procedures, only three of the eight logically possible cells are filled. No currently married individual, for example, defines his/her marriages as one in which high conflict occurs with low levels of interdependence, regardless of the ideological orientation of the individual. Although other cultures may have different definition of marriage, it appears that in North American culture, there are three basic approaches that individuals take to marriage: traditional, independent, and separate.

Three Basic Marital Definitions

Traditionals exhibit interdependence in their marriage for they have a high degree of companionship and sharing. This companionship is reinforced by the traditionals' use of time and space. A regular daily time schedule as well as a lack of autonomous physical space in the home facilitates interaction between these spouses. Traditionals place greater emphasis on stability than on satisfaction in marriage and hold conventional values about relationships. Such conventionality includes agreement with such statements as: a woman should take her husband's last name when she marries and spouses should care deeply about one another but not become overly demonstrative. Traditionals describe their communication style as nonassertive, although traditionals are willing to engage their spouses in conflicts when the issues are serious.

Independents maintain a high level of companionship and sharing in their marriages but of a qualitatively different kind than that of the traditionals. Although independents try to stay psychologically close to their spouses, independents are also careful to maintain separate physical spaces to achieve some control over the accessibility each has to the other. An additional limitation on accessibility and hence interaction is that independents have trouble maintaining regular daily time schedules. Independents are at the opposite end of the ideological continuum from the traditionals. Independents, for example, espouse a belief that relationships should not constrain an individual's freedom. Finally, independents report some assertiveness in their marriages and are apt to engage in conflicts with their spouses on a variety of issues, both large and small.

Separates maintain much less interdependence in their marriage than the other basic types. Separates are disengaged from one another in that they control accessibility both physically and psychologically. The major index of interdependence in this marriage is temporal regulation in that separates keep regular daily schedules. Separates are ideologically bivalent in that they can agree with both the importance of stability and the importance of satisfaction. In reference to their communication style, separates report some assertiveness in their marriage but they always try to avoid open conflict.

Couple Types

Couple or marital types are defined by comparing the relational definitions of husbands and wives. The couples' rather than individuals' self-reports and communication behaviors are compared and discussed because the former are a more meaningful analytic unit. In the study of personal and social relationships, dyadic-level constructs such as couple and marital types, can yield information about the relationship between partners that is significantly more predictive of communication patterns and outcomes than is an individual-level assessment.

The pure couple types (Traditional, Independent, Separate) are those in which the husband and wife share the same definition of the marriage. Approximately 60% of those couples who have completed the RDI agree on a definition of their marriage. To say that the couple type is a more meaningful unit of analysis than is the individual relational definition means that knowing how an individual views his/her marriage is less informative than knowing how both partners view the marriage. For example, the pattern of communication in the relationship between a traditional and an independent is significantly different than that in a pure Traditional or a pure Independent marriage. Such a difference is apparent only when couples rather than individuals are used as the unit of analysis.

The remaining 40% of the couples fall into the mixed category. The mixed types are those in which the husband holds one definition of the marriage and the wife another (e.g., Separate/Traditional). The overall 40% disagreement rate on dimensions of marriage is relatively consistent with the literature. In research on relationships in general (Duck, 1980) and on marriage in particular (Bernard, 1972), such discrepancies on the reports of partners concerning the relationship are relatively common. The major mixed type of couple uncovered in this program of research is the marriage in which the husband is a separate and his wife is a traditional. In a Separate/Traditional marriage the husband maintains some distance in the relationship although his wife is more interdependent and expressive. Both spouses support conventional ideological orientations to the marriage, although the husband is somewhat more likely to doubt these views.

Building a typology of marriage is an elegant and useless exercise unless the types of marriages relate to other dimensions of interest. The combination of relational dimensions that create the marital types (Table 7.1) predicts: the sex-role orientations of husbands and wives (Fitzpatrick & Indvik, 1982); their accuracy in predicting the responses of their spouses (Fitzpatrick & Indvik, 1979); their achieved level of marital adjustment and satisfaction (Fitzpatrick & Best, 1979); their levels of self-disclosure (Fitzpatrick, Vance, & Witteman, 1984); their evasive, cooperative, and confrontational behavior in both high conflict and casual marital discussions (Fitzpatrick, 1981; Fitzpatrick, Fallis, & Vance, 1982; Sillars, Pike, Jones, & Redman, 1983; Williamson & Fitzpatrick, 1985).

Table 7.1. Self-report and behavioral differences of the various couple types.

	Tradi-tional	Inde-pendent	Sepa-rate	Separate/ Tradi-tional	Mixed
Self-reports					
Fitzpatrick & Indvik (1979)					
Wife Coorientation Accuracy	+	+	−	+ +	+
Fitzpatrick & Best (1979)					
Consensus	+ +	−	+	+	−
Cohesion	+ +	+	−	+	+
Affectional expression	+ +	+	+	+ +	−
Marital Satisfaction	+ +	−	−	+	+
Fitzpatrick & Indvik (1980)					
Conventional sex role	+	−	+	+	Varies
Sex typed (H)	+	+	+	+	Varies
Fitzpatrick, 1981					
Ideal relationship	+ +	+	−	−	
Communication behaviors					
Fitzpatrick, Fallis, & Vance (1982)					
Frequent Pauses	−	−	+	−	−
Sillars, Pike, Jones, & Redman, (1983)					
Neutral affect (conflict)	+	−	+	No info.	No info.
Verbal avoidance (conflict)	−	+	+ +	No info.	No info.
Fitzpatrick, Vance, & Witteman (1984)					
Mind reading (Casual)	+	+	+	− −	No info.
High interaction duration	+	+	− −	No info.	No info.
Witteman & Fitzpatrick (1986)					
Compliance attempts	−	+ +	+	+	Varies

Note: The plus and minus signs indicate statistically significant differences among couple types in high (+) and low (−) directions. The Separate/Traditionals were discriminated from other couple types because often in analysis this couple shows a different pattern of response from other mixed types.

The range and diversity of the interaction differences among these couple types indicate that the typology is not artifactual. These couple types represent a description of patterned yet significantly different ways that individuals organize their marriages and their communication behaviors with the spouse. Not only do these couple types exist in the minds of married individuals and influence their behavior with the spouse, but these couple types appear to be psychologically real to other individuals as well. Giles and Fitzpatrick (1985) observed that when presented with patterns of communication found in actual couples of various types, individuals do relate these patterns to the conceptual dimensions that define the typology.

Based on the self-report data, the communication differences among these various types of couples, and the psychological reality that these couple types appear to have both in the minds of couples themselves and also in the evaluations that people in general make of marriage, it is reasonable to assume that couples in these various types approach decision making in markedly different ways. In the next section, we consider a special form of decision making in marriage, that is, how individuals convince the spouse to follow a course of action he or she has already decided.

Compliance-Gaining in Marriage

Most definitions of interpersonal communication include some notion of intersubjectivity and mutual influence. In other words, interpersonal communication is seen as a process in which persons engage in direct symbolic interaction in order to create meaning and to allow joint conduct. Central to this process are social actors constructing and producing messages in the service of some purpose or objective (Seibold, Cantrill, & Meyers, 1985). The study of compliance-gaining is that of those situations in which the actors communication is strategically directed toward achieving instrumental objectives. These instrumental objectives involve inducing or persuading another to comply behaviorally with a specific request or recommendation.

Marwell and Schmitt (1967) extracted five strategies of compliance-gaining behaviors that individuals said they would be likely to use when pursuing their instrumental objectives: rewarding activity; punishing activity; expertise; activation of impersonal commitments; activation of personal commitments. Closely resembling the bases of power identified by French and Raven (1960), these strategies have generated over 40 empirical pieces of research attempting to classify the strategies available to persuaders and to track the situational and individual differences that may impact on a persuader's choice of a strategic line of action (for summaries see Berger, 1985; Seibold, Cantrill, & Meyers, 1985). Two important lines of work are missing from the compliance-gaining literature. First, do the strategies isolated in the minds of respondents actually match the communication behavior of individuals in compliance situations? Second, do the compliance-gaining messages actually gain compliance. In studying persuasion between husbands and wives, I attend to both of these issues.

How do couples communicate with one another when attempting to persuade the spouse to comply? The study discussed in this chapter induced within each spouse a concern for his or her own outcomes: Spouses pursued their own position over that of the partner. Communication tactics used in these situations are called compliance-gaining moves. The research was designed to explore how couples in the various types confront one another in attempts to force a desired decision.

There are a myriad of ways for couples to be assertive with one another and these verbal strategies are captured in the Verbal Interaction Compliance-Gaining Scheme (VICS). A strategy is a conceptual route by which an actor makes his/her intentions manifest to the partner. Since all the messages in any given conversation do not serve a compliance-gaining function, a sieve-coding scheme was developed. This scheme is based on an analysis of the literature summarizing respondent perceptions of their compliance-gaining strategies as well as an analysis of the actual conversational ploys used by couples.

Compliance-gaining strategies contain, either implicitly or explicitly, the response intended for the partner to make and an inducement that provides a reason or motivation for doing what the speaker wants (Schenck-Hamlin, Wiseman & Georgacarakos, 1982). Compliance-gaining messages may be categorized according to one of three broad classes of reasons or motivations for complying (Witteman & Fitzpatrick, 1986). First, messages can induce compliance because of the expectancies or consequences associated with compliance or noncompliance. Second, messages can induce compliance because of the speaker's conception of the relationship and the requirements entailed by belonging to it. Third, messages can induce compliance because of the values or obligations held by the spouses. Because the couples used compromises frequently throughout their conversations, we included compromises, or the alternatives that speakers propose in an attempt to reach a solution, in the scheme (see Appendix 7.B).

There are a few differences between the observationally based categories and self-report compliance approaches. First, one notices the lack of focus in the self-report systems on the actor. Whereas many self-report categories focus on the receiver or target, corresponding to our *you* category, there are few categories that parallel our *me* category. Appeals such as "I need this" or "I always do it this way" are not represented in their categories. Second, very little attention is paid by these other schemes to the motivating force of appealing to the relationship between the parties as a reason for compliance. For married couples, the relationship is a resource that may motivate compliance from a mate. Third, although our *external* category does appear in other schemes in the forms of moral appeals and third-party approvals or condemnations, this category encompasses a much wider array of external agents and is expected to discriminate individuals who rely on external factors. Fourth, none of the compliance schemes includes an information-search category. In gaining compliance, information about the other's affective and cognitive states can be used by the actor in developing other messages. As such, *search* can be conceived of as a "prestrategy message."

Categories included in other schemes that do not appear in VICS appear to take two forms. The first set involves behaviors that would be difficult to pick up from observations of interactions. This group includes hinting, deceit, indirect strategies, suggesting, and withdrawal. Indirect attempts to gain compliance are not apparent in interaction. The second group consists of attempts at explanation, reasoning, and persuasion. These categories are often so broadly defined that they hold little promise for verbal message analysis. Explanation, reasoning, and persuasion can be better examined when the force behind the reason is specified.

The psychological thought unit (analogous to the sentence) is the unit of analysis yet, because all psychological thought units do not serve a persuasive function, this is a sieve-coding scheme. The reliability for the psychological units was .95 (Guetzkow, 1950) and each unit ($N = 2, 170$) was categorized into one of five main categories. That is, a psychological thought unit could represent an attempt to gain compliance, a statement refuting that attempt, a statement discounting the refutation, a simple agreement, or it could be none of the above. About 65% of the psychological thought units were coded as compliance-gaining behaviors. Cohen's (1960) Kappas for these five categories were comply (.74), refute (.69), discount (.65), agree (.80), and other (.73). Each of the compliance units was subsequently coded into one of the eight categories, or a final category called "compromise." The overall Cohen's kappa at this level of the scheme was .79, and the figures ranged from a high of .91 for *search* to a low of .62 for the *us* category.

Validation of the Coding Scheme

Since the coding scheme was developed for use in this experiment, some validation was necessary. This coding scheme was validated in two ways. First, we demonstrated that the selection of compliance-gaining messages was differentially related to the outcome of a persuasive transaction and the marital satisfaction and happiness of the communicators. Curiously, most of the compliance-gaining literature focuses on message selection and not the relationship between a given message and outcomes. Second, we translated the persuasive strategies defined in VICS into questions that could be used on a survey instrument. Married people were subsequently asked how likely they were to use these strategies in attempting to gain compliance from their spouses.

The first validation of this coding scheme explored which of the strategies "worked." How do these contentious strategies affect marital outcomes? Two coders classified the outcome of each interaction: husband wins, wife wins, compromise (Dillard & Fitzpatrick, 1984). The strategies were also related to the marital satisfaction and happiness of the couples. Simple correlation coefficients were calculated to assess the relationships among the use of the compliance-gaining messages and the outcomes. Adjustments were made for individual differences in verbal output and an arc-sine transformation was performed on each of the proportions to stabilize the variances (Winer, 1971).

As we can see in Table 7.2, the use of these messages leads to different outcomes. The husband's communication behavior was systematically related to the immediate outcome of the conflict more often than was the communication behavior of the wives. Yet the only strategy that enhanced the husband's likelihood of winning was the direct request. Implying that a wife should accede to her husband's wishes because of the nature of the relationship between them enhances the husband's chances of motivating his spouse

Table 7.2. Proportions of messages used at level two of verbal interaction compliance scheme (VICS) by outcome type.

	Outcome type							
	W wins		H wins		M res		No res	
	H	W	H	W	H	W	H	W
Expectancy								
Activity	22(+)	19(+)	16(−)	32(+)	34(+)	26(+)	28(−)	23(−)
Power	20	12(−)	24(+)	29	17(−)	17(−)	39(+)	42(+)
Relationship								
Us	11(−)	16	57(+)	37(+)	11(−)	16(−)	21(−)	32(+)
Direct	24(+)	16(−)	12(−)	34(+)	30(+)	24(+)	35	27(−)
Search	22(+)	15(−)	20(−)	33(+)	26(+)	23	32(−)	30
Value								
Me	20	22(+)	23(+)	23(−)	22(−)	25(+)	36(+)	31(+)
You	20	19(+)	12(−)	30	20(−)	16(−)	47(+)	35(+)
External	17(−)	21(+)	20	39(+)	20(−)	14(−)	43(+)	27(−)
Compromise	21(+)	19(+)	24(+)	24(−)	29(+)	31(+)	27(−)	26(−)

Note. The proportions sum to one across the rows of the table for husband or wife. Wife (W) wins, husband (H) wins, mutual resolution (M res), and no resolution (No res) are the outcome types. A plus or minus signifies that the Freeman-Tukey deviates associated with the frequency in each cell is $p < .001$. The sign in parentheses indicates whether the observed value is more or less, respectively, than that expected by chance.

to do what he wants. Reliance on messages in the values or obligations class tended to decrease the husband's chances of affecting a compromise.

When one looks at who won regardless of sex, winners tend to use more activity messages and more direct requests. Appealing to the positive or negative attributes of the proposed course of action and seeking information with which to build future compliance moves is associated with actually gaining compliance. Not surprisingly, compromise leads to more mutual resolutions of the situations.

The use of some message strategies is correlated to the happiness or satisfaction of one spouse and the distress of the other (Table 7.3). For example, the husband who uses external messages to gain compliance from his wife is himself less happily married, yet his use of these same messages is correlated to the marital happiness of his wife. When the husband used activity-focused attempts to gain compliance, these attempts were correlated to his wife's dissatisfaction. Please note: My colleagues and I cannot claim that compliance-gaining communication behaviors cause levels of marital satisfaction or distress, although we included marital satisfaction and marital happiness as "outcomes" in this study. We do not mean to imply by this choice that we are sure of the causal relationships between communication behavior and marital satisfaction.

There are systematic relationships between the use of these contentious messages and the outcomes of marital conversations. These findings show

Table 7.3. Correlations between spouse's use of verbal interaction compliance scheme (VICS) and relational state.

VICS	Speaker	Relational state			
		HSAT	HHAP	WSAT	WHAP
Expectancy					
Activity	H	.10	−.03	−.43*	−.01
Values					
Me	H	.13	−.25*	−.13	−.30*
You	W	.26*	−.24*	.03	−.02
External	H	−.46*	−.56*	.23*	.04
	W	−.29*	−.24	.03	−.02

Note. There are no significant correlations between the measures of marital satisfaction and happiness and the compliance-gaining messages that invoke the "relationship" as the force to comply. HSAT = husband satisfaction; HHAP = husband happiness; WSAT = wife satisfaction; WHAP = wife happiness.
*$p < .05$, $N = 51$.

that some contentious messages are more effective in the short run. The results also indicate, however, that the higher the frequency of contentious tactics, the less satisfied are the spouses with the marriage. Excessive concern for one's own outcomes over the outcomes of one's spouse is correlated with marital dissatisfaction.

The second validation of the coding scheme involved asking a sample of married people how likely they would be to use the message strategies in attempting to gain compliance from their spouse. I developed a self-report questionnaire concerning the likelihood of use of the tactics. Four separate questions were written for each of the 31 subcategories of the VICS. These questions were based on actual couple dialogue coded into each category but written to be used in a survey instrument. For example, one question was, "How likely are to you 'Tell your spouse he/she should do this because society expects it of him/her?'" This question measures the likelihood that an individual will appeal to external matters in the cultural values or moral class.

A random-sample telephone survey was conducted with 67 married individuals, approximately equal numbers of males and females (70% acceptance rate). One of the four versions of the survey instrument was chosen and respondents were asked how likely they would be to use the various message types when attempting to convince their spouse to follow a certain course of action. Thirty-one one-way analyses of variance were conducted ($p < .001$) to insure that the four questions for each category were similar in the minds of the respondents. There were no significant differences on likelihood of use indicating that the four versions of the questions were exemplars of the same tactic. Table 7.4 presents the mean likelihood of use of each tactic and the actual frequency of use of the behaviors in the compliance-gaining situation.

In general, married individuals, drawn from the same population as the

Table 7.4. Likelihood of use and actual use of compliance-gaining messages.

	Mean	Freq
Expectancies		
I. Activity		
a. Positivity of own	3.84	6% i
b. Negativity of own	3.34	1% i
c. Positivity of other	3.49	1% i
d. Negativity of other	2.24	3% c
II. Power		
a. Exclamation/cursing	1.75	1% c
b. Constraining self	2.09	7% c
c. Constraining other	1.83	1% c
Relationship		
III. Us		
a. Identity	2.99	2% c
b. Internal	2.34	1% c
c. Positive Feelings	2.89	0% c
d. Negative Feelings	1.53	0% c
e. Pet Names	2.81	1% c
IV. Direct		
a. Statement of Situation	3.88	19% c
b. Direct Request	3.60	6% i
V. Search		
a. Internal Information	4.27	10% c
b. External Information	4.03	1% i
Values		
VI. Me		
a. Positive-self	2.69	1% c
b. Negative-self	2.45	0% c
c. Identity	3.78	2% i
d. Internal	3.58	19% c
VII. You		
a. Positive-other	3.35	1% i
b. Negative-other	1.99	3% c
c. Identity	3.12	1% i
d. Internal	3.45	4% i
VIII. External		
a. Time	2.70	2% c
b. Cultural Norms	2.40	0% c
c. Third Parties	2.58	3% c

Note. The mean likelihood of use is on a scale of 1 (very unlikely) to 5 (very likely). The "c" assumes a mean likelihood of use under 3.00 and less than 10% of the overall compliance-gaining messages are the correct estimates of the behavior. The "i" represents incorrect estimates.

experimental subjects, are very good at predicting which tactics are likely to be used in compliance-gaining marital dialogues. Indeed, these respondents predicted behavioral data correctly about 70% of the time.

Married individuals say that they are not likely to use extreme negative tactics (any power tactic or focus on negative aspects of the other's idea, or person), and behaviorally couples *do not tend* to use these tactics. Married people also say they are not likely to use the relationship as a compelling reason for compliance, and they actually do not use any of the messages in the *us* category to any great degree. Finally, married people argue that they are not likely to use *external* messages and the behavioral data agree with this perception.

The married sample errs in predicting the likelihood of use of either the internal characteristics of themselves or any of the *you* messages that focus on characteristics or traits of the spouse. The survey data argue that these messages are very likely to be used, yet they are rarely used in the behavioral data. In thinking about how to get one's own way, one may use attributions about the spouse, although such attributional categories do not appear when actually engaged in message exchanges. Finally, the sample errs in predicting that they would focus on the characteristics of the activity as a primary means of getting their own way. Thus, the sample members may tend to see themselves as rational in focusing on the positive consequences of an activity yet actually do very little of this in compliance-situations.

The data indicate that social desirability arguments against the use of checklists and self-reports of compliance-gaining techniques may need to be modified. Falbo and Peplau (1980) argue that power strategies can be described on three continua: positive-negative; rational-irrational; direct-indirect. People appear to be able to correctly report the use of negative strategies. When people report that they do not use power strategies and negative tactics, it is because they actually use these techniques very rarely. Social desirability may enter the equation only when considering the dimension of rationality-irrationality. Here, for example in the activity category, people see themselves as referencing the "pro and con" of an issue more than they tend to in conversation. People also see themselves taking the other's needs and desires into account more than they do behaviorally.

Summary

The coding scheme developed to measure the various strategies that spouses use in conversations with one another in order to "get their own way" appears to be a valid representation of the ways that individuals in ongoing relationships attempt to persuade one another of a given course of action. Messages within the scheme can be clearly related to a set of outcomes of communication, and random samples of couples in similar populations readily can assess the likelihood they would use such strategies with their own spouses.

Two points can be made about persuasive tactics in personal relationships based on these results. First, the compliance-gaining perspective should be avoided. Spouses who have already decided what their position is and what outcome they must achieve, are arguing over positions and not negotiating the issues (Fisher & Ury, 1983). Such behavior may be detrimental to the relationship. Currently, partners may expect spouses to act in more egalitarian terms and discuss together a decision rather than make one independently and persuade the spouse to agree. Even in the most traditional of marriages today, the husband may have the last word, but his wife's opinion is expected to be taken into account in his decisions. The most persuasive strategy is to allow the partner to assume they have had an important influence on the decision, and were not merely told the position after the fact.

Second, when arguing over positions, the choice of tactics is important. Strategies that directly reference the relationship appear to be related to positive outcomes, although these strategies are rarely used by married people. Simply requesting compliance from the spouse also works well in the short run. Although the use of power messages may stop the spouse from winning, these strategies do not appear to benefit the user in the long or the short run. In the next section of this chapter, we describe the use of the VICS in a study of marital interaction in various types of couples.

Inducing Spousal Compliance

Individuals in close relationships often are reticent to discuss potential power differences in the marriage. Despite this fact, both the ideological orientations to male and female roles and the typical interactional styles used in conflict (Fitzpatrick, 1984) suggest that the bases of power and the techniques of influence differ for couples in the various types of marriages. Kipnis, Castell, Gergen, and Mouch (1976) have found differences in the reports that various types of husbands and wives make about the likelihood they would use certain persuasive strategies.

Traditionals are concerned with the stability of their marriage and tend to disclose their anxieties to their spouses. Traditionals say they are extremely well adjusted in their marriage and appear to have less intense and fewer conflicts than do other couples. In interaction, Traditionals quickly accede control to their spouses in conversations that do not involve important issues and appear to struggle with the spouse only when discussing serious issues of disagreement. Traditionals are not likely to employ compliance-gaining messages that disrupt the stability of the relationship by threatening the other, or bringing up doubts about the values held by the spouse. Thus, when Traditionals reference expectancies in attempts to gain compliance, they rely on activity messages rather than power messages. Given the shared-value orientations and the presumption of understanding in this marriage, Traditionals may be expected to employ more direct requests for compliance. When Traditionals want to invoke the relationship as a basis of power, direct requests allow the major premise to remain unspoken. Traditionals have little need to reinforce verbally the shared- and stable-value orientations each holds in common.

The Separates' communication style with one another can best be described as a guerrilla (hit-and-run) style in that one spouse may make a confrontational remark to the other but quickly withdraws if the other spouse responds. Additionally, the Separates tend to speak to one another for shorter periods of time than do couples in the other types. Thus, Separates are expected to use the compliance-gaining messages that take the least time—that is, power in the expectancies class and external messages in the obligation class. Power entails little discussion because it involves a strong assertion on the part of the spouse demanding compliance. External messages require little discussion because these messages make the claim that the issue is out of the control of the spouse demanding compliance. By the same reasoning, Separates will be unlikely to use *search* messages that may involve them in extended discussion. Given that these couples are emotionally distant, they are unlikely to use the relationship (i.e., *us* messages) as a reason for spousal compliance.

The Independents, defined by a commitment to openness and expressivity, are expected to have an active compliance-gaining repertoire. Their engagement style is structured in general around intense messages. They may tend to use power messages when referencing their expectations about the compliance act. The powerful identification of the Independents with one another should allow these couples to use the relationship as a means of influence. Since Independents are renegotiating their roles in the relationship, such couples are expected to employ messages that seek out information about the relationship and the other, and that appeal to the state of the marriage.

Unique among the mixed types are the Separate/Traditionals. These couples are the most conservative ideologically about family and marriage values and report a high degree of marital adjustment. Since both the husband and wife maintain similar values about the family, and these values are a major strength of the marriage, they are likely to reference such values when attempting to gain compliance. For the other mixed types, few specific predictions can be derived concerning their compliance-gaining behavior.

Fifty-one couples participated in this study. The average length of the marriages was 7.8 years (range, <1 year–33 years). On the average, husbands were 31.7 years old (range, 22–57 years), and wives were 30.4 years old (range, 21–55). In this sample, there were 13 traditionals, 10 separates, 6 Independents, 5 Separate/Traditionals, and 17 Mixed types. The distribution of the frequencies in this sample of the three pure types, the mixed types, and the Separate/Traditionals does not differ significantly from that of the major random sample of couples (Fitzpatrick & Indvik, 1982).

Couples were asked to carry out two role plays, each of which took 15 minutes. The role-play situations represent areas of conflict that occur in most marriages at some time. One role play concerned the sharing of time; the other involved forming new friendships. Before the experiment, interviewers helped couples make the role plays conform as much as possible to the overall structure of their relationship and interaction style. Roles for husbands and wives were assigned on the basis of rather extensive probes (Gottman, 1979, pp. 138–140). After the coaching session, couples

Table 7.5. Frequency of use and correlation between husband and wife compliance-gaining behaviors.

	Frequency	Correlation
Referencing expectancies		
Activity	14.75	.39*
Power	11.52	.07
Invoking the relationship		
Us	5.42	.28*
Direct	33.07	−.14
Search	15.39	.26*
Appealing to values		
Me	26.02	.27*
You	10.96	.34*
External	10.52	.16
Compromise	12.78	.27*

*$p < .05$

were brought into a simulated living room and instructed to try to gain compliance from their spouse for the course of action they had chosen. Compliance-gaining conversations were videotaped and transcribed. The manipulation checks indicated that all spouses saw themselves during these interactions as being natural and comfortable, and their behaviors as being similar to real-life situations. Because there were no significant differences in the perceptions of the respondents between the two discussion tasks, these two discussions were combined for analyses.

There were no significant differences in the number of psychological thought units coded for husbands and wives (Table 7.5). The frequency of use of the various strategies differed. By far, the most popular way of attempting to gain compliance was to make a direct request apparently unadorned by a rationale, whereas the least popular compliance-gaining message is *us*. In invoking the relationship, couples do so indirectly rather than explicitly. The correlations between husband and wife compliance strategies suggest that spouses cue one another in persuasive situations as to which strategies to use. Significant correlations hold for all but external, direct, and power strategies. The bluntness of the power and direct strategies may preclude a spouse from answering in kind, whereas external reasons could only apply to the speaker's situation.

We can now turn to the communication differences in the couple types. The average frequency counts for each communication category were analyzed using log-linear analysis (Bishop, Feinberg, & Holland, 1975). Because we expected couples in different types of marriages to use different compliance-gaining strategies, we focused on models involving couple types. All of these models contain sex-by-couple-type interaction because this interaction is automatically fixed by the sampling plan (see Swafford, 1980). A number of criteria was used to select the best-fitting model. The first was

Table 7.6. Proportions of messages used at level one of verbal interaction compliance-gaining scheme (VICS) by couple type.

| Message | Couple type | | | | |
	Traditional	Separate	Independent	Separate/ Traditional	Mixed
Comply	.18(+)*	.20(+)*	.19(−)*	.22	.21
Refute	.16(−)*	.22(+)*	.29(+)*	.13(−)*	.20
Discount	.13(−)*	.24(+)*	.35(+)*	.12(−)*	.17(−)*
Agree	.18	.17(−)*	.16(−)*	.27(+)*	.23(+)*
Other	.16(−)*	.17(−)*	.22(+)*	.26(+)*	.19(−)*

From Witteman & Fitzpatrick (1986).
Note. The proportions sum to one across the rows of the table. These indicate differences among the couple types in their usage of messages.
* Freeman-Tukey deviates associated with the frequency in each cell is $p < .001$. Positive or negative signs in parentheses indicate whether the observed value is more or less, respectively, than that expected by chance.

based on the probability level of the model. The appropriate probability level ranges from anything over .05 as implied by Brown (1983) and Kennedy (1983) to between .10 and .35 (Knoke & Burke, 1980). We used the latter, more conservative standard to obtain a moderately robust yet parsimonious model to explain the data. If no model falls within this range, the model with a level of probability above and closest to .35 was selected. This again insured parsimony. In addition, only the model that added a significant component chi-square was accepted. Once the best-fitting model was selected, the respective Freeman-Tukey deviates for the best-fitting model were examined. The deviates for the model were tested for significance at the $p < .001$ significance level (Bishop, Feinberg, & Holland, 1975).

Table 7.6 reveals the proportion of the messages used at level one of the coding scheme for each couple type. Independents tend to refute one another in situations involving a conflict of interest, whereas Traditionals use relatively few refutations and discounts. At this level of analysis, the Separates were the most assertive and contentious. These couples used a high proportion of compliance moves, refuted one another's attempts, and discounted one another's arguments. Notably, the Mixed types and the Separate/Traditionals tended to use a good deal of agreement and tended not to discount the arguments of the spouse. Like the Traditionals, and Separate/Traditionals tended not to refute what the spouse said.

In terms of specific compliance-gaining techniques, the independents are the only couple type who use all three bases of power when seeking spousal compliance, albeit a restricted range of messages within each category (Table 7.7). Independents demand compliance from their spouses in that they rely on *you* strategies and power plays when attempting to persuade their spouses. Independents are likely to offer compromises and to question the spouse about their needs and wants. Independents use fewer compliance-

Table 7.7. Proportions of messages used at level two of verbal interaction complicance-gaining scheme (VICS) by couple type.

| Message | Couple type | | | | |
	Traditional	Separate	Independent	Separate/ Traditional	Mixed
Expectancies					
Activity	.26(+)*	.19(−)*	.16(−)*	.16(−)*	.22(+)*
Power	.15(−)*	.25(+)*	.24(+)*	.11(−)*	.26(+)*
Relationship					
Us	.17	.16(−)*	.14(−)*	.33(+)*	.21
Direct	.20(+)*	.19(−)*	.18(−)*	.21(−)*	.23(+)*
Search	.20(+)*	.17(−)*	.24(+)*	.18(−)*	.22(+)*
Values					
Me	.14(−)*	.20	.19(−)*	.29(+)*	.18(−)*
You	.14(−)*	.22(+)*	.20(+)*	.29(+)*	.15(−)*
External	.17(−)*	.26(+)*	.17(−)*	.22	.18(−)*

From Witteman & Fitzpatrick (1986).
Note. The proportions sum to one across the rows of the table. These indicate differences among the couple types in their usage of the compliance-gaining messages.
* Freeman-Tukey deviates associated with the frequency in each cell is $p < .001$. Positive or negative signs in parenthesis indicate whether the observed value is more or less, respectively, than that expected by chance.

gaining techniques overall, yet will engage in defending themselves and refuting what the spouse says. The techniques the independents do use rely on a variety of power bases.

Traditionals talk about their expectancies in trying to gain compliance. Given the shared, conventional value system of these couples and their levels of interdependence, Traditionals can discuss the positive and negative outcomes of a given course of action. This shared-value orientation does not result in the Traditionals using any message in the values/obligations categories. Traditionals are significantly less likely than expected by chance to summon their values or any obligations in the relationship as a means to gain the compliance of a spouse. In attempting to get their own way, the Traditionals use the relationship and the identification that each has with the other as motivating forces to achieve compliance.

Separates avoid using identification or relationally based messages when seeking compliance from a spouse and tend to focus on the negative consequences of noncompliance. Only the Separates cite external reasons for spousal compliance. When Separates do engage in contentious behavior with the spouse, they use blatant attempts to constrain the behavior and sometimes even the internal states, like thoughts or feelings, of their spouses. Separates are not without intensity in their interactions but have a guerrilla-like communication style that demands acquiescence from the spouse without verbally staying to fight the whole battle.

Separate/Traditionals stress values and obligations and the relationship as means to gain compliance from a spouse. These couples ask the spouse to comply for them, for the spouse, and for the relationship. The Separate/ Traditionals was the only couple type to inhibit its attempts to compromise when attempting to gain compliance from a spouse. Separate/Traditionals do not prematurely yield to their spouses when they are attempting to get their own way. The other mixed types rely on references to the consequences of noncompliance; they also rely on power plays, direct requests, and compromises as strategies to gain spousal compliance.

Conclusion

Three general observations on decision making can be drawn from this research on compliance-gaining in various types of marriages. First, this research supports and expands the various gender models of marital interaction (e.g., Scanzoni & Scanzoni, 1976). Couples in more traditional sex-role relationships have fewer decisions to make because the roles, rules, and norms are more clearly established in the relationship. These couples fit the prototype of the Traditional couple. Traditional couples do not engage in power struggles with one another because, to some degree,the power matrix in the relationship is already established by the conventions and normative prescriptions of appropriate husband and wife behavior. Under conditions of disagreement, Traditionals try to conciliate and to avoid the discussion of conflict issues. Traditional couples handle important decisions on which they may disagree often by defining them as "trivial." Traditionals may tend to redefine serious problems rather than dealing with them. Once they have settled on a course of action, Traditionals seek compliance from one another by focusing on the rational pros and cons of an issue, and simply by asking their spouses to give in.

A gender model of marital interaction also predicts that couples who have little commitment to traditional sex roles are more likely to engage in manifest conflict, negotiation, bargaining, and decision making with the marital partner (Scanzoni & Scanzoni 1976). The roles, rules, and norms of this marriage need to be defined and renegotiated with changes in the relationship or the environment. These couples clearly fit the Independent prototype. Attempts on the part of Independent couples to establish new role patterns and less sex-stereotypic interaction routines bring a certain level of conflict, stress, and tension to the relationship. Couples like the Independents who deviate from well-established patterns experience more stress. Such couples may need help in handling these tensions within their own value orientations and comfortable levels of marital interdependence.

The marital typology expands the gender model of marital power to include Separate and Mixed-type couples. With their combined traditional sex-role expectations and lack of interdependence, Separates are emotionally divorced. The closeness of the Traditional relationship, as well as the certainty about traditional values, is missing in the Separate marriage. Separates do not openly discuss their conflicts and retreat immediately from the discussion of negative issues when the spouse begins to deal with any stressful topic. Separates externalize the reasons they seek compliance from a spouse and tend to be argumentative, yet retreat if the spouse responds. In one study, the Separates were found to be the least accurate in predicting how their spouses saw themselves (Fitzpatrick & Indvik, 1979). Separates may overattribute the causes of their spouses' behavior to sex-role stereotypes (e.g., "their feelings are just so easily hurt. That's just the way women are").

Mixed-couple types also have different interaction styles, suggesting different strengths and problems. In the Traditional/Independent marriage, for example, the husband may help keep conflict in the marriage within manageable bounds by strategically avoiding discussing issues that cannot be resolved; his wife may place fewer role burdens on him than would a more traditional wife. In general, however, couples in these mixed relationships tend to have control problems and hence difficulties in making decisions together.

The second major implication of this research for the study of marital decision making, negotiation, and problem solving is that couples in various types of marriages use different verbal strategies of confronting, retreating from, and resolving conflict. The research has demonstrated the importance of examining in more detail the various global strategies that couples can use in conflict. The time has come to move from making general statements about the positivity or negativity conveyed between spouses in verbal and nonverbal communication channels. This chapter has shown that researchers can profitably explore the specific message strategies and tactics that couples in a variety of different types of marriages use to handle their problems.

The third major implication for the study of marital processes in general is that this research underscores the importance of considering three levels of analysis in any systematic study of marital decision making: resources, process, and outcomes. The typology points to the resources that spouses bring to interaction, predicts the messages they choose to deal with conflicts, and suggests the outcomes each couple type can expect to achieve with these message strategies. The relations between interdependence and ideological orientations and open conflict and marital outcomes are complex; yet there seems to be little justification for assuming that high levels of conflict are necessarily associated with imbalances of power or with dissatisfaction in marriage.

Acknowledgment. The research reported in this chapter was funded by grants from the Wisconsin Alumni Research Foundation.

References

Berger, C (1985). Social power and interpersonal communication. In M. Knapp & G. R. Miller (Eds.) *Handbook of interpersonal communication* (439–499). Beverly Hills, CA.: Sage.

Bernard, J. (1972). *The future of marriage*. New York: Bantam.

Bishop, Y. M., Feinberg, S. E., & Holland, P. W. (1975). *Discrete multivariate analysis*. Cambridge, MA: MIT Press.

Brown, M. B. (1983). Frequency tables. In W. J. Dixon (Ed.), *BMDP statistical software* (pp. 143–206). Berkeley, CA: Regents of California.

Cohen, J. (1960). A coefficient of agreement for nominal scales. *Educational and Psychological Measurement, 20*, 37–46.

Dillard, J. P., & Fitzpatrick, M. A. (1984). *The short and long term outcomes of compliance gaining in marital interaction.* Paper presented at the annual meeting of the International Communication Association, San Francisco.

Duck, S. (1980). Personal relationship research in the eighties: Towards an understanding of complex human sociality. *Western Journal of Speech Communication, 44*, 114–119.

Ericson, P. M., & Rogers, E. L. (1973). New procedures for analyzing relational communication. *Family Process, 12*, 245–267.

Fisher, R. & Ury, W. (1983). *Getting to yes.* New York; Penguin.

Falbo, T & Peplau, L. A. (1980). Power strategies in intimate relationships. *Journal of Personality and Social Psychology, 38*, 618–628.

Fitzpatrick, M. A. (1976). *A typological approach to communication in relationships.* Unpublished doctoral dissertation, Temple University, Philadelphia.

Fitzpatrick, M. A. (1981). Directions for interpersonal communication research. In G. I. Friedrich (Ed.), *Education in the 80's: Speech communication* (pp. 73–81). National Education Association: Washington, D. C.

Fitzpatrick, M. A. (1984). A typological approach to marital interaction: Recent theory and research. In L. Berkowitz (Ed.), *Advances in experimental social psychology* (vol. 18, pp. 1–47). New York: Academic Press.

Fitzpatrick, M. A., & Best, P. (1979). Dyadic adjustment in traditional, independent, and separate relationships: A validation study. *Communication Monographs, 46*, 167–178.

Fitzpatrick, M. A., Fallis, S., & Vance, L. (1982). Multifunctional coding of conflict resolution strategies in marital dyads. *Family Relations, 31*, 611–670.

Fitzpatrick, M. A., & Indvik, J. (1982). The instrumental and expressive domains of marital communication. *Human Communication Research, 8*, 195–213.

Fitzpatrick, M. A., Vance, L. E., & Witteman, H. (1984). Interpersonal communication in the casual interaction of marital partners. *Journal of Language and Social Psychology, 3*, 81–95.

Folger, J. & Poole, M. S. (1984). *Communication and conflict.* Glenview, IL.: Scott Foresman.

Frost, J. H., & Wilmot, W. W. (1978). *Interpersonal conflict.* Dubuque, Iowa: W. C. Brown.

Giles, H. & Fitzpatrick, M. A. (1985). Personal, group and couple identities: Towards a relational context for the study of language attitudes and linguistic forms. In D. Schiffrin (Ed.) *Meaning, form and use in context: Linquistic applications* (1–25). Washington, DC: Georget own University Press.

Gottman, J. M. (1979). *Marital interaction*. New York: Academic Press.

Guetzkow, H. (1950). Unitizing and categorizing problems in coding qualitative data. *Journal of Clinical Psychology, 6,* 47–58.

French, J. & Raven, B. (1960). The bases of social power. In D. Cartwright & A. Zander (Eds.) *Group dynamics* (607–623). New York: Harper & Row.

Hess, G. & Handel, G. (1959). *Family worlds.* Chicago: University of Chicago Press.

Kennedy, J. J. (1983). *Analyzing qualitative data.* New York: Praeger.

Kipnis, D., Castell, P., Gergen, M., & Mauch, D. (1976). Metamorphic effects of power. *Journal of Applied Psychology, 61,* 127–135.

Knoke, D., & Burke, P. J. (1980). *Log-linear models.* Beverly Hills, CA: Sage Publishers.

Marwell, G., & Schmitt, D. R. (1967). Dimensions of compliance-gaining behaviors: An empirical analysis. *Sociometry, 30,* 350–364.

Scanzoni, L. & Scanzoni, J. (1976). *Men and women and change.* New York: Mc Graw Hill.

Schenck-Hamlin, W. J., Wiseman, R. L., & Georgacarakos, G. N. (1982). A model of the properties of compliance-gaining strategies. *Communication Quarterly, 30,* 92–100.

Seibold, D., Cantrill, & Meyers, R. A. (1985). Communication and interpersonal influence. In M. L. Knapp & G. R. Miller (Eds.) *Handbook of interpersonal communication* (551–614). Beverly Hills, CA.: Sage.

Sillars, A. L., Pike, G. H., Jones, T. S., & Redman, K. (1983). Communication and conflict in marriage. In R. N. Bostrom & B. H. Westley (Eds.), *Communication yearbook 7* (pp. 414–431). Beverly Hills, CA: Sage Publishers.

Sprey, J. (1979). Conflict theory and the study of marriage and the family. In W. L. Burr, R. Hill, F. D. Nye, & I. L. Reiss (Eds.), *Contemporary theories about the family* (volume 2, pp. 130–159).

Swafford, M. (1980). Three parametric techniques for contingency table analysis: A non-technical commentary. *American Sociological Review, 45,* 664–690.

Williamson, R. & Fitzpatrick, M. A. (1985). Two approaches to marital interaction: Relational control paterns in marital types. *Communication Monographs, 52,* 236–252.

Winer, B. J. (1971). *Statistical principles in experimental design.* New York: McGraw-Hill.

Witteman, H., & Fitzpatrick, M. A. (1984). Unpublished Codebook, University of Wisconsin-Madison, Center for Communication Research.

Witteman, H., & Fitzpatrick, M. A. (1986). Compliance-gaining in marital interaction. *Communication Monographs, 53,* 130–143.

Appendix 7.A. Representative Statements from the Relational Dimensions Instrument

Interdependence

Sharing

We tell each other how much we love or care about each other.
My spouse/mate reassures and comforts me when I am feeling low.
I think that we joke around and have more fun than most couples.

Autonomy

I have my own private workspace (study, workshop, utility room, etc.).
I think it is important for one to have some private space which is all his/her own and separate from one's mate.

Undifferentiated Space

I feel free to interrupt my spouse/mate when he/she is concentrating on something if he/she is in my presence.
I open my spouse/mate's personal mail without asking permission.
I feel free to invite guests home without informing my spouse/mate.

Temporal Regularity

We eat our meals (i.e., the ones at home) at the same time every day.
In our house, we keep a fairly regular daily time schedule.
We serve the main meal at the same time every day.

Ideology

Ideology of Traditionalism

A woman should take her husband's last name when she marries.
Our wedding ceremony was (will be) very important to us.
Our society as we see it needs to regain faith in the law and in our institutions.

Ideology of Uncertainty and Change

In marriage/close relationships there should be no constraints or restrictions on individual freedom.
The ideal relationship is one marked by novelty, humor, and spontaneity.
In a relationship, each individual should be permitted to establish the daily rhythm and time schedule that suits him/her best.

Conflict

Conflict Avoidance

If I can avoid arguing about some problems, they will disappear.
In our relationship, we feel that it is better to engage in conflicts than to avoid them.
It is better to hide one's true feelings in order to avoid hurting your spouse/mate.

Assertiveness

My spouse/mate forces me to do things that I do not want to do.
We are likely to argue in front of friends or in public places.
My spouse/mate tries to persuade me to do something that I do not want to do.

Appendix 7.B.

Verbal Interaction Compliance-Gaining Scheme (VICS)

References to Expectancies/Consequences

I. *Activity*: Force to comply comes from the nature of the specific activity, the importance of the activity, or from the outcome of the activity.
  A. Positivity/Importance of Own Activity or Compromise.
  B. Negativity/Unimportance of Own Activity or Compromise.
  C. Positivity/Importance of Other's Activity or Compromise.
  D. Negativity/Unimportance of Other's Activity or Compromise.
II. *Power*: Focus is on the exertion of control in the relationship. Control may be manifested in attempts to constrain behavior (both verbal and physical) and internal states or processes of either participant.
  A. Exclamations/Cursing.
  B. Constraining Self or Other.

Invocations of Identification/Relationship

III. *Us*: Force to comply comes from the relationship between the interactants.
  A. Identity. Relationship's more stable characteristics.
  B. Internal. Needs of the relationship.
  C. Feelings between Spouses—Positive.
  D. Feelings between Spouses—Negative.
  E. Pet Names or Terms of Address.
IV. *Direct*: Nonevaluative statement or questions expressing past, current, or future activity, or activities (excluding behavioral regularities of *me*, *you*, or *us*).
  A. Statement of Situation.
  B. Direct Request for Compliance.
V. *Search*: Information search in question form. Questions are evaluatively neutral.
  A. Relational/Self/Other Information.
  B. External Information.

Appeals to Values/Obligations

VI. *Me*: Force to comply comes from within the actor.
  A. Positive Self-Casting. The focus is on the actor as a "good" person.
  B. Negative Self-Casting. The focus is on the actor as a "bad" person.
  C. Identity. The focus is on the actor's stable characteristics.
  D. Internal. The focus is on the actor's transient characteristics.
VII. *You*: Force to comply comes from within the other.
  A. Positive Altercasting. The focus is on the target as a "good" person.

B. Negative Altercasting. The focus is on the target as a "bad" person.

C. Identity. The focus is on the target's stable characteristics.

D. Internal. The focus is on the target's transient characteristics.

VIII. *External*: Force to comply comes from a specific (enabling or disabling) agent or agents outside the participants or their relationship.

A. Time.

B. Cultural/Moral/Social Norms.

C. Third Parties.

From Witteman & Fitzpatrick (1984).

CHAPTER 8

Implicit and Explicit Decision-Making Styles in Couples

Alan L. Sillars and Pam J. Kalbflesch

Occasionally one finds a reference to decision making within couples or families, but the subject has not been pursued as systematically as, say, power, conflict, self-disclosure, companionship, and other blatantly expressive and emotive aspects of interaction. The nature of intimate relationships suggests this emphasis. Intimate relationships are formed for social and companionate reasons. Decision making is a by-product; something that is necessary to maintain the relationship but not a goal in-and-of itself. In contrast, many task and work relationships are formed basically for the purpose of decision making. Thus, the archetypal setting for the study of communication and collaborative decision making has been the task-oriented small group. One way of clarifying the subject of this chapter is to contrast the much studied task-oriented group with the decision making of couples.

Decision making as represented in group studies takes place during a formal meeting in which the decision is an explicit agenda item. The task-group meeting provides an isolated setting in which decision making can take place with minimal distraction, thereby allowing an organized approach to decisions. In contrast, decision making in couples tends be embedded in other activity and takes place with less self-conscious attention to the decision-making process (Sillars & Weisberg, 1987; Weick, 1971). Small-group studies are also based on a rationalistic model of decision making, not in the sense that groups always behave rationally but rather that their effectiveness is assessed relative to some baseline of optimal performance (e.g., Steiner, 1972). This assumes that decision-making outcomes can be compared objectively, which is often the case with task outcomes (e.g., investment strategies) but rarely the case with relational outcomes (e.g., having a child, getting a divorce, negotiating togetherness or separateness), which dominate much of the decision making of intimate couples. Given the emphasis on tangible outcomes, the main conceptual task of communication within the task-oriented group is to promote optimal use of the component resources of group members (i.e., the "pooling" of resources). The communication practices of "effective" task groups are those that facilitate the coordination of inputs by fostering an organized and collaborative approach to the task. By contrast, the primary function of communication between intimate couples is to preserve and enhance the relationship, which occurs largely through the implicit relationship-defining character of messages (Watzlawick, Beavin, & Jackson, 1967). Given the primacy of relationship-maintenance goals, intimate couples and families are less likely than task groups to press for quality solutions and are more apt to adopt norms against verbalizing disagreements, thus constraining innovation and information sharing (Aldous, 1971). In sum, group studies provide a model of optimal decision making that stresses orderly and explicit management of discussion. A similar model of optimal decision making may also apply to intimate couples. However, a rationalistic model of communication and decision making is less relevant to intimate couples because it cannot describe how couples actually make decisions much of the time.

If couples made decisions the way that effective task groups are thought to make decisions they would set aside a separate time and setting in which to discuss decisions, gather information systematically (e.g., read *Consumer Reports*), organize the discussion so that the generation of alternatives precedes criticism, maintain open channels of communication, tolerate and even encourage idea conflict, continue to evaluate while implementing, and so forth. Although an occasional couple does behave this way, typical decision making is less explicit and organized. For every couple who reads *Consumer Reports* and holds a planning session before buying a new furnace, I suspect that several others impulsively decide that their energy savings justify the monthly payments, after going to the store on an unrelated mission. Naturally, different decisions may invoke different patterns of decision making. For example, an organized and deliberative style of decision making is more likely to be used with decisions of major consequence (e.g., changing jobs, having a child, buying a house), although even these decisions often have a serendipitous element. Overall, the pattern is for couples to fluctuate between an implicit and explicit style of communication, with the implicit style predominating much of the time.

This essay contrasts the implicit, nonreflective forms of interaction found in many examples of couple decision making with the explicit, strategic communication processes found in others. Self-conscious and explicit communication about decisions is seen here as an occasional practice encouraged by specific situational, social, and cultural factors. More often, couples plod through decisions in a spontaneous and incremental fashion because of strenuous demands on time, energy, and other resources. Thus, the topic of communication and dyadic decision making must be viewed broadly, as single-minded attention to explicit discussion of decisions (analogous to the focus on formal meetings in small-group studies) will fail to represent basic properties of decision making. Initially this chapter describes decision-making styles, which range on a continuum from direct, explicit, organized, and proactive to indirect, implicit, impulsive, and incremental. Later, resource demands on intimate relationships that affect decision-making styles are discussed. Lastly, decision-making styles are related to situational and sociocultural factors, such as life stage and traditionalism.

Decision-Making Styles

The observations about implicit decision making in this chapter are partly a consequence of research focusing on communication and marital conflict (Sillars, Pike, Jones, & Redmon, 1983; Sillars, Pike, Jones & Murphy, 1984; Pike & Sillars, 1985; Burggraf & Sillars, 1987; Zietlow & Sillars, in press). In these studies my collegues and I have analyzed recorded conversations between spouses to reveal elements of couples' conflict styles. This research was not designed to assess decision making, yet it has produced some relevant observations. The couples in this research were given discussion topics composed of typical complaints and problem areas in marriage (e.g., inadequate time spent together, lack of affection or attention, disagreements about leisure activities) and were asked to discuss the status of each issue in their own relationship. A surprising outcome of these studies has been the lack of explicit decision-making or problem-solving comments. Although the couples were not specifically told to resolve their conflicts, one would expect some rudimentary efforts to do so once an issue had been raised. Relevant comments would include statements that initiate search for a solution to conflict (i.e., "problem solving"), express behavioral concessions ("concession"), or demand changes by the partner ("hostile imperative"). The content analytic scheme used to code the discussions identified such statements but the categories merely filled a logical niche in the coding system, as only a few examples were observed. Naturally, more explicit decision making would have taken place if we had instructed the couples to resolve disagreements, but this would have inflated the number of decision-making comments beyond normal proportions. This suggests that couples do not engage in much proactive discussion of relationship change unless something out of the ordinary prompts them to do so.

A second notable observation about the discussions was the diversity of couples' conflict styles. Some couples introspectively analyzed their relationship while others joked, obfuscated, pursued tangents, told "white lies," traded insults, and so forth. The patterning of styles also revealed differences between couples, for example, some conversations reflected a single style of conflict while others were characterized by complex cycles and phases (see Sillars, Wilmot, & Hocker, in press). The communication styles and patterns observed in these studies differ along a dimension of engagement versus avoidance of conflict, which has been a focal point of much previous research on communication and interpersonal conflict (see Raush, Barry, Hertel, & Swain, 1974; Sillars & Weisbery, 1987). Increasingly, it appears that engagement is part of an even more general tendency for couples to

Table 8.1. Characteristics of decision-making styles.

Explicit decision making	Implicit decision making
Explicit agreements	Silent arrangements
Prospective awareness	Retrospective awareness
Proactive planning	Incrementalism
Syntactic code usage	Pragmatic code usage
Explicit process management	Implicit process management
Conflict engagement	Conflict avoidance
Mastery orientation	Stoicism

emphasize implicit versus explicit patterns of adjustment and coordination. This is suggested by our investigations into the types of relationships in which engagement and avoidance patterns are observed. Couples who acknowledge and analyze conflict also appear in other respects to be verbal, introspective, and "communication sensitive." Open communication is occasionally such a pivotal value that it pervades every encounter. Couples who do not acknowledge conflict do not see interpersonal communication in the same terms. Relationships may be expected to occur more "naturally" or relationships may evolve from a more verbal state to a point where less effort is expended on explicit communication.

In addition to conflict engagement versus avoidance, explicit versus implicit adjustment is revealed by such things as self-disclosure, elaborated versus truncated linguistic codes, active versus passive problem solving and introspective awareness of communication. Each of these concepts appears to share a common relationship with exogenous variables such as traditionalism (Ellis & Hamilton, 1985; Fitzpatrick, 1983; Scanzoni & Szinovacz, 1980; Sillars & Weisberg, 1987). Two general styles of decision making are suggested by these concepts, one of which is explicit, analytic, proactive, and organized and the other more implicit and less reflective. The two styles are summarized in Table 8.1 and the style subdimensions are discussed in the forthcoming section.

Explicit Agreements and Silent Arrangements

Most obviously, implicit decision processes include "silent arrangements" (Scanzoni & Szinovacz, 1980; Strauss, 1978), which are decisions reached without verbal agreement. Scanzoni and Szinovacz (1980) describe several ways that silent arrangements occur. In the simplest case, silent arrangements reflect the playing out of standards learned from reference groups. This calls to mind traditional sex-role differentiation, for example, the wife does the laundry while the husband barbeques. In other cases these arrangements may reflect cultural norms besides sex roles (e.g., spouses do not take separate vacations) or expectations that partners share because of similar beliefs, backgrounds, and experiences (e.g., two graduate students who allow one another uninterrupted time during the busiest parts of the school year). If two people have the same expectations entering the relationship, then silent arrangements may be completely unconscious, that is, it never dawns upon the couple that they might do things differently. In effect, the decision is in place when the relationship is formed.

Silent arrangements may also evolve over time. For example, a wife might observe her husband's sarcastic grumbling about having to "babysit" on Saturdays. She may then silently conclude that unconventional child-care arrangements, such as having her husband stay home so that she can resume her career, are not a viable option. Explicit disagreements may also evolve into silent arrangements. This is illustrated by a mother who, after strenuously objecting to her daughter's announced intention to use birth control pills, silently agrees not to press the matter further (Scanzoni & Szinovacz, 1980). A silent agreement remains intact until the daughter tests its limits by bringing the boyfriend home to stay overnight (Scanzoni & Szinovacz, p. 111).

In some silent arrangements discussion leads toward but does not actually culminate in explicit agreement. The partners may "feel one another out" about an impending action, but stop short of negotiating the operational details (e.g., discussing a dinner party without agreeing on a time or date). One couple was increasingly confronted by the need to buy a new car. Although they discussed the purchace, no final decision was reached until the husband impulsively bought a car on his own. Despite the apparent arrogance of the husband's action, the wife later commented that she was surprised he had not purchased the car sooner, thus reflecting the fact that implicit consent to the decision had been given.

Finally, many silent arrangements evolve through the setting of implicit precedents. Watzlawick (1976) observes that relationship "rules" (basically, norms governing expected and required behavior) evolve through precedent-setting actions that may involve little or no explicit discussion. Essentially, if one partner initiates a course of action and it continues uncontested, over time the pattern of action and response evolves into an unarticulated relationship rule. Later deviation from the expected pattern is reacted to as if an explicit, agreed-upon decision had been violated. For example, if a husband purchases personal items without consulting the wife and no objections are raised, then he assumes the right to do so in the future. All interaction is said to have this rule-negotiating quality, although the process of rule negotiation gradually recedes into the background if there is no interruption in established patterns.

In a few of the examples we have observed, silent arrangements substitute for explicit agreement because it never occurs to the couple to behave in any manner other than the way they do. In the other cases silent arrangements are labor-saving devices. Silent arrangements are simpler and easier to accomplish generally than explicit agreements. As noted in a later section of this chapter, the sheer number of decisions handled by intimate couples would be overwhelming if explicit agreement was necessary on every matter. Potential decision-making overload is reduced substantially, for example, by treating implicit precedents as if they were explicit agreements. When discussion precedes a decision but does not culminate in explicit agreement (as in the car purchase example), the implicit arrangement circumvents the problem of explicitly negotiating minor operational details of the decision. Of course, glossing over details (e.g., the color of the car) can produce conflict later, but this strategy works well enough if two people think similarly. If two people have different preferences and expectations then "glossing the details" and "acting on implicit consent" will prove to be less adequate strategies. Divergent, free-thinking individuals are probably better off seeking explicit agreement as much as possible; however, the price of explicit agreement is greater time and effort devoted to decision making.

A final reason why silent arrangements may substitute for explicit agreements is that silent assent is a weaker form of agreement. On occasion, only a weaker form of agreement is possible to achieve. In the earlier example of the daughter using birth control pills, the silent arrangement allows the relationship to continue despite irreconcilable differences on an extremely divisive issue. By refusing to agree to the behavior but allowing it nonetheless, the mother is able to reach a middle-ground position that is consistent with her own values and responsive to the daughter's desire for decision-making autonomy.

While there is always a risk that partners will misperceive silent arrangements, it does not follow that explicit agreements are always clearer than silent arrangements. Surprisingly, there does not seem to be a strong association between explicit discussion and mutual understanding (Sillars, in press). Two studies (Sillars, Pike, Jones, & Murphy, 1984) found no relation between how much spouses disclosed and exchanged information about marital conflicts and how well they understood the other's feelings with respect to the same issues. Understanding appeared to be based more on internal cues (i.e., projection of one's own feelings to the spouse) and nonverbal communication (i.e., paralinguistic affect). Another study focusing on selective memory of conversations (Sillars, Weisberg, Burggraf, & Zietlow, 1987) found that recall of disclosive and informational statements by the spouse was related to understanding of the spouse's "instrumental" attitudes (i.e., attitudes pertaining to work, money, household tasks, and leisure activities) but not to more abstract and relational attitudes (pertaining to affection, irritability, togetherness, and communication). Finally, a study of life-stage differences in marital communication (Zietlow, 1986) revealed that elderly couples disclosed less and "projected" more than young couples; yet their understanding of one another was about the same. These studies suggest that silent arrangements are not inherently obscure. In fact, silent arrangements are sometimes as well understood as explicit agreements. This is most likely to be the case when two people are very similar or they share similar stereotypes about intimate relationships (e.g., "traditional" views of marriage), thereby allowing individuals to understand the partner on the basis of internal cues (i.e., self-perceptions and stereotypes).

Prospective/Retrospective Awareness

When couples engage in discussion with the clear goal of making a decision, their awareness of decision making is prospective. Retrospective awareness, on the other hand, occurs when couples do not self-consciously view themselves as making decisions except after the fact (Weick, 1971). Prospective awareness and explicit agreement are intuitively linked, since explicit agreement obviously requires explicit attention to issues. To some authors it is a contradiction of terms to speak of "unconscious decision making." Etzioni (1968, p. 251), for instance, would prefer to reserve the phrase "decision making" for a conscious choice between alternatives and to treat unconscious choice as something entirely different. However, it is not always clear what should count as a conscious choice. Although some decisions are obviously conscious ones and others are unconscious (note the discussion of silent arrangements), much of the decision making of couples involves partial awareness of the decision process. This stems from the fact that the decision making of couples tends to be embedded within and interrupted by other activities that compete for attention (Weick, 1971). Decision making occurs during meals, shopping trips, television shows, and trips to the laundromat. Only occasionally is couple decision making temporally isolated from other activities and managed as a separate event. Further, these other activities tend to be the dominant focus. Decision making may be only a brief phase within the larger sequence of activities (e.g., shopping) or it may be spontaneously elicited by something within the situation (e.g., a television show that sparks discussion of vacation plans). Although decision making of this sort is neither completely unconscious nor implicit, the dominant activity in the situation will often distract from, interrupt, and terminate conscious reflection about any decisions entailed. Thus, typical decision making may be prospective, but only in a weak sense.

On a theoretical level, the phenomena of prospective/retrospective awareness relate to the multifunctionality of communication. Messages may simultaneously accomplish several goals, for example, to impart information, manage impressions, express feelings, persuade, resolve conflict, regulate intimacy, or impart a sense of coherence to the conversation (Patterson, 1983; Street & Cappella, 1985). All of these functions are involved to some extent in decision making; however, prospective awareness of decision making occurs only to the extent that the decision itself is a salient goal. Since messages may accomplish several things simultaneously, the goals that are salient or problematic determine what aspects of the situation are monitored directly. Thus, couples seldom self-consciously view their actions as decision making, since other goals tend to be more immediate. Decisions may still emerge from encounters where decision making is not the primary goal; however, awareness of the decision will be more retrospective than prospective. This situation is especially likely to characterize routine decisions. During difficult decisions that provoke conflict or decisions that are not satisfactorily resolved, decision making becomes a more salient and consciously monitored goal. Members of the relationship are then more likely to be aware of the process through which a decision was reached (Aldous, 1971).

Proactive/Incremental Planning

Human decision making is said to be a blend of rationalist planning and muddling through changes in small increments (see Janis & Mann, 1977). Couples appear to do a great deal of muddling through. This might be reflected, for example, in a tendency to plan the budget a few purchases at a time, to buy on impulse, to make decisions at the last possible moment, or to incrementally commit to something (e.g., the decision to marry) through a succession of small steps (Janis & Mann, 1977). Deciding on impulse and drifting into decisions incrementally is not unique to couples. For example, policy groups often make decisions incrementally (Braybrooke & Lindblom, 1963; Janis & Mann, 1977), although sometimes for different reasons (i.e., among policy groups the need to make political compromises may prevent long-range planning). Incrementalism among couples is related to the factors previously mentioned, that is, much of the decision making of couples takes place with limited explicit communication or direct attention to the decision process. These factors are conducive to "spur-of-the-moment" decisions. Poole and Doelger (1986, p. 59) point out that when individuals share a clear, prospective understanding of a decision-making task, future steps are apt to be proactive and organized. When images of the task are unclear, incomplete, or fragmented, then decision making tends to occur in an "inchworm" (incremental) fashion. This sort of decision making occurs without a "master plan" and is collectively defined after the fact.

Even when decisions are highly salient, couples may not have the facility to recognize and account for all of the factors that impinge upon a decision. This is illustrated by the experiences of couples when buying a house. This particular decision may foster a great deal of explicit communication and prospective awareness because it is such a monumental investment for most couples. Thus, in an effort to proactively organize the decision, a couple may carefully establish criteria that the investment must satisfy (e.g., energy efficiency, a particular number of bathrooms, the absolute top amount they can spend) but end up buying a house, which, although it fails many of the explicit criteria, is suited to the self-identity of the couple and the style of life they fantasize having. The front porch and mature trees may touch a nostalgic desire for traditional family life or conveniences, such as an electric garage door opener and microwave oven, may appeal to their desire for an efficient and uncomplicated home life. Although very important to satisfaction with a decision, such considerations are not easily understood or articulated, so they may be neglected when criteria for the decision are laid down in advance.

Because they are difficult to articulate, subjective criteria for decisions are subject to much disagreement and misunderstanding. For example, the individual members of a couple may develop proactive decision plans but have difficulty systematically reconciling these to form a joint plan (Park, 1982). Park's (1982) research shows that individual members of home-buying couples can articulate a decision plan that specifies necessary or preferred attributes and trade-offs that would lead to a purchase offer. However, the decision plans of different spouses do not show a high degree of overlap and do not converge over time. As one would expect, there is less similarity with respect to subjective decision criteria (e.g., appearance, location, interior design) than with easily objectifiable criteria (e.g., number of bedrooms, age of home, central air conditioning). Disagreement is compounded by misunderstanding, for spouses tend to assume that their decision plans are similar (Park, 1982). There is comparable evidence outside the strict domain of decision making that spouses chronically overestimate similarity with the partner, particularly with respect to abstract versus concrete judgments (see Sillars, in press; Sillars & Scott, 1983). According to Park (1982), the lack of convergence among spouses' decision plans is evidence that couples do not maximize joint utilities (i.e., shared interests). Instead, they reconcile individual utilities using simple heuristics that minimize conflict and decision-making effort, for example, they seek agreement on easily objectified criteria first, they focus more on undesirable qualities in a house than on positive attributes, and they yield on criteria where the other person has stronger feelings or more expertise. The result, as Park notes, is a disjointed process of muddling through that exceeds couples' comprehension.

In some respects, cultural views of intimate relationships give license to spontaneous decision making. Some decisions, such as the decision to be together, are thought to suffer from too much rationality. Contemporary American society regards romantic love as the only truly acceptable reason for marriage (Gadlin, 1977) and "falling in love" is believed to be an intuitive and inexplicable matter, as suggested by the widely cited objections of U.S. Senator Proxmire to funding of research on romantic love (e.g., Knapp, 1984). While "falling in love" is the clearest example of relational decision criteria outweighing instrumental criteria, it is not the only such instance. Spontaneous decisions that bring unexpected rewards (e.g., a spur-of-the-moment purchase or trip) can break stale routines and endear individuals to one another more than well planned-out decisions (Aldous, 1971). Thus, Hill (1970) found that family consumer decisions were more personally satisfying when *less* carefully planned out.

Syntactic/Pragmatic Code Usage

A more implicit style of communication has a number of manifestations that extends beyond decision negotiation. Meanings generally may be relatively explicit in talk or implicit in context, silent arrangements being a special illustration of the latter. Further, the style of decision making should overlap with more pervasive communicative tendencies. As the previous discussion has noted, decision making is embedded within daily activities and it generally lacks a distinct beginning and end. Thus, the extent to which couples directly talk about and explicitly plan decisions should correspond with their construction of fully explicit messages in general.

Ellis and Hamilton (1985) suggest that diverse features of language are interrelated elements of more or less explicit linguistic codes. Building on the work of Bernstein (1975) and others, Ellis and Hamilton suggest that linguistic codes are more or less explicit and fully elaborated depending on the clarity of role expectations in a relationship. In a traditional marriage there are clearer guidelines for understanding the other person based on conventional role expectations. Consequently, there is less need to talk and the talk that does occur "does more work," for example, a few words may substitute for a complete sentence. These relationships are characterized by use of a "pragmatic" (versus "syntactic") code, in which much of the meaning is implicit in context. In the syntactic code, characteristic of nontraditional relationships, linguistic relations are more explicit and individual experience is more differentiated and fully elaborated. In the research reported by Ellis and Hamilton (1985), nontraditional married couples, in comparison with traditional couples, had greater use of personal reference ("I" words), more linguistic elaboration (uncommon adjective, nouns, descriptive adjectives, adverbs), greater structural complexity (subordinate clauses), more disfluency (indicative of verbal planning), more explicit cohesion relations (i.e., repetition, paraphrasing, and other devices that connect one utterance with another), and a more consistent utterance length (rather than many brief utterances and a few long ones). We will return to the discussion of traditionalism in a later section of this chapter, although the critical variable here is not traditionalism per se, but similarity of expectations. The implication of Ellis and Hamilton's research is that couples will adopt verbal shortcuts as permitted by similarity of expectations. When personal experiences are extensively shared then an explicit code is unnecessary, so communication is more efficient and less redundant. To the extent that individual experience is more private and unique, then a more explicit, elaborated, and effortful form of communication must take place.

Ellis and Hamilton's (1985) discussion of pragmatic and syntactic codes stresses the structural aspects of language (syntactic features and the like). Although more difficult to interpret, communication also has implicit *content*, which Hopper (1981) refers to as the "taken for granted." The taken-for-granted component refers to "messages not actualized in physical speech, but nevertheless understood in-common (or at least thought to be so understood) by the senders and receivers of the talk" (Hopper, p. 196). Taken-for-granted meaning within couples may be revealed by an inside joke, a nonverbal mannerism that reveals impending conflict, or a terse reference to a problem neighbor that provokes a stream of images and memories (Reiss, 1981, p. 178). Conversations that are high in taken-for-granted meaning are described by Hall (1977) as "high (versus low) context transactions." In a high context transaction much of the information is in the receiver and context and only minimal information is explicitly coded within the transmitted message. Low context transactions are the opposite. Within a high context transaction even silence may have a clear and specialized meaning depending on the context. In one context silence may indicate a refusal to go along with or even legitimize a request (e.g., as when one person "disconfirms" another; see Watzlawick, et al., 1967). In another context, silence may indicate consent, as in the case of some silent arrangements. Naturally, intimate couples tend to behave more like high context communication systems than say, strangers or acquaintances, because of the opportunity for intense bonding and sharing of intimate experiences over time. Again, however, couples vary a great deal. In some relationships, messages are truncated and highly efficient; in others, meanings are more fully and explicitly coded in talk to make up for a lack of spontaneous consensus.

Explicit/Implicit Process Management

A fifth contrast is between decision making that involves explicit management of the process of discussion and decision making that is guided by implicit rules only. At one extreme is the situation where there is an explicitly agreed upon set of procedures, that is, a formal "script" that may specify a time and place for discussion, leadership responsibilities, participation rules (e.g., parlimentary procedure), formal decision schemes (e.g., authority rule, majority vote), and so forth. Generally this calls to mind institutional decision making, although there are analogues within personal relationships, for example, the family that holds regular meetings according to the "family council" concept. More often, explicit process management among couples occurs in the form of explicit (i.e., verbal) metacommunication, for example, talking about the need to make a decision, clarifying intentions and meanings, commenting on the partner's nonverbal expression, and so forth. Such comments are frequent, yet vastly more metacommunication takes place at an implicit level, and some couples rely on implicit metacommunication almost exclusively.

The distinction between explicit and implicit metacommunication stems from the work of interactional communication theorists (see Raush, Grief, & Nugent, 1979; Wilder, 1979; Watzlawick et al., 1967). One foundation of interactional theory is the idea that all messages have both propositional content and relational meaning, the latter being a heavily contextual, implicit statement about how the interpersonal relationship is to be construed (e.g., as dominant or submissive, close or distant). Parallel distinctions are found elsewhere, for example, the concepts of "presentational" (Danziger, 1976), "illocutionary" (Searle, 1969), and "episodic" (Frentz & Farrell, 1976) meaning all allude to the implicit code that clarifies the social significance of language actions being performed (e.g., whether an utterance constitutes a request for information or a command; whether the previous speaker's comments are accepted, rejected, or disconfirmed). The implicit code is the primary vehicle through which couples resolve relationship issues, such as who has the right to make what decisions.

Explicit metacommunication will occur with greater frequency in either of two instances. First, couples who are more aware of, reflective about, and concerned with the process of communication will tend to engage in more explicit metacommunication. General sensitivity to interpersonal communication may reflect social science education, enrichment training, or the general emphasis on communication within society (see Kidd, 1975). In this case, explicit process management should overlap closely with the other facets of an explicit decision-making style, including explicit agreement, prospective awareness, syntactic code usage, and proactive planning.

The second situation in which metacommunication becomes more explicit is when there are fundamental disagreements about communication rules. Explicit metacommunication in this case is a sign of relationship trouble; it results from a failure of the implicit code (Watzlawick, et al., 1967). When explicit metacommunication is a consequence of conflict over communication rules then the correspondence between explicit process management and explicit decision making is unclear. Conflictive couples may even have a relatively implicit style of overall decision making. They may fruitlessly work at relabeling and redirecting the discussion while the lack of fundamental consensus blocks explicit agreement, disrupts proactive planning, and encourages fight-flight patterns of conflict (Raush et al., 1974; Sillars et al., in press). Thus, explicit process management may or may not reflect explicit decision making generally, depending on the factors responsible for explicit metacommunication (i.e., sensitivity to communication versus conflict over communication rules).

Engagement/Avoidance of Conflict

Although not synonymous, the areas of decision making and conflict are very close. Needless to say, decisions frequently entail conflict. Further, just as decision making may be more or less explicit, communication about conflict may be more or less direct. Explicit decision making is parallel to an engagement style of conflict where conflict issues are directly verbalized. Similarly, some silent arrangements (e.g., an agreement not to discuss an issue) very clearly represent avoidance of conflict (Scanzoni & Szinovacz, 1980). Of course, some implicit arrangements do not indicate conflict avoidance;

they are simply a less verbal mode of interaction. Similarly, conflict styles range on a continuum from maximally direct (i.e., threats and insults) to maximally indirect (i.e., outright denial of conflict). Between these extremes there are many variants, for example, people may partially acknowledge conflicts and partially obscure or deny them (e.g., by joking, intellectualizing, or speaking in contradictions). Thus, conflict styles are one further indication of how explicit two people are in addressing relationship issues.

The basic communicative moves during conflict are summarized by a category scheme presented in Table 8.2. This scheme was developed as a research tool for coding communication during interpersonal and marital conflict. Of the conflict styles identified in Table 8.2, "confrontive" and "analytic" remarks are the clearest examples of engagement styles. "Denial and equivocation," "topic management," and "noncommittal" remarks are nonengagement patterns, whereas "irreverent" and "conciliatory" styles are more ambiguous with respect to engagement. The term "style" refers here to the nature of communication at a particular moment, not to the enduring tendencies of an individual. Although some couples may use one style almost exclusively (Sillars, et al., in press), most couples use a variety of styles and often interchange them in rapid succession. The styles are briefly discussed below in order of increasing directness.

Denial and equivocation refers to statements that either directly deny the existence of a conflict, imply that there is no conflict, or present an evasive, self-invalidating response. Denial, really a form of lying, is the most blatant instance of conflict avoidance. Evasive remarks occur when one person asks a question or makes a statement about the existence of conflict and the other person responds ambiguously. Evasive remarks are related to the concept of "disqualification." Disqualification is the creation of a message that invalidates itself through obscurity (Watzlawick et al., 1967; Bavelas, 1983). The message may be vague, ambiguous, or paradoxical, thus providing an unclear statement about the interpersonal relationship. Disqualifying remarks mostly occur when people see themselves in "bind" (i.e., an approach-avoidance conflict). When given a choice between the awkward truth (e.g., "I don't like the gift you gave me and I am going to return it"), an outright lie (e.g., "The gift is perfect, I really love it,"), and a disqualifying response (e.g., "I appreciate your thoughtfulness") people usually say that they would choose the latter (Bavelas, 1983). *Topic management* is a further way of limiting explicit conflict. This includes topic changes that circumvent or terminate discussion as it begins to center on items of conflict.

Somewhere in between clear examples of avoidance and engagement are remarks that neither deny nor acknowledge conflict issues. *Noncommittal* remarks may take a variety of forms, including unfocused questions (e.g., "What do you think?"), abstract or vague generalities (e.g., "Nothing in life that is worthwhile comes easily"), "intellectualizing" (e.g., "The deeper the issue the more yourself is threatened"), discussion of friends, acquaintances, and relatives ("Mom always said that marriage is hard work"), procedural

Table 8.2. Summary of conflict codes.

Conflict codes	Illustrations
A. Denial and equivocation	
1. *Direct denial.* Statements that deny that a conflict is present.	"That's not a problem."
2. *Implicit denial.* Statements that imply denial by providing a rationale for a denial statement, although the denial is not explicit.	"We've never had enough money to disagree over." (In response to a question about disagreements over money.)
3. *Evasive remarks.* Failure to acknowledge or deny the presence of a conflict following a statement or inquiry about the conflict by the partner.	"That could be something that a person might resent but I don't know."
B. Topic management	
4. *Topic shifts.* Statements that terminate discussion of a conflict issue before each person has fully expressed an opinion or before the discussion has reached a sense of completion.	"Okay, the next issue is ..." (The preceding statement occurs before each person has disclosed his or her opinion on the topic.)
5. *Topic avoidance.* Statements that explicitly terminate discussion of a conflict issue before it has been fully discussed.	"I don't want to talk about that." "This isn't getting us anywhere. Let's move on."
C. Noncommittal remarks	
6. *Noncommittal statements.* Statements that neither affirm nor deny the presence of conflict and that are not evasive replies or topic shifts.	"The kids are growing up so fast, I can't believe it."
7. *Noncommittal questions.* Unfocused and conflict-irrelevant questions.	"What do you think?" "Was it last summer we went to Maine?" "All people are irritable sometimes."
8. *Abstract remarks.* Abstract principles, generalizations, or hypothetical statements that are not evasive remarks.	
9. *Procedural remarks.* Procedural statements that supplant discussion of conflict.	"It's your turn to talk." "You aren't speaking loud enough."
D. Irreverent remarks	
10. *Friendly joking.* Friendly joking or laughter.	"We need to clean the house or torch it [stated in a friendly tone of voice]."
E. Conciliatory remarks	
11. *Supportive remarks.* Statements that refer to understanding, support, acceptance, positive regard for the partner, shared interests and goals, compatibilities with the partner, or strengths of the relationship.	"I can see why you would be upset." "You don't stay irritable long."
12. *Concessions.* Statements that express a willingness to change, show flexibility, make concessions, or consider mutually acceptable solutions to conflicts.	"I think I could work on that more." "I think we have a good chance of working this out."

Table 8.2. (*continued*)

Conflict codes	Illustrations
13. *Acceptance of responsibility.* Statements that attribute responsibility for conflict to self or to both parties.	"I think we've both contributed to the problem." "Okay. that one's my fault, I guess."
F. Analytic Remarks	
14. *Descriptive statements.* Nonevaluative statements about observable events related to conflict.	"I criticized you yesterday for getting angry with the kids."
15. *Disclosive statements.* Nonevaluative statements about events related to conflict that the partner cannot observe, such as thoughts, feelings, intentions, motivations, and past history.	"I swear I never had such a bad week as that week." "I didn't think we'd be able to talk about the kids without yelling."
16. *Qualifying statements.* Statements that explicitly qualify the nature and extent of conflict.	"Communication is mainly a problem when we're tired."
17. *Soliciting disclosure.* Nonhostile questions about events related to conflict that cannot be observed (thoughts, feelings, intentions, motives, or past history).	"What were you thinking when you said ..."
18. *Soliciting criticism.* Nonhostile questions soliciting criticism of oneself.	"Does it bother you when I stay up late?"
G. Confrontative Remarks.	
19. *Personal criticism.* Remarks that directly criticize the personal characteristics or behaviors of the partner.	"Sometimes you leave and you don't say goodbye or anything. You just walk right out." "I can't believe you let that one incident ruin our whole evening."
20. *Rejection.* Statements in response to the partner's previous statements that imply personal antagonism toward the partner as well as	"Oh come on." "You're exaggerating."
21. *Hostile imperatives.* Requests, demands, arguments, threats, or other prescriptive statements that implicitly blame the partner and seek change in the partner's behavior.	"If you're not willing to look for a new job then don't complain to me about it."
22. *Hostile jokes.* Joking, teasing or sarcasm at the expense of the partner.	"Its very easy to say, 'Gee I *really* appreciate you'" [said mockingly].
23. *Hostile questions.* Directive or leading questions that fault the partner.	"Who does most of the cleaning around here?"
24. *Presumptive remarks.* Statements that attribute thoughts, feelings, motivations, or behaviors to the partner that the partner does not acknowledge.	"You're purposefully making yourself miserable."
25. *Denial of responsibility.* Statements that minimize or deny personal responsibility for conflict.	"That's not my fault." "You can't blame me for everything."

comments about the process of discussion ("You'll have to speak up so that I can hear you"), and other forms of abstract, vague, or tangential discussion. All of these styles put psychological and emotional distance between the person and the conflict issue without actually denying or directly evading it. In some contexts noncommittal remarks may be seen as acts of conflict avoidance. Shifting the level of abstraction, for example, is one way that individuals can avoid conflict without seeming to ignore an issue altogether. However, noncommittal remarks may also be used to express conflict cautiously and indirectly and, in other instances, such remarks are simply a reflection of what is on the speaker's mind at the moment.

Irreverence is not within the traditional focus of research on conflict and related topics such as decision making or problem solving. Generally we assume that these topics are serious matters. Weick (1971) wryly notes that subjects recruited to be in studies of problem solving or conflict occasionally fail to grasp the seriousness of the situation and play with the researcher's well-designed instructions. One interpretation is that these individuals have gone outside the boundaries of the research and are performing something other than conflict. On the other hand, humor can also be construed as a basic conflict management strategy. As Weick point out, levity enables individuals to redefine "problems" as "annoyances," which are dealt with more easily and with less fretting. Recognizing the absurd element in an absurd situation improves one's response to it, whereas taking the situation too seriously produces a maladaptive response (Weick, 1971, p. 18). Humor is not a clear instance of avoidance or engagement as it potentially serves several roles. Some individuals use humor to manage tension and to work through conflicts in a less threatening way. On the other hand, lampooning an idea is one form of tangential response, so humor is sometimes linked to conflict avoidance. Humor can also be verbally competitive and abusive as in the case of the biting sort of humor that we identify under the confrontive style (i.e., hostile joking).

Conciliatory remarks are statements that seek reconciliation, for example, through concessions, compliments, statements empathizing with the partner's feelings or point of view, or statements acknowledging the speaker's own contribution to the conflict. These are essentially relationship repair messages that are the direct counterpart of demands, criticism, ridicule, and accusations. Conciliatory remarks represent a more direct style of conflict than other styles considered thus far, as conciliation generally implies that the existence of a conflict has been acknowledged. Still, conciliation is primarily aimed at relationship repair. It does not necessarily lead to a direct discussion of the content issues at hand, particularly if a person concedes simply to end further consideration of the conflict. Kilmann and Thomas (1975) describe conciliatory behavior (i.e., "accommodation") as a cooperative but nonassertive style of conflict, which is similar in the latter respect to conflict avoidance. Conciliatory messages can also be a form of "passive resistance," as in the case where one partner admits guilt without any commitment to change (i.e., "You're right, I'm no damn good").

The obvious alternative to avoidance and confrontation is to *analyze* the conflict from a collaborative standpoint. Behaviors affiliated with this style include self-disclosure and descriptive statements of a nonevaluative nature, nonhostile questions soliciting information from the other party, statements that explain, "document," or qualify general feelings and observations, and suggestions that are presented for mutual consideration without the speaker assuming a strong advocacy role. As the term "analytic" implies, the essence of this style is to give and seek information in the interests of coming to a better understanding of the issues. The analytic style is naturally aligned with the cultural metaphor of communication as "work" (as in "working on one's relationship" or "working out difficulties"), which is associated with expressive norms for communication (Katriel & Phillipsen, 1981).

Virtually all communication texts and training programs encourage individuals to practice some version of the analytic style, assuming it to be the most underdeveloped and underutilized style for many individuals. Married couples have utilized this style as much as 43% percent of the time in one study and as little as 16% percent in another. Across four samples of married couples, the rate of analytic (sometimes called "informational") remarks has averaged 25%, which compares with an average of 25% confrontive remarks (also called "distributive"), 8% conciliatory remarks (also called "supportive"), and 42% for the combination of various forms of avoidance, indirect or noncommittal statements, and humor (Sillars et al. 1983; Burggraf & Sillars, 1987; Zietlow & Sillars, in press). These figures suggest that, although couples use the analytic style of communication frequently, it is far from the primary style in most cases.

Confrontive remarks refer to the type of verbally competitive acts that we most associate with hostile, abusive, and destructive conflicts, that is, criticism, demands, hostile jokes and questions, denial of responsibility, "mind reading," and so forth. Although confrontive remarks are maximally expressive, they are embedded within overall patterns that may or not be highly explicit. Most confrontive exchanges we have observed are very brief. In some relationships, confrontive comments are interspersed with analytic and irreverent remarks (Zietlow & Sillars, in press). This is perhaps the modal form of conflict engagement among basically compatible couples. The overall pattern is expressive and somewhat intense but escalation sequences are counterbalanced by positive forms of engagement. On the other hand, dissatisfied couples often vacillate between confrontive and avoidance remarks in a "hit-and-run" manner (Pike & sillars, 1985; Raush et al., 1974). Complaints are expressed, but not in the context of a sustained attempt to air relationship issues. Thus, this pattern in not indicative of a generally explicit style of interaction.

All of the conflict styles described above refer to verbal behavior. There are even more implicit forms of conflict that are nonverbal, for example, swallowing pride, suppressing feeling, or walking away. While the styles we have considered presume that there is some verbal communication, the styles are more or less explicit in relation to a particular issue. When confronted with a situation that virtually requires overt communication, couples nonetheless demonstrate a broad repertoire of strategies for obscuring, avoiding, or softening the issue. Some couples in some situations, however, are quite explicit in negotiating the terms of their relationship. These tend to be couples who are more "communication-sensitive" in general (Sillars et al., 1983).

Mastery Orientation/Stoicism

The final contrast refers to two opposite ways that people may respond to problems. That is, they may accept the problem (stoicism) or attack it (mastery). Mastery, being the more overt response, requires more explicit communication between decision-making partners. Stoicism is an individual response that often substitutes for explicit problem solving. A mastery orientation is more responsive to sources of information and other cues originating in the external environment. Mastery may also result in a tendency to initiate change within the relationship (i.e., the "work" metaphor).

Stoic and mastery orientation reflect different interpretation of interpersonal competencies in relation to the environment. Mastery is the interpersonal counterpart of psychological locus of control (Rotter, 1966). A mastery orientation assumes that people are able to control and change their situation, whereas a stoic orientation is fatalistic. Stoic individuals may assume that some aspects of life are beyond their control or that the effort and other costs required to change situations are excessive. Stoicism also implies lower standards for satisfaction, that is, the attitude that one can make do with less. Thus, some issues that are seen as problems to solve given a mastery orientation (e.g., not going out on the town often enough) may not be identified as problems from a stoic value system. Stoic values naturally lead to an emphasis on relationship maintenance functions of interaction over problem-solving functions. Respect, consideration, and conformity are apt to be valued and expressivity is likely to be devalued under a stoic orientation.

The above comments are partly based on Reiss' (1971, 1981) description of family problem-solving styles. Reiss observed that certain families, referred to as "environment-sensitive," view problems as intellectual challenges. These families delay closure until all the available evidence has been examined and arrive at solutions through the sharing of ideas. Intellectual conflict may be welcomed by such families. Other families (labeled "consensus-sensitive") view problems as a threat to internal cohesion. These families emphasize agreement over optimal problem solving. Similarly, McLeod and Chaffee (1972) identify one family type ("pluralistic") that values open expression and critical thought over agreement, and another family type ("consensual") with the opposite priorities. Blue-collar families and many ethnic groups tend to be consensus-sensitive and stoic (Komarovsky, 1962; McGoldrick, 1982; Rubin, 1976; Sillars & Weisberg, 1987). White-collar families are more likely to adopt an activist approach to problem solving that leads to explicit discussion and negotiation.

Either stoicism or active problem solving may be a functional pattern in a given situation. Although biting one's lip is clearly not the best response to all problems, it is equally evident that: (1) not all problems can be solved, (2) some problems are not worth the effort it takes to solve them [Watzlawick, Weakland, & Fisch (1974) refer to the latter as "irritations" rather than "problems"], and (3) some problems are made worse by focusing on and communicating about them. Problems that stem from unemployment, sex discrimination, personality disorders, ill health, basic incompatibility, and so forth may be beyond the practical control of individuals. The problems that couples and families can resolve are often ones that are less important (Aldous, 1971). Therefore, stoicism may represent the most adaptive response to some situations. Indeed, we found in a recent study (Sillars, Weisberg, Burggraf, & Wilson, 1987) that satisfied married couples often demonstrated an attitude of stoicism in their comments to one another, whereas less satisfied couples were more likely to become mired in extended conversation about individual personalities and roles.

Thus far I have suggested that several aspects of communication and decision making reflect a general contrast between implicit and explicit decision processes. Implicit functioning is reflected in silent arrangements, limited awareness and planning of decisions, implicit process management, taken-for-granted meaning, nonengagement modes of conflict, and stoicism. The forthcoming section provides a theoretical account of the factors that elicit implicit functioning. These factors include characteristics that intimate relationships tend to share (e.g., problematic resource allocation) and factors that vary among types and stages of intimacy (i.e., stability and homogeneity).

Eliciting Conditions

Some of the factors that lead to implicit decision making apply to most couples. These considerations help to account for differences between the way couples and other social groups make decisions. The hypothesis offered here is that the decision-making resources of couples (i.e., expertise, time, energy) are often inadequate in relation to the potential demands on these resources. This creates a problem of decision overload that, although not done intentionally, is managed by use of implicit forms of adjustment. Implicit decision making is the baseline pattern, as it represents the path of least effort. Explicit decision making, on the other hand, occurs when implicit adjustment does not occur smoothly.

Other influences on decision making reflect the nature of particular relationships. Especially germane to implicit and explicit styles of decision making are the stability and homogeneity of relationships. In the forthcoming section, general demands on decision-making resources within intimate couples are first considered, then the factors that influence decision making within different types of couples are discussed.

Resources and Demands

Decision overload is a significant factor for intimate couples, as couples typically make do with fewer resources (i.e., time, energy, expertise) while processing a greater number and variety of issues than other decision-making bodies. Naturally, the adequacy of decision making in classic terms is a function of the fit between resources and demands (number and variety of decisions). To the extent that more decisions are processed with fewer resources, each decision will be given less careful consideration and shortcut strategies will be adopted that circumvent explicit, organized decision making. Because of the pressing need to dispense with decisions quickly and move on to other business, couples may be more concerned with lowering immediate tensions to a comfortable level than with comprehensively analyzing decision options (Aldous, 1971; Janis & Mann, 1977). An exception to this may occur among couples who have a favorable balance between resources and demands (e.g., an affluent and highly educated couple without children) and can therefore isolate and attend to individual decisions more adequately.

The vast number and variety of decisions made by couples is a consequence of relationship *breadth*, that is, the tendency of intimate relationships to embrace a wide spectrum of topics deemed mutually relevant (Altman & Taylor, 1973). Thus, the focus of decision making is diffuse. Couples must coordinate with respect to careers, children, sex, money, television shows, breakfast cereals, drapes, and so forth. In addition to these issues that are more recognizable as decisions, there are also less tangible and more abstract decisions concerning the structure of the relationship (e.g., who has the right under what conditions to make a particular decision). Decisions about the structure of the relationship are a part of all interpersonal or group interactions, but they are especially salient within intimate couples because of the intensity and longevity of relations and because of the lack of formal rules limiting decision making, such as those found in institutional contexts (e.g., formal role responsibilities, lines of authority, decision schemes). Among intimate couples all procedural matters are open to negotiation, being constrained only by implicitly accepted cultural standards insofar as these apply (e.g., traditional gender roles). In sum, intimate couples make innumerable decisions covering substantive (e.g., where to go at Christmas) as well as procedural issues (e.g., how to decide where to go at Christmas). Each such issue can be clearly and carefully deliberated only to the extent that decision-making resources are adequate.

Decision-making resources consist of expertise (i.e., knowledge and skill), time, and energy. The breadth of decision making by couples has an obvious consequence concerning expertise. Couples cannot be expected to have adequate expertise about every important decision, particularly decisions involving specialized or technical competence (e.g., buying mutual funds, hiring a contractor, caring for an infant). Some major life decision points (e.g., having a child, changing careers, buying and/or selling a house) saturate couples with demands for technical competence in legal, economic, sociological, and other matters. Other decisions, for example, placing a child in day care, choosing a mechanic, or buying a refrigerator, do not demand technical expertise as much as basic information about the available choices. Nonetheless, the information must be acquired through an investment of time and energy. Finally, optimal decision making places a demand on couples for "process" expertise, that is, communication and negotiation competencies. These skills are difficult to define because of their highly situational nature, but they appear to include behavioral flexibility, perspective-taking ability, and interaction management skill (Argyle, 1969; Spitzberg & Cupach, 1984; Wiemann, 1977). Paradoxically but understandably, the attributes that contribute to process competence are at low ebb during stressful events, when decisions are often of the greatest consequence (Janis & Mann, 1977; Schroder, Driver, & Streufert, 1967).

The second resource, time, is taxed by the sheer abundance of decisions within couples, in combination with numerous competing and overlapping activities. Work, recreation, personal and household maintenance, and sleep constitute a full schedule for most couples. Couples with school-age children are particularly said to suffer from a "time-crunch" because the outside activities of children increasingly add to an already full agenda (Harry, 1976; Rollins & Galligan, 1978). Adding to the problematic allocation of time for decision making is the fact that decision making within couples tends to be embedded within other activities. Thus, time is split between decision making and one or more additional activities that tend to be at the center of attention.

A special instance of split attention occurs due to the confounding of content and relationship issues within communication. Concerns over abstract relational issues (e.g., dominance and autonomy in the relationship) are played out through the discussion of specific surface issues (e.g., who should cook dinner). Since a few basic relational issues may lie behind numerous specific content issues, fundamental disagreements about core relationship issues may have a "rippling" effect, causing conflict over many peripheral issues (Altman & Taylor, 1973; Watzlawick et al., 1967). Communication in the absence of fundamental consensus about the relationship will tend to lack topical coherence or continuity (Sillars & Weisberg, 1987; Sillars et al., in press) and may reflect "cross-complaining" (Gottman, 1979), where complaints by one person bring forth new, unrelated complaints from the partner. Needless to say, dyadic decision making in this environment is chaotic.

There are several further consequences of the fact that decision making within couples competes and overlaps with other activities. First, because of the distracting effects of competing activities, decision making frequently occurs spontaneously with little information gathering, critical idea testing, or strategic management (note the earlier discussion of awareness and planning). Second, the decision making of couples may lack continuity, since it is initiated when stimulated by events in the situation and terminated as the situation shifts or becomes too hectic. The more that different events are crowded together in time and space, the less continuity can be expected in decision making. The focus of attention may also drift owing to a lack of explicit process management and to the way a variety of issues may be called forth successively by the same situation (as in the case of cross-complaining). For example, getting the kids off to school may bring up decisions about bedtime, breadfast, laundry, work schedules, evening activities, and so forth. Third, more stressful situations provoke more decision making, as crises bring decisions to the forefront. Naturally, optimal decision making becomes more difficult as a crisis becomes more immediate (see Janis & Mann, 1977). Fourth, different individuals will tend to focus on different decisions. Particular issues (e.g., whether to get the couch re-upholstered or to attend a couples' enrichment workshop) are often of greater interest to one partner than to the other. Consequently, when one person perceives a need for immediate discussion of a decision, the other will often regard the situation as inappropriate or find more pressing business elsewhere in the situation.

The final resource, energy, is something that may be in short supply among couples because their greatest abundance of energy is expended either outside of the relationship (e.g., at work, school, aerobics, Kiwanis, Cub Scouts) or within the relationship on routine maintenance tasks (e.g., cleaning, cooking, repairing, remodeling, recreating, disciplining, and educating). Social scientists fail to show much sensitivity to this factor as the many social competencies that couples are urged to acquire (e.g., political competencies, parenting skills, television viewership skills, conflict-management skills) all require an investment of energy beyond routine functioning. If there is an implicit ideal family in the social science literature, it is the Newbolds, one of five families in Hess and Handel's (1959) classic analysis of family life. Energy in this family is an inexhaustible reservoir, as suggested by the mother's account of a typical day:

We get up. That hour before the older boy goes to school is one split. Getting everything done, getting breakfast, checking on books, being sure they have warm enough clothing ... Then straighten up the kitchen and leave the house about ten for some civic job. I never leave without the house being in good order—beds made. Also the phone has rung at least five times in that hour. Some of the messages will have to be cared for right away.

I try to get home for lunch with Curt. Afternoon it's either civic responsibilities or something here: ordinary housework, serving, marketing, or cooking. There's always somebody dropping in for coffee. Then it's three and the children come home. They talk constantly about their day. Then the boys go to the club or some-thing ... Then it's dinner ... everybody has something to say. Always something in-teresting. I sometimes wish there weren't so many things going on. Father goes back to the office. Boys straighten up the kitchen and do homework and then bed.

After the house is quiet and everybody's in bed I do some desk work and wait for Mr. Newbold to come home ... There are nights when I have to go out to dinner—dinner meetings, mostly. On those days I plan to have things in the oven, and the boys can handle it from there on" (pp. 187–188).

The abundance of energy and variety reflected in the Newbold's daily routine contrasts with the experience of many couples who feel "spent" after devoting the better part of the day to career and household tasks. This suggests another contrast with the organized task group. As Weick (1971) points out, task groups typically address decisions at a time when their mental facilities are most lucid. Couples and families make decisions mostly at times when their energy level is lowest, that is, early or late in the day.

Since a large number and variety of issues compete for limited expertise, time, and energy, decision shortcuts are apt to be used when applicable. These shortcuts correspond to implicit decision processes.

Stability and Homogeneity

Communication becomes more implicit and less conscious to the extent that background assumptions are in alignment. Highly implicit transactions are limited to more homogeneous and stable social relationships where the shared experiences of individuals allow them to fill in considerable taken-for-granted meaning. For example, among "closed" groups who share similar values, persuasive arguments tend to have a telegraphic quality in the sense that important premises and conclusions are omitted but are nonetheless understood (Hart, 1984). Similarly, members of some non-Western cultural groups, such as the Japanese, rely less on explicitly stated meaning and more on implicit, contextual meaning than the typical American (Gudykunst & Nishida, 1984; Ting-Toomey, 1985). This is apparently tied to the fact that Japanese society reinforces uniformity of unstated values and assumptions.

In Western society, intimate relationships promote uniformity of experi-ence as much as any social arrangement. Extensive sharing of personal ex-periences during relationship development (Altman & Taylor, 1973) and screening out of dissimilar others during mate selection (Duck, 1977; Ker-ckhoff & Davis, 1962) fosters homogeneity and leads to implicit, idio-syncratic, and efficient forms of communication (Bell, Buerkel-Rothfuss, & Gore, 1987; Cushman & Whiting, 1972; Hopper, Knapp, & Scott, 1981; Knapp, 1984). The stability of intimate relationships also impacts decision making. The divorce rate notwithstanding, marital relationships often last much of a person's life span. The sheer repetitiveness of interactions encour-ages less conscious and explicit decision making (i.e., redundant interactions will tend to become "scripted" or "mindless"; see Langer, 1978).

While all couples utilize some forms of implicit decision making, the variation among couples is considerable. To some extent, this variation is situational. Any disruption in routine interaction, such as individual maturation or crisis, will promote more explicit and reflective forms of interaction. Watzlawick et al. (1967, p. 52) speak of explicit relationship communication as a symptom of relationship trouble, since relationship issues are taken for granted unless there is conflict. Similarly, Reiss (1981) sees the emergence of explicit rules as an initial stage in family disorganization. The ability to function implicitly is an indicator of family organization, according to Reiss. During stressful events, families lose their repertoire of background understandings, assumptions, traditions, secrets, and rituals that previously made it possible to function implicitly. Implicit functioning is replaced by the setting of explicit rules, discussion of unclear events, and explicit planning and monitoring. The family becomes preoccupied with itself and, at least temporarily, becomes like a collection of individuals (Reiss, 1981, p. 184). Emergence of the explicit family may be initiated by benign and temporary disruptions in daily routines, such as the family vacation, or it may be the intitial phase leading to complete reorganization or breakup of the family in response to a deep crisis. The family's preoccupation with itself may be maladaptive in some respects, for example, the proliferation of explicit rules can become overbearing and tyrannical. However, the emergence of explicit functioning may also lead to new insights that contain the "seeds of healing" (Reiss, 1981, p. 184).

While most couples become more explicit during times of confusion or crisis, there are also persevering differences between couples and families. Some relationships foster stability and homogeneity, other relationships promote uncertainty, change, and individuality. Relationships of the latter type have more need for explicit negotiation and conscious monitoring of interactions. These relationships also have less ability to function implicitly. The pertinent differences in the definition of intimacy are related to sociocultural factors, including traditionalism, social network, life stage, and remarriage following divorce.

Traditionalism

Historians note that modern society's concept of intimacy is pluralistic (Gadlin, 1977; Hareven, 1982). Traditional relationships have not been replaced as much as they have been supplemented. The characteristics of traditional relationships include conventionality, togetherness, temporal regularity, and a preference for stability in the relationship over uncertainty and change (Fitzpatrick, 1983; 1984). There is also less need for explicit communication among traditional couples because conventional role expectations constrain behavior and clarify many issues (Spiegel, 1960). Role expectations may be taken for granted and never consciously analyzed (Scanzoni & Szinovacz, 1980). Thus, traditional couples are not likely to analyze and verbalize relationship issues to the same extent as nontraditional couples.

Traditional role orientations constrain outcomes, divide decision-making domains, and determine which issues are to be individually versus mutually decided. This is not simply a matter of the male subjugating the female in all decision making, as some traditional wives are submissive whereas others are not (Scanzoni & Szinovacz, 1980). Rather, decision-making authority is divided along sex-stereotypic lines, with the wife having primary authority over within-home tasks and the husband having responsibility for out-of-home tasks. For example, American wives tend to be more responsible for decisions regarding furniture, groceries, and family health care, whereas husbands are more responsible for car and life insurance (Childers & Ferrell, 1981; Green, Verhage, & Cunningham, 1981). This segregation of roles reduces the effort that must be expended negotiating decisions through delegation of decision making to individuals (Spiegel, 1960).

Traditional couples are to be contrasted with other couple types, such as the "independent" and "separate" couples described by Fitzpatrick (1983, 1984). Separate couples are similar to traditionals in the respect that they maintain separate roles and have stereotyped views of male and female behavior. However, the coordination of separate spouses is based less on traditional marital ideology than it is on individual autonomy. Separates lack the clear marital ideology, consensus, and close coordination of roles found in traditional couples. Autonomous decision making pervades the separate relationship.

The independent relationship is both interdependent and nontraditional. These couples are highly communicative. Whereas the stable and conventional roles of traditional couples limit the need for explicit decision making, independents place a high value on uncertainty, novelty, and change, which virtually requires frequent discussion and explicit negotiation of the relationship. Independents have many issues to resolve with few a priori guidelines for doing so. Every small matter (e.g., how to arrange the furniture or shop for auto parts) is potentially a joint decision, so there are many sources of conflict. However, negotiation of every detail is not necessarily implied. Independents may also establish some degree of role segregation, although along less stereotypic lines than traditional couples. For example, the husband may do all of the cooking and shopping and the wife may file tax returns. Although a nonconventional arrangement such as this must be negotiated at some point, it eventually serves the same function as traditional sex-role differentiation, which is to economize the time and energy devoted to decision making.

Research on communication within couple types has confirmed that independents have a more explicit style of interaction than traditional and separate couples. In comparison to traditional couples, independents use a more elaborated linguistic code with explicit syntactic relations (Ellis & Hamilton, 1985), they have more explicit cohesion relations linking speaking turns (Ellis & Hamilton, 1985; Sillars et al., 1987), which is partly indicative of explicit process management, and they adopt a more direct, engagement style of conflict (Burggraf & Sillars, 1987). Of the three couple types, independents are the most disclosive during casual conversations (Fitzpatrick, Vance, & Witteman, 1984) and they refer most often to the external environment during conflict discussions (Sillars et al., 1987), which may indicate a mastery orientation. In contrast, the content themes of traditional couples indicate a stoic view of marital conflicts (Sillars et al., 1987).

Traditionals show an interesting tendency to contradict themselves as far as conflict engagement is concerned. Traditional couples do not describe themselves as conflict avoiders on self-report scales (Fitzpatrick, 1983). However, they behave like conflict avoiders when their conversations are being recorded (Burggraf & Sillars, 1987; Sillars et al., 1983), perhaps because of an overriding concern for tactfulness and discretion in communication (Fitzpatrick, 1983). Independents are less apt to censor themselves because they believe open communication to be of fundamental importance. Both self-report and observational studies indicate that independents are highly communicative and direct in addressing conflict issues (Fitzpatrick, 1983; Burggraf & Sillars, 1987).

Unlike either traditional or independent couples, separates think of themselves as conflict avoiders. Avoidance of conflict is consistent with the premise of high individual autonomy in these relationships. In actual conversations, separates use topic management to avoid conflict (Sillars et al., 1983) and they speak less than other couples (Fitzpatrick, Fallis, & Vance, 1982; Fitzpatrick et al., 1984), although they are also confrontive at other moments (Burggraf & Sillars, 1987). In this particular case, the confrontation probably occurred because the research situation encouraged more explicit discussion of conflict than separate couples are accustomed to.

We have seen that the role of communication is substantially different in traditional and "separate" relationships than in the more "growth-oriented" view of intimacy (i.e., independent couples). In the former, adjustment is presumed to happen implicitly. Extensive negotiation is, therefore, symptomatic of a breakdown in the underlying, implicit consensus. In contrast, couples following the independent pattern are more disposed to incorporate explicit negotiation into their normal style of interacting.

Network Influences

Bott's (1971) distinction between "segregated-role" and "joint-role" couples parallels the traditional and independent couple types. As the name suggests, segregated-role couples have conventional, sex-linked roles. Joint-role couples are more egalitarian, communicative, and self-reflective. Bott assumes that these traits are an outgrowth of the social network characteristics of each couple type. Segregated role arrangements are most common in highly stable and interconnected communities, such as many rural, working-class, and ethnic neighborhoods. Joint-role arrangements are more common among highly mobile individuals, such as urban professionals, whose social network ties are more loose-knit. When social network ties are extensive, extended family, neighbors, and friends support and stabilize intimate relationships (Reiss, 1981). The network becomes a source of companionship (especially through close relationships between individual spouses and same-sex parents or friends), instrumental support (e.g., babysitting and the like), and crisis support (see Albrecht & Adelman, 1987; Eggert, 1987). The social network also has a homogenizing effect, as networks promote communal and conventional social norms (Bott, 1971; Gadlin, 1977). As a consequence, extensive social networks tend to foster conformist (Cohler & Geyer, 1982), sex-role stereotypic (Bott, 1971; Richards, 1980; Spiegel, 1982), and homogeneous (Cohler & Geyer, 1982; Oliveri & Reiss, 1982) relationships. As with traditional couples generally, there is less need for explicit negotiation within such relationships because much decision making takes place implicitly.

The opposite is true of joint-role couples. These couples are more autonomous from the surrounding community, indeed they may jealously guard their privacy and resent intrusions of outsiders into their affairs. With the lesser influence of outsiders comes greater freedom and uniqueness but, again, this comes at the price of decision-making effort and ambiguity. As in the case of the independent couple type, there are more issues to resolve and fewer a priori guidelines for resolving them. Consequently, joint-role couples should engage in more self-conscious and explicit communication about decisions relative to segregated role couples.

Life Stage

Most studies of couple communication are studies of young couples. The few studies that include a broad spectrum of age and life stages indicate some intriguing differences between younger and older couples. Young couples are the most disclosive, self-analytic, and argumentative of couples in different life stages. Young spouses report higher self-disclosure to their mate (Jourard, 1971; Swenson, Eskew, & Kohlhepp, 1981) and they engage in more direct discussion of conflict issues (Zietlow & Sillars, in press). Late life stage couples, such as "empty nest" (i.e., parents whose grown children have left home) and retired couples, are passive and inexpressive by comparison, although their understanding of one another is about the same as among young couples (Zietlow, 1986) and they tend to express higher marital satisfaction than couples at any stage past the newlywed period (Anderson, Russell, & Schum, 1983; Sporakowski & Hughston, 1978). The expressivity of young couples reflects explicit negotiation of the relationship while the relative passivity of older couples shows a tendency to rely on implicit consensus primarily. Middle-aged couples are harder to characterize but they tend to fall between extreme expressivity and passivity (Zietlow & Sillars, in press).

It is difficult to say exactly what accounts for life-stage differences in expressivity, since there are at least three plausible explanations. The three explanations refer to (1) cohort differences in perceptions of interpersonal communication, (2) reduced stress and conflict during later life stages, and (3) intrinsic developmental processes (i.e., the natural evolution of communication patterns over time). Cohort effects are important here primarily because they coincide with different cultural perceptions of intimacy. Assuming that older couples are more influenced by pre-1960s popular culture, they are less likely to value self-disclosure and open expression of conflict in marriage than younger couples (Ellis, 1979; Kidd, 1975; Knapp, 1984). As in the case of traditional- and segregated-role couples, earlier concepts of intimacy were predicated on conformity to clear role standards, whereas the contemporary vision of intimacy emphasizes the dynamic nature of relationships and the need for open communication. Young couples are, therefore, more apt to be enculturated within a view of intimacy that emphasizes the value of explicit negotiation.

Marital stress at different points in the life cycle is greatly affected by children. Among couples with children, marital stress and conflict tends to center on child-raising issues and activities. Apparently, this accounts for the finding that older couples, whose children have matured, are relatively harmonious and satisfied. Marital satisfaction is high among newlywed and childless couples, but it subsequently declines to a low point at either the preschool 2nd school-age child-rearing stages (Anderson et al., 1983; Burr, 1970; Medling & McCarrey, 1981; Miller, 1976; Terman, 1938), the launching stage (Bernard, 1934; Rollins & Feldman, 1970), or the empty-nest stage (Gurin, Veroff, & Feld, 1960; Rollins & Feldman, 1970) before increasing into retirement. Naturally, not all elderly couples are highly satisfied. Those with a high-quality marriage appear to experience a decline in satisfaction during child rearing and then bounce back, whereas low-quality marriages stay low (Ade-Ridder & Brubaker, 1983). The presence of children proliferates the number of decisions and potential conflicts, for example, decisions involving day care, ballet lessons, bedtime, curfew, and delinquency are added to those that childless couples face. Decisions are also made more complex and difficult as the number of competing interests and preferences affected by family decisions increases (e.g., dining options must be expanded to include *McDonalds* and *Burger King*). Although their perceived influence is less than parents, parents acknowledge that children affect decisions, such as when to go on vacation and where to stay (Filiatrault & Ritchie, 1980). Further, because children progress through developmental changes more rapidly than adults, they add instability to family relationships. Children create a need to absorb new activities periodically into the family calender and to adjust decision making as children become more competent, autonomous, and assertive. Thus, the presence of children forces many issues to the surface. Although this encourages more explicit couple communication, it does not necessarily lead to organized and proactive decision making, because couples with children may particularly suffer from decision overload.

Developmental processes include the sheer amount and repetitiveness of communication over time, leading to increasingly efficient, unconscious, and implicit communication. Older spouses tend to have more similar personal goals than young spouses (Atchley & Miller, 1983) and they rely more on personal intuition (i.e., the "projection" phenomena spoken of earlier) as a means of understanding the partner (Sillars, in press; Zietlow, 1986). Young couples require more explicit negotiation simply because their relationships are at less advanced stages of development. Although older couples may rely on implicit adjustment primarily, crises, conflicts, and life-stage transitions temporarily alter implicit patterns. Transitions in the life cycle, such as the children leaving home or the onset of retirement, disrupt daily routines and force adaptation to new circumstances. The couple may face decisions they have not faced previously, such as how to spend additional time subsequent to retirement. In addition, marital roles may shift as a function of personal changes that accompany life-cycle transitions. For example, the change in daily routines subsequent to retirement promotes a softening of sex-typed behavior, particularly for husbands (Blood & Wolfe, 1960; Gutmann, 1975; Lieberman, 1978; Treas, 1975; Zietlow, 1986; Zube, 1982). Explicit and self-reflective decision making is apt to reemerge during such periods when marital roles are recalibrated.

Although older couples tend to be harmonious, there is also some indication that these couples have less flexible communication patterns (Illig, 1977; Zietlow & Sillars, in press). The elderly in one study enacted one extreme pattern of behavior or another, that is, either no acknowledgement of conflict whatsoever or constant bickering (Zietlow & Sillars, in press). There was little indication, as was the case among young and middle-aged couples, of elderly spouses shifting in and out of a problem-focused, analytic style of discussion. Elderly couples seem inclined to diffuse potential conflicts by making individual adjustments to the other spouse. However, when there are serious, persistent conflicts in the marriage, these couples sometimes lack an adequate repertoire of alternative strategies for expressing conflict without provoking an escalatory spiral or conflict avoidance.

Remarried Couples

Remarried couples are described as more self-conscious, less spontaneous, and more apt to engage in explicit negotiation in comparison with intact married couples (Duberman, 1975; Kompara, 1980; Rosenbaum & Rosenbaum, 1978; Visher & Visher, 1978; Walker & Messinger, 1979; Weisberg, 1983). Several factors appear responsible. Most obviously, the dramatic role transitions associated with divorce and remarriage create intense introspection about relationship processes. Weiss (1975) observes that divorced and separated spouses may be consumed by questions about "what went wrong." Their retrospective accounts seem partly motivated by a desire to construct predictability out of chaos and thereby avoid future mistakes (Weiss, 1975). The experience of a previous divorce may create hyper-sensitivity to relational conflicts. For example, disagreements are more quickly seen as a prelude to divorce rather than simple bickering (Asmundson, 1981). In contrast, the experiences of intact couples are less tumultuous, more stable, and more continuous, so monitoring of the relationship may subside with time.

Although personal crisis and reorganization is, at least initially, the dominant influence on remarried couples, other factors may continue to affect decision making even after reorganization has been achieved. First, remarried couples tend to be more heterogeneous in age, religion, and education (Dean & Gurak, 1978) and less traditional (Duberman, 1975; Messinger, Walker, & Freeman, 1978) than intact couples. Consequently, there is less foundation for spontaneous consensus and more need to explicitly communicate. Traditionalism may decline because of personal reorientations that individuals go through following divorce. Women tend to see themselves as more independent and desirous of an egalitarian relationship, whereas men see themselves as more nurturing following divorce (Messinger et al., 1978). Thus, roles are more achieved and less ascribed in remarried couples (Walker & Messinger, 1979).

A second continuing influence on remarried couples is the reduced impact of social networks. Divorce tends to disrupt social networks, since friends who previously interacted as couples must now relate to one another as individuals (Weiss, 1975). Thus, remarried men and women report fewer friends outside the marriage (White, 1979). When children are involved, divorce and remarriage complicates interaction with extended family, for example, holiday visits may be coordinated with as many as four sets of grandparents. Since extensive social network ties have a homogenizing and stabilizing influence on marital roles, the weakening of these ties may further promote explicit rule negotiation.

Third, step-parent arrangements may complicate reintegration of the family unit, thus providing a continuing impetus for explicit rule setting and negotiation of family decisions. Characteristic problems within blended families include coalition formation between children and biological parents, conflicts over parental authority, and conflicts involving the relationship of the ex-spouse to the family (Asmundson, 1981; Duberman, 1975; Messinger, 1976). The obvious conflicts involving children in blended families are aggravated by the sudden formation of new parental and sibling bonds without the opportunity for gradual adjustment that exists in intact families. As a result of such factors, decision making will tend to require much explicit attention and effort from remarried couples, since implicit forms of adjustment will often be inapplicable or inadequate.

Summary and Conclusion

Beyond the infinitely complex variations in the way individual couples make decisions, resolve conflicts, and communicate generally, there appear to be some broad similarities. To the extent that conditions permit, couples rely less on effortful, explicit, and reflective forms of adjustment. From this perspective, styles of decision making are but one consequence of more or less efficient and implicit communication. More implicit adjustment is revealed in several areas, for example, silent arrangements, retrospective awareness, incrementalism, taken-for-granted meaning, implicit process management, conflict avoidance, and stoicism. Silent arrangements may tend to be conservative (i.e., it is difficult to conceive of radically new roles evolving implicitly) but no less adequate than explicit agreement in some other respects.

Implicit forms of adjustment are possible due to the homogeneity of most intimate relationships, along with the opportunity for efficient communication to develop over time. Implicit or marginally explicit decision making is further encouraged by the fact that decision resources (expertise, time, energy) often do not stack up well against demands (i.e., the abundance and breadth of potential decisions), thus presenting a need to dispense with issues quickly and move on to other business. Decision making overlaps and competes with other goals and activities, which draws attention away from decision making as an event in its own right. In some cases implicit or impulsive decisions result from relationship maintenance goals taking precedence over content issues, for example, spouses may yield to the partner with stronger feelings or make spur-of-the-moment decisions that bring unexpected rewards and build affection. In general then, decision making and communication can be characterized as indirect, implicit, nonreflective, and incremental, verus direct, explicit, self-reflective and proactive, with couples operating toward the former end of the continuum much of the time.

A highly explicit style of decision making occurs in response to certain relational conditions. These conditions include instability, heterogeneity, and sensitivity to communication processes. Although largely situational, these variables also reflect broad, enduring characteristics of relationships. All couples will tend to become more explicit when undergoing transitions or crises, but some relationships establish a higher base rate of change. These relationships, for example, the "independent" prototype, also have more expressive norms for communication and (probably) more extensive monitoring of the relationship, because implicit consensus is not assured. Traditional and stable relational forms, on the other hand, have less need for explicit negotiation.

The main implication of this chapter is that dyadic decisions are only partly mainfested in explicit thought and talk. Decisions may be systematically deliberated and consummated in explicit agreement or they may evolve by partly unspoken and mysterious means. Either pattern potentially says a great deal about the nature of relationships and the role of interpersonal communication therein.

References

Ade-Ridder, L. A., & Brubaker, T. H. (1983). The quality of long-term marriages. In T. H. Brubaker (Ed.), *Family relationships later in life*. Beverly Hills: Sage.

Albrecht, T. L., & Adelman, M. B. (1987). *Communicating social support*. Newbury Park, CA: Sage.

Aldous, J. (1971). A framework for the analysis of family problem solving. In J. Aldous, T. Condon, R. Hill, M. Straus, & I. Tallman (Eds.), *Family problem solving: A symposium on theoretical, methodological, and substantive concerns*. Hinsdale, IL: The Dryden Press.

Altman, I., & Taylor, D. (1973). *Social penetration*. New York: Holt, Rinehart & Winston.

Anderson, S. A., Russell, C. S., & Schumm, W. R. (1983). Perceived marital quality and family life-cycle categories: A further analysis. *Journal of Marriage and the Family, 45*, 127–139.

Argyle, M. (1969). *Social interaction*. Chicago: Aldine.

Asmundson, R. (1981). Blended families: One plus one equals more than two. In C. Getty & W. Humphreys (Eds.), *Understanding the family: Stress and change in American family life*. New York: Appleton-Century-Crofts.

Atchley, R. C. & Miller, S. J. (1983). Types of elderly couples. In T. H. Brubaker (Ed.), *Family relationships in later life*. Beverly Hills: Sage.

Bavelas, J. B. (1983). Situations that lead to disqualification. *Human Communication Research, 9*, 130–145.

Bell, R. A., Buerkel-Rothfuss, N. L., & Gore, K. E. (1987). "Did you bring the yarmulke for the cabbage patch kid?": The idiomatic communication of young lovers. *Human Communication Research, 14*, 47–67.

Bernard, J. (1934). Factors in the distribution of success in marriage. *American Journal of Sociology, 40*, 49–60.

Bernstein, B. (1975). *Class, codes and control* (Vol. 3). London: Routledge & Kegan Paul.

Blood, R. O., & Wolfe, D. M. (1960). *Husbands and wives: The dynamics of married living*. Glencoe, IL: Free Press.

Bott, E. (1971). *Family and social network*. New York: The Free Press.

Braybrooke, D., & Lindblom, C. E. (1963). *A strategy of decision: Policy evaluation as a social process*. New York: The Free Press.

Burggraf, C. S., & Sillars, A. L. (1987). A critical examination of sex differences in marital communication. *Communication Monographs, 54*, 276–294.

Burr, W. R. (1970). Satisfaction with various aspects of marriage over the life cycle sample. *Journal of Marriage and the Family, 26*, 29–37.

Childers, T. L., & Ferrell, O. C. (1981). Husband-wife decision making in purchasing and renewing auto insurance. *The Journal of Risk and Insurance, 48*, 482–492.

Cohler, B., & Geyer, S. (1982). Psychological autonomy and interdependence within the family. In F. Walsh (Ed.), *Normal family processes*. New York: Guidion.

Cushman, D., & Whiting, G. C. (1972). An approach to communication theory: Toward consensus on rules. *The Journal of Communication, 22*, 217–236.

Danziger, K. (1976). *Interpersonal communication*. New York: Pergamon.

Dean, G., & Gurak, D. (1978). Marital homogamy the second time around. *Journal of Marriage and the Family, 40*, 559–570.

Duberman, L. (1975). *The reconstituted family: A study of remarried couples and their children.* Chicago: Nelson-Hall.

Duck, S. W. (1977). *The study of acquaintance.* Farnborough: Gower.

Eggert, L. L. (1987). Support in family ties: Stress, coping, and adaptation. In T. L. Albrecht & M. B. Adelman (Eds.), *Communicating social support.* Newbury Park, CA: Sage.

Ellis, D. A. (1979). *Til' divorce do us part: Communication descriptions and prescriptions in popular magazines, 1968–1978.* Unpublished master's thesis, Purdue University Lafayette, IN.

Ellis, D., & Hamilton, M. (1985). Syntactic and pragmatic code choice in interpersonal communication. *Communication Monographs, 52*, 264–278.

Etzioni, A. (1968). *The active society: A theory of societal and political processes.* New York: The Free Press.

Filiatrault, P., & Ritchie, J. R. B. (1980). Joint purchasing decisions: A comparison of influence structure in family and couple decision-making units. *Journal of Consumer Research, 7*, 131–140.

Fitzpatrick, M. A. (1983). Predicting couples' communication from couples' self-reports. In R. N. Bostrom (Ed.), *Communication yearbook 7.* Beverly Hills: Sage.

Fitzpatrick, M. A. (1984). A typological approach to marital interaction: Recent theory and research. In L. Berkowitz (Ed.), *Advances in experimental social psychology.* New York: Academic Press.

Fitzpatrick, M. A., Fallis, S., & Vance, L. (1982). Multi-functional coding of conflict resolution strategies. *Family Relations, 31*, 611–670.

Fitzpatrick, M. A., Vance, L. E., & Witteman, H. (1984). Interpersonal communication in the casual interaction of marital partners. *Journal of Language and Social Psychology, 3*, 81–95.

Frentz, T. S., & Farrell, T. B. (1976). Language-action: A paradigm for communication. *Quarterly Journal of Speech, 62*, 333–349.

Gadlin, H. (1977). Private lives and public order: A critical view of the history of intimate relations in the United States. In G. Levinger & H. Raush (Eds.), *Close relationships: Perspectives on the meaning of intimacy.* Amherst: University of Massachusetts Press.

Gottman, J. M. (1979). *Marital interaction: Experimental investigations.* New York: Academic Press.

Green, R. T., Verhage, B. J., & Cunningham, I. C. M. (1981). Household purchasing decisions: How do American and Dutch consumers differ? *European Journal of Marketing, 15*, 68–77.

Gudykunst, W. B., & Nishida, T. (1984). Individual and cultural influences on uncertainty reduction. *Human Communication Research, 51*, 23–36.

Gurin, G., Veroff, J., & Feld, S. (1960). *Americans view their mental health.* Basic Books: New York.

Gutmann, D. L. (1975). Parenthood: Key to the comparative psychology of the life cycle? In N. Datan & L. Ginsberg (Eds.), *Life span developmental psychology.* New York: Academic Press.

Hall, E. T. (1977). *Beyond culture.* Garden City, NY: Anchor.

Hareven, T. K. (1982). American families in transition: Historical perspectives on change. In F. Walsh (Ed.), *Normal family processes.* New York: Guidion.

Harry, J. (1976). Evolving sources of happiness for men over the life cycle: A structural analysis. *Journal of Marriage and the Family, 38*, 289–296.

Hart, R. P. (1984). Communication and the maintenance of public values. In C. C. Arnold & J. W. Bowers (Eds.), *Handbook of rhetorical and communication theory*. Boston: Allyn and Bacon.

Hess, R. D., & Handel, G. (1959). *Family worlds: A psychosocial approach to family life*. Chicago: University of Chicago Press.

Hill, R. (1970). *Family development in three generations: A longitudinal study of changing family patterns of planning and achievement*. Boston: Shenkman & Co.

Hopper, R. (1981). The taken-for-granted. *Human Communication Research, 7*, 195–211.

Hopper, R., Knapp, M. L., & Scott, L. (1981). Couples' personal idioms: Exploring intimate talk. *Journal of Communication, 37*, 23–33.

Illig, D. P. (1977). *Distributional structure, sequential structure, multivariate information analysis, and models of communicative patterns of elderly and young, married and friendship dyads in problem-solving situations*. Unpublished doctoral dissertation, Pennsylvania State University, University Park, PA.

Janis, I. L., & Mann, L. (1977). *Decision making: A psychological analysis of conflict, choice and commitment*. New York: Free Press.

Jourard, S. M. (1971). *Self-disclosure: An experimental analysis of the transparent self*. New York: John Wiley.

Katriel, T., & Phillipsen, G. (1981). "What we need is communication": "Communication" as a cultural category in some American speech. *Communication Monographs, 48*, 301–317.

Kerckhoff, A. C., & Davis, K. E. (1962). Value consensus and need complementarity in mate selection. *American Sociological Review, 27*, 295–303.

Kidd, V. (1975). Happily ever after and other relationship styles: Advice on interpersonal relations in popular magazines, 1951–1973. *Quarterly Journal of Speech, 61*, 31–39.

Kilmann, R., & Thomas, K. (1975). Interpersonal conflict-handling behavior as a function of Jungian personality dimensions. *Psychological Reports, 37*, 971–980.

Komarovsky, M. (1962). *Blue-collar marriage*. New York: Random House.

Kompara, D. R. (1980). Difficulties in the socialization process of stepparenting. *Family Relations, 29*, 69–73.

Knapp, M. L. (1984). *Interpersonal communication and human relationships*. Boston: Allyn & Bacon.

Langer, E. (1978). Rethinking the role of thought in social interaction. In J. H. Harvey, W. J. Ickes, & R. F. Kidd (Eds.), *New directions in attribution research*, (Vol. 2). Hillsdale, NJ: Lawrence Erlbaum.

Lieberman, M. A. (1978). Social and psychology determinants of adaptation. *International Journal of Aging and Human Development, 9*, 115–126.

McGoldrick, M. (1982). Normal families: An ethnic perspective. In F. Walsh (Ed.), *Normal family processes*. New York: Guilford Press.

McLeod, J. M., & Chaffee, S. H. (1972). The construction of social reality. In J. T. Tedeschi (Ed.), *The social influence processes*. Chicago: Aldine-Atherton.

Medling, J. M., & McCarrey, M. (1981). Marital adjustment over segments of the family life cycle: The issue of spouses value similarity. *Journal of Marriage and the Family, 43*, 196–203.

Messinger, L. (1976). Remarriage between divorced people with children from previous marriages: A proposal for preparation for remarriage. *Journal of Marriage and Family Counseling, 2,* 193–200.

Messinger, L., Walker, K. M., & Freeman, S. J. (1978). Preparation for remarriage following divorce: The use of group techniques. *American Journal of Orthopsychiatry, 48,* 263–272.

Miller, B. C. (1976). A multivariate developmental model of marital satisfaction. *Journal of Marriage and the Family, 38,* 643–657.

Oliveri, M. E., & Reiss, D. (1982). Family styles of construing the social environment: A perspective on variation among nonclinical families. In F. Walsh (Ed.), *Normal familiy processes.* New York: Guilford Press.

Park, C. W. (1982). Joint decisions in home purchasing: A muddling-through process. *Journal of Consumer Research, 9,* 151–162.

Patterson, M. L. (1983). *Nonverbal behavior: A functional perspective.* New York: Springer-Verlag.

Pike, G. R., & Sillars, A. L. (1985). Reciprocity of marital communication. *Journal of Social and Personal Relationships, 2,* 303–324.

Poole, M. S., & Doelger, J. A. (1986). Developmental processes in group decision-making. In R. Y. Hirokawa & M. S. Poole (Eds.), *Communication and group decision-making.* Beverly Hills, CA: Sage.

Raush, H. L., Barry, W. A., Hertel, R. K., & Swain, M. A. (1974). *Communication and conflict in marriage.* San Francisco, CA: Jossey-Bass.

Raush, H. L., Greif, A. C., & Nugent, J. (1979). Communication in couples and families. In W. R. Burr, R. Hill, F. I. Nye, & I. L. Reiss (Eds.), *Contemporary theories about the family* (Vol. 1). New York: The Free Press.

Reiss, D. (1971). Varieties of consensual experience 1. *Family Process, 10,* 1–27.

Reiss, D. (1981). *The family's construction of reality.* Cambridge, MA: Harvard University Press.

Richards, E. F. (1980). Network ties, kin ties, and marital role organization: Bott's hypothesis reconsidered. *Journal of Comparative Family Studies, 11,* 139–151.

Rollins, B. C., & Feldman, H. (1970). Marital satisfaction over the family life cycle. *Journal of Marriage and the Family, 32,* 20–28.

Rollins, B. C., & Galligan, R. (1978). The developing child and marital satisfaction of parents. In R. M. Lerner & G. B. Spanier (Eds.), *Child influences on marital and family interaction: A life-span perspective.* New York: Academic.

Rosenbaum, J., & Rosenbaum, V. (1978). *Stepparenting.* New York: E. P. Dutton.

Rotter, J. B. (1966). Generalized expectancies for internal versus external control of reinforcement. *Psychological Monographs, 80* (1, whole No. 609).

Rubin, L. B. (1976). *Worlds of pain: Life in the working class family.* New York: Basic Books.

Schroder, H. M., Driver, M. J., & Streufert, S. (1967). *Human information processing: Individuals and groups functioning in complex social situations.* New York: Holt, Rinehart & Winston.

Scanzoni, J., & Szinovacz, M. (1980). *Family decision-making: A developmental sex role model.* Beverly Hills: Sage.

Searle, J. R. (1969). *Speech acts.* London: Cambridge University Press.

Sillars, A. L. (in press). Communication, uncertainty and understanding in marriage. In B. Dervin, L. Grossberg, B. O'Keefe, & E. Wartella (Eds.), *Rethinking communication: Vol. 2. Paradigm exemplars.* Newbury Park, CA: Sage.

Sillars, A. L., Pike, G. R., Jones, T. S., & Murphy, M. A. (1984). Communication and understanding in marriage. *Human Communication Research*, *3*, 317–350.

Sillars, A. L., Pike, G. R., Jones, T. S., & Redmon, K. (1983). Communication and conflict in marriage. In R. Bostrom (Ed.), *Communication yearbook 7*. Beverly Hills: Sage.

Sillars, A. L., & Scott, M. D. (1983). Interpersonal perception between intimates: An integrative review. *Human Communication Research*, *10*, 153–176.

Sillars, A. L., & Weisberg, J. (1987). Conflict as a social skill. In M. E. Roloff & G. R. Miller (Eds.), *Interpersonal processes: New directions in communication research*. Newbury Park, CA: Sage.

Sillars, A. L., Weisberg, J., Burggraf, C. S., & Wilson, E. A. (1987). Content themes in marital conversations. *Human Communication Research*, *13*, 495–528.

Sillars, A. L., Weisberg, J., Burggraf, C. S., & Zietlow, P. H. (1987). *Communication and understanding revisited*. Unpublished manuscript, University of Montana, Missoula, MT.

Sillars, A. L., Wilmot, W. W., & Hocker, J. L. (in press). Communication strategies in conflict and mediation. In J. Wiemann & J. A. Daly (Eds.), *Communicating strategically: Strategies in interpersonal communication*. Hillsdale, NJ: Erlbaum.

Spiegel, J. (1960). The resolution of role conflict within the family. In N. W. Bell & E. F. Vogel (Eds.), *A modern introduction to the family*. New York: The Free Press.

Spiegel, J. (1982). An ecological model of ethnic families. In M. McGoldrick, J. K. Pearce, & J. Giordano (Eds.), *Ethnicity and family therapy*. New York: Guilford Press.

Spitzberg, B. H., & Cupach, W. R. (1984). *Interpersonal communication competence*. Beverly Hills, CA: Sage.

Sporakowski, M. J., & Hughston, G. A. (1978). Prescriptions for a happy marriage: Adjustments and satisfactions of couples married for 50 or more years. *The Family Coordinator*, *27*, 321–328.

Steiner, I. D. (1972). *Group process and productivity*. New York: Academic Press.

Strauss, A. (1978). *Negotiations: Varieties, contexts, processes and social order*. San Francisco: Jossey-Bass.

Street, R. L., & Cappella, J. N. (1985). *Sequence and pattern in communicative behaviour*. London: Edward Arnold.

Swenson, C. H., Eskew, R. W., & Kohlhepp, K. A. (1981). Stage of family life cycle, ego development, and the marriage relationship. *Journal of Marriage and the Family*, *43*, 841–853.

Terman, L. M. (1938). *Psychological factors in marital happiness*. McGraw-Hill: New York.

Ting-Toomey, S. (1985). Toward a theory of conflict and culture. In W. Gudykunst, L. Stewart, & S. Ting-Toomey (Eds.), *Culture and organizational processes: Conflict, negotiation and decision-making*. Newbury Park, CA: Sage.

Treas, J. (1975). Aging and the family. In D. Woodruff & J. Birren (Eds.), *Aging: Scientific perspectives and social issues*. New York: Van Nostrand.

Visher, E. B., & Visher, J. S. (1978). Common problems of stepparents and their spouses. *American Journal of Orthopsychiatry*, *48*, 252–262.

Walker, K. N., & Messinger, L. (1979). Remarriage after divorce: Dissolution and reconstruction of family boundaries. *Journal of Family Process*, *18*, 185–192.

Watzlawick, P. (1976). *How real is real?: Confusion, disinformation, communication*. New York: Random House.

Watzlawick, P., Beavin, J., & Jackson, D. D. (1967). *Pragmatics of human communication: A study of interactional patterns, pathologies and paradoxes.* New York: Norton.

Watzlawick, P., Weakland, J. H., & Fisch, R. (1974). *Change: Principles of problem formation and problem resolution.* New York: Norton.

Weick, K. E. (1971). Group processes, family processes, and problem solving. In J. Aldous T. Candon, R. Hull, M. Straus & I. Tallman (Eds.), *Family problem solving: A symposium of theoretical, methodological and substantive concerns.* Hinsdale, IL: Dryden Press.

Weisberg, J. (1983). *Communication in blended families.* Unpublished manuscript, Ohio State University, Columbus.

Weiss, R. S. (1975). *Marital separation.* New York: Basic Books.

White, L. K. (1979). Sex differentials in the effects of remarriage on global happiness. *Journal of Marriage and the Family, 41,* 869–876.

Wiemann, J. J. (1977). Explication and test of a model of communicative competence. *Human Communication Research, 3,* 195–213.

Wilder, C. (1979). The Palo Alto group. *Human Communication Research, 5,* 171–186.

Zietlow, P. H. (1986). *An analysis of the communication behaviors, understanding, self-disclosure, sex roles, and marital satisfaction of elderly couples and couples in earlier life stages.* Unpublished doctoral dissertation, Ohio State University, Columbus.

Zietlow, P. H., & Sillars, A. L. (in press). Life stage differences in communication during marital conflicts. *Journal of Social and Personal Relationships.*

Zube, M. (1982). Changing behavior and outlook of aging men and women: Implications for marriage in the middle and later years. *Family Relations, 31,* 147–156.

CHAPTER 9

The Structuring of Dyadic Decisions

Marshall Scott Poole and Julie Billingsley

A Picture of Dyadic Decision Making

At the turn of the century, the German sociologist Georg Simmel (1950) offered a penetrating analysis of dyadic relationships. He argued that dyads were truly unique social units, different from groups of three or more and not reducible to individual phenomenology. Crucial to Simmel's argument was his observation that if one member of a dyad withdraws (either physically or psychologically), the dyad perishes. This puts considerable pressure on the dyad, and can lead in either of two directions.

On one hand, the dyad may smooth over differences and hide important interests and feelings in an effort to protect the relationship. In decision making, this strategy results in fast and often token agreement, incomplete sharing of information about problems and reactions, and little real problem solving. Often a "midpoint" compromise is reached or one member gives in to the other. Ultimately, this may increase tensions, because underlying issues are not addressed. These tensions are usually dealt with by smoothing and by developing an ideology to cover the divergence. Simmel discusses the poignant situation of highly "intimate" couples who use the ideology of closeness to maintain the distance between them.

Alternately, a dyad may overcome relational threats by developing a relationship of great intimacy and openness. Members attempt to minimize the possibility of disagreement by creating a mutually shared perspective. Problem solving is promoted by open information flow and "talking through" disagreements. This, too, can be harmful, because the dyad may become too narrow and ignore outside information and ideas. The carefully constructed and strenuously maintained consensus may shut the dyad into a world of its own.

These two cases are extreme types, but they illustrate the range of dyadic relationships, as reflected in the variety of dyadic decision units: superior-subordinate, husband-wife, teacher-student, counselor-patient, salesperson-customer. Dyadic relationships range from great formality and constraint to extreme intimacy and openness. Of course, each dyad defines a more or less unique relationship. An important property of dyadic relationships is their idiosyncracy, in the sense that each pair adapts social norms in ways specific to the dyad. In addition, the quality of a given dyadic relationship may vary over time, as members "restructure" it.

This discussion highlights a key point: It is impossible to understand dyadic processes without taking into account the nature of the dyadic relationship under consideration. The dyadic relationship is the ground against which all dyadic decisions must be considered.

Just as the dyadic relationship differs from other social units, so dyadic decision making is different from individual or group decision making. The most common unit of analysis in decision research is the individual. Many insights regarding dyadic and group decisions can be gleaned from individual decision-making research. However, except for studies of decision making by "divided selves" [e.g., Lewin's (1951) studies of decisional conflict; Janis & Mann, 1977], there is only one voice in individual decision-making research. It is assumed that the decision maker has a single, more or less consistent perspective. This rules out conflicts in point of view, partial withholding of information, and outright deception that often occur in dyadic decisions. Nor does individual decision-making research take into account the pressure to manage and maintain relationships. Social pressure plays a key role in dyadic decisions that is not taken into account in studies of individual decision making. Also, attention management is less of a problem for an individual than for a dyad. Members of a dyad may find it hard to focus on the matter at hand if they are "out of synch" in thinking, as when one focuses on defining the problem, while the other talks about solutions. Studies of group decision making have shown lack of synchronization to be a major problem in reaching a conclusion (Hewes, Planalp, & Streibel, 1980). So many of the assumptions of classical individual decision-making research—focused attention, a clearly defined problem and set of options, relatively full information—have to be relaxed when considering dyads.

Nor are dyads equivalent to decision-making groups. Groups have a much shorter "attention span" for a given topic than do dyads. With only two points of view, it is easier for a dyad to focus on a common topic than it is for a group, whose members may have many different perspectives and concerns. Shifts to unrelated topics are quite common in groups, and it is relatively easy for a group to get sidetracked and lose the thread of a discussion. Also, members of a dyad have greater influence over the decision than does the average group member. Especially as groups get larger, influence tends to be concentrated in a few members (Bales, Strodtbeck, Mills, & Rosenborough, 1951). Because of their unique leverage, dyad members have greater latitude for influence. Relationships between members are also more salient and critical in dyads than in groups. While the importance of the socioemotional dimension of groups is unquestionable, a group is not a collection of dyads; some members may have only cursory relationships that are relatively unimportant to the functioning of the group. Whether dyadic relationships are distant or close, they are of crucial importance to the dyad's work. There is always pressure on dyad members to be "present," whereas group members may take advantage of their partial inclusion to miss discussions and let their attention wander. We can take many ideas from group research into the dyad—the dynamics of social pressure, the necessity for dealing with multiple perspectives, problem redefinition, problems with synchronizing members' thought processes—but dyads are clearly distinctive.

In general, dyadic decision processes are less orderly than individual decision making, but more orderly than group decision behavior. In dyadic interaction, the decision is continuously open to restructuring. As has been found for both individual (Klein, 1983) and group decisions, decision rules and schemes may shift as the decision evolves. The social process of interpreting the decision task and restructuring it is crucial in the development of a common orientation for the dyad. And the dyadic relationship always looms in the background. As the dyad works, members use their relationship as a resource for structuring and making a decision, and the decision process simultaneously serves to validate the relationship or to alter it (Watzlawick, Bevin, and Jackson, 1967). The dyadic relationship cannot be isolated from the larger social context. Dyads are nearly always part of some larger social unit—a business, school, community group, friendship group, family. Norms, interpretive schemes, and power structures from these units will be imported into the decision, though the dyad will develop its own idiosyncratic versions of these over time.

So, to capture dyadic decision making accurately, a theory would have to meet the following criteria:

1. It would have to acknowledge the primary influence of the dyadic relationship. This relationship has qualities unique to the dyad and is negotiated between members. Dyadic relationships cannot be viewed as static, but may be altered by the decision. Relationships constrain dyadic decision making, but they are also influenced by the decision process.
2. It would have to focus on decision processes in addition to outcomes such as quality and acceptance. The same outcomes may be produced by different processes. And two decision with the same outcomes are qualitatively different if arrived at by different processes. Therefore a focus on the development of decisions is crucial.
3. It would have to incorporate a mechanism for the restructuring of the decision task and decision rules. This would acknowledge the active role of participants in generating a decision. Members cannot be reduced to "role markers," driven by outside determinants; some room for autonomous action must remain.
4. It would have to allow for divergence in members' perspectives and for lack of synchronization in their decision-making efforts.
5. It would have to recognize the constraints the social context of the dyad

places on relationships and decision processes. But it would also have to take into account the fact that dyads adapt these constraints to their own situations and needs.

In the next section of this chapter we will introduce a general perspective that attempts to fulfill these requirements. Following that we will develop a theory of dyadic decision making.

The Theory of Structuration

To meet these requirements, a theory would have to incorporate both the active role of members in creating the decision and the deterministic forces that constrain the dyad. One theory that does this is the theory of structuration (Giddens, 1976; 1979; Poole, Seibold, and McPhee, 1985 and 1986). It views decisions as the product of members' actions and as generated and restructured during the entire decision interaction. But members are not completely free agents—their actions are constrained by various factors, including the nature of the decision task and the surrounding social organization, that limit the roles members can assume and their power. These factors act as causal constraints on the decision. The theory of structuration offers a means of encompassing the role of action and determinism in a common frame, rather than considering them as independent acting in parallel. In so doing, it can provide a truly processual theory of dyadic decision making. Our discussion of structuration will be necessarily brief. More detailed descriptions applied to decision making can be found in Poole, et al. (1985, 1986).

The concept of structuration is developed in the work of several social and literary theorists (Barthes, 1971; Bordieu, 1978; Giddens, 1976, 1979; see one account in Coward & Ellis, 1977). Applied to social contexts, structuration refers to *the production and reproduction of social systems via actors' use of generative rules and resources.* This definition rests on several key distinctions and assumptions.

First, it is necessary to distinguish system and structure, which are used in somewhat unusual ways. *System* refers to observable, "regularized relations of interdependence between individuals and groups" (Giddens, 1979, p. 66). In this case the observable relations between members of a dyad, including their decision behavior, are a system and systemic properties or indicators that include their interaction rates, the "pecking order," and their level of expressed affection. The dyad's decision behavior can be defined as a social system of a very limited sort. This system can be depicted as a series of activities that reflect members' efforts to make (or postpone, or act like they're making) the decision. *Structures* are rules and resources that form the basis for action in the system. Structures are not directly observable, but must be inferred through analysis of social systems. They exist at a "deep" level, in the sense that they generate the social system. Examples of rules are turn-taking conventions (Sacks, Schegloff, & Jefferson, 1974) and norms governing the degree of control husbands have in family decision making (Klein & Hill, 1979). Resources include formal authority, money, and knowledge.

A system has coherency because it is continuously produced and reproduced through members' use of rules and resources. Members use structures to act and to reflexively monitor and adjust activity. Members' actions are necessary for the system to exist at all (i.e., they produce it); without members' interaction a dyad could not exist. This production process creates the conditions that dyads draw on to sustain their relationship (i.e., to reproduce it). Reproduction may maintain the relationship in a more or less steady state, or it may involve continuous change or evolution of the system. In the theory of structuration both stability and change are explained in the same terms. Stability cannot be taken for granted; there must be a process generating stability.

It is not simply a matter of members' using structure to produce and reproduce the system. Structures are themselves produced and reproduced along with the system. A central assumption of the theory of structuration is the dual nature of structures: They are both the medium and the outcome of action. They are its medium because people have to draw on structures to interact; structures are what make social action possible. They are its outcome, because rules and resources only exist through being applied and oriented to in interaction—they have no reality independent of the social practices they constitute (Taylor, 1971). Thus, structuration operates in a recursive fashion, the rules and resources used to generate a system are themselves outcomes of action in the system.

Where do structures come from? In some cases they are created de novo, but more often they are appropriated by actors from larger social institutions. In the case of dyadic decisions, two examples of relevant institutions are the family and the organizational hierarchy. Institutions shape the possibilities for a society, including the range of possible or conceivable social relationships and the topics and forms of decisions. Actors appropriate aspects of institutions for use in concrete, situated practices. Giddens (1979) terms these appropriations *modalities of structuration*, particular manifestations of general social institutions that inform or generate a situated social system. The modalities are the operative locus of structure in interaction.

Institutions are not simply imposed on action in a deterministic manner; actors influence the appropriation process, and in some cases may even control it consciously. Intentionally or unwittingly, members select the particular combinations of institutional elements that structure a system. And there is no definitive control on how members use, interpret, and combine structures; members may adopt institutional features in ways quite different from the "normal form" of the institution. For example, although the institution of formal hierarchical authority is commonplace, particular superior-subordinate relationships may enact this institution in different ways. All draw on the structure of legitimate authority, but how this authority is used and what sorts of relationships it generates vary widely in specific contexts. In each particular superior-subordinate pair, the dyad creates its own social system, idiosyncratic to some extent. In some cases the modality of structuration may preserve the typical forms of legitimate authority quite faithfully, while in others it may transform this structure. Of course, this does not mean that actors completely determine the nature of structural modalities. Appropriating a given structural feature, such as a majority voting rule, carries with it a number of accompanying features of which members may be aware. These are generally imported into the system without members' awareness and constrain their behavior.

Giddens (1979), following traditional distinctions in sociology, distinguished three general types of modalities of structuration, which represent different ways in which institutions can be appropriated. Institutionalized structures may serve as *interpretive schemes* in communicative interaction, as *norms* coordinating and providing a moral order for interaction, or as *facilities*, supporting power moves. These are connected to three generally acknowledged social institutions, orders of signification (language, symbolic structures), legitimation (religion, ethics, law, social custom), and domination (privileges, resource allocation). Giddens (1976, p. 122) provides the following diagram, which illustrates the modalities as mediators between interaction and institutions:

INTERACTION	Communication	Power	Morality
(MODALITY)	Interpretive scheme	Facility	Norm
STRUCTURE	Signification	Domination	Legitimation

At the same time interaction draws on institutionalized structures in the modalities, it is also reproducing the institutions. Institutionalized structures only exist because they are produced and reproduced in action throughout a society. Although institutions may be embodied in concrete form (e.g., language in dictionaries and laws in the legal system), ultimately they exist only because they are used in many interaction systems throughout the society. If people use language differently, language changes; if superior-subordinate relationships are enacted differently, ultimately the institution of legitimate authority will change.

So, to understand structuration, we must be able to trace how actors appropriate social institutions and how they use these to produce and reproduce social systems, in this case a dyadic decision. The particular trajectory a structurational process takes is influenced by two major classes of factors: (1) forces that influence and constrain action, and (2) interstructural influences, in which different structural features shape, constrain, and change one another.

In the case of dyadic decision making several constraints on *individual action* are evident. First, the nature of the dyadic relationship influences members' scope of action, including the roles they can take and the balance of power in the decision process. Second, the nature of the decision task limits what members can do. Previous decisions can serve as precedents that lock the dyad into certain courses of action. A highly complex situation may overload the dyad's information processing capacities, limiting how "rational" the decision can be. Other task effects are also possible. Third, preexisting decision structures may determine how the dyad goes about making the decision. For example, a past compromise may require a "trade-off" on the current decision. Because previous structural modalities are salient to members and assumed by others, they tend to be drawn on and reproduced in present conduct, and in this way circumscribe and condition that conduct. Previous structures constrain later ones and perpetuate themselves, thus limiting members' ability to alter or adapt them. Finally, members' level of understanding of the structuring process determines their latitudes of action. Members unaware of processes generating a system are subject to control by the system, whereas those with some "penetration" of its working can use this to regulate structuring. Clearly, if one member has an understanding of the system, while the other does not, this gives the first power over the second.

Structural dynamics also shape processes of structuration. Particularly important are two dyamics, mediation and contradiction. In *mediation*, one structure mediates the action of another. For example, in a dyad sensitive about its relationship, every decision move may be interpreted in light of its implications for the relationship. In this case, members may attempt to apply rules of reasoning, but any arguments would be translated into terms of what they say about the dyad's relationship. A logical argument might be interpreted not as a reason for making the decision, but as an attempt by one party to control the other. The structure of the relationship transforms what reasoning means and mediates its ultimate effect on the relationship and on the decision. In *contradiction*, structuration occurs through two structural elements that require each other, but ultimately work against each other to undermine the stability of the system. In dyads, one commonly noticed contradiction is between processes requiring fusion of the two individuals into a common relationship and processes of individual development. Individual development is necessary for effective functioning of the dyad, but it can only go so far within a tightly constraining dyad. So individual development may undermine the very conditions in the dyad that initially promoted it.

The best way of demonstrating the value of the structurational approach is to develop a specific analysis of dyadic decision making. However, some general advantages can be reviewed briefly: (1) Structurational theory recognizes the role of action in social processes. Decisions are not simply determined by exogenous conditions; they are shaped according to actors' choices in a given social context; (2) At the same time, the theory realizes that actors act in a world that is not totally of their own making or totally under their control. Causal factors condition action, limiting and shaping how members can structure a decision; (3) The theory recognizes that causal constraints and the structures underlying decisions may be reproduced or altered by the decision process itself. It allows for the emergence and negotiation of decision problems and solutions and even of the rules of decision making.

A Model of the Structuring of Dyadic Decisions

The structuring of dyadic decisions is accomplished through the interaction of two modalities—*task representations and dyadic relationships.* In brief, these modalities are configurations of rules and resources members use to organize work on the decision, to interpret each other, and to influence the decision. As the decision evolves, the modalities themselves are produced and reproduced. Depending on the nature of dyadic interaction and the constellation of forces constraining the system, the modalities will either be stabilized or changed. The production and reproduction of the decision system and modalities is accomplished through *structural operations* embodied in members' discourse and actions. These operations access and invoke the modalities to structure the process, move from one topic to another, exert influence, etc. The operations are the motive force in the structuration of decisions, the medium of members' activity in producing and reproducing the system. As such, the operations also mediate the influence of causal constraints on the decision. This section of the present chapter will be divided into four parts. First, we will discuss the two modalities. Following this, we will explicate structural operations and how the structuration of dyadic decisions occurs. Third, we will work through an example of dyadic decision making. Finally, we will present summary propositions derived from the theory.

Modalities of Decision Structuration

Task Representations

A task representation is a theory regarding the "nature of the task, its objective, the means to employ to carry out the task, and the behaviors conducive to effectiveness" (Abric, 1971, p. 313). The dyad's representation of its decision task guides and organizes its decision behavior. Task representations vary in comprehensiveness; some have relatively complete descriptions, with all the elements Abric mentions, whereas others are vague and incomplete. There is no necessary correspondence between objective characteristics of tasks and task representations. Abric (1971) was able to induce different groups to interpret the same stimulus materials as a creativity task and a problem-solving task. In the case of a dyad, there may be both individual and collective task representations. The individual task representation is an interpretation; in the collective, it is a social construction. As with all social constructs, there may be conflict over the task representation; there may be competing theories of decision-making in the dyad, with obvious consequences for decision behavior and outcomes (Poole, 1985).

Task representations can be divided into several components, which will be described below. But at any point in time, the task representation incorporates a dynamic between two horizons, *what-is-to-be done* and *what-has-been-accomplished*. Against these two constructs, the dyad evaluates its progress and reorganizes or reemphasizes the directions it is taking. As the dyad moves through the decision, there is a continuous process of discursive accounting that ties the two horizons together. The has-been-accomplished is redefined as a means of redefining the what-needs-to-be-done. As the decision proceeds, the horizon of the to-be-done wanes, while the has-been-done waxes. The to-be-done is disposed of in two phenomenological "receptacles": the must-be-done and the what-should-be-done-in-the-future. This latter category holds aspects of the decision the dyad does not find feasible or exigent to handle at the time, but that would be desirable in the best of all possible worlds. In some cases there is an honest intent to accomplish the what-should-be-done-in-the-future, and in other cases this category is simply rhetorical.

It is important to distinguish individual from collective task representations, although in reality the two blend into each other. Individual task representations are mental representations developed and held by individuals. Because they are individualized, individual representations can disagree. An individual's task representation helps him or her decide on conduct in the decision session (Grosz, 1977). As a mental construct, individual task representations are inaccessible to researchers. Our only recourse is to get at them through members' discourse, as expressed in decision-making sessions.

On an entirely different plane, there exists a *collective* task representation, of similar form to individual representations but commonly held and publicly displayed in the dyad's interaction. The collective representation is instantiated and developed through such devices as goal statements, agendas, and process-related comments (which we will revisit as "structural operators" below). Sometimes the collective representation is entirely laid out as a plan or agenda; more often it is only partially realized and may unfold as the discussion proceeds. In still other cases the collective representation may be an object of contention.

Collective representations are determined partly by individual representations, but they are neither an average of individual views nor simply a substitute term for agreement between individual representations. Collective representations are discourse-based and objectifiable; they are not simply a perception shared by members. Several studies support the existence of collective task representations in their own right. Meyer (1984) identified several shared, public "theories of decision making" in his analysis of deliberations over hospital equipment purchases. Davis (1973) reports extensive evidence for the existence of social decision schemes, normative decision procedures holding for populations of groups. Finally, studies of group decision development (Poole & Doelger, 1986) identified phasic sequence that may represent "stock" task representations.

Collective task representations give coherency to dyadic work. They define the phases dyads go through and requirements for finishing the task. Grosz (1977) has related task representations to "focus spaces," which organize task-related discourse. Indeed, *the task representation is what the dyad works on in the case of decision making*. Decision tasks cannot be defined entirely in objective, material terms or in terms of physical operations. Decisions are intangible, even though they may have concrete outcomes. So, as the dyad acts, it operates on the task representation. Each completed period of activity alters the task representation and, when the dyad redefines the task representation in such a way that its previous behavior has fulfilled task requirements, the decision process stops. Rather than considering observable actions or speech acts as the primary stuff of decision, this view construes them as a surface level generated according to the task representation.

Task representations are made up of three classes of structural elements: formal decision requirements, material decision requirements, and issues.

Formal Decision Requirements

Formal decision requirements correspond to what Poole (1985) called a decision logic, and can be defined as a scheme depicting the process by which a decision is made. Formal decision requirements are determined by the interplay of two components. First, the *framing* of the task by persons external to the dyad provides important cues for dyadic interpretation. These cues may come from a variety of sources: an experimenter who defines the dyad's task as "negotiation"; a job manual that terms superior-subordinate meetings "goal-setting and feedback sessions"; a culture that views family problem solving as a setting for the father to reassert his dominance. Maier (1970), Abric (1971), Moscovici (1976), and Billig (1976), among others, have documented the powerful effects external framing has on task perception and definition.

Formal decision requirements may be shaped, second, by members' *implicit theories of decision making*. Here we will define an implicit theory as a scheme depicting how a decision should be made, that is, the strategy for decision in a particular situation. Implicit theories provide individuals with structures for organizing and understanding group activity. Perhaps the best-known implicit theory is the rational model, which assumes that the best way to make a decision is means-ends analysis. In observation of numerous decisions we have discerned at least four implicit decision theories (see also Meyer, 1984):

Assumed consensus—Members assume they agree on basic values and on the nature of their problem or task. Their orientation is to find a solution as quickly as possible and work out the details.

Political—Members assume that decision making is a process of winning adherents for their own preferred alternative. Their primary criterion is political acceptability, and originality or effectiveness take secondary status. Their orientation is to fasten onto their own preference early, win adherents, and shoot down other positions. This may require them to hide their own preferences until other positions are destroyed.

Rational—This orientation aims at making the best possible solution in the technical sense of the term. It employs rational standards and means-ends analysis and implies a sequence like the following: problem definition, problem analysis, solution search, solution evaluation and selection, and implementation.

Reactive—Members may have no expectations. They look to others for cues and "ad hoc" their way through the decision.

This is a fairly limited list; we are currently developing an instrument for identifying additional implicit theories.

Framing and implicit decision theories will have varying degrees of influence depending on several factors. Framing will tend to have more influence for dyads that are strongly controlled by external organizations, in dyads without much history (as in experimental situations), and in dyads whose relationships are closely modeled on social stereotypes. Implicit theories will have more influence for dyads with stronger inner control, particularly those who have defined their relationship in a unique manner and have good understanding of the structuring process.

Material Decision Requirements

These are the dyadic resources the decision requires. Two resources are particularly important: time and effort. The energy a dyad puts into a decision and members' motivation level are influenced by estimates of how long the decision will take and the amount of effort needed (Zander, 1971). Time estimates include both an assessment of the length of time the decision will take and an assessment of whether or not the dyad has sufficient time to reach a decision. Motivation level will be highest if the time available for the decision corresponds to the time needed. Members may redefine formal requirements so the time needed fits the time available. Estimates of effort include assessment of the degree of effort needed for a satisfactory outcome and assessment of the effort the group is capable of marshaling. Again, motivation will be highest if the effort needed and effort available are more or less consistent.

Issues

The term "issues" refers to a content-based agenda of issues specific to the decision. These issues include the information needed, analysis required to understand the problem and generate solutions, requirements for implementation of the decision, and division of labor during the decision process. For example, in a decision to purchase a home computer, several issues might be important to a young married couple, including relative cost, ease of operation, maintenance demands, and need for training. The wife might be delegated to gather information from computer stores and libraries, and after sufficient information has been accumulated, the value of various computers must be weighed vis-a-vis financial considerations. The issues a dyad will consider depend on the subject area of the decision and on the level of experience members have with the task. The more experienced the dyad is with decision making, the more likely it will have a model of the decision task. The model influences the issues considered and filters out alternative concerns.

Interplay of the Elements of the Task Representation

Together formal requirements, material requirements, and issues define a task representation that implies the order of activities and the intensity of the decision (i.e., how quickly the decision must be made and how much energy it will take). Generally, a task representation is pieced together from parts appropriated from institutions, although somtimes a task representation may be appropriated whole cloth. As noted above, the dyad's previous task representations are likely to shape the present one. For example, a married couple happy with previous decisions in which the husband took the "traditional" dominant role is likely to attempt to reproduce that arrangement in current or future decisions. Task representations may also be assembled by the dyad. In a performance appraisal, the boss may attempt to appropriate an implicit decision theory in which the superior dictates and the subordinate accepts, while the subordinate, having read the self-help literature, may want more control. Each may have their own issues, and the combination may look very different from what either envisioned at the outset.

Three points are important here. First, the task representation evolves throughout the decision. It is rare for task representations to be fully defined at the outset. Members add elements, move elements from what-is-to-be-done to has-been-done status, and delete elements in a continuous discursive accounting process. Below we will discuss factors relating to the completeness of task representations.

Second, there may be disagreements among members over the correct collective task representation. Disagreements may be over any part, formal requirements, issues, and, less often, material requirements. There may be two or more competing task representations in the discourse or one member may simply attack the one being discussed. This conflict must be worked out in interaction. The longer the conflict, the more complex the dyad's decision path. There are two dangerous responses to such conflict. One case is when members operate according to different task representations throughout the decision without trying to work out their differences. This results in a pseudo-decision, in which members think or say they are in agreement, when in fact they are not. In the second case, the dyad avoids conflict when one member capitulates and adopts the other's perspective. A real decision is made, but it does not address the other's concerns. How the dyad handles conflict determines how creative and effective their decision making can be (Klein & Hill, 1973; Folger & Poole, 1983).

Third, there is pressure for consistency among the elements of task representations. If the dyad believes time is short, there is pressure to reduce the number of issues and streamline formal requirements. If there are a lot of important issues and a short time-frame, a dynamic tension is set up and the dyad must cope with its negative effects. Members may do this in a number of ways—by dutifully trying to do the task against all odds, by redefining the task, by fighting—their response will be reflected in interaction. This is one important contradiction that shapes the course of interaction and the structuration of decisions.

Dyadic Relationship

The second modality, the dyadic relationship, is important in the structuring of decisions. As Watzlawick et al. (1967) showed, every message carries two levels of meaning: a *literal* level devoted to issues such as the decision, and a *relational* level, which displays, defines, and can redefine the dyadic relationship.

Numerous studies have focused on basic dimensions of relationships and relational communication (Leary, 1957; Foa, 1961; Wish, Deutsch, & Kaplan, 1976; Wish & Kaplan, 1977). They have consistently found two dimensions (though they have called them by different names): dominance (the degree to which one partner controls the relationship) and affiliation (the amount of friendliness or hostility in the relationship). A third dimension found by several studies is relevant for our purposes, that is, task orientation (the degree to which the relationship is focused on work as opposed to social or intimate bonding). Depending on how relationships vary in terms of these dimensions, they may be used differently in the decision process. Three major influences on decision structuring can be distinguished.

First, the nature of the relationship influences who controls the decision process and how control is exerted in the structurational process. If one party dominates the other, that party can control decision structuring (insofar as the dominant party understands the structuring process). Control is different in task-oriented and socially oriented relationships. In task relationships control is grounded on instrumental and legitimate bases, whereas in social relationships control is more diffuse, stemming from history of relationship, tradition, and culture. Control is also enacted differently in friendly and hostile relationships.

The nature of the relationship also influences the degree of openness in the decision process. If the relationship is equal as opposed to dominated, then decision making is more likely to exhibit open exchange of information and ideas (Walton & Dutton, 1969). Other things equal, openness is also more likely in social as opposed to task relationships. Concern with politics and reward in task relationships sometimes makes parties less willing to pass on relevant information (Monge & Eisenberg, 1987). Degree of openness is important not only because openness generally promotes better decision making, but also because it promotes control by members over the structuring process. Above, we noted that members' knowledge of the structures and processes generating a system was an important prerequisite for reflexive control over the structuring of decisions. Greater openness facilitates members' penetration of the structuring process.

The nature of the relationship effects the likelihood that the relationship will mediate, and potentially distort, dyadic reasoning and argumentation. Relational definition may become more important to parties than making the decision itself. The focus of their efforts, though apparently on the decision, can shift to relational issues. In this case the relationship mediates the task modality in parties' interpretations, normative regulation of the decision, and influence attempts. Arguments that are putatively addressed to the decision are seen as comments on the relationship; attempts to coordinate action become efforts to enforce relational norms; influence attempts are construed as control moves. The relationship is more likely to become salient in cases where it is unequal, socially based, and hostile.

As noted above, the use of the relational modality to structure decision making produces and reproduces the relationship. By invoking certain aspects of relationships in decision making, members may strengthen or inadvertently undermine their own dyad.

Structural Operators

Members' use of a structural modality produces and reproduces it, and hence may either stabilize or change it. *Structural operators* are the instruments of this process. Actors' appropriations of structural elements operate on them such that they are either preserved or altered. For example, when a superior gives an employee orders or feedback, she is appropriating the institution of legitimate authority. She may use legitimate authority in a way consistent with the accepted notion, for example, to give a work-related order. She may also appropriate it in a way inconsistent with the normal range of uses, for example, to obtain personal favors. If the subordinate accedes to the latter's orders, the superior has expanded the range of legitimate authority in this particular relationship. The particular moves she used to expand the structure are what we term structural operators. (Over the course of the relationship this change may be preserved or altered, depending on how the two actors appropriate the relational modality.

Structural operators, the instruments of structuration, are embodied in interactional moves, such as calling for a vote or stating a goal. Structural operators are closely related to other interaction moves used for the management of discourse, formulations (Garfinkel & Sacks, 1970), and alignment devices (Ragan, 1983). To repeat a point made above, one key to explaining the course of structuration is to elucidate how the application of structural operators is influenced by forces that constrain action and structural dynamics. This will be the focus of the remainder of this essay. But first, it is necessary to describe structural operators and how they might be identified.

An institutional structure can be described in terms of two aspects: its spirit and its specific features. Spirit is the intended, generally recognized purpose of the structure. For example, the rules of logical argument are intended to help members choose an alternative on the basis of "good reasons" that can be adduced to support it. The specific features are the operations the structure requires and the timing and sequence of operations. For example, in the case of argument, providing evidence, marshaling reasons, making a clear point, and being responsive to the other's arguments.

In appropriating the structure there are four possibilities: (1) an actor may stick closely to both the spirit and operations; (2) an actor may act in a way consistent with the spirit, but change and reinterpret operations; (3) an actor may violate the spirit of the structure, but retain its operations, using them in unintended ways (e.g., using argument to exhaust the other so much that he or she simply agrees to get the discussion done); (4) the actor may alter both the spirit and operations of the structure. Options (1) and (2) are *faithful* appropriations, whereas (3) and (4) are *ironic* appropriations. It is important to emphasize that the group may not be aware of how it is appropriating structures; uses are not always planned, and members may alter a structure considerably without intending to do so.

Since the appropriation and reproduction of structures occurs in interaction, it can be traced with interaction coding and discourse analysis procedures. Table 9.1 contains sample categories from a coding scheme that we are developing to identify how members use structure in interaction (Poole & DeSanctis, 1987). The categories represent ways in which intended structures can be preserved, changed, or reinterpreted by the dyad. These general moves are accomplished through the speech acts listed in the right-hand column of Table 9.1. For example, if a dyad member said, "We have to make this decision based on the facts," and then consistently pushed his preferences as justifications for various choices, his acts would be coded as an instance of *substitution by metonymy* (because the member substituted preferences for facts, but still treated them as arguments). If the dyad knows its time is short and one member repeats, "Time flies, time flies," it would be coded as *enlargement by metaphor* (since it adds meaning to the time-requirement estimate). Not every act is a structural operator, but those that are can be assigned two codes with the system, one pertaining to whether it is a faithful or ironic appropriation and one indicating the type of appropriation it represents.

From these codings and further analysis, we can derive indices of group structuring processes such as the following:

Degree of faithful versus ironic use;
Degree to which there is preservation versus reinterpretation versus change of structures;
Degree of conflicting or inconsistent appropriations by members;

Table 9.1. General categories of structural operations with corresponding speech acts.

Structural operators	Example speech acts
Structural preservation	
Direct appropriation	Explicit appropriation—open talk about how to use structure
	Implicit appropriation—indirect use of structure
Structural change	
Substitution (adopt one structure in place of another or in spirit of another)	Synechdoche-part for whole
	Metonymy—substitute related structure
	Catechresis—substitute unrelated structure (misuse)
Combination (combining two structures)	Composition—mix two structures
	Periodic chain—series of structures that add together cumulatively
	Paradox—combine contrary structures
	Antagogue—adopt one structure as corrective for a problem in another
Structural reinterpretation	
Enlargement (understand one structure in terms of another)	Metaphor—relation of two structures in which one is used to gain understanding of structure in use
	Addition of consistent elements
Constraint (direct and focus use of structure)	Periphrasis—use of description for name
	Definition—explain the structure directly
	Polarization—all-or-nothing approach to structure; reject any change
	Diagnosis—identify a problem in the use of structure; comment on how it is working; ask question about structure
	Ordering—specification of order among structural components
Contrast (definition of structure in terms of what it is not or should not be)	Litotes—express thought by denying its contrary
	Antithesis—explicit contrast of structures with the one that is favored
	Criticism—critical comment on how structure is used
Reaction	
Affirmation	Agreement with adoption of structure
Negation	Disagreement with adoption of structure

Degree to which the use of structures changes over time;
Degree to which members are aware of how they use structures.

The temporal pattern of appropriation can also be studied to see how the production and reproduction of structure occurs and who controls it. It is important to remember that relational structure is also appropriated and reproduced through these moves.

The Structuring of Dyadic Decisions

The Basic Model

The modalities and structural operators figure in the following generative mechanism for dyadic decisions. A dyad develops a task representation early in the decision process. The task representation may be explicitly set forth in a "problem and procedure" statement, or it may be implicit, as in a suggested solution. This representation guides dyadic activities and helps members understand and evaluate what they have done. As the decision progresses, members alter the task representation, moving items from to-be-done to has-been-accomplished. They do this through discursive accounting moves such as summaries, process statements, the introduction of solutions, criticisms, and other reactions. All these embody structural operators, which stabilize or change the task representation. These moves and others described below can be traced in the dyad's discourse.

Dyad members build individual and collective task representations of structural elements drawn from institutions and their own prior experience. The collective representation is constituted in the dyad's discourse and emerges from the interaction of members' representations. A well-defined collective representation serves as a steering mechanism to guide the dyad through a specified sequence of activities. However, two problems may militate against coordination and coherency in dyadic decision behavior: incompleteness of the task representation and conflict over the "correct" task representation. In both cases, the dyad's attempts to cope with problems may work against effective decision making.

A complete task representation is one in which (1) there are no major gaps or uncertainties in the dyad's task theory, (2) elements of the task representation are specific and concrete, and (3) the task representation is stable in the sense that its elements are well-defined enough that they are not undergoing continual metamorphosis. A complete representation has both benefits and costs. The more complete the task representation, the greater the possibility of planned and coordinated action. Without a fairly specific, relatively stable task representation, dyadic action may swing aimlessly and add up to nothing. But if a task representation is too complete, stable, and well-defined, it may stifle creativity and the dyad's ability to adapt to additional demands as they arise, resulting in lower quality decisions. So the key would be to maintain a relatively complete task representation that is "fuzzy around the edges," to allow for new ideas and problems. However, certain conditions make it difficult to achieve a complete task representation. The dyad will be less likely to formulate a complete representation if members are unfamiliar with the decision task, if the decision is very complex (i.e., if it requires working with multiple perspectives, many issues, or a difficult problem), if time is short, or if their relationship is unstable. When these conditions hold, the dyad is likely to have a much more complicated decision path, with repetitions of earlier steps and operations. The possibility of conflict is also enhanced. Finally, the quality of the decision is likely to be lower than if a relatively complete task representation has been achieved.

When members disagree on the task representation, the dyad must resolve the divergence, and this complicates the development of the decision considerably (except for the special case where one member forces the other to accept his or her representation at the outset). Members may try to follow two or more different task representations at once or to hybridize task representations, which results in a more complex developmental sequence and may affect decision quality. The dyadic relationship provides rules and resources that serve a critical role in the management of these differences.

An example involving a traditional family in which the husband is task-oriented and dominant and the wife socially oriented and submissive, may illustrate some of the possibilities in cases of representational conflict. The husband has greater resources to control structuring of the task representation and, other things equal, he would set the initial representation and control its development. However, given the intimate nature of the relationship it is always possible that the relationship will achieve high salience and mediate work on the decision itself. The husband (and in some cases the wife) must expend energy to keep this from happening, and in many cases the desire to keep the relationship in the background provides a counterweight for the wife to the husband's task control. She can use the relationship and his fear that it will obstruct the decision to exert some control, indirectly on representation structuring.

When there is conflict over the task representation, the dyad's decision path will be complicated. The dyad's progress toward a decision will not be "rational" or step-by-step, but will exhibit halting, shifting patterns of activity with periods where the dyad cycles back to previous issues and reworks them. Conflicts over substantive issues are common arenas for relational conflict and change (Walton, 1969). So, as the dyadic relationship is used as a modality for working on the task representation, it is reproduced and may be altered. The quality of the decision will vary depending on how the conflict is managed. However, generally the following predictions can be ventured for the case of representational conflict: For simple decision tasks with few perspectives and little time to make the decision, a dominant, one-sided relationship will lead to higher quality decisions than will other types of relationships. For more complex tasks, a more equal relationship will result in higher quality.

Influences and Constraints on Structuration

The factors that channel and constrain structuration will vary greatly depending on the context of the decision. They can be roughly divided into constraints on action and structural dynamics. Here are some of the most important, drawn in part from earlier discussion:

1. The nature of the *decision task* is a constraint on dyadic action. Although the dyad operates on a task representation, the representation derives from objective demands of the decision situation. To the extent that the collective task representation is not commensurate with the objective demands of the task, decision quality will be lowered and the dyad will experience failure. These failures will force the dyad to backtrack and make its decision path more complicated.

2. *Limits* placed on the dyad by an organization or by authority figures, such as experimenters, also constrain action. These constraints dictate elements of the task representation and may constrain how much control members have over appropriation of the representation.

3. The intrusion of *relational concerns* into the decision arena can also affect the decision process. When this occurs, the relational modality mediates the task representation. This structural dynamic transforms the meaning of statements concerning the decision so that they apply to the dyadic relationship instead. Work on the decision proceeds, but it is overshadowed by relational work.

4. A second structural dynamic is the contradiction of elements in the task representation, such as cases where the dyad defines the representation so that there are too many issues for the available time, more issues than the decision logic can handle, too little time for the decision logic, etc. In this case, separate aspects of the structure, both important for a quality decision, work against each other. This creates problems with which the dyad must cope. Such coping attempts are reflected in behaviors such as doubling back, conflict, skipping or tabling issues, etc. If the contradiction goes far enough and takes suffiencient energy to cope with, the group will have to alter its task representation. Contradictions in a representation may ultimately undermine it.

An Illustration

An example should help illustrate some aspects of dyadic decision structuring. The decision(s) in question were made during a telephone conversation between Watergate conspirators John Ehrlichman and Herbert Kalmbach on April 13, 1973. Kalmbach was called to testify before the Watergate committee and a grand jury and Kalmbach called Ehrlichman to work out some details of the testimony he gave. The conversation is summarized in Appendix 9.A and the structural analysis of the development of the decision is in Appendix 9.B.

Initiating the task representation (refer to Appendix 9.B, T1 and T2) Kalmbach introduces the issues. Implicitly, these statements develop the following formal requirements: this is a telephone call, subject to constraints imposed by a different channel than face-to-face communication (Williams, 1977); the decision frame is the goal of defending the Administration; the implicit theory is that the decision must be made by coordinating their stories and that Ehrlichman has some legitimate authority and therefore can give *serious* advice; there is sufficient time, but a decision must be made during the call; no specific agenda of issues is laid out—Kalmbach introduces the purpose of the call and the issues unfold throughout the session; the relationship is introduced explicitly only in move 7. Structuring moves are indicated at the bottom of the diagram (see the key explaining codings at the beginning of the chart). The framing of the decision as a coordination problem reduces the likelihood that we will encounter persuasive or other compliance-gaining moves in this conversation. Instead, the decisions will be made through more subtle means.

Several moves from the chart are interesting. In move 6, Ehrlichman introduces change by metonymy by shifting the frame to the defense of Kalmbach (implied by summarizing the threat to Kalmbach and by Kalmbach's later remarks and agreements). In the same move a rule is added to the implicit decision theory: Kalmbach must show his behavior to be "lawyerly," that is, consistent with legal principles. Move 6 also constrains the issues on testimony by defining the issues Kalmbach must respond to more completely. A single statement thus contains multiple structural operations. This is fairly common, as several other instances show (moves 9, 12, 14, 16, 18, and 21).

The evolution of formal requirements can also be traced. In terms of implicit decision theory, it starts with Kalmbach asking advice to coordinate his testimony with Ehrlichman, therefore placing the decision subject to rules of coordination and legitimate authority. As it proceeds, three more rules for Kalmbach are spelled out: he must show how his actions conform to legal requirements, are based on orders, and are authorized by Dean, who is in the process of "opening up" to investigators. Legitimate authority is expanded by combination in move 12, when protection is added as an obligation of Ehrlichman (and implicitly the President) to Kalmbach. Note the chaining together of rules. Paradoxically, this multiplication of rules may make Kalmbach and Ehrlichman's position more difficult, because it depends on more premises.

Framing of the decision shifts three times through metonymy that focuses interaction on three successive goals: protect the administration (move 1), protect Kalmbach (move 6), and protect the President (move 16). There is great potential for contradiction here, though it is glossed over in the interaction. These shifts in frame leave the outcome of the decision somewhat ambiguous, especially in cases where the goals are inconsistent. The vagueness of the formal requirements is advantageous in that it permits Kalmbach and Ehrlichman to define more than one desideratum for the decision; but it is disadvantageous in that it renders the task representation unstable. Explicit discussion would have helped in this case, but instead the members acted as though they could handle several goals simultaneously. They did not consider the possibility that the three framings might collide (as they did during questioning of Kalmbach). This contradiction is exhibited in the exchanges after move 16, in which Ehrlichman emphasizes protection of the President and Kalmbach stated that he acted only on orders (note the code as combination by paradox). No conflict is in evidence in the discussion, but the tension it introduced came out clearly during Kalmbach's testimony.

This contradiction is potentiated by a tension in the relational modality. Kalmbach has previously been a friend and colleague, but in move 18 he stresses the employee-employer relationship, in a substitution by catachresis. The tension between the employee role and the friend-colleague role reflects a different level of the contradiction mentioned in the previous paragraph.

Throughout the session items move from the to-be-done to the has-been-done, especially on the issue aspects of the task representation. In move 15 Kalmbach explicitly shifts previous issues and decision requirements into the has-been-done through a summarization-action statement. Note that just after this, Kalmbach and Ehrlichman go over the decision again, cycling back through the same story (practicing?). This would be expected with a complex task and with the developing contradictions. Another such accounting move can be seen in statement 21, a topic shift.

The cycling back may be necessary to gloss over contradictions in framing, between framing and issues, and between framing and relationships. Unfortunately, the recycling just makes the contradiction worse.

This analysis shows the process by which the dyad worked out its decision, also illustrating tensions and contradictions that were to put Kalmbach in a dilemma during questioning in front of the panel.

Propositions

In this section of the present chapter we will summarize some basic predictive propositions from the model. These do not constitute an exhaustive list, but they give some idea of the types of predictions the model can support. It is important to note that few of these propositions are deterministic hypotheses in the form, "the greater the X, the greater Y." Instead they represent tendencies in the action system that the structurational process will generally follow. However, there will be deviations from these predictions, as actors generate their own particular attack on the decision.

Propositions Concerning Task Representations

1. Task representations are likely to be vague or incomplete if the decision is unfamiliar, if it is complex, if there is little time in which to make the decision, and if the parties have little understanding of how task representations should be structured.
2. Members' task representations are likely to differ if the decision in unfamiliar, if it is complex, if there are relational problems, and if the re-

lationship is equal (i.e., if there is no dominant member), especially if it is hostile.

3. Difficulty in resolving task representational differences is greater if task representations are well defined, if the relationship mediates work on the decision, if there are relational problems, and if members have little understanding of the structuring process.

4. The relationship is more likely to mediate direct work on the decision when the relationship is unequal, when it is socially oriented and intimate as opposed to task-oriented, when it is hostile as opposed to friendly, and when one member uses it repeatedly in attempts to control the decision.

5. Contradictions in task representations are more likely if the task is complex, if the task representation is incomplete or vague, and if there were differences in members' task representations that have to be resolved.

6. Control over the task representation is likely to be unequal if the relationship is dominated by one party and the other has no countervailing relational strengths, if one party has superior understanding of the structuring process and does not use it for the benefit of both, and if one party is familiar with the decision and the other is not.

7. Parties' efforts to control problems in propositions 1–5 will be most effective under the following interaction processes: faithful appropriation, a moderate amount of change in the structure over time, if structural changes do not introduce contradictions, and if members do not conflict in the way in which they appropriate structures.

Propositions Relating to Outcomes

1. The dyadic decision path will be more complex if the task is complex, members' task representations differ, there are contradictions in task representations, the relationship mediates direct work on the task, and members' appropriations of task representations are conflicting and inconsistent.

2. The quality of dyadic decisions will be lowered if there are contradictions in the task representation, if the relationship mediates direct work on the task, if task representations differ and members cannot deal with these in an open and constructive way, if there is a large amount of ironic use of structures, if members' appropriations of task representations are conflicting and inconsistent, and if the task representation is not incommensurate with the objective demands of the task.

3. Members' acceptance of a dyadic decision will be lowered if the relationship mediates direct work on the decision, if there have been many differences and contradictions in task representations, if there has been a large amount of ironic use of structures, if members' appropriations of task representations are conflicting and inconsistent, if the dyad has trouble making progress on the task, and if there are relational problems.

Propositions Related to Practice

1. One way to influence dyadic decision making is to affect framing of the decision and the dyad's implicit decision theories.
2. Improvement of how dyads appropriate decision structures is one key to improving dyadic decision making. Improving members' understanding of the structuring process can enhance their ability to control and guide a decision. Emphasis on faithful appropriation of decision structures may help, though for low-power parties, ironic appropriations may be more effective since they cover over power moves. It may also make members more effective if we teach them to recognize and avoid contradictions.
3. Relationships mediating dyadic decisions are a major problem. But for purposes of influence or persuasion, invoking the relationship may be an effective tactic—if we can get the dyad to focus on their relationship, it may blind them to some implications of the decision content.
4. Timing of contributions is very important. If a member invokes a structure at the beginning of a discussion it sets the parameters of the decision, though it may be altered in subsequent interaction. For more controversial issues or rules, it may be better to tie them to accepted structures by combination, so they will not raise objections.

The propositions concerning task representations and outcomes provide a means of evaluating the structurational model. If it is correct, the pattern of results should support the predictions. However, predictive accuracy would not be sufficient to support the theory; it would also be necessary to show how the model governs temporal evolution of the decision.

Conclusion

An important implication of this theory is that dyadic decision outcomes cannot be predicted with a deterministic model. Instead, we must take the process of decision into account. The theory of structuration focuses our attention on a particular aspect of decision process—how the dyad structures its work on the decision. This is in large part controlled by the actors, so there will always be an element of indeterminacy in any dyadic decision. This indeterminacy is not due to "error," but to the essential nature of dyadic action. With respect to dyadic decision making, the best we can do is to reconstruct action post hoc. We must focus on the devices actors use to structure their decisions, on the structures they use, and on how they appropriate them. These structures are drawn from social institutions, and they are both the medium and outcome of dyadic action in any specific dyad.

So the theory becomes a theory of how various styles of action and choices influence the structuring of decisions and the production and reproduction of the system. Modalities of structuration are where the real action of decision making takes place. The degree of members' understanding of the structuring process is therefore of critical importance. Another implication of the theory is that the task definition and procedures may change over the course of the decision. The dyad may redefine the decision, shift decision rules, alter its estimate of how long the decision may take, and shift its focus from the task representation to the relationship. Again, these alterations are not just sources of "error" in prediction, but fundamental to the decision process.

Actors do not have total freedom in the decision process; they operate under definite sets of constraints, which include constraints on action such as the task, members' level of experience, preexisting structures, and structural dynamics such as mediations and contradictions. These factors shape structuration, though their effects are mediated by interaction itself.

The structurational approach links action and institutions, and micro and macro levels. It gives researchers a mandate to investigate institutional influences on action. Depending on the structures members appropriate and how they do so, a decision may be "rational" or not. Much has been made of the rational model—premised on defining the problem, generating a range of solutions, deciding on the best solution on the basis of "good reasons," and planning implementation (usually in that sequence). As a normative model it has become a Western institution, and it has been advanced as a descriptive model as well. However, according to the current analysis, this model is not always appropriate. The rational model will only be an accurate description if members see fit to appropriate it as an implicit decision theory, and there are many cases where they will not do so. The rational model will be normative only if members adopt it as a standard, explicitly or implicitly.

Discourse analysis is time-consuming and presents analytical problems, but this type of close analysis is essential if we are to trace the impact of action on decision-making. This impact is manifested in the sequences of structural operations that move the group through a decision. Two useful sources of data can be garnered from procedures such as those illustrated above: (1) overall summary properties of the session, such as the proportion of ironic appropriations, the balance of control over appropriations, and the amount of change in the task representation; (2) sequential properties, such as where contradictions occur and how the dyad responds to them, and how patterns of control over appropriation shift over time. These, as well as analysis of specific content and its evolution, can be related to the complexity of the dyadic decision path, differences in decision quality and acceptance, and relational properties to evaluate the usefulness of the theory.

The theory of structuration is a theory focused on action and interaction, their role in producing and reproducing social systems, and the forces that shape these processes. Communicative interaction plays a major role in these structuring processes. It is this focus that makes the theory so promising for the study of dyadic decision-making, for as Simmel (1950) wrote:

[The] dyad is inseparable from the immediacy of interaction; for neither of its two elements is the super-individual unit which elsewhere confronts the individual, while at the same time it makes him participate in it (p.126).

If Simmel was wrong in any respect, it was in his underestimation of the role of social structures external to the dyad. The theory of structuration tries to retain the interactional focus, while adding a concern with institutions and culture to the study of dyadic decision making.

Acknowledgment. We would like to thank Lisa O'Dell for her comments on this essay.

References

Abric, J. C. (1971). An experimental study of group creativity: Task representation, group structure, and performance *European Journal of Social Psychology, 1,* 311–26.

Bales, R. F., Strodtbeck, F. L., Mills, T., & Rosenborough, M. E. (1951). Channels of communication in small groups. *American Sociological Review, 16,* 461–468.

Barthnes, R. (1971). *S/Z.* New York: Hill and Wang.

Billig, M. (1976). *Social psychology and intergroup relations.* London: Academic Press.

Bordieu, P. (1978). *Outline of a theory of practice.* Cambridge: Cambridge University Press.

Coward, R., & Ellis, J. (1977). *Language and materialism: Development in semiology and the theory of the subject.* Boston: Routledge and Kegan Paul.

Davis, J. H. (1973). Group decision and social interaction: A theory of social decision schemes. *Psychological Review, 80,* 97–125.

Foa, U. (1961). Convergences in the analysis of the structure of interpersonal behavior. *Psychological Review, 68,* 341–353.

Folger, J. P. & Poole, M. S. (1983). *Working through conflict.* Glenview, IL: Scott, Foresman.

Garfinkel, H., & Sacks. H. (1970). On formal structures of practical actions. In J. C. McKinney & E. A. Tiryakin (Eds.), *Theoretical sociology: Perspectives and developments.* New York: Appleton-Century-Crofts, pp. 337–366.

Giddens, A. (1976). *New rules of sociological theory.* New York: Free Press.

Giddens, A. (1979). *Central problems in social theory.* Berkeley, CA: University of California Press.

Grosz, B. J. (1977). *The representation and use of focus in dialogue understanding.* Unpublished doctoral dissertation, University of California, Berkeley.

Hewes, D., Planalp, S., & Streibel, M. (1980). Analyzing social interaction: Some excruciating models and some exhilirating results. In D. Nimmo (Ed.), *Communication Yearbook, IV.* New Brunswick, NJ: Transaction Press.

Janis, I., & Mann, L. (1977). *Decision-making.* New York: Free Press.

Klein, D. M., & Hill, R. (1979). Determinants of family problem-solving effectiveness. In W. R. Burr, R. Hill, F. J. Nye, & I. L. Reiss (Eds.), *Contemporary theories about the family.* New York: Free Press.

Klein, N. M. (1983). Utility and decision strategies: A second look at rational decision-making. *Organizational Behavior and Human Performance, 31,* 1–25.

Leary, T. (1957). *Interpersonal diagnosis of personality.* New York: Ronald.

Lewin, K. (1951). *Field theory in social science.* New York: Harper and Brothers.

Maier, N. R. F. (1970). *Problem-solving and creativity.* Belmont, CA: Brooks-Cole.

Meyer, A. (1984). Mingling decision-making metaphors. *Academy of Management Review, 9,* 6–17.

Monge, P. R., & Eisenberg, E. M. (1987). Emergent communication networks. In. F. M. Jablin, L. L. Putnam, K. H. Roberts, & L. W. Porter (Eds.), *Handbook of Organizational Communication: An Interdisciplinary Perspective.* Beverly Hills, CA: Sage Publ. 304–342.

Moscovici, S. (1976). *Social influence and social change.* London: Academic Press.

Poole, M. S. (1985). Tasks and interaction sequences: A theory of coherence in group decision-making interaction. In R. L. Street & J. N. Cappella (Eds.), *Sequence and pattern in communicative behaviour.* London: Edward Arnold, pp. 206–224.

Poole, M. S., & DeSanctis, G. (1987). Group decision support systems and group decision-making. Unpublished manuscript, University of Minnesota, Management Sciences Department.

Poole, M. S., & Doelger, J. (1986). Developmental processes in group decision-making. In R. Y. Hirokawa & M. S. Poole (Eds.), *Communication and group decision-making.* Beverly Hills: Sage.

Poole, M. S., Seibold, D. R., & McPhee, R. D. (1985). Group decision-making as a structurational process. *Quarterly Journal of Speech, 71,* 74–102.

Poole, M. S., Seibold, D. R., and McPhee, R. D. (1986). A structurational approach to theory-building in group decision-making research. In R. Y. Hirokawa & M. S. Poole (Eds.), *Communication and group decision-making.* Beverly Hills, CA: Sage Publ. 237–264

Ragan, S. (1983). Conversational analysis of alignment talk in job interviews. In R. Bostrom (Ed.), *Communication Yearbook 7.* Beverly Hills, CA: Sage.

Sacks, H. Schegloff, M., & Jefferson, G. (1974). A simplest systematics for the organization of turn-taking in conversation. *Language, 50,* 696–733.

Simmel, G. (1950). *The sociology of Georg Simmel.* K. Wolff (Ed.), New York: Free Press.

Taylor, C. (1971). Interpretation and the sciences of man. *Review of Metaphysics, 25,* 1–52.

Walton, R. (1969) *Interpersonal peacemaking: Confrontatiations and third party consultation.* Reading, UA: Addison-Wesley.

Walton, R., & Dutton, J. M. (1969). Management of interdepartmental conflict: A model and review. *Administrative Science Quarterly, 14,* 73–84.

Watzlawick, P., Bevin, J., & Jackson, D. (1967). *Pragmatics of human communication.* New York: Norton.

Williams, E. (1977) Experimental comparisons of face-to-face and mediated communication: A review. *Psychological Bulletin, 74,* 963–976.

Wish, M., & Kaplan, S. (1977). Toward an implicit theory of interpersonal communication. *Sociometry, 40,* 234–246.

Wish, M., Deutsch, M., & Kaplan, S. (1976). Perceived dimensions of interpersonal relations. *Journal of Personality and Social Psychology, 33,* 409–420.

Zander, A. (1971). *Motives and goals in groups.* New York: Academic Press.

Appendix 9.A.

Ehrlichman–Kalmbach Telephone Call
April 19, 1973

The following is an abstracted transcript of a telephone conversation between John D. Ehrlichman and Herbert W. Kalmbach. Ehrlichman recorded the conversation and provided the transcript to the Senate Watergate Committee.

Move	Person	Content
		(Ehrlichman greets K.)
1	Kalmbach	I'm pretty good. I'm scheduled for 2 tomorrow afternoon. {Ehrlichman asked where, and Kalmbach provided time and place.}
2	Kalmbach	Yeah. I just wanted to run through quickly several things, John, in line with our conversation. I got in here last night and there was a telephone call from O'Brien. I returned it, went over there today and he said the reason for the call is LaRue has told him to ask him to call me to say that he had to identify me in connection with this and he wanted me to know that and so on.
3	Ehrlichman	Did he tell about Dean?
4	Kalmbach	Well, Dean has totally cooperated with the U.S. Attorney in the hopes of getting immunity. Now that he says or how he says nobody seems to be able to divine but he. {They discuss the extent of Dean's disclosures and that Dean is implicating mostly Ehrlichman and another.}
5	Ehrlichman	And taking the position that he was a mere agent. Now on your episode he told me before he left, so to speak, he, Dean, told me that really my transaction with him involving you was virtually my only area of liability in this thing and I said, well, John, what in the world are you talking about? {Ehrlichman summarized supposed liability in money transaction with Kalmbach and Dean.}
6	Ehrlichman	I don't understand the law but I don't think Herb entered into this with any guilty intent and I certainly didn't and so I said I just find that hard to imagine. Now since then I've retained counsel. {Ehrlichman details hired lawyer's opinion of his lack of guilt.}

7	Kalmbach	And also that you know I was your friend and you know I was the President's attorney.
		{They discuss Ehrlichman's involvement}
8	Ehrlichman	So that Mitchell and Stans both know that there wasn't any point in calling you direct because we had gotten you out of that on the pretext that you were going to do things for us.
		{Ehrlichman details more of points of liability and involvement.}
9	Kalmbach	You know, when you and I talked and it was after John had given me that word, and I came in to ask you, John is that an assignment I have to take on? You said, yes it is period and move forward. Then that was all that I needed to be assured that I wasn't putting my family in jeopardy.
10	Kalmbach	And I would just understand that you and I are absolutely together on that.
		{Ehrlichman agrees}
11	Kalmbach	Yeah, Well and when we talked you know that I was about to do, you know, to go out and get this dough for this purpose; it was humanitarian.
	Ehrlichman	It was a defense fund.
12	Kalmbach	... he said that there is a massive campaign evidently under way to indict all the lawyers including you, Herb, and I was a little shocked and I guess that I need to get from you, John, is assurance that it is not true.
13	Ehrlichman	Well I don't know of any attempt to target you at all. (Ehrlichman guesses the committee is trying to get to him through Kalmbach)
14	Ehrlichman	Yeah, and the point that I undoubedly never expressed to you that I continually operated on the basis of Dean's representations to me. {discussion of Dean's liability as house lawyer.}
15	Kalmbach	And it's just unbelievable, unthinkable. Now shall I just—I'll just if I'm asked by Silver I'll just lay it out just exactly that way.
16	Ehrlichman	Yeah, I wouldn't haul the President into it if you can help it. {K agrees}
17	Ehrlichman	But I think the point that which I will make in the future if I'm given the chance that you were not under our control in any sort of slavery sense but that we had agreed that you would not be at the beck and call of the committee.
18	Kalmbach	And, of course, too, that I act only on orders and, you know, on direction and this is something that you felt

		sufficiently important and that you were assured it was altogether proper, then I would take it on because I always do it and always have. And you and Bob and the President know that.
19	Ehrlichman	Yeah, well as far as propriety is concerned I think we both were relying entirely on Dean.
20	Ehrlichman	I made no independent judgement.
	Kalmbach	Yep. Yep.
	Ehrlichman	And I'm sure Bob didn't either.
	Kalmbach	Nope, and I'm just, I just have the feeling, John, that I don't know if this is a weak reed, is it? {more on same by both.}.... And the only inquiries I made, John was to you after I talked to John Dean.
	Ehrlichman	And you found that I didn't know just a whole helluva lot.
	Kalmbach	You said this is something I have to do and ...
	Ehrlichman	Yeah, and the reason that I said that, as you know, was not from any personal inquiry but on the basis of what had been represented to me.
	Kalmbach	Yeah, and then on—to provide the defense fund and take care of the families of these fellas who were then ...
	Ehrlichman	Indigent. {more in same vein}
21	Kalmbach	Now, can I get in to see you tomorrow before I go in there at 2?
22	Ehrlichman	If you want to. They'll ask you. {...} they'll ask you to whom you've spoken about your testimony and I would appreciate it if you would say you've talked to me in California because at that time I was investigating this thing for the President. {Kalmbach and Ehrlichman discuss Ehrlichman's plan for his account of his investigation. Kalmbach requests and receives assurance of good faith. Ehrlichman expresses his feeling of persecution. Kalmbach briefly reviews again. Conversation closes.}

Appendix 9.B.

Key to Decision Diagram

Each of the first four rows represent elements of the task representation structure. If a comment has an operator that initiates or changes the entry, the substance of the comment is entered into the row, along with the comment number in parentheses. Along the top of the diagram the discrete time periods are marked. These do not correspond to real time, but to each time at which some change is made in the decision representation.

If an entry is carried on to the next time period, it is marked with a series of dots (. . . .). If the entry is moved to the has-been-done from the to-be-done it is labeled with the Scandinavian zero sign (   ). If the entry is dropped or replaced by the next remark, it is marked with a capital x (X). If there is no entry in a row, it means nothing in the discourse had any effect on that row.

The fifth row, entitled "Structural Operators," lists the operators that worked on the task representation in brackets. From top to bottom they correspond to the row entries that are changed as we move from the top of the first row down. So, if there are two entries in the structural operators row, there should also be two entries under the time period in the four rows above; the top entry in the structural operator row corresponds to the top entry above, while the bottom entry in the operator row corresponds to the lower entry above. We have also made notes of which structural elements are combined in any combination moves and which are introduced in any addition or introduction moves.

The bottom row contains comments about patterns in the structural operators.

When an entry is carried from one page to another, an arrow on the right hand margin indicates it.

Time	T1	T2	T3	T4	T5	T6	T7	T8	T9
Formal Requirements — Frame	Telephone call (0)	K: defense of Administration (2)		•X	X E: defense of K (6)				K: be sure absolutely together
Implicit Theory		K: coordinate story (2)			E: must show consistent with law (6)			K: given order (9)	
		K: check on information (implied)							
		K: accept advice from E based in legitimate authority (2)							
Material Requirements — Time		K: sufficient time bad decision must be made during call							
Effort									
Issues	K: Scheduled to testify. Run through testimony (1)		→ E: Should know about Dean (3,4)	→ E: transaction is only liability (5)	→ E: K may have broken law (6)		E: Mitchell, Stans knew they couldn't call direct (8)	→ K: You gave me the word to do it (9)	
Relationship		K: friend and colleague (implied)				K: Knew I was only a friend and President's attorney (7)			
Structural Operators	[addition]	[indirect appropriation] [direct appropriation] [indirect appropriation] [indirect appropriation]	[addition]		[Change by metonymy] [addition plus direct appropriation of legal code] [constraint by definition]	[direct appropriation] [Plus 2 affirmations by Ehrlichman]	[addition]	[combination by composition: legal + authority structures] [addition] [E: affirmation]	
Comments:		Invokes structures of coordination and legitimate authority			Adds a new decision rule to implicit theory and a new goal to framing				

Time		T10	T11	T12	T13	T14	T15	T16	T17	T18
Formal Requirements	Frame						x E: Defense of Nixon (16)			↑
	Implicit Theory		K: protected by authority (12)		E: nothing illegal. Dean's word (14)				K: reinforce authority (18)	E: nothing illegal; acted on Dean's word (19)
Material Requirements	Time									↑
	Effort			Ø						
Issues		K: money was for humanitarian purposes (11) / E: defense fund (11)		K: assurance that there is no indictment (12) → E: No attempt to target you (13)	E: I operated on basis of Dean's representation (14)	Ø K: If asked by Silver I'll do it that way (15)	E: Don't haul President in (16)	→ E: Not in slavery, not at back and call	→ K: I act only on orders (18)	→ E: orders given on Dean's authority (19)
Relationship									K: employee (18)	↑
Structural Operators		[Enlargement by metaphor]	[Combination by composition authority plus protection [addition]]	[addition]	[Combination by Periodic chain: legal + authority + expertise affirmed by K (twice) and E (once) [addition]]	Ø [Conclusion by Formation – More topics to has-been-done.]	[metonymy] [affirm by K] [addition]	[Enlargement by Metaphor]	[direct appropriation Paradox: not slave, but ordered substitution by catachresis]	[direct appropriation [addition]]
Comments				A long chain of issues and arguments is more complex			Note the metonymy, which introduces an ambiguity— should K. defend himself or Administration	There is a contradiction here between acting on orders yet not being a slave.		

Time		T19	T20	T21	T22	END
Formal Requirements	Frame { Implicit Theory	• • •	• •	• • •	• • •	
			Check on information (21) Accept advice (21)			
Material Requirements	Time	•	X Not enough time. Need to check again (21)	X Enough time	•	END
	Effort					
Issues		•	K: Now (21)			
			K: Can I get in to see you tomorrow before I go in there at 2? (21)	→ E: They'll ask you (22)	→ E: Say you talked to me in California (23)	
Relationship {		•	•	•	•	
Structural Operators		Reinforce and Repeat Previous Sequence (20)	Move to has-been-done (21)	[?] [Negation] [affirmed by K]	[addition]	
			[indirect appropriation] [indirect appropriation] [?] [addition]			
Comments						

Part 4
Sociological Perspectives

CHAPTER 10

Joint Decision Making in the Contemporary Sexually Based Primary Relationship

John Scanzoni

"Whatever its 'commitment,' the current interpersonal relationship must include a commitment to continuing negotiation" (Raush, 1977, p. 182).

A fundamental premise of this chapter is that commitment to negotiation is as vital as any other kinds of commitments made by the dyadic pair. We will elaborate the validity of that proposition first, by describing the basic elements of dyadic decision making; second, by describing the basic elements of the contemporary sexually based primary relationship; third, by analyzing the ways decision making assumes a pivotal role (driving force) within that type of relationship.

The Contemporary Primary Relationship

The Kelley et al. (1983, p. 38) definition of a *close* relationship—mutually contingent interdependence between A and B so that what A does influences B and vice versa—makes it quite indistinguishable from two long-standing traditions in sociology. One of these is the idea of *primary* relations traceable to Cooley (1909); the other is the broader field of micro-sociology (Turner, 1985) traceable in turn to Simmel (see Levine, Carter, & Gorman, 1976). In sociology the primary relationship or micro *situation* is always understood to be influenced by its environment—the meso and macro milieu. Over time in feedback fashion the situation is understood to influence its environment as well. Prior investigations have identified at least four types of close or primary relations: those based on *propinquity* (neighbors, coworkers, etc.), *friendship* (emotional intimacy, companionship, etc.), *blood* (sibs, kin, parents, children), and *sexual* interdependence.

Space permits attention solely to the sexually based primary relationship (Scanzoni, 1987; Scanzoni, Polonko, Teachman, & Thompson, 1988). According to Kelley et al. (1983, p. 38) the close or primary relationship in general is characterized by exchanges that are frequent, diverse, intense, and of duration. In particular, the sexually based primary relationship (SBPR) is the genre in which participants define sexual exchanges as a legitimate and normative feature (basis/bond) of their relationship. This interdependence makes their primary relationship intrinsically distinctive from the three remaining types of primary relationships. Nonetheless although the SBPR is unique, it is not necessarily exclusive. Persons may simultaneously be in more than one SBPR. SBPR becomes the generalizing construct used to subsume all manner of sexually based primary relationships whether heterosexual or homosexual. These relationships (as distinct from casual encounters) may sometimes be accompanied by a marriage license, and sometimes not. They may sometimes occur among persons coresiding whether legal or not. Sometimes coresiding persons do not maintain SBPR even though they are legal. And of course SBPR may occur among persons not coresiding whether legal or not. As discussed later on, the elements of legal status as well as coresidence sometimes become variables helping to express SBPR. Also intrinsic to the understanding of SBPR are decision-making elements. These particular elements become part of the driving force or engine (Gulliver, 1979) underlying SBPR.

Elements of Joint Decision Making

For heuristic and research purposes, Strauss (1978) and also Weiss (1978) divided dyadic decision making, or decisioning, into three categories: context, processes, and outcomes. The first and third of these categories have been the most easily—and thus the most widely—studied. But what Hicks, Hansen, & Christie (1983) call the "black box" of process dynamics is the least understood and most difficult to investigate.

Context

In Giddens's (1981) view the context is both constraining and enabling. Certain context variables acting alone and/or in combination may either restrain or facilitate process dynamics and their ensuing decisioning outcomes. The context of the contemporary primary relationship is made up of at least 12 clusters of variables.

Economic/occupational variables consist not only of measures of partners' education, occupational status, and income (if currently employed), they also include assessments of satisfactions with current life-style, including their partners' (if any) contribution to it (Scanzoni, 1978). Equally significant are measures of current occupational achievement and aspirations and expectations for future achievement. It is essential that this entire array of measures be gotten for women as well as men. The continuing movement of white women into the role of *worker* (a role that black women have occupied since Emancipation) necessitates this strategy.

Compositional issues include not only legal status but also whether a household has one or two adults present. If only one adult, does Actor maintain SBPR with another person residing in a separate household in the same or different locale? A separate question is whether Actor has a primary relationship with an Other that may be described as either propinquitous or as a friendship because, for example, Other contributes to child support and/or has child visitation and/or custody rights? Composition also sub-sumes numbers and ages of children in the household, including whether they are his, hers, or theirs.

Length of relationship can be measured from at least four different points in time: since first meeting; since becoming sexually involved; since coresi-dence (if it has occurred); since legalization (if at all).

The socioemotional or expressive dimension consists of three interrelated and multifaceted components: satisfactions with companionship activities during nonpaid working hours; sexual satisfaction; and satisfactions with emotional intimacy including love/caring (Rubin, 1983).

The religious devoutness dimension pertains to degree of Actor's religio-sity as assessed by indicators relevant to the contemporary U.S. religious scene. According to D'Antonio (1983) religiosity has taken on renewed sig-nificance in predicting variation in primary relationship issues (Morgan & Scanzoni, 1987a).

Gender-role preferences assess desired interchangeability between the sexes and are a major component in accounting for the pervasiveness of deci-sioning throughout contemporary primary relationships (Scanzoni & Szino-vacz, 1980). Variation in these preferences also help explain differences in process behaviors such as bargaining modes (Arnett, 1987).

Individualism pertains to the degree to which Actor favors relationship maintenance at the expense of his or her own interests (Bellah, Madsen, Sul-livan, Swidler, & Tipton, 1985; Veroff, Douvan, & Kulka, 1981). Persons who are more individualistic or pragmatic (Scanzoni, 1968; Morgan & Scan-zoni, 1987b) are less likely to favor stability for its own sake, as well as less likely to believe that obligation is the basis for relationship stability. Instead they are more likely to favor relationship termination in the event their own interests appear to be in jeopardy.

Whereas individualism, like gender-role preferences, is a generalized orientation, commitment to one's current partner is highly specific. Com-mitment is a behavioral indicator of the degree to which one is willing to continue working at or to persevere in one's relationship in the expectation that it will (continue to) pay off (Scanzoni & Arnett, 1987).

According to Pleck (1985) satisfactions with the partner's performance of routine household chores, as well as participation in child care, are becom-ing increasingly important dimensions of the contemporary close relation-ship, owing, among other things, to women's growing participation in the paid labor force.

Also growing increasingly significant in terms of its potential impact on decisioning processes is Actor's sense of autonomy or self, whether this is conceptualized as self-esteem (Hill & Scanzoni, 1982), or whether one's locus of control is located in self, spouse, or fate (Scanzoni & Arnett, 1987).

Actor's evaluations of prior decisioning processes and outcomes also constitute a crucial context dimension. If those kinds of evaluations tend to be negative, their impacts on current decisioning are likely to be different than if those evaluations have been positive.

Finally, just as Actor's own economic resources may be considered as alternatives to those provided by Other, Actor may also possess significant others external to the relationship that also may be considered as alternatives in various senses. Kin (including children), friends, coworkers, counselors, and so forth may provide sources of nonerotic primary type gratifications in addition to any supplied by one's partner. In addition, Actor may be obtaining sexual gratifications from persons other than one's partner. The notion of alternatives or options of any sort has long played a role in our conceptual understanding of Actor's decisioning behaviors (Thibaut & Kelley, 1959).

Since our concern is with joint decisioning, it is necessary to obtain measures from both partners on each of the variables that appear within each cluster. Whenever possible the research goal is to make the pair the unit of analysis instead of focusing solely on female partners as is usually done, or on female and male partners separately. One way to operate at the dyadic rather than the individual level of analysis would be to examine degree of congruence/disparity over certain variables. Assuming that congruence/disparity exists on a continuum, the expectation is that a high degree of congruence over certain variables will influence process variables differently than will relatively high amounts of disparity. Nonetheless, at this early stage of research into such issues, it remains very much an empirical question as to when and under what conditions disparity/congruence is a better predictor of process dynamics than is an individual measure of some variable taken alone.

Processes

While not quite as extensive as the array of context variables, the numbers of process variables can be large as well, but we choose to limit them to four. The first of these is communication style. Following the Raush, Barry, Hertel, & Swain (1974) schema, at least three components of style may be identified: cognitive, affiliative, and coercive. Persons higher on the first two and lower on the third dimension may be said to exhibit *positive* communication styles. Persons lower on the first two and higher on the third may be said to exhibit *negative* styles. In contrast to context variables that can be collected from each partner separately and simultaneously by their completing a questionnaire while being monitored by the interviewer, communication style must be assessed by one form or another of observation techniques. In our research, after the partners completed the questionnaires we brought them together and, following a protocol, we asked them to interact over some specific matter (e.g., money) and tape-recorded their verbal interactions. Coding the transcripts and tapes then permits assignment of the Raush et al. (1974) codes (Godwin & Scanzoni, in press).

A second process variable is labeled *bargaining mode*, and is based on the work of Pruitt (1981). Also obtained by coders working with tapes and transcripts, Pruitt suggests a continuum along which are found four kinds of bargaining behaviors that he labels as: problem-solving, compensatory, compromise, and competitive.

A third process variable is labeled *process power* and is closely linked with bargaining mode. However it differs in that here the coder working from transcripts and tapes attempts to assign codes assessing Zartman's (1976) formal definition of process power: the "ability of one party to produce ... movement or re-evaluation ... or ... change of behavior" on the part of the other. "'Power is present' in a negotiation situation when one party shifts another from its initial positions toward the positions of the first party, because the first party has caused the other to move. Such a notion allows the analyst to compare the movement effected by each party as an index of the ability of each to cause the other to change, or, in other words, of their power."

A fourth type of process variable is not assessed by the coder, that is, Olson's (1977) "outsider," but instead is obtained from the respondents themselves, that is, Olson's "insider." At the completion of the pair's episodic interactions regarding a particular matter (e.g., money), each partner once again completes a questionnaire separately from the other. Among the questions asked are items designed to assess Actor's perception of how Other behaved during that particular episode with regard to maximum *joint* profit (concern for the interests of both of them while discussing/bargaining) versus maximum *individual* profit. In the latter instance Other is seen as being more concerned for his/her own individual interests than for joint interests. What is being measured is perceptions of the focus of each partner upon *collective* versus *individualistic* interests (Scanzoni, 1978).

Outcomes

As with context and process segments, the outcomes of joint decisioning are multifaceted. The most obvious dimension lies with actual behaviors. For instance, if the pair was discussing whether or not a nonemployed wife should enter the paid labor force, her actual entry or continued nonemployment represents a *behavioral* outcome of their decisionings. Nonetheless, the investigator cannot naively assume a snapshot stance toward that behavior. Instead of viewing it in static or fixed terms one must consider any particular decisioning episode regarding issues such as money, companionship, wife employment, or whatever as part of an ongoing set of developmental episodes regarding that broad issue area. In effect, the outcomes of a particular episode regarding, for example, employment, becomes part of the context for subsequent episodes.

That episodic image is owing chiefly to the reality that alongside objective behaviors at outcome time X, subjective outcomes occur simultaneously that significantly influence the stability of any objective behaviors. One of these is called degree of perceived *consensus/dissensus* regarding the issue. That is, Actor may report that she and her partner are in complete agreement regarding whatever behavioral outcome has emerged, whereas Other reports they are in total disagreement. Amount of perceived agreement lies of course on a continuum and partners may diverge from each other to a greater or lesser degree.

A second subjective outcome pertains to each partner's perception of the *fairness/equity* of the current behavioral outcome. These sorts of perceptions also exist on a continuum ranging from "very fair" to "very unfair" and once again partners may diverge to a greater or lesser degree regarding where they fall on this continuum. A third subjective orientation is called *outcome power*, and assesses each partner's perceptions regarding "how much" s/he got of what s/he actually "wanted" during the recorded episode regarding the particular issue under discussion. Each partner can also be queried as to "how much" of what Other wanted Other was able to get during that episode. Once again partners can diverge more or less in terms of both aspects of outcome power. A final subjective outcome orientation assesses the impact, if any, of the particular episode's interactions upon each partner's current feelings for Other. Did the particular interactions make him/her feel "closer," "distant," resentful," "loving," "indifferent," "neutral," and so forth? Once more, partners can diverge/converge to a greater or lesser extent regarding their perceptions of impacts on their feelings.

Explicit/Implicit Sequences

The preceding discussion has assumed that joint decision making has been carried on in explicit or verbal fashion. But sometimes, particularly within primary relationships, decision making takes place in what Strauss (1978) calls *implicit, silent,* or *tacit* fashion. Often based on cues, clues, body language, and other nonverbal means, implicit understandings may become critical elements alongside more explicit interactions. According to Strauss, it is important to identify if and when the boundaries of silent arrangements are transgressed by Actor, thus functioning as a catalyst triggering an explicit or verbal response on the part of Other. Once made explicit the partners may seek to arrive at some mutually acceptable outcome. However, over time, one or both partners may stray from that explicit outcome agreement and, although tacitly aware of that divergence, avoid making it explicit until once again Other goes "too far" and transgresses certain understood boundaries.

Quantitative/Qualitative Analyses

The model in question can be tested either by quantitative or qualitative techniques, or by some combination of the two (Hill & Scanzoni, 1982;

Deal, 1986; Kingsbury & Scanzoni, in press; Arnett, 1987; Fishel & Scanzoni, in press). In either case, the hypotheses are that context influences processes, and that in turn context and processes together influence outcomes. Over time, outcome variables become part of the fresh context influencing subsequent process dynamics. In one study, for example, a qualitative in-depth approach is being utilized to compare decision making between couples who have sought professional counseling (i.e., "distressed") with those who have not (Waldruff, in preparation). In another more quantitatively oriented study, advanced and innovative statistical techniques such as LISREL are being explored in terms of their potential to satisfactorily test linkages among the numerous variables displayed by the model in question (Godwin & Scanzoni, in press).

Joint Decision Making Within the Sexually Based Situation

Having described SBPR and also the basic elements of a joint-decisioning model, the final question pertains to how the two are joined. How can it be said that joint decisioning is the "engine" that drives the *sexually based close relationship situation in development?*

Relationship Development

In classic sociological thought (Buckley, 1967) there are four questions addressed to every situation: How does it form; how is it maintained; how does it change: how does it dissolve? In the close-relationship literature some researchers have approached both friendship and romantic situations by asking these same kinds of questions (Perlman & Duck, 1987; Mueller & Cooper, 1986). In our schema we reduce them to three by identifying conditions of formation; maintenance/change (MC); dissolution. The assumption is that, sexually based/bonded relationships are in continual development, for example, into formation, out of formation into MC or dissolution, within MC, from dissolution to MC, and so forth. A further assumption is that persons' degree of commitment to one another is a prime element influencing relationship development. A final assumption is that the character of prior decisioning processes and outcomes is a significant factor predicting interpersonal commitments. It is in this sense that Raush (1977, p. 182) is correct when he places so much emphasis on continuing negotiation. Decisioning processes/outcomes influence interpersonal commitment, which in turn drives situational development.

Joint Decision Making and Situational Development

Figure 10.1 graphically displays SBPR, and the most efficient way to make sense of Figure 10.1 is to trace some potential paths throughout it that persons/partners may take, and to describe how those paths may be signifi-

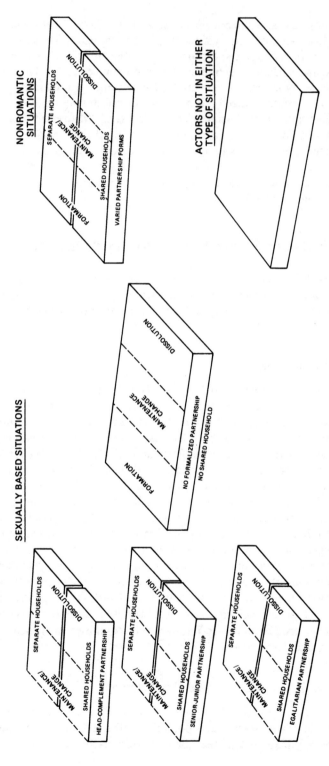

Figure 10.1. Elements of the sexually based primary relationship in development, in conjunction with nonromantic primary relationships, and with Actors not in either type of situation. Transition is possible from any set of circumstances to any other set at any time in the life span. Children may or may not be present within any of the primary relationship circumstances. They may or may not be birth-children of adult(s) in household. The technical classification "single-parent" may appear in many sets of primary relationship circumstances. Legal status of persons in varied circumstances is open-ended. Varied circumstances may include heterosexuals or homosexuals.

cantly influenced by commitment, which in turn is impacted by decisioning context/processes/outcomes (cf Scanzoni, Polonko, Teachman & Thompson, 1988). For example, persons may move into the formation phase of SBPR (center block) from either the upper-right block (nonromantic friendship) or move into it apart from a prior friendship. Assuming Actor and Other had no prior friendship they possess no history of joint decision making. Let us further assume that they enter into their sexually based situation via implicit decisioning—apart from much if any verbal discussion regarding their decision to establish sexual interdependence.

The task of the researcher begins by making an operational distinction between pre-SBPR and SBPR. To do so one would operationalize the four formal criteria of *close* from Kelley et al. (1983) described above. Specifically as the sexual interdependence *continues* and is relatively *frequent*, two of the criteria are met. *Strength and intensity of feelings* is a third criterion to consider, plus the final indicator of *additional exchanges*. Based on these four indicators, a judgment is made that the partners have passed into a formation phase. Very likely, frequency, duration, and additional exchanges are decided more or less implicitly. At this point a minimal but identifiable level of commitment exists between the partners because of these satisfactory exchanges. Exploration of additional exchanges and possible expansion into them characterizes the ongoing development of the formation phase (Scanzoni, 1979). The increasing tempo of exchanges in the formation phase is characterized by continued implicitness. Costs that in a later MC phase might generate explicit conflict and decisioning tend to be ignored. However, the range of potential gratifications is necessarily finite and at some point the tempo slows and evaluation of cost/reward ratios begins in earnest. Exchanges perceived as costly are then likely to generate explicit decisioning. The issue as to just how much thought versus "mere emotional feeling" occurs at such points remains unsettled. As Duck and Perlman (1985, p. 12) put it, "the little-researched fact [is] that people think about their relationships, both in advance and afterwards, both at the time of their conduct and at other times." A viable hypothesis is that degree of thought, calculation, evaluation, etc., varies positively with degree of individualism and degree of gender-role modernity.

The character of those decisioning *processes* and *outcomes* is likely to drive the relationship either into MC or into dissolution. If emergent communication styles are perceived as highly affiliative and cognitive and less coercive, if bargaining mode is oriented toward problem solving, if process power is relatively symmetrical, if Other is seen as oriented towards maximum joint profit, and if decisioning outcomes are perceived as consensual, equitable, and so forth, then the situation is likely to shift from formation into an MC phase. In short, a prime indicator of having developed into MC is effective explicit decisioning over specific interests that are vital to each partner. Commitment to effective decisioning is assumed to enhance commitment to one another and thus to the continuation of the MC phase of the relationship.

Furthermore the delicate balance between maintenance and change is achieved by means of ongoing discussions/negotiations. For example, at any given point in time particular arrangements over certain interest areas may remain constant. However, arrangements regarding other interest areas are being renegotiated, some areas are being dropped entirely, and/or new exchanges are being incorporated into the relationship. Both the constancy and the alterations are likely to result from explicit decisioning, but in certain instances the decisioning may also incorporate implicit elements. As long as the partners evaluate the decisioning processes and outcomes positively, commitment to one another is likely to be maintained or to grow.

In contrast to being driven into MC, SBPR can also be driven from formation into a dissolution phase if process dynamics and outcomes are deemed ineffective. Ineffective would be characterized by negative interaction processes (i.e., the opposite of above—less affiliative and cognitive and more coercive with respect to communication style; more competitive, less problem solving with respect to bargaining mode; as well as negative-type measures on the remaining process and outcome variables). Thus a prime indicator of having developed into a dissolution phase (from either formation or MC) is ineffective explicit decisioning over specific interests that are vital to each partner. While there may or may not be commitment to effective decisioning, it simply does not exist (owing very likely to combinations of certain context variables). *Consequently commitment to one another as well as to the relationship becomes problematic.* The relationship may continue in a dissolution phase for a period of time after which the emergence of more effective decisioning may drive or develop the relationship on to an MC phase. If negative decisioning processes and outcomes continue, the resulting minimal gratification levels may erode their interpersonal commitment so greatly that gradually all exchanges—including the sexual—cease; hence the situation (SBPR) will in effect have been terminated.

Expanding the Model's Elements

The logic describing joint decisioning and situational development within and between the remaining numerous paths in Figure 10.1 is essentially the same as that just outlined. The Figure 10.1 model addresses three additional dimensions that are subsumed by and contribute to the broader, more abstract notion of SBPR development just described.

The first of these we call *partnership* status and includes the production and consumption of material resources. Equally significant are nonmaterial matters dealing with preferences for behaviors in both market and home places. In effect partnership status subsumes many of the elements described earlier. Partnership status exists on a continuum, which one pole identifies as equal partners. On the material side both partners in this arrangement are economically autonomous and self-sufficient, and on the nonmaterial side both partners share preferences for parity of socioeconomic interests.

Among these interests, for example, is the notion that each partner possesses a high degree of occupational commitment—that the occupational endeavors of one are not a priori more significant than those of the other. Needless to say from these values flow norms of interchangeability with regard to parenting and household chores.

Located in the center of the partnership continuum are the *junior/senior partner* statuses characterized chiefly by the primacy of one partner's occupation (most commonly the male's) vis-a-vis Other's occupation. Given continuing trends in married women's labor force participation, this center portion of the continuum contains the largest proportion of U.S. (and Western) marriages.

At the continuum's opposite pole is the *head-complement* arrangement characterized chiefly by the woman's absence from the paid labor force. Although once the prevailing form of marriage both in behavior and ideals, it is now in behavioral as well as normative decline. In sum the partnership realm revolves around the many issues raised by feminists and others regarding the critical question of gender inequality (Ashmore & Del Boca, 1986). A basic assumption is that there cannot be anything approaching gender equality throughout the larger society apart from equity between the sexes within SBPR (Gerson, 1985).

Several decades ago decisions regarding what sort of partnership legal couples would maintain were largely implicit and nonproblematic. White persons simply took it for granted that they would live in head-complement arrangements. To be sure, conflicts and decisions arose over how to consume the resources produced by the male sole provider, but tended to be resolved by males according to the levels of resources they supplied (Blood & Wolfe, 1960). Today the presence of two additional partnership options involving not merely consumption issues but more fundamental production issues requires extensive explicit joint decisioning. The varieties and complexities of partnership issues requiring decisioning by contemporary couples could not have been envisioned by analysts of an earlier era (Pitts, 1964).

The two remaining dimensions identified in Figure 10.1 were at one time even more nonproblematic but now, as with partnership status, have fallen into the realm of the uncertain, which requires joint decisioning. We address them simultaneously, although in fact they are empirically distinct, because they tend to be closely identified not only in the minds of laypersons, but among professionals as well. These are the issues of residential status and of legal status (see above). In terms of the conjugally based conventional family paradigm, these two matters are considered basic defining attributes. Relationships in the nonlegal and/or separate residence category have been considered qualitatively different from those in the legal/coresidence category (Macklin, 1983). On the other hand, from the perspective of a SBPR paradigm, partners *make decisions* regarding residence and legality within the course of their ongoing development (formation, MC, dissolution), and also in conjunction with their partnership status. The broader, more abstract construct becomes the micro *situation* subsuming more concrete matters such as partnership, residence and legal status. The latter types of questions become some of the dimensions that concretely express or describe the larger situation.

For example, residence can readily be reconceptualized as "degree of physical proximity" and treated as a variable measured, for example, by numbers of overnights spent together in any one week or month. For centuries legal husbands have spent large numbers of nights away from their wives, although it was highly unlikely that wives ever participated in negotiations with their husbands over these matters. As did Abigail Adams, they simply accepted lengthy separations as inevitable (Butterfield, Friedlander, & Kline, 1975). Recently increasing numbers of partnered women and men (some legal partners; others nonlegal partners) have resided in separate locales owing to employment constraints (Gerstel & Gross, 1984; Winfield, 1985). Proportions of nonlegal persons residing together in the same locale are also steadily increasing (Gwartney-Gibbs, 1986). Although data may not yet be available, one could conclude that there are growing proportions of partners in sexually based primary relationships residing in the same locale and maintaining two households, but nonetheless sharing many overnights per week or month. Thus residence or degree of proximity becomes an issue of potential discussion/negotiation in terms of increasing, decreasing, or else maintaining the partners' present levels of proximity. Falling into this vein are current coresiders' decisions to move to *separate* residences whether or not the partners are legal.

Similarly, persons in ongoing sexually bonded relationships make decisions (often implicitly) regarding whether or not to legalize their behaviors. And of course ever-increasing numbers of persons who are now legal are negotiating the termination of that status. Hence, as with proximity/residence, legal status becomes ever more problematic and much less taken for granted as an understood given. It too becomes an issue to be decisioned alongside partnership and residence matters. To the degree that residence, partnership, and legal status matters are decisioned effectively, to that degree is interpersonal commitment enhanced, and situational development influenced in terms of a MC mode. Conversely, to the extent these clusters of matters are decisioned ineffectively, to that extent does continuity in the MC mode become less likely.

Permutations and Life-Course Chronology

Returning specifically to the SBPR model in Figure 10.1, it is plain that the permutations of possible life-course circumstances is quite large; second that there can be no predetermined chronology whatsoever governing movement among those life-course circumstances; third, there is no guarantee of having but one partner while developing within and among the circumstances.

Given the wide range of options regarding circumstances, timing, and partners, as well as the fluidity inherent to such matters, it is equally plain why it appears valid to assert that awareness of decisioning dynamics in terms of their context/processes/outcomes, as well as commitment to their complexities, become the sine qua non of the contemporary sexually based relationship. For instance, although persons in the center block, MC phase, do not possess a shared household, partnership, or legal status (with each other), they engage in decision making over these and related matters that might drive or develop them into one of the left-block circumstances. In one instance, they may develop into left-middle block, nonshared household, and remain nonlegal. That is they may negotiate an economic partnership of a senior/junior type, even though they maintain two dwellings. Moreover one or both partners may have (a) child(ren) residing with him/her (or with a former partner) and thus also be involved in a primary relationship based on blood. In turn that blood tie has a significant impact on decision making between the adult partners. For instance, while they were in MC phase center block, they may have been trying to negotiate whether to shift to a shared or nonshared household in left block. (Nonshared household in left block implies some sort of economic partnership or interdependence, yet apart from coresidence.) The presence and ages of their children influenced them to negotiate a nonshared household arrangement. On the other hand, many contemporary partners decide to blend households (coreside) and children, and thus the literature is replete with the difficulties of discipline and decision making inherent within such arrangements (Chilman, 1983).

Remaining permutations within Figure 10.1 while not limitless become exceedingly numerous. In addition to movement within and across circumstances, persons may be located in more than one circumstance at a time, thus further enlarging the range of complications. One possibility implied in the above discussion is that a woman could be located in the upper-right block, shared household with her child, at the same time that she is located in the center block in a sexually based relationship with a man. Complicating the picture further is the possibility that she may be legally married to yet another man. But since they have ceased to be sexual they are by definition no longer in SBPR. Instead, because they remain friends, they may both be located in upper-right block/nonshared household, and maintaining a friendship-type primary relation in which, for example, he contributes to the economic support of their child. At the same time her center-block male partner may be in a SBPR in left block, shared household, legal marriage to a head complement. However, that relationship may be in its dissolution phase.

Underlying the particular SBPR circumstances, whatever they may be, is the interplay between decision making and interpersonal commitment described above. Partners satisfied with both the processes and outcomes of decision making over specific issues are more likely to enter a formation phase, shift to an MC phase, and avoid a dissolution phase. Conversely, persons dissatisfied with decisioning processes and outcomes are less likely in the first place to enter a formation phase. If they did enter a formation phase because decisioning satisfactions were acceptable, they are likely to enter into a dissolution phase if those sorts of satisfactions begin to falter. Similarly persons in MC are also more likely to enter into a dissolution phase if and when previously acceptable levels of decision processes and outcomes falter. Consequently how partners carry on the process dynamics of decision making regarding particular issues appears to be just as critical as the outcomes themselves. Both the *how* (processes) and the *what* (outcomes) influence commitment, which in turn significantly affects situational development.

Summary

This chapter's thesis is that commitment to contemporary primary relationships based on sexual interdependence is significantly influenced by the character of the joint decision making carried on by the dyadic pair. Decision making is analyzed in terms of its three major components: context, processes, and outcomes. The context consists of a number of dimensions that may either enable or constrain process dynamics. In turn process dynamics, along with context, significantly affect decisioning outcomes. Decisioning processes/outcomes perceived as effective by the participants tend to enhance interpersonal commitment. Commitment, in turn, affects the developmental phases of the partners' relationship—whether formation, maintenance/change, or dissolution. Situational development is a broad construct subsuming potential concrete expressions of the sexually based primary relationship. These expressions include legal status, residential status, and partnership status. Many of the specific issues over which partners must make decisions regarding their primary relationships are subsumed by these three statuses. Thus as Figure 10.1 suggests, throughout their life courses persons may, with one or more partners, experience a number of kinds of SBPR circumstances, and experience the same circumstance more than once. Their joint decision making with their partner(s) is seen as simultaneously influencing and being influenced by these continually developing life-course circumstances.

References

Arnett, C. E. (1987). *The relation of marital partnership status to husband/wife bargaining mode.* Unpublished doctoral dissertation, University of North Carolina-Greensboro.

Ashmore, R. D., & Del Boca, F. K. (Eds.). (1986). *The social psychology of female-male relations: A critical analysis of central concepts.* New York: Academic Press.

Bellah, R. N., Madsen, R., Sullivan, W. M., Swidler, A., & Tipton, S. M. (1985).

Habits of the heart: Individualism and commitment in American life. Berkeley: University of California Press.

Blood, R., & Wolfe D. M. (1960). *Husbands and wives.* New York: Free Press.

Buckley, W. (1967). *Sociology and modern systems theory.* Englewood Cliffs, NJ: Prentice-Hall.

Butterfield, L. H., Friedlander, M., & Kline, M. J. (1975). *The book of Abigail and John: Selected letters of the Adams family, 1762-1784.* Cambridge: Harvard University Press.

Chilman, C. S. (1983). Remarriage and stepfamilies: Research results and implications. In E. D. Macklin & R. H. Rubin, (Eds.), *Contemporary families and alternative lifestyles* (pp. 147-165). Beverly Hills: Sage.

Cooley, C. H. (1909). *Social organization.* New York: Scribner's.

D'Antonio, W. V. (1983). Family life, religion, and societal values and structures. In W. V. D'Antonio & J. Aldous (Eds.), *Families and religions: Conflict and change in modern society* (pp. 81-108). Beverly Hills: Sage.

Deal, T. R. (1986). *Divorce mediation: Factors influencing the choice of mediation and their respective objective and subjective outcomes.* Unpublished doctoral dissertation, University of North Carolina-Greensboro.

Duck, S., & Perlman, D. (1985). The thousand islands of personal relationships: A descriptive analysis for future exploration. In S. Duck & D. Perlman (eds.), *Understanding personal relationships: An interdisciplinary approach.* Beverly Hills: Sage.

Fishel, A., & Scanzoni, J. (in press). *Context, process and outcome dynamics regarding child-custody conflicts. Journal of Divorce.*

Gerson, K. (1985). *Hard choices: How women decide about work, career and motherhood.* Berkeley: University of California Press.

Gerstel, N., & Gross, H. (1984). *Commuter marriage: A study of work and family.* New York: Guilford Press.

Giddens, A. (1981). Agency, institution and time-space analysis. In K. Knorr-Cetina & A. V. Cicourel (Eds.), *Advances in social theory and methodology* (pp. 161-174). Boston: Routledgo & Kegan-Paul.

Godwin, D., & Scanzoni, J. H. (in press). Couple decision-making: Commonalities and differences across issues and spouses. *Journal of Marriage and Family.*

Gulliver, P. H. (1979). *Disputes and negotiations: A cross-cultural perspective.* New York: Academic Press.

Gwartney-Gibbs, P. A. (1986). The institutionalization of premarital cohabitation: Estimates from marriage license applications, 1970 and 1980. *Journal of Marriage and Family, 48,* 423-434.

Hicks, M. W., Hansen, S. L., Christie, L. A. (1983). Dual-career/dual work families: A systems approach. In E. D. Macklin & R. H. Rubin (Eds.), *Contemporary families and alternative life styles* (pp. 164-179). Beverly Hills: Sage.

Hill, W., & Scanzoni, J. (1982). An approach for assessing marital decision-making processes. *Journal of Marriage and Family, 44,* 927-941.

H. H. Kelley, E. Berscheid, A. Christensen, J. H. Harvey, T. L. Huston, G. Levinger, E. McClintock, L. A. Peplau, D. R. Peterson, 1983 "Analyzing close Relationships," pp. 20-67 in H. H. Kelley et al. (eds.). *Close relationships.* New York: Freeman.

Kingsbury, N., & Scanzoni, J. H. (in press). *Process power and decision outcomes among dual career couples.* Journal of comparative family studies.

Levine, D. N., Carter, E. B., & Gorman, E. M. (1976). Simmel's influence on American sociology. I. *American Journal of Sociology, 81,* 813–845.

Macklin, E. D. (1983). Nonmarital heterosexual cohabitation: An overview. In E. D. Macklin, & R. H. Rubin (Eds.). *Contemporary families and alternative lifestyles.* Beverly Hills: Sage.

Morgan, M. Y., & Scanzoni, J. H. (1987a). Religious orientations and women's expected labor force continuity; *Journal of Marriage and Family, 49,* 367–379.

Morgan, M. Y., & Scanzoni, J. (1987b). Values about divorce: Assessing variation in permanence/pragmatism orientations. *Journal of Divorce,* 11: 1–24.

Mueller, E. C., & Cooper, C. R. (Eds.). (1986). *Process and outcome in peer relationships.* New York: Academic Press.

Olson, D. H. (1977). Insiders' and outsiders' views of relationships: Research strategies. In G. Levinger & H. L. Raush (Eds.), (pp. 115–136). *Close relationships: Perspectives on the meaning of intimacy.* Amherst: University of Massachusetts Press.

Perlman, D., & Duck, S. (Eds.). (1987). *Intimate relationships: Development, dynamics, & deterioration.* Newbury Park: Sage.

Pitts, J. R. (1964). The structural-functional approach. In H. T. Christensen (Ed.), *Handbook of marriage and the family* (pp.51–124). Chicago: Rand McNally.

Pleck, J. H. (1985). *Working wives/working husbands.* Beverly Hills: Sage.

Pruitt, D. G. (1981). *Negotiation behavior.* New York: Academic Press.

Raush, H. L. (1977). Orientations to the close relationship. In G. Levinger & H. L. Raush (Eds.), *Close relationships: Perspectives on the meaning of intimacy* (pp. 163–188). Amherst: University of Massachusetts Press.

Raush, H. L., Barry, W. A., Hertel, R. K., & Swain, M. A. (1974). *Conflict and marriage.* San Francisco: Jossey-Bass.

Rubin, L. B. (1983). *Intimate strangers: Men and women together.* New York: Harper & Row.

Scanzoni, J. (1968). A social system analysis of dissolved and existing marriages. *Journal of Marriage and Family, 30,* 452–461.

Scanzoni, J. (1978). *Sex roles, women's work and marital conflict: A study of family change.* Lexington, MA: D. C. Heath/Lexington Books.

Scanzoni, J. (1979). Social exchange and behavioral interdependence. In T. L. Huston & R. L. Burgess (Eds.), *Social exchange and developing relationships* (pp. 61–98). New York: Academic Press.

Scanzoni, J., & Arnett, C. (1987). Enlarging the understanding of marital commitment via religious devoutness, gender role preferences and locus of marital control. *Journal of Family Issues, 8:* 136–156.

Scanzoni, J., & Szinovacz, M. (1980). *Family decision-making: A developmental sex role model.* Beverly Hills: Sage.

Scanzoni, J. (1987). "Families in the 1980s: Time to refocus our thinking." Journal of Family Issues. 8: 394–421.

Scanzoni, J., Polonko, K., Teachman, J., & Thompson, L. (1988). *The sexual bond: Rethinking families and close relationship.* Newbury Park: Sage.

Strauss, A. (1978). *Negotiations: Varieties, contexts, processes and social order.* San Francisco: Jossey Bass.

Thibaut, J. W., & Kelley, H. H. (1959). *The social psychology of groups.* New York: Wiley.

Turner, R. H. (1985). Unanswered questions in the convergence between structuralist and interactionist role theories. In H. J. Helle & S. N. Eisenstadt (eds.), *Micro-sociological theory: Perspectives on sociological theory* (Volume 2, pp. 22–36). Beverly Hills: Sage.

Veroff, J., Douvan, E., & Kulka, R. A. (1981). *The inner American: A self portrait from 1957 to 1976.* New York: Basic Books.

Waldruff, D. (in preparation). *Assessing the decision making processes of distressed couples.* Doctoral Dissertation, University of North Carolina-Greensboro.

Weiss, R. L. (1978). The conceptualization of marriage from a behavioral perspective. In T. J. Paolino, Jr. & B. S. McCrady (Eds.), *Marriage and marital therapy* (pp. 165–239). New York: Brunner-Mazel.

Winfield, F. (1985). *Commuter marriage.* New York: Columbia University Press.

Zartman, I. W. (1978). Negotiation as a joint decision-making process. In I. W. Zartman (Ed.), *The negotiation process: Theories and applications* (pp. 67–86). Beverly Hills: Sage.

CHAPTER 11

Dyadic Models of Contraceptive Choice, 1957 and 1975

Elizabeth Thomson

Married couples are often theoretically and analytically treated as a single unit rather than as an interacting dyad. This is particularly common in studies of marital fertility, since births occur (at least socially) to couples. However, married couples do not always agree about whether and when to have children (Beckman, 1984; Czajka, 1979; Muhsam and Kiser, 1956; Westoff, Mishler, & Kelley, 1957; Westoff, Potter, Sagi, & Mishler, 1961), and there seem to be few real compromises between having and not having a(nother) child. They are therefore often faced with decisions about "joint" contraceptive behavior. Even though specific actions to prevent pregnancy may be undertaken by one or the other spouse, the other's marital fertility is inhibited. If neither spouse contracepts, they share the risk of conception and birth.

Though studies of women's fertility motives, goals, and intentions have dominated research on contraceptive behavior and fertility, several investigators have collected data from both wife and husband in order to understand the couple's fertility behavior. The typical model specifies additive effects of each spouse's motives or goals on the couple's fertility behaviors or outcomes (e.g., Beckman, Aizenberg, Forsythe, & Day, 1983; Fried & Udry, 1979; Udry, 1981). Additive models confound two very different effects, those of shared motives/goals and those involving a choice or compromise. When goals are shared, it is not clear that they should be specified as two distinct variables; when they differ, there is no reason to assume that the resulting behavior or outcome is an additive function of the two goals. When agreeing and disagreeing couples are lumped together, the effects of shared goals may be underestimated, since they are more likely to be directly translated into couple behavior and outcomes than one or the other of two competing motives/goals. On the other hand, choices or compromises between different goals may be obscured, because the overall association between each spouse's motive/goal and couple behavior is dominated by the identical associations for couples whose motives or goals are the same.

Interaction models are required to correctly specify both the effects of shared goals and choices between competing goals on joint behaviors and outcomes (Thomson, in press). In this chapter, I specify and estimate interaction models of marital contraception, using survey data collected from wife-husband pairs. The models provide not only estimates of the effects of shared goals on contraceptive use, but also evidence of various decision "rules" that couples may use to resolve disagreements about having children. The analyses use data collected during two important periods in the history of U.S. fertility, the Baby Boom of the 1950s and the Baby Bust of the 1970s.

Resolution of Fertility Disagreements

Since the dyad has no majority, couples must use some other decision "rule" when they disagree about a joint behavior or outcome. Several alternative rules have been investigated by family scholars; each implies a different pattern of association among spouses' goals and couple behavior.

Patriarchal rule is perhaps historically the most common way of resolving marital disagreements—husbands' goals prevail. Although the structure of modern society continues to support male dominance (Gillespie, 1971), most wives and husbands today do not believe that the goals of husbands should automatically be preferred to those of wives.

The "sphere of interest" decision rule is that each spouse wins all or most of the time about goals in her/his sphere of interest (Scanzoni, 1979). In the husband's sphere of interest, behaviors and outcomes will be consistent with his goals, while wives "win" in their spheres of interest. Because children and family are assumed to be in wives' sphere of interest, this rule implies that wives' fertility goals supersede those of husbands. There is perhaps more normative support for this type of decision, particularly since women incur the costs of pregnancy and childbirth, as well as potentially greater involvement in child rearing.

Some decisions appear to be made de facto. At any given time, the couple's behavior produces outcomes that may not be consistent with one spouse's goals. When goal attainment requires behavioral change, disagreement may be resolved by doing "nothing," that is, by continuing the status quo. Neal and Groat's (1980) theory of social drift assumes that disagreement prevents couples from making a decision to contracept, and therefore results in pregnancy. Davidson and Beach (1981) propose a theory of inertia in which the same decision rule may apply, but the starting point is different; that is, couples are already contracepting and must change behavior in order to conceive a child.

Additional considerations or "rules" may come into play when a couple is deciding which specific contraceptive method to use. Some methods require cooperation while others may be used by wives without the cooperation, and perhaps without the knowledge, of their husbands [i.e., oral contraceptives and intrauterine devices (IUDs)]. What appears to be a sphere-of-influence outcome (wives win) may in fact be the outcome of the wife's unilateral decision to avoid pregnancy using these methods of contraception. Other important attributes of contraceptive methods are their side effects; particular methods may produce negative side effects primarily for the wife, primarily for the husband, or equally for both spouses. When the couple disagrees about preventing pregnancy, an equity rule might be used to choose a method that has more negative effects for the spouse who wants to prevent conception than for the spouse who would like to have a child.

Interaction Models of Individual Goals and Contraceptive Behavior

Sometimes we may be able to obtain direct measures of couples' fertility decision rules; however, we will still want to test reports of those rules by observing the couple's fertility behavior and outcomes in relation to their individual goals. When we have no direct measures of decision rules, they must be inferred from those relationships. The problem is that different decision rules may lead to the same observed behavior; we must specify models that distinguish identical behaviors based on different rules. Such inferences are often possible only if we contrast the behavior of couples whose goals differ to that of couples with the same goal.

Models of marital contraceptive choice pose another analytic problem, since the dependent variable is not continuous. Although alternative methods may be ordered on a theoretical dimension of interest (e.g., effectiveness, severity of side effects for the wife or the husband), they must be analyzed as discrete choices. There is no real midpoint between using condoms and using a diaphragm; conceptual as well as empirical discontinuities exist no matter what continuum we specify to underlie the discrete choice of one method or another. If we are willing to dichotomize contraception into use and nonuse, it is relatively easy to estimate interaction models of wives' and husbands' fertility goals, but then considerable information is lost. In particular, we cannot distinguish unilateral female decisions nor analyze the equity rule for choice among methods with different side effects for women and men.

Table 11.1 presents a model of direct and interaction effects of spouses' desires for another child on contraceptive choice. The dependent variables (columns) are contrasts between the use of each method and using no method at all; for simplicity's sake (and in relation to available data), three method categories are specified: oral contraceptives and IUDs, foam and/or diaphragm, and condoms. Oral contraceptives and IUDs are combined because they can both be used unilaterally by women and because their side effects are experienced only by women. Both spouses must cooperate to some extent in using the other methods, and they all may affect the couple's sexual spontaneity; however, condoms may have additional effects on men's sexual pleasure, while diaphragm and foam are more trouble for women.

Table 11.1. Loglinear model of contraceptive choice.

Desire for another child	Contrast		
	Oral contraceptives, IUDs vs. no method	Diaphragm, foam vs. no method	Condoms vs. no method
Husband "no"	b1[a]	b2	b3
Wife "no"	b4	b5	b6
Both "no"	b7	b8	b9

[a] Coefficients b1–b9 represent effects of individual or shared desires to prevent pregnancy on the log-likelihood of being in the top method category, rather than using no contraceptive method.

(Male and female categories of voluntary sterilization could also be specified, but since the analyses below are limited to reversible methods of fertility control, they are not included in this example.)

The independent variables in Table 11.1 are combinations of spouses' desires to prevent a birth: husband only, wife only, and both spouses desire no child (at this time). The omitted category is couples who both want another child (now.). The coefficients in Table 11.1 represent the effects of one or both spouses' desires to prevent a birth on the likelihood of using each method, relative to the likelihood of using no method at all. Each decision rule discussed earlier implies a different pattern of effects:

Patriarchal Rule

Method use and choice depend only on husband's goal, and effects are the same, regardless of the wife's goal:

$$b4 = b5 = b6 = 0$$

$$b7 = b1 > 0$$

$$b8 = b2 > 0$$

$$b9 = b3 > 0$$

Sphere-of-Influence Rule

Method use and choice depend only on wife's goal and effects are the same, regardless of the husband's goal:

$$b1 = b2 = b3 = 0$$

$$b7 = b4 > 0$$

$$b8 = b5 > 0$$

$$b9 = b6 > 0$$

De-Facto Decisions

The direction of effects depends on the contraceptive status quo. If the couple is not using contraception regularly, disagreement inhibits method use; only couples who both want to prevent a birth will be more likely to use a contraceptive method than the omitted category, couples who want to conceive:

$$b1 = b2 = b3 = 0$$

$$b4 = b5 = b6 = 0$$

$$b7, b8, b9 > 0$$

If contraception is the status quo (Bumpass, 1973), effects of shared desires to prevent pregnancy should be the same as that of a single desire; disagreement would be associated with contraceptive use and pregnancy prevention (Townes, Beach, Campbell, & Wood, 1980):

$$b1 = b4 = b7 > 0$$

$$b2 = b5 = b8 > 0$$

$$b3 = b6 = b9 > 0$$

Unilateral-Female Decision

If we consider only method use per se, we cannot distinguish sphere-of-influence decision rules from unilateral decisions of wives to use oral contraceptives or IUDs. However, with the three categories specified in Table 11.1, we may be able to distinguish the two rules. Unilateral-female decisions are reflected primarily in effects of wives' goals on use of oral contraceptives and IUDs. By implication, such decisions may depress use of condoms, diaphragm, or foam among couples who disagree. Thus, evidence for unilateral female decisions would be provided by the following pattern:

$$b1 = 0$$

$$b7 = b4 > 0$$

$$b8 > b5, b2$$

$$b9 > b6, b3$$

Equity Rule

Evidence for this rule depends on differences in effects of spouses' desires on use of "female" versus "male" methods. Husbands' desires to prevent conception should increase the likelihood of condoms or perhaps decrease the likelihood of any method, since husbands have no options for unilateral contraception. Wives' desires to prevent conception should increase the likelihood of diaphragm and foam, as well as oral contraceptives and IUDs.

Thus, we would look for the following pattern of effects:

$$b4 > b7 > b1$$
$$b5 > b8 > b2$$
$$b3 > b9 > b6$$

Models of this form can be estimated with multinomial logistic regression. This technique produces simultaneous estimates of the effects of independent variables (including control variables such as social and economic characteristics) on the log-odds of being in one category of contraception rather than another (Aldrich & Nelson, 1984; Knoke & Burke, 1980). If there are n possible categories of the dependent variable, effects on n-1 independent contrasts can be estimated. The contrasts can be specified in theoretically meaningful ways. For example, rather than contrasting different method types to no method as in Table 11.1, we might contrast the "cooperative" and no-method categories to orals and IUDs in order to estimate potential effects of unilateral female decisions. The primary advantage of multinomial logistic regression is that we use all the information available about associations among independent variables, even when estimating a dichotomous contrast between any two particular method categories; we are not limited to a subset of the cases falling into categories and therefore obtain better estimates of variable effects.

The relation between spouses' fertility goals and their contraceptive choice was examined with survey responses from U.S. couples in 1957 and 1975. A critical difference between these two time points is that oral contraceptives and IUDs were not available in 1957, so that unilateral female contraception was not possible. As a result, the 1957 data provide somewhat better evidence of the equity decision rule, since so many more couples were using either the diaphragm or condoms than in 1975. First, I present analyses of the 1975 survey data, and then those for the earlier period. Similarities and differences between the two sets of findings are discussed in the concluding section.

Desires for Children and Marital Contraception, 1975

The U.S. Value of Children Survey was conducted in 1975 (Hoffman, Thornton, & Manis, 1978). A nationally representative sample was drawn of married women under 40 years of age. The response rate was 79%. Husbands of 434 of these respondents were also interviewed.[1] Analyses reported here were based on 308 nonpregnant, fecund couples; couples in which one

---

[1] Of the 1,569 female respondents, 576 were selected to have their partners interviewed. It is unclear whether attempts were made to obtain the partner's participation in all of these cases. The minimum possible response rate is 76%, making the minimum estimate of the "couple" response rate 60%.

or the other spouse was sterile, or who reported fertility "problems" were excluded. Although the effects of spouses' fertility goals on voluntary sterilization (especially male vs. female) are relevant to the theoretical questions addressed herein, they cannot be estimated with cross-sectional data. Sterilized couples may rationalize their inability to conceive by reporting they want no more children; any association between spouses' goals and choice of sterilization could then be due to the effects of that prior decision on current goals, rather than to the effects of prior goals on that decision.

Measures of each spouse's desire for another child were constructed from responses about desired family size, current family size, and desired timing of the next child. For respondents who said they would like more children, desired family size was computed as current number of children plus the number of additional children desired "if you could have just what you wanted." For respondents who said they would not want more children, and who said their current family size was "about right," desired family size was set equal to current family size. Respondents who wanted no more children and who did not say their current family size was "about right" were asked how many children "you think you would have preferred," and this number was used for desired family size.[2] Respondents who desired more children than they currently had were asked: "When would you want your next child to be born?" On the basis of these responses, respondents were divided into three categories: desire no more children; desire another child "later" (in 2 or more years); desire another child "now" (within a year of the survey, "as soon as possible," or "anytime").[3]

Measures of contraceptive choice were based on the wife's report and initially categorized as follows: no method, rhythm, condoms, diaphragm or foam, oral contraceptives, or IUD. In order to control for possible spurious associations between spouses' desires and contraceptive choice, reports were obtained from the wife of her education, age, race (black/nonblack), parity, number of prior marriages, and duration of current marriage.

---

[2] This measure attempts to capture the respondent's underlying feelings about childbearing and not her/his intended or expected family size. Respondents' intentions or expectations about having another child are more likely to take into account any known differences in desires of wife and husband, as well as the respondent's beliefs about how those differences were being or would be resolved. The wording "if you could have just what you wanted" was designed to explicitly remove consideration of partner's desires in stating own desires. Of course, this wording may have removed consideration of other aspects of the respondent's life situation that we might not want to be disregarded, such as age. Therefore, the responses may incorporate elements of "ideal" family situations. (However, see footnote 3.)

[3] One wife and two husbands who had initially indicated they desired another child recanted when asked to specify a preferred time for the child to be born. These respondents were therefore classified as desiring no more children on the timing variables. The fact that only three respondents changed their responses in this way suggests that the initial measure of desire for another child does not represent an abstract ideal.

Table 11.2 presents the distribution of contraceptive method by spouses' desires for the timing of another child (no, later, now). As shown in the bottom row of Table 11.2, a little more than half of couples share the desire for another child, while less than one-third agree they want no more children. Substantial minorities disagree about whether (16%) or when (13%) to have another child. Turning to the column percentages, 74% of couples who both desire another child "now" are not contracepting, compared with only 16% of disagreeing couples and 15% of couples who agree on no additional children. The latter group may consist of couples who believe they are not fecund (even though the wife reported no "fertility problems") or couples who would ideally like to avoid a birth but do not feel strongly enough to use contraception. Similarly, some of the couples who both desire another child "now" but are using contraception may believe they will be able to conceive very soon after stopping contraception.

Although some of the predicted patterns of contraceptive choice seem to emerge in Table 11.2, there are too few cases in several categories to test the statistical significance of the relations between couple's desires and method use. In order to do so, it was necessary to combine the "cooperative" methods of rhythm, condoms, foam and diaphragm, even though these methods differ in their relative side effects for wife and husband. The small number of couples using rhythm were also included in this category. Thus, the multinomial regression analysis estimates effects of spouses' fertility goals on only two contrasts: "female" methods (orals, IUDs) versus no method, and "cooperative" methods versus no method.

Couples' desires for another child are represented in the analysis by six dummy variables constructed from wife's and husband's indicators of desired timing: wife desires another child "now" and husband desires postponement, wife desires postonement and husband desires another child "now," both partners desire another child "later," only the wife desires another child, only the husband desires another child, both partners desire no more children. The reference category includes couples who both desires another child "now."

Table 11.3 presents estimates of the effects of the couple's desires on the log-odds of using "female" or "cooperative" methods, in comparison with using no method, and in comparison with one another. (Note that the latter contrast is simply a linear function of the first two.) The logistic regression coefficients and their standard errors are presented for each comparison. Positive coefficients indicate that the particular combination of wife's and husband's desires increases the likelihood that the couple is in the top category of method use rather than the bottom, in comparison with couples who both desire a child now; negative coefficients indicate the reverse.

Desire by either partner to postpone or avoid a birth increases the likelihood of using some contraceptive method. We must therefore reject hypotheses that patriarchal or sphere-of-influence rules underlie the couple's contraceptive behavior. Instead, these findings are consistent with a de facto de-

Table 11.2. Desires for another child and contraceptive method.

Method	N	Couple's desire for a(nother) child						
		Neither	W No H yes	W yes H no	Both later	W later H now	W now H later	Both now
None	63	14.8%	13.6%	8.3%	9.7%	18.8%	33.3%	73.7%
Rhythm	6	3.4	0.0	0.0	2.8	0.0	0.0	2.6
Condoms	17	9.1	0.0	4.2	6.9	0.0	9.5	2.6
Diaphragm, foam	26	11.4	4.5	25.0	5.6	0.0	9.5	0.0
Orals, IUD	169	61.4	81.8	62.5	75.0	62.5	47.6	21.1
		100.0	100.0	100.0	100.0	100.0	100.0	100.0
Total	281	88	22	24	72	16	21	38
Percent	100.0	31.3	7.8	8.5	25.6	5.7	7.5	13.5

Note. From U.S. Value of Children Survey, 1975. W = wife; H = husband.

Table 11.3. Effects of desires for another child on contraceptive choice.

Desires for child timing	"Cooperative"[a] vs. no method	"Female" vs. no method	"Female" vs. "cooperative"
Husband later, wife now			
Logit[b]	1.94*	1.53**	−0.41
S.E.	(1.00)	(0.71)	(1.01)
Husband now, wife later			
Logit	3.06**	2.95**	−0.11
S.E.	(1.14)	(0.85)	(1.05)
Both later			
Logit	3.33**	3.28**	−0.05
S.E.	(0.93)	(0.64)	(0.88)
Husband no, wife yes			
Logit	4.88**	4.19**	−0.69
S.E.	(1.22)	(1.03)	(0.95)
Husband yes, wife no			
Logit	3.10**	4.73**	1.63
S.E.	(1.50)	(0.98)	(1.34)
Both no			
Logit	4.74**	4.82**	0.07
S.E.	(1.02)	(0.78)	(0.92)

Note. From U.S. Value of children Survey, 1975.

[a] "Cooperative" methods are condoms, diaphragm, foam, and rhythm. "Female" methods are oral contraceptives and IUD.

[b] Logit coefficients; control variables are wife's education, age, race (black/nonblack), parity, duration of current marriage, and number of prior marriages; standard errors (S.E.) in parentheses.

* One-tailed t-test, $p < .05$.

** Two-tailed t-test, $p < .05$. Note, however, that the tests of significance for each comparison are not independent of the tests for the other two comparisons.

cision rule in which the status quo is contraception (Davidson & Beach, 1981); disagreement is associated with contraceptive use, and spouses are most likely to stop contracepting when both desire another child "now."

On the other hand, there appears to be support for a weak form of the sphere-of-influence rule, in which disagreements are more likely to be resolved in the wife's favor. The coefficients for couples in which only the husband desires postponement are smaller than those for couples in which only the wife desires postponement; and the latter are very similar to estimated effects for couples who both desire postponement. However, when the dummy variables representing categories of spouses' desires were recoded to represent successive (top to bottom) contrasts, the "husband now, wife later" group was not significantly more likely than the "husband later, wife now" group to contracept.

Turning to the decision rules based on method attributes, there is no evidence of unilateral female decisions to contracept. Such decisions would require that "husband no, wife yes" couples be less likely (negative rather than positive coefficient) and that "husband yes, wife no" couples be equally likely (nonsignificant coefficient) to use "female" methods in comparison with couples who both desire no additional children. (Parallel patterns would be expected for disagreements about timing.) However, using the contrast-coded independent variables, there were no significant differences between successive pairs of the last three categories.

There is some support for the equity decision rule based on the side effects of female or cooperative methods. Using contrast coding, "husband yes, wife no" couples were significantly less likely than "husband no, wife yes" couples to use "cooperative" methods, in comparison with "female" methods or no method at all. That is, disagreements about having a(nother) child (ever) shift method choice toward oral contraceptives and IUDs when the wife doesn't want the child, but toward condoms and diaphragm (see Table 11.2) when the husband wants to avoid a birth. The spouse whose goals are met by method use may be more willing than otherwise to incur its negative side effects.

The relative size of coefficients for postponement desires (first three rows) and avoidance desires suggests that the de facto decision rule is less strong for disagreements about timing than it is for disagreements about occurrence of a birth. However, the coefficients for the "both later" category are not significantly different from those for categories of desires to avoid a birth.

Desires for Children and Marital Contraception, 1957

The first wave of the Princeton Fertility Surveys was conducted in 1957 (Westoff et al., 1961). Randomly selected married women whose second birth occurred in September 1956 were interviewed 5 to 7 months after the birth. All wives resided in one of the eight largest standard metropolitan areas of the United States, excluding Boston. Wives and their husbands were both white, married only once, and living together with no expectation of being separated for 6 months or longer in the near future. At the time of the interview, the wife did not believe herself to be pregnant. The husbands of 941 respondents completed mailed, self-administered questionnaires.[4] Analyses reported here were based on 882 fecund couples.

Measures of each partner's desire for another child were constructed from responses about desired family size and desired or expected timing of the next child. Each spouse was asked "How many children do you want to have altogether, counting the two you now have?" Those who reported a desired family size of two were coded as desiring no additional children. Wives who reported a desired family size of three or more were asked "How long from

---

[4] This number constitutes an 81% response rate among the 1,165 couples in which the wife had been interviewed.

now would you personally like to have your next child born?" However, husbands were asked how soon they expected another child. Although husbands who desired only two children often reported they expected a third child at some time, they were coded as wanting no more children; for those whose desired family sizes were greater than two, timing desires were assumed to be equal to expected timing.[5] For both wives and husbands, timing desires/expectations of less than 24 months, as well as such responses as "don't care," were coded "now," responses of 24 months or more, "later."

The measure of contraceptive choice was drawn from the wife's report. Respondents were allowed to specify up to four different methods. The numerous options presented were collapsed into five categories: no method; rhythm, douche, or irregular use of other methods; regular use of "male" methods (condoms, withdrawal); regular use of "female" methods (diaphragm, foam, jelly, suppository, pessary); regular use of both "male" and "female" methods (in combination or alternately).[6] Control variables include the wife's reports of her own education and age, and of marital duration.

Table 11.4 presents the distribution of contraceptive method by spouses' desires for the occurrence and timing of a third birth. Slightly more than half agree they want another child, and about one-quarter share the desire to stop at two. Almost as many disagree about having a third child (21%) or about the birth's timing (16%). Approximately two-thirds of couples who both want a child now use no method, relatively ineffective methods, or contracept irregularly, while a similar proportion of couples who both desire no more children use relatively effective methods on a regular basis. Spouses who differ in wanting another child seem just as likely to use effective methods as those who both desire no more children. On the other hand, disagreements about the timing of the next (desired) birth have the opposite effect; those couples are almost as likely to use no method or ineffective methods as couples who are willing to conceive "now," while shared desires

---

[5] Of the 319 husbands who desired no more children, 97 expected to have a child later and 26 expected to have a child now. In contrast, only two wives gave inconsistent responses on the desired family size and desired timing variable. The 123 husband who expected children they did not desire were recoded as desiring no additional children on the couple timing variable. The timing variable therefore assumes that husbands who want additional children desire to have them at the same time as they expect them. The measure is not exactly comparable with the wife's measure, but alternative approaches (such as not recoding the 123 discrepant husbands) did not produce substantially different results.

[6] Several alternative categorizations were also considered. For example, couples who used both male and female methods were randomly assigned to the male or female category. This had virtually no effect on the results. Including irregular with regular use of male or female methods also made little difference. Finally, weak methods used irregularly were combined with no method; since some differences between weak or irregular methods and nonuse could be detected, this approach was rejected.

Table 11.4. Desires for another child and contraceptive method.

Method	N	Neither	W No H yes	W yes H no	Both later	W later H now	W now H later	Both now
					Couple's desire for a(nother) child			
None	107	9.0%	5.1%	10.2%	8.1%	18.8%	13.5%	36.4%
Rhythm, douche	242	20.9	19.0	19.4	31.5	40.0	38.5	29.9
Withdrawal, condoms	315	46.4	41.8	48.1	32.2	23.5	23.1	16.9
Diaphragm, foam	186	22.3	26.6	19.4	23.0	16.5	19.2	14.3
Diaphragm, condoms, etc.	32	1.4	7.6	2.8	5.2	1.2	5.8	2.6
		100.0	100.0	100.0	100.0	100.0	100.0	100.0
Total	882	211	79	108	270	85	52	77
Percent	100.0	23.9	9.0	12.1	30.6	9.6	5.9	8.7

Note. From Princeton Fertility Survey, Wave 1, 1957.

Table 11.5. Effects of desires for another child on contraceptive choice.

Desires for child timing	Low Effective[a] vs. no method	"Male" method vs. no method	"Female" method vs. no method	"Male and "female" method vs. no method
Husband later, wife now				
Logit[b]	1.13**	1.20**	1.16**	1.57
S.E.	(0.53)	(0.59)	(0.62)	(1.03)
Husband now, wife later				
Logit	.95**	1.00**	.84	.00
S.E.	(0.42)	(0.48)	(0.52)	(1.28)
Both later				
Logit	1.45**	2.07**	1.91**	2.12**
S.E.	(0.38)	(0.42)	(0.44)	(0.82)
Husband no, wife yes				
Logit	.96**	2.36**	1.73**	1.63**
S.E.	(0.48)	(0.48)	(0.53)	(1.00)
Husband yes, wife no				
Logit	1.74**	2.99**	2.85**	3.53**
S.E.	(0.64)	(0.63)	(0.67)	(1.00)
Both no				
Logit	1.41**	2.63**	2.28**	1.54
S.E.	(0.41)	(0.44)	(0.47)	(0.99)

Note. From Princeton Fertility Survey, Wave 1, 1957.
[a] Low effective methods are rhythm and douche, or irregular use of other methods; "male" methods are regular use of condoms or withdrawal; "female" methods are regular use of diaphragm, jelly, and/or foam.
[b] Logit coefficients; control variables are wife's education, age, and duration of current marriage; standard errors (S.E.) in parentheses.
* One-tailed *t*-test, $p < .05$.
** Two-tailed *t*-test, $p < .05$. Note, however, that the tests of significance for each comparison are not independent of the tests for the other two comparisons.

to postpone a birth are associated with levels of method use almost as high as that for couples who both want no more children.

Table 11.5 presents the multinomial logistic regression estimates and standard errors for each method contrast. Almost all of the coefficients are significant and positive, so we must again reject hypotheses that either husbands' or wives' goals are more likely to prevail. Regardless of method type, the likelihood of use is increased by either spouse's desire to postpone or avoid a birth. De facto decisions from a starting point of contraceptive use are consistent with this pattern of effects. (The pattern of effects on use of both "male" and "female" methods is slightly different, but the small number of couples in this category and the resulting larger standard errors make it unwise to draw conclusions from the difference.)

There is no evidence here that the equity rule applies to contraceptive choice. The effects of spouses' goals on the relative likelihoods of "male" and "female" methods are very similar, and contrasts between them were not statistically significant. (Recall, however, that those tests are not independent of the tests reported in Table 11.5.)

Disagreements about birth timing are associated with lower likelihood of regularly using "male" and "female" methods than are disagreements about having a third child. That is, there is a significant difference between the effects on method use of "husband now, wife later" goals and those of "both later" goals. On the other hand, shared desires to postpone a birth have essentially the same effect on contraception as shared desires to have only two children or as disagreements about (ever) having a third child. The likelihood of using less effective methods or contracepting irregularly is increased about the same by desires to postpone or avoid pregnancy.

Desires for Children and Marital Contraception, 1957 and 1975

In the United States, marital fertility behavior appears to be influenced by the desires of both wife and husband. In 1957 and 1975, either spouse's desire to postpone or avoid a birth increased the likelihood of contraceptive use, in comparison with couples who both wanted another child "now." There was no evidence for either period that wives' or husbands' fertility goals were more likely to prevail, and therefore no evidence of decision rules based on male dominance or wife's sphere of influence. For the 1970s, when IUDs and oral contraceptives gave wives the option of unilateral decisions to contracept, there is no evidence that they did so.

This evidence of de facto decisions under the status quo of contraception is consistent with previous findings for the Baby Bust period that disagreement about having a child decreased the likelihood of a subsequent birth (Townes et al., 1980). Based on these analyses of 1957 data, it seems that the corresponding contraceptive pattern also prevailed during the Baby Boom. However, it is important to remember that the 1957 data come from urban, Protestant couples who already had two children. Had the effects of disagreement on contraceptive use been estimated for a more heterogeneous population, the results could have been different.[7] The 1957 respondents do exhibit the fertility pattern toward which high-fertility populations shifted in the 1970s, so it is not terribly surprising that the heterogeneous 1975 sample revealed similar patterns of fertility goals and contraceptive use. (Note, for example, that the distribution of desires for another child is quite similar for the two samples, despite the great differences in their composition.)

---

[7] On the other hand, these differences were to some extent statistically controlled by including religion, race, number of prior marriages, and parity in the analysis of the 1975 data, and by controlling in both analyses for marital duration and wife's age and education. It was not possible to analyze data for a subset of the 1975 couples who were similar to those surveyed in 1957; only 43 couples were white, married only once, with exactly two children, the youngest child under 2 years of age, and wife not pregnant at the time of interview.

No evidence was found in the 1957 data for "equitable" choices of contraceptive method, based on the direction of disagreement and side effects of different methods for wives versus husbands. Couples were just as likely to use "male" as "female" methods, regardless of which spouse wanted to prevent pregnancy. In 1975, on the other hand, there was some evidence that "female" methods of IUDs and oral contraceptives were more likely to be used when only the wife wanted no more children, and "cooperative" methods when only the husband wanted no more children. Several explanations for the difference between the two findings are plausible. First, the 1957 couples were both Protestant, married only once, and had just had their second child; perhaps such couples are more likely than more heterogeneous couples to think of themselves as a unit, even when they disagree, and therefore less likely to be concerned about individual equity in choosing a contraceptive method. Second, the potential side effects of IUDs and oral contraceptives are much more serious than those of the "female" methods of the 1950s, and are therefore more likely to be taken into account as a component of equitable contraceptive decisions. Third, marriage in the 1970s may have been viewed in more individualistic terms for all couples; increasing female autonomy and changing marital roles might have increased the salience of equity in marital decisions.

One difference in the two sets of findings probably reflects real social change. In 1975, disagreements about birth timing among couples who both wanted another child, did not significantly reduce the likelihood of contraceptive use, in comparison with couples who both wanted a child "later"; in 1957, the reduction was significant, and disagreements about timing led to contraceptive behaviors similar to those for couples who agreed they wanted another child "now." These findings are consistent with the increased use of contraception in the 1970s for spacing as well as for stopping births (Westoff & Ryder, 1977). They suggest that at least some of the early births reported by Baby Boom mothers were on time for fathers, and that mothers and fathers in the 1970s were more likely to experience births too late for at least one parent.

These analyses also have more general methodological and theoretical implications. The interaction models specified to represent effects of different decision rules enabled tests of potential differences between the effects of wives' and husbands' fertility goals on joint contraceptive behavior. A simple additive model would not allow us to draw such conclusion. In addition, the multinomial specification of the dependent variable, contraceptive behavior, enabled the drawing of inferences about unilateral female decisions, and about decisions based on an equitable distribution of method side effects. Such evidence would not be provided in models using an ordinal or interval measure of method effectiveness or using a dichotomous measure of use/nonuse.

The results suggest a dyadic version of Davidson and Beach's (1981) theory of inertia, in which irreversible decisions (such as to stop contraception and attempt to conceive) are not made until a relatively high threshold of motivation is reached. It is likely that both spouses must attain some threshold of desire for a child before they make the appropriate change in behavior of stopping contraceptive use. Of course, with these data, we don't know what that threshold might be, since we have only a dichotomous measure of each spouse's desire. The different effects in 1957 of desires for timing versus occurrence demonstrate, further, that the outcome of "inertia" depends on the behavioral status quo. When couples are not contracepting (as was common between desired births during the Baby Boom), disagreeing couples may experience fertility outcomes similar to those for couples who both want another child; when contraception is the status quo (in order to stop having children in the 1950s and for both stopping and spacing in the 1970s), disagreeing couples will be more like couples who both desire to postpone or avoid another birth.

Acknowledgment. This research was supported by Grant 1-R01-HD-17190 and by Center Grant HD-05876 from the Center for Population Research, NICHHD, and by a grant from the Wisconsin Alumni Research Foundation. Thanks are also due to Richard Williams for his able research assistance and useful comments on earlier versions of this paper. Preliminary analyses of the 1975 data were presented at the annual meetings of the Population Association of America, Minneapolis, Minnesota, May 1984, and in Working Paper 83–8, Center for Demography and Ecology, University of Wisconsin, Madison, Wisconsin.

References

Aldrich, J. H., & Nelson, F. D. (1984). Linear probability, logit, and probit models. Sage University Paper series on Quantitative Applications in the Social Sciences (no. 45). Beverly Hills, CA: Sage.

Beckman, L. J. (1984). Husbands' and wives' relative influence on fertility decisions and outcomes. *Population and Environment, 7,* 182–197.

Beckman, L. J., Aizenberg, R., Forsythe, A. B., & Day, T. (1983). A theoretical analysis of antecedents of young couples' fertility decisions. *Demography, 20,* 519–533.

Bumpass, L. L. (1973). Is low fertility here to stay? *Family Planning Perspectives, 5,* 67–69.

Coombs, L. C., & Chang, M. (1981). Do husbands and wives agree? Fertility attitudes and later behavior. *Population and Environment, 4,* 109–127.

Czajka, J. L. (1979). Husband-wife agreement on desired family size in the United States. Unpublished doctoral dissertation, University of Michigan, Ann Arbor, MI.

Davidson, A. R., & Beach, L. R. (1981). Error patterns in the prediction of fertility behavior. *Journal of Applied Social Psychology, 11,* 475–488.

Fried, E. S., & Udry, J. R. (1979). Wives' and husbands' expected costs and benefits of childbearing as predictors of pregnancy. *Social Biology, 26,* 265–274.

Gillespie, D. L. (1971). Who has the power? The marital struggle. *Journal of Marriage and the Family, 33*, 445–458.

Hoffman, L. W., Thornton, A., & Manis, J. D. (1978). The value of children to parents in the United States. *Journal of Population, 1*, 91–132.

Knoke, D., & Burke, P. J. (1980). *Log-linear models.* Sage University paper series on Quantitative Applications in the Social Sciences (no. 20). Beverly Hills, CA: Sage.

Muhsam, H. V., & Kiser, C. V. (1956). The number of children desired at the time of marriage. *Milbank Memorial Fund Quarterly, 34*, 287–312.

Neal, A. G., & Groat, H. T. (1980). Fertility decision making, unintended births, and the social drift hypothesis: A longitudinal study. *Population and Environment, 80*, 221–236.

Scanzoni, J. (1979). Social processes and power in families. In W. R. Burr, R. Hill, F. I. Nye, & I. L. Reiss (eds.), *Contemporary theories about the family: Vol. 1. Research-Based Theories* (pp. 295–316). New York: The Free Press.

Thomson, E. (in press) Two into one: Modeling couple behavior. In T. W. Draper & A. C. Marcos (eds.), *Family variables: Conceptualization, measurement and use.* Beverly Hills, CA: Sage.

Townes, B. D., Beach, L. R., Campbell F. L., & Wood, R. L. (1980). Family building: A social psychological study of fertility decisions. *Population and Environment, 3*, 210–220.

Udry, J. R. (1981). Marital alternatives and marital disruption. *Journal of Marriage and the Family, 43*, 889–897.

Westoff, C. J., & Ryder, N. B. (1977). *The contraceptive revolution.* Princeton, NJ: Princeton University Press.

Westoff, C. F., Mishler, E., & Kelly E. (1957). Preferences in size of family and eventual fertility twenty years after. *American Journal of Sociology, 62*, 491–497.

Westoff, C. F., Potter, R. G., Jr., Sagi, P. C., & Mishler, E. G. (1961). *Family growth in metropolitan America.* Princeton, NJ: Princeton University Press.

CHAPTER 12

Decision-Making on Retirement Timing

Maximiliane Szinovacz

Introduction

When approaching the retirement years, men and women tend to be married and active members of the labor force.[1] This means that timing of retirement frequently involves decision making between spouses, and that adjustment to retirement depends not only on the retiree's own life circumstances but on those of his or her spouse as well. Yet family sociologists and gerontologists rarely view retirement from a dyadic decision-making perspective.

In contrast to the prevailing individualistic approach, this chapter applies a couple perspective and views retirement timing of married couples as a decision outcome evolving from influence and negotiation processes between spouses. Given the paucity of research on retirement as a couple event, the purpose of this chapter is twofold: the first part of the chapter is devoted to a theoretical exploration of retirement timing decision-making processes and a reevaluation of previous research from this perspective; the second part provides some preliminary empirical analyses of couples' retirement timing.

The Retirement Timing Decision-Making Process

Family power researchers agree that adequate investigation of marital decision making requires consideration of the decision-making *process* (McDonald, 1980; Scanzoni, 1979; Szinovacz, 1987). This means that decision-making research cannot be restricted to decision outcomes but must include

---

[1] According to recent statistics, 81.2% of men aged 55 to 64 years, and 78.9% of men aged 65 to 74 years are married. The respective percentages for women are 67.0% and 49.1% (U.S. Bureau of the Census, 1986). Among men, labor-force participation (currently employed) decreases from 86.6% for the 45 to 54 age-group to 64.9% for those aged 55 to 64 years and to 24.4% for those aged 65 to 69 years. The respective labor-force participation rates for women are 64.4%, 40.4%, and 13.8% (U.S. Department of Labor, 1987).

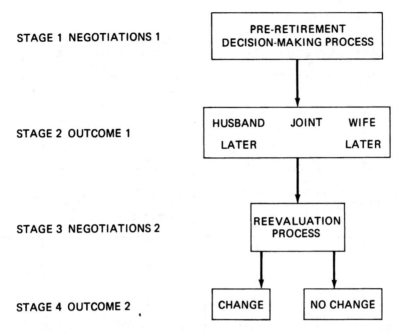

Figure 12.1. Steps of the retirement decision-making process.

analyses of spouses' negotiations before a decision is reached as well as rene-gotiations of outcomes and potential outcome changes deriving from such renegotiations (Scanzoni & Szinovacz, 1980).

Application of this perspective to couples' retirement timing implies at minimum a four-stage process (see Figure 12.1).[2] Spouses' negotiations about the timing of retirement (stage 1) precede the retirement of one or both spouses (stage 2). Once the first decision is implemented (i.e., when one or both spouses retire), the outcome is reevaluated and, if found dissatisfactory by one or both spouses, a new series of negotiations may start (stage 3) resulting either in the maintenance or change of the previous decision (stage 4). Further negotiations and outcome changes may occur if the new outcome again dissatisfies one or both spouses, provided such changes are still possible.[3]

Exchange theorists view the outcome of decision-making processes (or

---

[2] Further stages in the decision-making process are, of course, possible and likely to occur. Furthermore, as outlined in Scanzoni and Szinovacz (1980), the negotiation process itself may involve several "decisioning" stages.

[3] In contrast to other marital decisions (e.g., division of household work), the transition to retirement may be irreversible. For instance, once the husband quits his job, he may not be able to return to the labor force. The impact of nonvoluntary factors on retirement decision making is addressed in a later section of this paper.

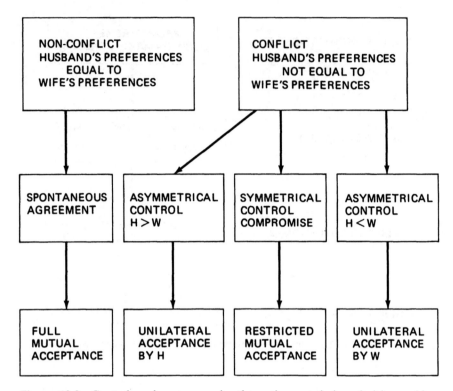

Figure 12.2. Control and outcomes in the retirement-timing decision-making process.

negotiations) as a function of the discrepancy between actors' preferences and their relative power over selected issues.[4] As shown in Figure 12.2, high convergence between spouses' preferences (nonconflict) is expected to result in a mutually agreed-upon outcome and to involve minimal negotiations ("spontaneous agreement," Scanzoni & Szinovacz, 1980). In the conflict situation (preferences are different) spouses may either reach a compromise or one partner may impose his/her preferences on the other. Compromise outcomes will typically reflect a more symmetrical exertion of power than the noncompromise solutions.[5]

In terms of the retirement-timing decision, the nonconflict situation should lead to retirement timing that is mutually accepted by and satisfac-

---

[4] For a detailed description of this approach and its application to marital power relationships, see Szinovacz (1987). The conceptualization of power as the ability to achieve *desired* outcomes is, perhaps, most clearly expressed in Nagel's (1975) work.

[5] Decision outcomes are not necessarily determined by power advantages. The more powerful partner may choose not to impose his position on the partner, or other circumstances may render control attempts impossible or ineffectual.

tory to both spouses (see Figure 12.2). In contrast, the noncompromise conflict situations are expected to generate unilateral acceptance and discrepancies in spouses' satisfaction with the outcome, that is, satisfaction on the part of the "winning" and dissatisfaction on the part of the "losing" spouse. By definition, the compromise situation implies mutual acceptance of the retirement-timing decision, but it may be less satisfactory to both spouses than outcomes achieved through spontaneous agreement.[6]

Analyses of exchange and power relations presume that actors are free to choose among outcomes. Situational factors (e.g., pension coverage, work conditions) may inform but not determine actors' choices. However, retirement timing can be nonvoluntary as in the case of mandatory retirement or severe illness or disability of one or both spouses. Under such circumstances, the retirement-timing decision models outlined in Figures 12.1 and 12.2 do not hold.[7] Specifically, the model shown in Figure 12.1 assumes that a couple's retirement-timing decision takes into account when each spouse should retire *in relation to the other spouse*. If one spouse's retirement is nonvoluntary, the decision-making process will focus on the retirement timing of the other spouse (provided he or she is not subject to nonvoluntary retirement) and the nonvoluntary retirement will, by definition, be independent of both spouses' preferences (see Figure 12.3). It is probably rather rare for both spouses to simultaneously experience nonvoluntary retirement (i.e., both spouses simultaneously experience mandatory retirement or severe illness). However, nonvoluntary retirement of one spouse may require the other spouse to leave the labor force or to postpone retirement, regardless of his or her preferences (e.g., the spouse's illness demands extensive caregiving). Consequently, as shown in Figure 12.3, nonvoluntary retirement of one spouse (in this example, the wife) implies that spouses' preferences and their negotiations will focus exclusively on the retirement of the other spouse (the wife); that the conditions associated with the nonvoluntary retirement will affect spouses' negotiations concerning retirement timing of the other spouse; that possibilities of outcome changes will be restricted. Under these conditions, acceptance of and satisfaction with retirement timing will be a function of the extent to which the decision on the wife's retirement reflects each spouse's preferences, the conditions associated with the husband's nonvoluntary retirement such as lack of income, illness, or care-

---

[6] The proposed relationship between type of retirement timing, decision making, and satisfaction with decision outcomes relies on the assumption of a positive linear relationship between outcome control over this decision and outcome satisfaction. At least in the marriage literature, this assumption requires empirical support. For instance, asymmetrical decision making on major issues such as timing of retirement could have negative consequences for the marital relationship, which in turn may reduce the controlling partner's outcome satisfaction ("If I hadn't made her retire, things would be much better between us").

[7] Several authors stress the nonapplicability of exchange theory to nonvoluntary situations (Blau, 1964; Chadwick-Jones, 1976; Gratton & Haug, 1983).

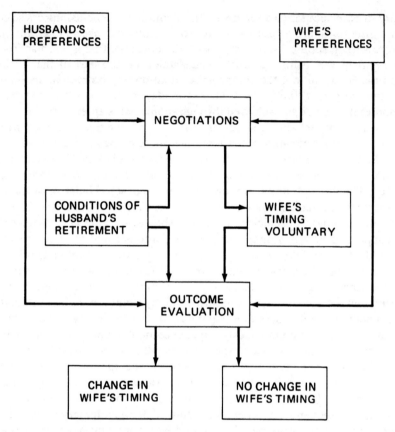

Figure 12.3. Outcome evaluation of combined voluntary and nonvoluntary retirement timing.

giving responsibilities, as well as the degree to which the husband's non-voluntary retirement timing is perceived to be off-time and/or to prevent achievement of work or life goals (Neugarton & Hagestad, 1976; Atchley, 1982).

Previous Research

The retirement-timing model discussed above relies on three major assumptions. It assumes, first, that both spouses' retirement timing constitutes a decision-making unit. Consequently, timing outcomes for both spouses are contingent on both spouses' preferences and/or nonvoluntary timing determinants. Finally, each spouse's evaluation of timing outcomes will depend on the extent to which his or her preferences were implemented and whether or not the transition was voluntary. Restrictions in the design of previous research (cf. Gratton & Haug, 1983) do not allow an assessment of this model and its assumptions. However, some previous findings on the retirement timing and retirement satisfaction of men and women may shed some light on the validity of the above assumptions and on needs for future research. Studies pertaining to these issues are discussed in the following pages; selected research findings from a recent study by the author are presented later in this chapter.

Retirement Timing

Using data from the Longitudinal Retirement History Study (LRHS),[8] several researchers investigated factors associated with the retirement-timing decision (measured as discontinuation of labor-force participation) of male respondents and their wives (Anderson, Clark, & Johnson, 1980; Clark, Johnson, & McDermed, 1980; Henretta & O'Rand, 1980, 1983). Major findings from this research indicate: a tendency toward joint retirement of spouses (i.e., spouse's labor-force status constitutes a significant determinant of respondent's labor-force status that cannot be attributed to other variables); the impact of selected characteristics of both spouses on labor-force status; the prevalence of health, age, and economic considerations (including social security and pension benefits, income or support of dependents) on retirement timing. Henretta and O'Rand (1983) further show symmetrical effects of spouses' pension coverage, age, and wages on retirement-timing patterns, and Anderson et al. (1980) suggest that dual-worker couples delay retirement to implement a joint-retirement transition.

Based on these findings, the authors stress the importance of viewing labor-force participation and retirement decisions within a household framework (Anderson et al., 1980, p. 124) and retirement "as a process that involves the family unit" (Henretta & O'Rand, 1983, p. 515). Their finding of symmetrical effects of selected spouse characteristics on retirement timing leads Henretta and O'Rand (1983, p. 516) to the additional conclusion that spouses' retirement decision making reflects "a certain amount of equality in decisions to retire."

Other studies confirm that wives consider their husband's retirement timing in their own plans. Prentis (1980) reports that close to one-half of his sample of white-collar working women indicated that they would follow their husband's retirement. Middle-aged women surveyed in the National Longitudinal Surveys (NLS) did not plan to retire at the same time as their husbands, but they did note that their husbands' retirement might propel their own retirement transition (Shaw, 1984). Similar trends toward joint retirement are reported by Atchley and Miller (1983) and Campione (1987).

---

[8] For a description of the Longitudinal Retirement History Survey see Schwab and Irelan (1981) and the references cited in this section.

How much women adjusted their retirement plans to those of their husbands was affected by social security and pension eligibility, income, husband's health, and the age differences between spouses (Shaw, 1984; Prentis, 1980; Gratton & Haug, 1983).

How do these findings relate to the decision-making models described above? They clearly support the assumption that spouses plan and implement the timing of retirement in relation to each other. They also demonstrate—as does other research (Kimmel, Price, & Walker, 1978; Palmore, George, & Fillenbaum, 1982)—the multidimensionality of retirement reasons: Spouses' retirement preferences tend to be based on and reflect a complex set of motives, including more objective factors such as economic considerations, work conditions, or health, as well as more subjective factors such as occupational goals and leisure plans. What these studies do not show is husbands' and wives' relative influence on retirement-timing decisions. Some studies suggest that a noteworthy number of women incorporate husbands' expected retirement time into their own plans (Prentis, 1980; Shaw, 1984), but similar questions were not asked of men.[9]

Adjustment to Retirement

Whereas some research on retirement timing incorporates a couple perspective, the literature on retirement adjustment remains tied to an individualistic approach (Gratton & Haug, 1983; Szinovacz, 1984a). At best, studies compare the retirement adjustments of men and women, at worst, they focus on the adjustment of one sex or ignore the sex of respondents (Szinovacz, 1982). Investigations comparing the retirement adjustments of men and women have yielded divergent results. Whereas some studies indicate lower adjustment on the part of women (Atchley, 1976; Seccombe & Lee, 1986; Streib & Schneider, 1971), other research shows no significant sex differences (Atchley, 1982; Atchley & Miller, 1983; Gratton & Haug, 1983).

Previous research also failed to provide a consistent picture of sex differences in the predictors of retirement adjustment. For instance, Atchley (1982) reports women to be more vulnerable than men to situational influences, whereas George, Fillenbaum, & Palmore (1984) find more effects of retirement on various outcomes for men than for women, and Seccombe and Lee (1986) show no sex differences in predictors of retirement adjustment. In-

---

[9] Henretta and O'Rand (1983) infer equality in the decision-making process from symmetric statistical effects of selected spouse characteristics on retirement timing. The symmetry pattern may reflect equality, but it could also imply that one spouse imposes an economically feasible solution on the other spouse. In other words, the husband could say: "Given *our* income, pension coverage, and age, I will continue to work until age 64 and then we will both retire together." This example may produce the symmetrical effects described by Henretta and O'Rand even though it suggests that the husband imposes his preferences on his wife. Unless spouses' preferences are assessed, conclusions about spouses' relative power in the negotiation process are unwarranted.

vestigations of the impact of husbands' retirement on wives demonstrate great variability in wives' reactions and in their adaptation to husbands' needs (Fengler, 1975; Keating & Cole, 1980; Hill & Dorfman, 1982; Heyman & Jeffers, 1968).

The applicability of these studies to the relationships between retirement-timing decision making and satisfaction outlined in the preceding section of this chapter is quite limited. Not only were the predictors of retirement adjustment included in these studies modeled on early research on male retirement (e.g., health, income, leisure, or social activities), they rarely included spouse or couple characteristics. Also, research findings on the effects of husbands' retirement on housewives cannot be generalized to dual-worker and dual-retirement couples (Szinovacz, 1980; Dobson, 1983; Brubaker, 1985; Atchley & Miller, 1983). The one truly applicable study (Atchley & Miller, 1983) partially supports implications of the decision-making model for retirement adjustment: It demonstrates that spouse's characteristics have some effect on the retiree's life satisfaction. However, it does not show an effect of couple's retirement-timing patterns on the couple's postretirement life satisfaction.[10] In summary, it seems appropriate to conclude with Gratton and Haug (1983, p. 70) that the "most fruitful and useful source for subsequent research on female retirement clearly lies in the analysis of retirement decisions of married couples" and that such research is yet to be conducted.

Sex Differences in Retirement Timing and Adjustment: Some Preliminary Findings

To test the decision-making model outlined above and to overcome limitations in previous research, it would be necessary to obtain couple data that include information on spouses' retirement-timing preferences, their objective, as well as subjective reasons for retirement and their adjustment to this life transition. No study to date fulfilled all of these requirements. The data presented in the following sections of this chapter provide some of the needed data but also share limitations of previous research.[11] Specifically, the study relies on data from unrelated men and women and contains only limited information on spouse characteristics. Its cross-sectional design further

---

[10] The decision-making model relates retirement-timing patterns to each spouse's adjustment; Atchley and Miller (1983) used couple satisfaction scores, which may suppress discrepancies in spouses' adjustment. Their findings indicate, however, that low life satisfaction is reported most often by couples with a working wife and a retired husband. The highest satisfaction scores occurred for couples with a retired wife and an employed husband.

[11] The major purpose of the present investigation was to assess the impact of life-event accumulation on retirement adjustment (Szinovacz, 1984a). Restrictions on the length of the instrument did not allow for more complete inclusion of spouse characteristics.

may result in some retrospective bias, especially on subjective assessments of preretirement and retirement transition events (e.g., self-reported health, retirement motives). Nevertheless, the study does offer information pertinent to retirement-timing decision making that was only rarely included in previous research (e.g., the relative retirement timing of spouses, marital and familial retirement reasons). Given these limitations, the following analyses address a selected range of research questions pertinent to couples' retirement decision making:

Retirement timing: How do spouses time their retirement in relation to each other? How important does spouse's retirement feature among the retirement motives of men and women?

Retirement adjustment: How does spouses' relative retirement timing relate to satisfaction with retirement timing and adjustment to the retirement transition? Does retirement to accomodate one's spouse reduce retirement adjustment?

Methodology

Sample and Data Collection

Data for this study were collected by mailed questionnaires in the Winter and Spring of 1983/1984. The sample consists of recent retirees (retired between 1979 and 1983) who were covered by Florida's state retirement system. Respondents were identified from the state's retirement system files. In selecting respondents, random sampling stratified by sex, retirement date, and income category (low, medium, high, estimated on the basis of years of service and amount of pension) was applied. Questionnaires were mailed in two waves: the first wave of 1,626 questionnaires was sent out in late 1983 and early 1984. A second wave of 525 questionnaires was mailed later in the Spring of 1984. This later mailing oversampled groups with high non-response rates to the first mailing, namely, low-income men and high-income women. The final study population consists of 912 retirees. Of the total 2,145 contacted individuals, 1,127 failed to respond (52.5%), another 51 (2.4%) questionnaires were returned for other reasons (e.g., moved, died) and 53 questionnaires (2.6%) were deleted from the sample because they either failed to meet sampling criteria or were only partially completed. While stratification goals were generally met, the sample slightly under-represents men, respondents in the middle-income category, and respondents retiring prior to 1981. Data for this chapter rely on the subsample of married retirees; also excluded were respondents who reported full-time employment at the time of the survey.[12] This subsample consists of 611 respondents, 336 men and 275 women.[13]

---

[12] The Florida Retirement System permits state retirees unlimited employment in the private sector; such employment does not affect pension payments.

[13] For a detailed description of the sample and data collection see Szinovacz (1984a).

Measures

The major groups of variables included in the following analyses are demographic and other background characteristics, retirement timing, retirement motives, and adjustment to retirement. Measurement of these variables is described below.

Demographic and Background Information

Income. Respondents' postretirement household income was used in the analyses. Current rather than preretirement household income was chosen because current income level is probably more important than preretirement income for respondents' retirement adjustment. Also, retirement timing is likely to be influenced by expected income adequacy after retirement, which is better reflected in current than preretirement income. Data for this variable were collected by asking subjects to choose among 26 income categories ranging from under $2,000 to over $50,000. These income categories were presented in $2,000 increments. Means and standard deviations of these and the other variables are shown in Tables 12.5 and 12.6.

Occupational Status. In addition to the income variables, respondents' occupational prestige was taken into consideration. This variable was based on written-in job descriptions and coded according to the classification used in the National Opinion Research Center (NORC) surveys. High scores indicate high prestige.

Pension Coverage. By definition, all respondents were covered by the state pension plan. However, not all respondents were eligible for full pension coverage. The Florida Retirement System's requirements for pension coverage are based on a combination of age and years of service. Except for certain special-risk annuitants, full coverage is achieved if an employee reaches age 62 with at least 10 years of state service (such service need not be continuous) *or* if a member reaches 30 years of service regardless of age. Members with at least 10 years of service may retire prior to age 62; however, their pension will be reduced by 5% for each year of retirement prior to their 62nd birthday. This reduction is not applied if members accumulated 30 years of state service. For the purposes of this study, one dummy variable was created to measure achievement of full pension coverage. Respondents who had either reached age 62, or 30 years of state service at the time of retirement were coded 1.

Community Size. While research findings relating community size to retirement adjustment are somewhat contradictory, there is agreement that environmental factors related to community size may importantly affect the elderly (Coward & Lee, 1985). To control for such effects, community size was considered in the analyses coded from 1 (small town under 10,000) to 5 (big city, over 500,000).

Length of Retirement. Length of retirement was included in the analyses to control for a potential "honeymoon effect" on retirement adjustment

(Atchley, 1976; Beck, 1982). Given sampling criteria, length of retirement could range from under 1 to 5 years.

Retirement Age. Retirement age was measured by subtracting length of retirement from respondents' age at the time of the survey. Because the sample contains only recent retirees, age at retirement and respondents' age are highly correlated ($r = .96$). Consequently, only retirement age was included in the analyses.

Presence of Extended Family Members. Several studies on retirement timing show relationships between continued labor-force participation and number of dependents (cf. Henretta & O'Rand, 1983). To control for such effects, the present analyses included a dummy variable on the presence of extended family members in the household. Extended family members residing with the respondents were primarily their children and their parents, but also included siblings, grandchildren, or nieces and nephews. Presence of an extended family member was coded 1.

Health. Several measures of health status were obtained in the survey. Spouse's health status was measured indirectly through a list of life events. Respondents indicated whether or not and when their spouse had experienced a major illness or injury. Based on responses to this item, a dummy variable was created. A code of 1 was assigned to those respondents whose spouse suffered a major illness or injury up to 3 years prior to or at any time after respondents' retirement. Respondents' current and preretirement health status was assessed through a series of questions on life problems. Based on this question, respondents indicated whether they had experienced a specific problem (in this case, health problems) prior to and/or after retirement and how serious they considered this problem to be. For the present analysis, a dummy variable measuring respondents' current health status was created. Codes of 1 were assigned if respondents indicated "somewhat serious" or "very serious" health problems after retirement, regardless of their preretirement health status.

Retirement Timing

The major purpose of this analysis is to examine spouses' relative retirement timing and the impact of such timing patterns on retirement adjustment. Based on information on respondents' own and their spouses' retirement date, a six-category variable was created: spouse currently employed full time, spouse retired 12 months or more after the respondent, spouse retired within 11 months before or after the respondent (joint retirement), spouse retired 12 months to 5 years prior to the respondent, spouse retired over 5 years before the respondent and spouse is a housewife. For the regressions these variables were transformed into dummy variables, treating housewives and spouses retiring more than 5 years prior to the respondent as the omitted category.[14]

Retirement Motives

The present investigation differs from many previous studies in its assessment of respondents' subjective retirement reasons. The questionnaire contained a question asking respondents to indicate how important 14 listed retirement reasons were for their own retirement. Answer categories were presented in a four-category Likert format, ranging from "very important" to "not important." In addition, respondents were asked to rank the three most important reasons, and they were encouraged to write in reasons not contained in the 14-item list. The answers to these questions were combined as follows: all reasons ranked among the three most important ones were coded as "very important"; all open responses that could be incorporated into the 14-item list were treated as responses to the pertinent item; if respondents' importance ranking for the open question differed from their answer to the specific precoded item, the higher score was assigned.

For some analyses, selected motives were combined as follows: family (family needed me, had to take care of ill relatives), spouse (spouse retired, spouse didn't want me to work), and self (wanted more time for myself, wanted to do other things). Intercorrelations among the motives combined into these categories ranged from $r = .55$ to $r = .80$. Since several motives were ranked infrequently as "very important" and showed a U-curve distribution, the combined motives were recoded into dummy variables assigning a code of 1 to respondents describing the motive as "very important" or "somewhat important."

Retirement Satisfaction

Two variables focusing on different aspects of retirement satisfaction were considered in the data analyses: satisfaction with timing of retirement and retirement adjustment. The first variable was measured with a single-item question asking respondents whether they would have preferred to retire later, at the same time, or sooner than their actual retirement. The original question was presented in five answer categories and later recoded into a dummy variable (1 = later).

Retirement adjustment was assessed with a modified version of Thompson's (1958) job deprivation scale. Scale scores were obtained by summing item scores and dividing the sum by the number of valid responses. Subjects were assigned a missing value if they failed to respond to less than 12 of the 16 items. The reliability for the entire sample is .92 (Cronbach's alpha).

---

[14] Inclusion of housewives as a separate dummy variable in the regressions for men did not alter the findings. Only the regressions with the combined omitted category are presented below.

Results

Timing of Retirement

The first research question addressed here concerns sex differences in retire-ment-timing patterns and their correlates. Data are presented that dem-onstrate the distribution of retirement-timing patterns within this popula-tion and that show relationships of timing patterns to selected respondent characteristics.

Sex differences in retirement timing are summarized in Table 12.1. To allow comparisons for dual-work couples, men's retirement timing was computed twice, once for the entire group of married men (row 1) and then for men in dual-earner couples (row 2). As shown in Table 12.1, the majority of couples were in a dual-retirement or dual-nonworking marriage at the time of the survey: Only about one-quarter of both men and women (33% for men in dual-earner couples) reported continuing employment of their spouse at the time of the survey.

Comparisons of spouses in previously dual-earner couples reveal sig-nificant sex differences in spouses' relative retirement timing. In general, women tend to retire later than their husbands (42% compared with 25%) and men retire earlier than their wives (49% compared with 35%). This means, of course, that men in dual-work couples are more likely than women to enter retirement while their spouse continues to work. Women, on the other hand, tend to retire into a dual-retirement situation. About one-quarter of both male and female respondents retired simultaneously, that is, within 1 year of each other. This proportion rises to two-fifths if a time period of 2 years is considered (not shown in Table 12.1).

Despite their tendency to retire later than their husbands, wives are bound to retire "early": They are significantly younger at retirement than men (59 compared with 62 years, $p < .01$), they are significantly less likely to reach full pension eligibility (47% vs. 70%, $p < .01$), and they are more apt than men to indicate preferences for later retirement (47% vs. 37%; $p < .05$).

To further explore these trends, spouses' retirement timing was related to

Table 12.1. Retirement timing by sex.

	Timing of retirement relative to respondent						
	Currently employed	Retired later	Retired at same time	Retired up to 5 years earlier	Retired over 5 years earlier	Housewife	(N)
Men	23%	11%	18%	8%	9%	31%	(288)
Men (dual earner)	33%	16%	26%	12%	13%		(198)
Women	25%	10%	23%	23%	19%		(251)

Chi-square (dual-earner men vs. women): 16.21, $p < .01$.

Table 12.5. Regression on retirement adjustment (men).

	b (1)[a]	b (2)[a]	$\overline{X}$	SD	r
Health	−0.25**	−0.22**	0.25	0.44	−0.35**
Spouse health	−0.07	−0.06	0.12	0.33	−0.12*
Community size	0.01	0.02	2.45	1.28	0.02
Household dependents	−0.09	−0.09	0.21	0.41	−0.10
Income	0.22**	0.19**	11.57	6.39	0.27**
Occupational status	0.07	0.06	46.92	16.50	0.26**
Retirement length	−0.06	−0.05	3.04	1.33	−0.08
Retirement age	−0.04	−0.09	62.13	4.62	−0.02
Timing-employed	−0.17**	−0.13*	0.20	0.40	−0.11*
Timing-later	−0.05	−0.05	0.09	0.29	−0.00
Timing-same	−0.03	−0.03	0.16	0.36	0.04
Timing-to 5 years earlier	−0.00	−0.03	0.07	0.25	−0.00
Motive spouse	−0.02	0.00	0.21	0.41	0.04
Motive family	−0.04	−0.04	0.21	0.41	−0.09
Motive self	0.18**	0.08	0.57	0.50	0.30**
Preferred later ret.		−0.28**	0.37	0.48	−0.40**
Family x later			0.08	0.27	−0.20**
Spouse x later			0.06	0.24	−0.13**
Retirement adjustment			2.79	0.53	
R	0.51	0.56			
R2	0.26	0.32			
F	7.48**	9.34**			
F change		27.85**			

[a] Standardized coefficients.
*$p < .05$. **$p < .01$.

holds. For women, positive and close to significant relationships also show with community size, retirement date, and occupational prestige. Among the three retirement motives only personal reasons are positively and significantly related to the retirement adjustment of both sexes. Men score significantly lower on adjustment if their spouses are currently employed, whereas women tend to report slightly higher adjustment if they retired jointly with their husbands.

In general, these trends remain after preference for later retirement is entered into the equations. Introduction of this variable somewhat enhances the impact of retirement age on men's adjustment, and it predictably reduces the effect of personal retirement reasons for both sexes (in the case of men to an insignificant level). Preference for later retirement is strongly negatively related to the retirement adjustment of both men and women. As noted above, interaction terms of marital and familial retirement reasons by preference for later retirement are nonsignificant for both sexes. However, the bivariate relationships are significant and in the predicted direction, that is, retirement for marital or familial reasons that is associated with preference for later retirement reduces adjustment. The first model accounts for 26% of

Table 12.6. Regression on retirement adjustment (women).

	b (1)[a]	b (2)[a]	b (3)[a]	X̄	SD	r
Health	−0.14*	−0.11*	−0.13*	0.19	0.39	−0.25**
Spouse health	0.04	0.02	0.02	0.18	0.38	0.02
Community size	0.09	0.10	0.12*	2.52	1.30	0.13*
Household dependents	−0.06	−0.07	−0.05	0.18	0.38	−0.04
Income	0.06	0.06	0.06	12.80	6.10	0.16**
Occupational status	0.11	0.07	0.09	49.06	12.70	0.21**
Retirement length	0.11	0.09	0.10	2.95	1.37	0.09
Retirement age	0.05	0.03	0.00	59.34	4.54	−0.04
Timing-employed	0.09	0.10	0.04	0.23	0.42	0.10
Timing-later	0.01	0.02	−0.00	0.09	0.28	−0.01
Timing-same	0.12	0.13	0.13*	0.21	0.41	0.01
Timing-to 5 years earlier	0.08	0.09	0.10	0.21	0.41	0.02
Motive spouse	−0.05	−0.04		0.56	0.50	0.01
Motive family	0.00	0.03		0.40	0.49	−0.01
Motive self	0.31**	0.18**	0.18**	0.60	0.49	0.36**
Motive family needs			0.09	0.37	0.48	−0.01
Motive care ill relative			−0.15*	0.19	0.40	−0.13*
Motive spouse retired			−0.14*	0.48	0.50	−0.02
Motive spouse against work			0.04	0.33	0.47	−0.01
Preferred later ret.		−0.31**	−0.31**	0.47	0.50	−0.43**
Family x later				0.20	0.40	−0.23**
Spouse x later				0.26	0.44	−0.23**
Retirement adjustment				2.84	0.55	
R	0.46	0.54	0.56			
R2	0.22	0.29	0.31			
F	4.75**	6.49**	6.43**			
F change		25.77**				

(N = 275).
[a] Standardized coefficients
*p < .05. **p < .01.

the variance in men's and 22% of the variance in women's adjustment. Introduction of preference for later retirement raises these percentages to 32% and 29%, respectively.

To further explore the impact of marital and familial retirement motives, the same set of regressions was repeated replacing the combined marital and familial retirement reason measures with their noncombined counterparts. Given the low frequency of these retirement motives for men, this detailed analysis was only performed for women (equation three in Table 12.6). In this regression, retirement to take care of ill relatives and retirement due to spouse's retirement reach significant effects. Both motives are associated with a reduction in women's adjustment.

These results show the income and health contingencies of satisfactory retirement reported in previous research; they also demonstrate the positive effect of a planned, leisure-oriented retirement on subsequent adjustment. In

Table 12.2. Spouses' relative retirement timing and other aspects of retirement timing.

	Spouse's relative retirement timing				
	Currently employed	Retired later	Retired at same time	Retired up to 5 years earlier	Retired over 5 years earlier/ housewife	
Men						
Full pension coverage	61%	77%	71%	83%	75%	5.96[a]
Preferred later retirement	55%	32%	37%	13%	29%	17.65***[a]
Retirement age ($\overline{X}$)	59.9	62.0	62.3	63.6	63.0	5.83**[b]
(N)	(66)	(31)	(52)	(23)	(116)	
Women						
Full pension coverage	28%	46%	40%	49%	70%	19.10***[a]
Preferred later retirement	45%	46%	55%	44%	52%	2.10[a]
Retirement age ($\overline{X}$)	56.0	59.7	59.1	60.1	62.6	18.54**[b]
(N)	(64)	(20)	(58)	(57)	(48)	

[a] Chi-square.
[b] F-ratio.
** $p < .01$.

their pension eligibility, preference for later retirement, and retirement age (Table 12.2). These data reveal significant relationships between spouses' retirement timing and respondents' retirement age: Men and women whose spouses are still working retired at a younger age than respondents whose spouses have retired, whereas respondents whose spouses retired more than 5 years earlier than themselves and/or men with housewives retired relatively late. Men with employed wives are also more likely to indicate preferences for later retirement than husbands of retired wives or housewives. For women, retirement timing is not significantly related to preference for later retirement. Even though men's pension eligibility is not significantly related to retirement timing, men with currently employed wives are less likely than others to have reached full pension coverage. The same—and significant—pattern shows for women. They are most likely to have achieved full pension coverage if their spouse retired much earlier than they themselves.

What do these data tell us about trends in and correlates of spouses' relative retirement timing? The results support previous findings indicating a tendency toward joint retirement, but they also demonstrate complexity and differences in spouses' retirement-timing patterns. One group of couples seems to opt for independent and/or separate retirement timing. In this situation, one spouse tends to retire early, often without reaching full pension coverage, whereas the other spouse seems to choose a relatively late retirement, perhaps to ensure pension benefits and an adequate retirement income for the couple. Also, men express regrets about their early retirement if their spouse continues to work.

Taken together, these results offer some—though certainly preliminary—insights into couples' retirement decision-making processes and negotiation outcomes. The first pattern—separate retirement—could evolve from the following negotiation/outcome scenarios: (1) one spouse decides (or is forced) to retire early, and this decision is reached regardless of the other spouse's preferences (unilateral decision); or (2) both spouses consent either through spontaneous agreement or through a compromise that one spouse will quit work while the other remains employed (or delays retirement). The dissatisfaction of male retirees with continued employment of their wives may be evidence of spouses' disagreement on retirement timing (i.e., the husband retires and his wife refuses to follow suit), it may result from husband's nonvoluntary retirement and his resentment of necessary shifts in provider-role responsibilities brought about by this situation, or it may signify a reevaluation of a mutually accepted outcome on the part of the husband that has not yet led to an outcome change. In the case of simultaneous retirement, retirement timing seems to follow the husband's "normative" retirement schedule: This pattern is associated with relatively early retirement and nonachievement of full pension coverage on the part of women. As will be discussed in more detail below, this timing pattern may either signify a mutually agreed upon decision (spontaneous agreement or compromise) or it may constitute a unilateral decision by the husband. Wives, on the other hand, seem less apt to pressure their husbands into joint retirement.

Retirement Motives

Analyses of retirement reasons by sex are shown in Table 12.3. These data indicate respondents' *subjective* assessment of why they quit the labor force; they also allow—at least indirectly—some inferences concerning subjects' ability to implement retirement-timing preferences.

As shown in Table 12.3, both men and women name normative retirement timing (age, time seemed right) among their most important retirement reasons. In addition, man mention their age and sufficient income as major retirement motives. Personal interest reasons for retirement (wanted more time for myself, wanted to do other things) also feature among the more frequently named retirement motives for both sexes. Sufficient income and work-related motives (feeling tired, tired of work, problems at work) are indicated somewhat less frequently. It is in the areas of nonvoluntary and family-related retirement that pronounced sex differences emerge. Men are significantly more likely than women to be subject to nonvoluntary retirement (mandatory retirement and illness); women, on the other hand, are significantly more likely than men to perceive marital and/or familial obligations as major retirement reasons.

These data suggest at least some asymmetry in the degree to which

Table 12.3. Retirement motives by sex.

Motives	Men Important & very important	Women Important & very important	Chi-square
Mandatory	22.8%	12.6%	9.59**
Tired of work	32.1%	39.3%	3.00
Problems at work	29.0%	28.1%	0.02
Had enough money	34.9%	29.6%	1.62
My health	53.9%	43.5%	5.91*
Family needed me	19.4%	37.4%	22.89**
Felt tired	38.9%	38.9%	0.00
Time right	73.5%	78.1%	1.51
My age	57.4%	44.1%	9.95**
Spouse retired	11.7%	48.5%	96.12**
Spouse didn't want me to work	14.5%	33.3%	28.37**
Had to take care of ill relatives	7.4%	19.6%	18.31**
Wanted more time for myself	47.8%	48.1%	0.00
Wanted to do other things	50.6%	57.0%	2.19
(N)	(324)	(270)	

* Sex differences significant at $p < .05$. ** sex differences significant at $p < .01$.

spouses adapt their retirement toward each other; women seem more bound than men to adjust their retirement timing to that of their spouse and/or to family needs. This does not necessarily mean that wives are less apt than husbands to implement retirement-timing preferences, that is, they may *wish* to adapt their own retirement to the retirement of the spouse.

How does retirement for marital reasons relate to spouses' retirement timing? Cross-tabulations between retirement timing and marital retirement motives are shown in Table 12.4. As can be expected, retirement for marital reasons is mentioned less frequently if the spouse is still employed or retired after the respondent. Nevertheless, close to one-fifth of the wives of employed spouses indicate that their husbands wanted them to stop working. Furthermore, men mention marital reasons most frequently if their spouse retired somewhat earlier than they themselves, but somewhat less often in the case of joint retirement. The opposite trend holds for women; they mention marital retirement reasons most frequently if the couple opted for joint retirement timing and somewhat less frequently if their husbands retired prior to the wife.

What do these patterns mean in terms of the decision-making models discussed above? Since marital reasons become an important factor in men's retirement timing only after their wives have been retired for some time, it seems that spouses' retirement is considered primarily at later stages in the decision-making process (i.e., at the reevaluation or renegotiation phase) and, perhaps, only in combination with the achievement of other retirement

Table 12.4. Spouse's relative retirement timing and marital retirement reasons.

Percent mentioning marital reasons	Spouse's relative retirement timing						
	Currently employed	Retired later	Retired at same time	Retired up to 5 years earlier	Retired over 5 years earlier	Housewife	F
Men	5%	10%	37%	57%	23%	18%	36.59***[a]
Women	19%	29%	86%	77%	63%		76.04**

[a] Chi-square for men based on husbands in previous dual-earner families.
** $p < .01$.

circumstances such as full pension coverage. Women, on the other hand, are most likely to note marital reasons in the case of joint retirement, indicating consideration of spouse's retirement during the initial negotiation stage and, if separate retirement was planned or did occur, a more accelerated reevaluation and renegotiation process. In other words, employed wives of retired husbands seem to be under considerably more pressure to retire jointly with or soon after their spouse than are employed men of retired wives.

Predictors of Retirement Adjustment

The decision-making model described in the first section of this chapter proposes that aysmmetrical control combined with unilateral acceptance of the retirement-timing decision will result in reduced retirement adjustment on the part of the "losing" spouse. As noted, the present data do not contain information on spouses' retirement decision-making processes. Based on the model we can predict, however, that respondents feeling "pushed into" retirement by their spouse or by family needs will score lower on adjustment than respondents who retired for voluntary reasons.

To test for these relationships (which essentially propose an interaction effect between retirement for marital/family reasons and preference for later retirement) as well as the impact of specific timing patterns on retirement adjustment, regressions on retirement adjustment were performed separately for men and women. Included in the regressions were selected control variables, retirement-timing patterns coded as dummy variables, as well as marital, familial and personal retirement reasons (using dummy variables for the combined motive variables). All variables were forced into the equations. In subsequent steps, preference for later retirement (coded 1 = later) and the interaction terms of marital or familial reasons by preference for later retirement were entered. Since the interaction terms proved nonsignificant, only results for the first two equations are shown in Tables 12.5 and 12.6.

The first equations confirm the importance of good health and (in the case of men) postretirement income on retirement adjustment. In addition, men tend to report slightly higher adjustment if they live in nonextended house-

Table 12.5. Regression on retirement adjustment (men).

	b (1)[a]	b (2)[a]	$\bar{X}$	SD	r
Health	−0.25**	−0.22**	0.25	0.44	−0.35**
Spouse health	−0.07	−0.06	0.12	0.33	−0.12*
Community size	0.01	0.02	2.45	1.28	0.02
Household dependents	−0.09	−0.09	0.21	0.41	−0.10
Income	0.22**	0.19**	11.57	6.39	0.27**
Occupational status	0.07	0.06	46.92	16.50	0.26**
Retirement length	−0.06	−0.05	3.04	1.33	−0.08
Retirement age	−0.04	−0.09	62.13	4.62	−0.02
Timing-employed	−0.17**	−0.13*	0.20	0.40	−0.11*
Timing-later	−0.05	−0.05	0.09	0.29	−0.00
Timing-same	−0.03	−0.03	0.16	0.36	0.04
Timing-to 5 years earlier	−0.00	−0.03	0.07	0.25	−0.00
Motive spouse	−0.02	0.00	0.21	0.41	0.04
Motive family	−0.04	−0.04	0.21	0.41	−0.09
Motive self	0.18**	0.08	0.57	0.50	0.30**
Preferred later ret.		−0.28**	0.37	0.48	−0.40**
Family x later			0.08	0.27	−0.20**
Spouse x later			0.06	0.24	−0.13**
Retirement adjustment			2.79	0.53	
R	0.51	0.56			
R2	0.26	0.32			
F	7.48**	9.34**			
F change		27.85**			

[a] Standardized coefficients.
*$p < .05$. **$p < .01$.

holds. For women, positive and close to significant relationships also show with community size, retirement date, and occupational prestige. Among the three retirement motives only personal reasons are positively and significantly related to the retirement adjustment of both sexes. Men score significantly lower on adjustment if their spouses are currently employed, whereas women tend to report slightly higher adjustment if they retired jointly with their husbands.

In general, these trends remain after preference for later retirement is entered into the equations. Introduction of this variable somewhat enhances the impact of retirement age on men's adjustment, and it predictably reduces the effect of personal retirement reasons for both sexes (in the case of men to an insignificant level). Preference for later retirement is strongly negatively related to the retirement adjustment of both men and women. As noted above, interaction terms of marital and familial retirement reasons by preference for later retirement are nonsignificant for both sexes. However, the bivariate relationships are significant and in the predicted direction, that is, retirement for marital or familial reasons that is associated with preference for later retirement reduces adjustment. The first model accounts for 26% of

Table 12.6. Regression on retirement adjustment (women).

	b (1)[a]	b (2)[a]	b (3)[a]	X̄	SD	r
Health	−0.14*	−0.11*	−0.13*	0.19	0.39	−0.25**
Spouse health	0.04	0.02	0.02	0.18	0.38	0.02
Community size	0.09	0.10	0.12*	2.52	1.30	0.13*
Household dependents	−0.06	−0.07	−0.05	0.18	0.38	−0.04
Income	0.06	0.06	0.06	12.80	6.10	0.16**
Occupational status	0.11	0.07	0.09	49.06	12.70	0.21**
Retirement length	0.11	0.09	0.10	2.95	1.37	0.09
Retirement age	0.05	0.03	0.00	59.34	4.54	−0.04
Timing-employed	0.09	0.10	0.04	0.23	0.42	0.10
Timing-later	0.01	0.02	−0.00	0.09	0.28	−0.01
Timing-same	0.12	0.13	0.13*	0.21	0.41	0.01
Timing-to 5 years earlier	0.08	0.09	0.10	0.21	0.41	0.02
Motive spouse	−0.05	−0.04		0.56	0.50	0.01
Motive family	0.00	0.03		0.40	0.49	−0.01
Motive self	0.31**	0.18**	0.18**	0.60	0.49	0.36**
Motive family needs			0.09	0.37	0.48	−0.01
Motive care ill relative			−0.15*	0.19	0.40	−0.13*
Motive spouse retired			−0.14*	0.48	0.50	−0.02
Motive spouse against work			0.04	0.33	0.47	−0.01
Preferred later ret.		−0.31**	−0.31**	0.47	0.50	−0.43**
Family x later				0.20	0.40	−0.23**
Spouse x later				0.26	0.44	−0.23**
Retirement adjustment				2.84	0.55	
R	0.46	0.54	0.56			
R2	0.22	0.29	0.31			
F	4.75**	6.49**	6.43**			
F change		25.77**				

(N = 275).
[a] Standardized coefficients
*p < .05. **p < .01.

the variance in men's and 22% of the variance in women's adjustment. Introduction of preference for later retirement raises these percentages to 32% and 29%, respectively.

To further explore the impact of marital and familial retirement motives, the same set of regressions was repeated replacing the combined marital and familial retirement reason measures with their noncombined counterparts. Given the low frequency of these retirement motives for men, this detailed analysis was only performed for women (equation three in Table 12.6). In this regression, retirement to take care of ill relatives and retirement due to spouse's retirement reach significant effects. Both motives are associated with a reduction in women's adjustment.

These results show the income and health contingencies of satisfactory retirement reported in previous research; they also demonstrate the positive effect of a planned, leisure-oriented retirement on subsequent adjustment. In addition, the findings lend some support to the assumption that spouses' relative retirement timing and obligatory (marital/familial) retirement reasons play a part in the retirement-adjustment process. The most pronounced effect is clearly the lower adjustment among men whose spouses remain employed. Men seem to resent the continued employment of their wives and the reversal in the provider role associated with this situation. Women, on the other hand, tend to be slightly less satisfied with retirement if the transition was brought about by the retirement of their spouse or by the care needs of ill relatives. If these motives are controlled, joint retirement timing seems to enhance women's adjustment.

From the perspective of the decision models described at the beginning of this chapter, these results suggest that both the *content* of negotiation outcomes and *how they were reached* influence adjustment. First, retirement for self-oriented motives and perceptions of "on-time" retirement have a pronounced effect on the retirement adjustment of both sexes. This finding supports the assumption that implementation of personal retirement preferences (which may or may not coincide with those of the spouse) is essential for adjustment. Secondly, specific outcomes seem to inhibit adjustment, most notably the continued employment of the wife. Given this situation, we may expect retired husbands to exert some pressure on their wives to leave the labor force as soon as economic considerations permit. Also it is, perhaps, the lack or discontinuation of such pressures combined with joint couple leisure pursuits that lead to the positive association between joint retirement timing and retirement adjustment in women. Case-study materials from previous investigations by the author (see Szinovacz, 1980, 1986/87) support this interpretation.[15] Several women interviewed for these studies described retired husbands' discontent with the wife's continued employment and husbands' efforts to get the wife to retire:

I wanted to work on ... (but) he felt he should work as long as I and vice versa, so he insisted that I retire when he retired and he said my mother needed me. I sort of wanted to work on ... (253B)

He supported my working because I had to. But he also wanted me to stop. He did not want me to work. When I got financially able to quit, this was it. We just looked over the whole financial picture ... and came to conclude that this would be better and it thrilled him to death. He was more excited than I was. (676B)

At first he wanted me to work but then he wanted me to quit. We talked about it and decided that when I reached enough (benefits) that I could retire, then I would go ahead and retire. I guess I would have backed out. (771B)

Well, he retired 15 months before I did and he was just ... lonesome at the house by himself ... He was just really glad when I retired. (633B)

---

[15] Descriptions of the study for all case studies marked A can be found in Szinovacz (1980), and a detailed description of case-study materials marked B can be found in Szinovacz (1986/7).

Women report lower adjustment if they adapted their retirement to their husband's or if they retired to fulfill familial care needs. In contrast, retirement for general family needs and because of the husband's objection to the wife's employment do not lead to lowered adjustment. The first variable may represent voluntary familial retirement, which would not be expected to lower adjustment. In the second case, potential negative effects of wives being pushed into retirement by their husbands may be obliterated by the resolution of preretirement conflicts concerning this issue. The following case-study materials illustrate this relationship from the viewpoint of both spouses:

Husband: I quit at 3:30–4:00 and she didn't come home till 5:00–5:30, you know. There you are, nobody home, beds aren't made, the house a wreck, the sink full of dishes—it just irritates you right off the bat. And then she'd come in and say something, I'd say something, and pretty soon out the door I'd go. Mostly when she worked I'd get a sandwich or anything that I felt like, hollering and bitching like a crazy man. Because there was no supper there and when she did get it ready, I didn't want any, I'd already eaten. Now when I come home hungry from work, I just wash, sit down and eat. I'm still a good cook—I'm a better cook than her, I believe—but, I don't know, you sort of have a wife, you want her home, you know.

Wife: I was tired at night, I didn't feel like cleaning so good. That kind of bugged him because he likes everything clean. But after I cleaned rooms all day for students, you know, I didn't feel much like coming home and wading into it at night. It's easier to do that now because he gets up and leaves and in a couple of hours I can have it all cleaned up. (116, 216A)

Finally, inherent ambiguities in the retirement-reason measures may have reduced the effect of marital/familial reasons on retirement adjustment. The measures did not assess how retirement for marital or familial reasons was perceived by the respondent or how the retirement-timing decision had been reached (e.g., agreement, compromise, or coercion). The decision-making model predicts negative consequences of such reasons primarily for situations representing asymmetrical control and unilateral acceptance (see Figure 12.2). As indicated by the following case-study examples, some wives view retirement for the husband's sake in a quite positive light:

I was glad my husband was here (alive) and I was retiring. I could pay more attention to him ... I could take care of him better. (683B)

My husband had already been retired for 4 years and having to get up and go to work and leave somebody at home was kind of hard. (553B)

I didn't dread it (retirement) nor did I look forward to it because I was happy on my job. But ... I began to notice that my husband was going down and I thought I would rather spend more time with him. (83B)

Also, changes in postretirement conditions (e.g., reduction in the care needs of relatives, satisfaction with leisure endeavors, or enhanced marital satisfaction) may weaken the association between marital/familial retirement and *current* retirement adjustment (Szinovacz, 1986/7).

Conclusions

The purpose of this paper was to address the retirement transition process from a couple perspective. To this effect, models of couples' retirement-timing decision making were developed and some data from a study of recent retirees were presented. It should be emphasized that the empirical analyzes did not constitute a test of the decision models; however, they provided some insights into the viability of these models and their underlying assumptions, as well as into data requirements for future research.

Two major conclusions can be drawn from this study. First, the data indicate a trend toward joint retirement of spouses, but they also demonstrate the existence of other couple retirement patterns. Specific retirement-timing outcomes seem to be associated with differences in couples' negotiations and in their retirement circumstances. Apparently, joint retirement is reached more through adaptations by the wife than by the husband to the other spouse's retirement timing: Wives retiring jointly with their husbands tend to retire early without achieving full pension coverage and were most likely to mention marital retirement reasons. Separate retirement timing, on the other hand, seems related to pronounced discrepancies in spouses' retirement age (and, perhaps, age differences between partners), that is, respondents with currently employed spouses retired relatively early while respondents whose spouses retired earlier report a relatively high retirement age. The early retirement of one spouse seems to involve reliance on the other spouse for achievement of an adequate postretirement income, especially if it is the wife who retires early (only 28% of retired wives with currently employed husbands achieved full pension coverage). Men tend to experience some difficulties in adjusting to later retirement of their spouse as long as the wife continues to work. In this situation, they also seem to exert some pressure on their wives to retire, and wives who reluctantly submit to such pressures can experience lowered retirement adjustment.

Second, the results show effects of sex-role norms on retirement-timing patterns and adjustment processes. Significant sex differences occurred in regard to spouses' retirement age, achievement of full pension eligibility, preferences for later retirement, their retirement motives, and the acceptance of spouses' continued employment. These sex differences are all consistent with a normative pattern that stresses men's traditional provider role and women's marital and familial roles.[16] These results have important implications for research on gender differences in retirement; they suggest that specific retirement-timing patterns have different meanings for men and women and that especially women's retirement timing must be viewed within a familial context (see also Brody, Kleban, Johnsen, Hoffman, & Schoonover, 1987).

What are the implications of these findings for future research on retirement? There can be little doubt that both retirement timing and retirement adjustment ought to be investigated from a couple and sex-role perspective. The decision-making models outlined at the beginning of this chapter may provide a fruitful framework for such research. To test these models, *couples* must be followed from the preretirement stage (both spouses employed) through the retirement transition and, for some, postretirement period to allow assessment of negotiations and outcome changes. Such research should include both *objective* measures pertinent to the retirement process as well as *subjective* assessments of retirement reasons, negotiations, and implementation of preferences.

If couples' retirement transition is viewed from a power/decision-making perspective, it will also be necessary to include in future research adequate measures of power processes and factors that have been shown to influence marital power relations (e.g., sex roles, spouses' relative resources; see Scanzoni, 1979; Szinovacz, 1987) and to apply methodologies appropriate for couple designs (Brown & Kidwell, 1982). The viability of the couple perspective of retirement should further be tested through comparisons of couples' retirement processes with those of unmarried individuals. Consequently, research designs should contain either matched groups of married and nonmarried individuals or rely on stratified random samples that include sufficient numbers of married and nonmarried men and women. Finally, the impact of sex-role norms and other familial conditions such as support of or care for dependents and extended family members requires further investigation.

During the last decade, research on retirement has gone through several stages. We recognized in the late 1970s that more attention should be paid to female retirement; more recently, we have turned to consider couple characteristics in research on retirement timing. The research agenda for the late 1980s and 1990s will be to treat retirement research from an integrated perspective that pays tribute to individual life transitions as well as to marital/familial decision making and adaptations, and that acknowledges the interconnections among these processes.

Acknowledgment. This study was funded by a grant from the American Association of Retired Persons (AARP) Andrus Foundation.

References

Anderson, K., Clark, R. L. & Johnson, T. (1980). Retirement in dual-career families. In R. L. Clark (Ed.), *Retirement policy in an aging society.* Durham, NC Duke University Press.

Atchley, R. C. (1976). Selected social and psychological differences between men and women in later life. *Journal of Gerontology, 31,* 204–211.

---

[16] We must remember that the current generation of retirees was typically raised in a sex-role traditional environment (1920s and 1930s) and married during the 1940s and 1950s.

Atchley, R. C. (1982). The process of retirement: Comparing women and men. In M. Szinovacz (Ed.), *Women's retirement: Policy implications of recent research.* Beverly Hills, CA: Sage.

Atchley, R. C., & Miller, S. J. (1983) Types of elderly couples. In T. H. Brubaker (Ed.), *Family relationships in later life.* Beverly Hills, CA: Sage.

Beck, S. H. (1982). Adjustment to and satisfaction with retirement. *Journal of Gerontology, 37*, 616–624.

Blau, P. M. (1964). *Exchange and power in social life.* New York: Wiley.

Brody, E. M., Kleban, M. H., Johnsen, P. T. Hoffman, C., & Schoonover, C. B. (1987). Work Status and parent care: A comparison of four groups of women. *The Gerontologist, 27*, 201–208.

Brown, L. H., & Kidwell, J. S. (Eds.). (1982). Methodology: The other side of caring [Special issue]. *Journal of Marriage and the Family, 44.*

Brubaker, T. H. (1985). *Later life families.* Beverly Hills, CA: Sage.

Campione, W. A. (1987) A married woman's retirement decision: A methodological comparison. *Journal of Gerontology, 42*, 381–386.

Chadwick-Jones, J. K. (1976). *Social exchange theory: Its structure and influence in social psychology.* London: Academic Press.

Clark, R. L., Johnson, T., & McDermed, A. A. (1980). Allocation of time and resources by married couples approaching retirement. *Social Security Bulletin, 43*, 3–17.

Coward, R. T., & Lee, G. R. (Eds.). (1985). *The elderly in rural society.* New York: Springer.

Dobson, C. (1983). Sex-role and marital role expectations. In T. H. Brubaker (Ed.), *Family relationships in later life.* Beverly Hills: Sage.

Fengler, A. P. (1975). Attitudinal orientation of wives toward their husbands' retirement. *International Journal of Aging and Human Development, 61*, 139–152.

George, L. K., Fillenbaum, G. G. & Palmore, E. (1984). Sex differences in antecedents and consequences of retirement. *Journal of Gerontology, 39*, 364–371.

Gratton, B., & Haug, M. R. (1983). Decision and adaptation: Research on female retirement. *Research on Aging, 5*, 59–76.

Henretta, J. C., & O'Rand, A. M. (1980). Labor force participation of older married women. *Social Security Bulletin, 43*, 10–16.

Henretta, J. C. (1983) Joint retirement in the dual worker family. *Social Forces, 62*, 504–520.

Heyman, D. K., & Jeffers, F. C. (1968). Wives and retirement: A pilot study. *Journal of Gerontology, 23*, 488–496.

Hill, E. A., & Dorfman, L. T. (1982). Reaction of housewives to the retirement of their husbands. *Family Relations, 31*, 195–200.

Keating, N. C., & Cole, P. (1980). What do I do with him 24 hours a day? Changes in the housewife role after retirement. *The Gerontologist, 20*, 84–89.

Kimmel, D. C., Price, K. F. & Walker, J. W. (1978). Retirement choice and retirement satisfaction. *Journal of Gerontology, 33*, 575–585.

McDonald, G. W. (1980). Family power: The assessment of a decade of theory and research, 1970–1979. *Journal of Marriage and the Family, 42*, 841–854.

Nagel, J. H. (1975). *The descriptive analysis of power.* New Haven: Yale University Press.

Neugarten, B. L., & Hagestad, G. O. (1976). Age and the life course. In R. H. Binstock & E. Shanas (Eds.), *Handbook of aging and the social sciences.* New York: Van Nostrand Reinhold.

Palmore, E. B., George, L. K. & Fillenbaum, G. G. (1982). Predictors of retirement. *Journal of Gerontology, 37,* 733–742.

Prentis, R. S. (1980). White-collar working women's perception of retirement. *The Gerontologist, 80,* 90–95.

Scanzoni, J. (1979). Social processes and power in families. In W. R. Burr, R. Hill, F. I. Nye, & I. L. Reiss (Eds.), *Contemporary Theories About the Family* (Vol. 1). New York: Free Press.

Scanzoni, J., & Szinovacz, M. (1980). *Family decision-making. Sex roles and change over the life cycle.* Beverly Hills: Sage.

Schwab, K., & Irelan, L. M. (1981). The Social Security Administration's retirement history study. In N. G. McCluskey & E. F. Borgetta (Eds.), *Aging and retirement: Prospects, planning and policy.* Beverly Hills: Sage.

Seccombe, K., & Lee, G. R. (1986). Gender differences in retirement satisfaction and its antecedents. *Research on Aging, 8,* 426–440.

Shaw, L. B. (1984). Retirement plans of middle-aged married women. *The Gerontologist, 24,* 154–159.

Streib, G. F., & Schneider, C. J. (1971). *Retirement in American society.* Ithaca: Cornell University Press.

Szinovacz, M. (1980). Female retirement: Personal and marital consequences. A case study. *Journal of Family Issues, 1,* 423–440.

Szinovacz, M. (1982). Introduction: Research on women's retirement. In M. Szinovacz (Ed.), *Women's retirement. Policy implications of recent research.* Beverly Hills: Sage.

Szinovacz, M. (1984a). Life events, retirement preparation and adjustment to retirement. A comparative study. Final Report submitted to the AARP Andrus Foundation, Washington, D.C.

Szinovacz, M. (1984b). Changing family roles and interactions. *Marriage and Family Review, 7,* 163–201.

Szinovacz, M. (1986/7). Preferred retirement timing and retirement satisfaction in women. *International Journal of Aging and Human Development, 24,* 301–317.

Szinovacz, M. (1987). Family power. In M. B. Sussman & S. K. Steinmetz (Eds.), *Handbook of Marriage and the Family.* New York: Plenum Press.

Thompson, W. E. (1958). Pre-retirement anticipation and adjustment in retirement. *Journal of Social Issues, 14,* 35–45.

U. S. Bureau of the Census. (1986). *Current population reports, series p-20, No. 410, marital status and living arrangements: March 1985.* Washington, D.C.: U.S. Government Printing Office.

U. S. Department of Labor. (1987). *Employment and earnings.* Washington, D.C.: U. S. Government Printing Office.

Part 5
A Reprise

CHAPTER 13

Multiple Perspectives on Dyadic Decision Making

David Brinberg and James Jaccard

Introduction

As may be seen from the chapters in this volume, dyadic decision making can be approached from numerous points of view. Each view provides a well-articulated and detailed perspective on dyadic decision making. In this chapter, we will discuss general trends in the area of dyadic decision making. We will first characterize the research in several disciplines—communication, bargaining and negotiation, and family relations—that pertain to the interaction processes in dyadic decision making. We will discuss the prominent theories and methods in each field, and highlight some substantive findings that address the interaction process in dyadic decision making. We will then describe methods of data collection for studying dyadic decisions. In the third section, we will propose a research agenda for examining dyadic decision making.

Interaction Analysis

Numerous research areas have examined the interaction among dyads (e.g., anthropology, bargaining and negotiation, counseling psychology, communication, comparative and developmental psychology, family relations, and marketing). We will characterize research in three of these areas—communication, bargaining, and family relations—because of the insights they provide for examining dyadic decision making. Our presentation of each area will be brief and will simply highlight some of the main issues.

Relational Communication

Historical perspective

This area of research focuses on two concurrent levels of communication between members of a dyad: (1) the content (report) of the communication, and (2) the relationship form (command) between couple members. The second level of communication—often referred to as metacommunication—is a level of interaction that modifies the content level. As an example, Bateson (1972) invented the principle of the "double bind," that is, command information that is inconsistent with the content information. The key ingredients of the double bind are: (1) two or more people in an important relationship, (2) repeated experience so that the double bind becomes a habitual expectation, (3) a primary negative injunction, and (4) a secondary injunction conflicting with the first at a more abstract, typically nonverbal level (Wilder, 1979). The classic example is as follows. A hospitalized man is recovering from an acute schizophrenic episode. When visited by his mother, he impulsively put his arm around her shoulder and she stiffened. When he withdrew his arm she asked, "Don't you love me anymore?" When he then blushed, she said, "Dear, you must not be so easily embarrassed and afraid of your feelings" (Wilder, 1979). The double bind is impossible to obey without disobeying.

Prominent Theories

The primary underlying dimension that characterizes this research is the notion of control or dominance. Bateson and associates have described relational communication as not "what" but "how" something is said, with the key dimension as dominance. A distinction is made between control and power. Control deals with the interaction process, not the resources or the outcome. Power is a function of resources, process, and outcome, and occurs in a relationship; that is, power does not exist outside of a relationship (Millars & Millars, 1979).

Three types of communication styles are delineated: dominant (i.e., seek to define the relationship), equivalent (avoid acceptance or assertion of definition), and submissive (accepts relational definition). Dominance is characterized by acts such as assertions, talk-over, nonsupport, and orders. Equivalence is characterized by acts such as the presentation of "facts," or answering questions. Submissiveness is characterized as questions and assertions that provide support. With these three categories, four patterns exist: competitive symmetry, where each person performs a dominant act; neutralized symmetry, where each person performs an equivalent act; submissive symmetry, where each person performs a submissive act; and complementarity, where one person performs a submissive act and the other person performs a dominant act.

Numerous postulates have been suggested about relational communication and individual difference variables. For example, Emery (1982) examined the relationship between internal-external locus of control and the patterns of communication (competitive symmetry, complementarity, and neutralized symmetry). Emery found that high internal dyads were more likely to respond in competitive symmetry as opposed to other patterns of interaction. High internal high external dyads were more likely to respond in a complementary pattern.

Parks (1977) describes a series of postulates concerning relational communication patterns and conflict resolution strategies. For example, greater competitive symmetry is likely to lead to greater unilateral actions, greater frequency of conflict, threats, intimidation and message rejection, than other patterns (e.g., neutrality, complementarity). Further, he hypothesized that greater rigidity (i.e., less frequent changes in the patterns of interaction throughout the course of an interaction) will lead to less frequent attempts to define the relationship.

Researchers also have found the primary relational communication patterns (e.g., symmetry, complementarity) to be related to nonverbal behaviors such as gaze (Burgoon & Hale, 1984) and physical distance. Further, researchers in this area (e.g., Millars & Millars, 1979) have examined the relationship between domineering (the ratio of the number of one-up acts to the total number of acts) and dominance (the number of one-down acts, given a preceding one-up act) with satisfaction and role strain and have found: (1) husband dominance related to higher levels of satisfaction and less role strain, (2) when husband performs a one-up act, he provides more supportive statements, and (3) when the wife is domineering, there is greater role strain and less satisfaction.

Several authors (e.g., Burgoon & Hale, 1984, 1987) have argued that multiple dimensions, rather than the single dimension of dominance/control, underlie relational communication. These authors have postulated 12 dimensions (e.g., intimacy, dominance-submission, emotional arousal, similarity, task-social orientation) to underlie relational communication and in a series of factor analytic and experimental studies (which manipulated certain nonverbal cues such as gaze, voice tone) have provided support for at least 4 to 7 of these dimensions.

Prominent Methods and Coding Systems

Two major coding systems have been proposed to study relational communication: (1) Rogers-Farace (RF) system and (2) Ellis's (E) system. Each system involves three sets of codes: (1) who speaks, (2) the grammatical form of the act (i.e., assertion, question, talk-over (interrupt), noncomplete, other, and (3) the person's response to the act (i.e., support, nonsupport, extension, answer, order, disconfirmation, topic, initiation/termination, other). The unit of analysis is the dyadic exchange, that is, an act and a react (Trujillo, 1981). The major distinction between the two systems is that RF allows for the double coding of a unit, whereas E does not.

Bargaining and Negotiation

Research on bargaining and negotiation has much of its historical roots in communication, consumer behavior, psychology, and sociology. Our focus in this section of the chapter will examine research in consumer behavior and psychology. Chapters by Fitzpatrick, Sillars and Kalbflesch, and Poole and Billingsley in this volume examine aspects of bargaining from a communications perspective.

Historical Perspective

Work in the area of bargaining and negotiation has an important basis in small-group research conducted in psychology. This research provides some context for understanding work on bargaining and negotiation. McGrath (1984) has provided an insightful discussion of the evolution of research on small groups and our presentation borrows from his description. The initial phase of small-group research was characterized by theory development, with little emphasis on empirical testing (see, for example, Allport's 1954 description of this research). The second phase of research focused almost exclusively on empirical tests, with little regard for the development (or evaluation) of broad-sweeping theories. Three research traditions were established in this phase. One tradition focused on "groups as a vehicle for delivering social influence" and may be found in the work by Lewin (1951), Festinger (1950), Thibaut and Kelley (1959), and others. A second tradition focused on "groups as structures for patterning social interaction" and may be found in the work of Bales and his associates (e.g., Bales and Cohen 1979). The third research tradition focused on "groups as task performance systems" and may be found in the work of Steiner (1972), Fiedler (1967), Davis (1969), and others.

Research in bargaining and negotiation has borrowed from each of the traditions and has created some unique perspectives. Bales and his associates conducted much of the early work on bargaining in their analysis of the interaction process of small-group task performance. Although this work did not focus exclusively on bargaining and negotiation, some of the empirical findings (e.g., phase shifts during group interaction) do provide insights for understanding bargaining and negotiation. A second major stream of research that has affected our understanding of bargaining and negotiation has its roots in game theory (e.g., Thibaut & Kelley, 1959; Luce & Raiffa, 1957). This research has examined the effect of incentives, initial resources, level of communication, the individual's motivational orientation, feedback, and numerous other independent variables on the types of choices made by the individual (e.g., a competitive/cooperative choice) and the pattern of those choices. Bargaining and negotiation research also has been affected by a third research tradition—conflict resolution. That tradition has examined a wide range of issues (e.g., Pruitt & Rubin, 1986; McGrath, 1984). Our focus, however, will be much more narrow; that is, the development, perception, and use of conflict resolution strategies and social judgment theory in bargaining and negotiation.

Prominent Theories

No single theory has been developed that can account for bargaining and negotiation between dyads. We will describe briefly, and point to, several theories that speak to these issues. One major theory (or set of theories) is classified as exchange theory. The seminal work in this area was conducted by Thibaut and Kelley (1959), Homans (1961), and subsequently by Foa & Foa (1974), and focused on the maintenance of relationships vis-a-vis resource allocation within the relationship. Thibaut and Kelley (1959) introduced two key concepts—comparison level and comparison level for alternatives. The former addresses the individual's level of satisfaction; that is, the standard against which the member evaluates the "attractiveness" of the dyadic relationship. The latter concept is the standard the individual uses in deciding whether to remain or to leave the relationship (Thibaut & Kelley, 1959). If the utility of a relationship falls below an individual's comparison level for alternatives, then the individual will leave the relationship; that is, for a relationship to exist, each member of the dyad must believe there is more to lose than to gain by *not* remaining in the relationship.

One important component of exchange theory is the norms (expectations) that govern the exchange. Several norms (allocation expectations) appear to regulate exchange. Adams (1965), for example, described the use of an equity norm—the allocation of resources gained in the context of a relationship—should be a function of the initial resource distribution. Other researchers (e.g., Foa & Foa, 1974) describe the use of a reciprocity norm—the exchange of like resources. Still other researchers (e.g., McGrath, 1984) describe the use of equality norms—the allocation of resources independent of the initial resource distribution. The type of norm elicited is contingent on the task, environmental constraints, type of individual, and numerous other factors. Thus, the prediction of which allocation rule will be evoked is actor, behavior, and context specific.

A second component of exchange theory is the role expectations for each person in the dyad. Role theory has received substantial attention in the communication and psychological literature. A role may be viewed as a set of affective, cognitive, and behavioral expectations, rights, and privileges for an individual who holds a particular position in a social system or social relationship. Because of changing role expectations in married couples (e.g., Buss & Schaninger, in press), issues associated with role strain may affect (intrude on) bargaining and negotiation. McGrath (1984) summarized three dimensions of role strain: conflict, load, and ambiguity. Load represents too many role demands and competition between roles. Conflict is the discrepancy between role demands and values or ability. Ambiguity is represented by unclear behavioral expectations or changing roles. Each of these problems may affect the exchange of information and, thus, affect the outcome of a negotiation or dyadic decision. Some current research (e.g., see, Fitzpatrick, this volume) has developed an instrument (called the Relational Dimensions Inventory) that categorizes couples into types (i.e., roles) and has examined the relation of these roles to a wide range of factors (e.g., communication styles, conflict resolution strategies, levels of disclosure).

One important modification of early exchange theory has been the specification of the types of resources that can be exchanged between two (or more) individuals. Foa and Foa (1974) have proposed a circumplex typology of six resources: *love*—an expression of affectionate regard, warmth, or comfort; *status*—an evaluative judgment conveying high or low prestige, regard or esteem; *information*—any advice, opinion, or instructions; *money*—any coin or token that has some standard of exchange value; *goods*—any product or object; *services*—activities directed at the individual. Two dimensions are hypothesized to underlie these six resources: particularism and concreteness. Several researchers (e.g., Brinberg & Wood, 1983; Brinberg & Castell, 1982; Foa & Foa, 1974) have found empirical support for these two dimensions and the underlying hypothesized structure.

The exchange theories provide one type of broad framework for examining bargaining and negotiation between dyads. For instance, the type of norm evoked in a situation would imply certain types of exchanges (e.g., demands or concessions). Moreover, the type of resource exchanged and the comparison level for alternatives each is likely to affect the pattern and outcome of a bargaining situation. In the last section of this chapter, we will propose several hypotheses concerning the role of exchange theory on bargaining and, subsequently, on dyadic decision making.

A second major class of theories that influences bargaining and negotiation is game theory. The roots of game theory can be traced to the classic work of Von Neumann and Morgenstern (1947) and Thibaut and Kelley (1959). Much of the early research proposed normative theories and solutions to bargaining situations. A major strength of game theory is that it allows the researcher to specify "optimal" solutions. A substantial body of literature (e.g., Rubin & Brown, 1975), however, has found that individuals do not respond in a manner consistent with normative theory. We will focus on the empirical (rather than purely theoretical) approaches to develop hypotheses concerning dyadic decision making.

Two mixed-motive game approaches have received impressive empirical attention—the prisoner dilemma paradigm and coalition research. Useful summaries of each paradigm may be found in Pruitt and Kimmel (1977) and Komorita (1976). In the prisoner dilemma paradigm, researchers have examined the extent to which individuals will adopt cooperative versus competitive orientations toward the garnering of resources. The research has found that (1) competitive choices by each individual dominate, (2) shifts in the relative pay off for cooperative (C) and competitive choices influence the proportion of C choices, (3) situational factors (e.g., pay off, interaction patterns) have a greater affect on the proportion of C choices than personal factors (e.g., gender, status, personality characteristics), and (4) the strategy of the partner (e.g., tit-for-tat, consistently cooperative or competitive response) has a great influence on the individual's proportion of C choices.

In the coalition paradigm, researchers have examined the influence of initial resource distribution (e.g., resources like power, status, income) on the distribution of the group outcome (e.g., the allocation of money to the group members). Allocation norms (e.g., equity, equality) have been found to affect resource distribution depending on the individual gender. Women seem to prefer an equality distribution, whereas men prefer an equity distribution.

Game theoretic approaches, especially prisoner dilemma and coalition research, provide insight into decision making among dyads. The pattern of interaction, the initial distribution of resources, and the individual's gender all influence the group's (dyad's) final outcome.

A third major theoretical perspective that may be used to examine bargaining and negotiation is social judgment theory. A description of this theory and its many uses can be found in Hammond and Wascoe (1980). Social judgment theory has its roots in the work of Egon Brunswik (1955). At the level of the individual, the underlying assumption of social judgment theory is that individuals use cues (or information) from the environment to make judgments about an event. Researchers have examined how individuals use cues in making judgments as a function of the number and redundancy of cues as well as the relationship of the cues to the criterion in the environment. This model can be used to estimate the weights an individual places on a cue when making a judgment, as well as the combinatorial rule used to organize these cues.

For dyadic decision making, this theory can be used to identify the judgment strategy of each member of the dyad prior to interaction. After each individual policy is delineated, any differences in the weights, combinatorial rule, or consistency in the use of the cues can become the content for a negotiation between the individuals in order for them to arrive at a dyadic decision. McGrath (1984) provides a useful discussion on the application of this theory for conflict resolution in groups. One nonintuitive finding is that group members abandon their own judgment policy rapidly, although they do not have one to replace it. A consequence of that action is the inconsistency in which the group's judgments are made. One (obvious) potential solution would be to encourage the individual to maintain his/her own judgment policy until he/she becomes proficient in the use of another policy.

Prominent Methods and Measures

Two strategies dominate the research on bargaining and negotiation— laboratory experiments on concocted groups who perform relatively unimportant tasks, and field studies on natural groups who perform relatively important tasks. The strengths and weaknesses of each of these strategies has been discussed, in detail, by numerous authors (e.g., Runkel & McGrath 1972; Brinberg & McGrath, 1985) and will not be presented here. One research strategy that has received relatively little attention in bargaining and negotiation is that of field experiments; that is, the systematic manipulation of some aspect of the environment in a natural setting.

Family Research

Much of family research has focused on the dynamics of family interaction and family relations, and the development of clinical/counseling strategies for treating family problems and improving marital relations. In this section of the chapter we will provide a brief overview of research in this area and highlight those theories/empirical findings that provide insight into dyadic decision making.

Historical Perspective

Research in the family area has its roots in three disciplines—sociology, communication, and psychology (see Gottman, 1979, for an extended discussion of these historical roots). The sociological tradition was characterized by large-scale surveys of married couples that focused on the effects of variables such as income, culture, and children on mate selection, marital satisfaction, marital stability, and sexual behavior (e.g., Terman, Buttenwieser, Ferguson, Johnson, & Wilson, 1938; Locke 1951). The communication tradition focused on the role of relational communication in family therapy. In the family therapy area, this research tradition has been used to classify therapist type (e.g., conductors and reactors), to treat clincally diagnosed couples, and to examine channel inconsistency in information exchange. A third research tradition has its origin in social learning theory in psychology. An early application of learning theory in the family area may be found in the work of Patterson (1978), Weiss (1974), and their associates. These researchers focused on both a detailed analysis of observational data (which resulted in a marital interaction coding system) and the use of learning theory principles to modify maladaptive (targeted) behaviors.

Prominent Theories

There are several major theoretical approaches to the analysis of families and family decision making. We will consider briefly three such approaches.

Developmental psychologists have become increasingly interested in family dynamics as a means of broadening traditional analyses of mother-infant relationships. This work has resulted in a broader conceptualization of children's social networks including fathers, siblings, grandparents, and peers (e.g., Lewis & Feiring, 1981). An emerging major perspective in developmental psychology is to view the family as a system and to draw concepts from general systems theory (e.g., Miller, 1978) as a way of analyzing family dynamics. Systems theorists recognize that social relationships within the family are complex and characterize such relationships in terms of bi-directionality, reciprocity, complementarity, situational sensitivity, indirect or second order influences, and integration within larger ecological contexts. System theory approaches to the family are described in detail by Lewis and Feiring (1981). This trend in developmental psychology is compatible with current thinking about how best to assess and treat families and children clinically (e.g., Epstein & Bishop, 1982).

Sociological theories of the family, in contrast to developmental psychology approaches, tend to view the family as a social unit and speculate about the nature of families and their role in society. The analysis focuses on the description of the missions of families (e.g., intergenerational transmission of information, management of resources) and the dimensions along which families differ. This research rarely considers the development of individual family members and how this development influences the family unit. Rather, the focus is on the family per se as the unit of analysis.

One example of a prominent sociological theory of the family which bears on dyadic decision making is that of Olson and his colleagues (e.g., Olson, 1985; Olson, Sprenkle, & Russell, 1979). The theory is referred to as the "circumplex model" and focuses on three family processes: cohesion (emotional bonding of family members), adaptability (ability to change in response to situational and developmental stress), and communication. Family cohesion is characterized by four levels, from disengaged, to separated, to connected, to emeshed. Family adaptability is dimensionalized into rigid, structured, flexible, and chaotic categories. For both areas, the two intermediate levels are considered good and associated with positive family outcomes, while the extreme levels are predicted to cause problems. The circumplex model also considers communication styles within the family. According to the model, certain communication styles foster balanced levels of cohesion and adaptability, while others mitigate against such balanced states.

Landesman, Jaccard, and Gunderson (1988) have presented a model of family dynamics that integrates psychological and sociological perspectives. The model focuses on six classes of outcome variables that describe different domains in which families function: cognitive development of family members, social development of family members, emotional development of family members, moral development of family members, physical care and health of family members, and aesthetic and cultural development of family members. Four major classes of variables describe family factors that influence these outcomes: the goals of family members, the strategies that members form to achieve the goals, the resources that families have available to them, and the individual experiences that each member brings to the family. Landesman et al. (1988) describe in detail the dimensions of each of these variables and how they can be used to analyze family functioning from both a micro as well as macro level.

Prominent Methods

Four research strategies dominate the research in the family area—survey research, laboratory experiments, observational methods, and intervention approaches—some using case studies. Several books (e.g., Gottman, 1979;

Yin, 1984) provide an analysis and description of the case approach. Landesman et al. (1988) describe the limitations with several of the traditional approaches to studying families, especially as used by developmental psychologists.

Part Summary

Each of the three disciplines described—communication, bargaining and negotiation, and family relations—provide insights into components of dyadic decision making. The application and integration of the prominent theories and methods in each area to dyadic decision making should provide a solid conceptual and methodological foundation for future research. Such research should consider what the individual brings to the situation (e.g., resources, preferences, perceptions), the relationships between the individuals (e.g., perceived role relations, communication styles), and the impact of the joint decision on future actions (e.g., decision satisfaction, decision quality). We will discuss these issues in greater detail in the last section of this chapter.

Translating Interaction Information into Empirical Data

A major constraint when examining dyadic decision making is the complexity in transforming the ongoing, continuous behavioral stream into discrete units. Other contributors in this volume (e.g., Kumar & Dillon; Kenny & Acitelli) have described several techniques for the analysis of interaction (i.e., sequential) data. This section of our chapter will describe a variety of techniques that generate the data needed for these analyses.

Forms of Empirical Evidence

A wide variety of measures and methods exist for the assessment of dyadic decision making. Several facets can be used to organize these assessment procedures and to identify some of their strengths and weaknesses. One facet is the source of the information; that is, whether each member in the dyad provides a self-report about his/her own cognitive, affective, or behavioral states, or whether an outside observer provides that assessment. A second facet is the role of time in the assessment procedure; that is, whether the assessment occurs prior to, concurrently, or subsequent to the actual occurrence of the event. A third facet is the relationship between the assessment procedure and the natural, unfolding events; that is, the extent to which the procedure affects that which it assesses. A fourth facet is the depth/richness of the assessment procedure; that is, the extent to which the researcher examines each member of the dyad, and their interaction on repeated occa-

Table 13.1. Facets for organizing empirical evidence.

	Subject			Observer		
	Past	Present	Future	Past	Present	Future
Detail						
Obtrusive	1	2	3	4	5	6
Unobtrusive	7	8	9	10	11	12
Cursory						
Obtrusive	13	14	15	16	17	18
Unobtrusive	19	20	21	22	23	24

sions, different contexts, and at different levels of analysis (e.g., in-depth probes vs. brief interviews). Table 13.1 contains a summary of these facets.

Combinations of these facets describe different measurement and assessment procedures. For instance, questionnaire measures of conflict resolution strategies typically (but not always) are (1) a subject's self-report, (2) concerning the occurrence of past events, (3) is relatively unobtrusive because the assessment did not interfere with the behavioral events, and (4) somewhat superficial in its assessment of conflict resolution strategies. This procedure would be classified in cell 19 of Table 13.1. An alternative approach toward the assessment of conflict resolution could be direct observation of a couple in a conflict situation. This assessment procedure (1) uses an outside observer as the source of information, (2) is concurrent with the occurrence of the behaviors, (3) is somewhat obtrusive if the respondents are aware they are being observed, and (4) can provide a rich data set, *if* the coding system allows for a variety of unique codes and multiple streams of information (e.g., verbal, nonverbal, spatial information). This measurement procedure would be classified in cell 5 of Table 13.1. A third approach for measuring conflict resolution is to use an experiential sampling procedure. This assessment procedure (1) uses the respondent as the source of information, (2) is concurrent with the occurrence of the behaviors, (3) is obtrusive because the assessment disrupts the ongoing, behavioral stream, and (4) provides some richness in data if multiple observations are collected across a range of situations. This measurement procedure would be classified in cell 2 of Table 13.1.

One potentially useful feature of these facets is that different combinations may suggest alternative assessment procedures for examining dyadic interaction. For instance, one assessment procedure not used currently is experiential sampling with an outside observer (e.g., a family member), rather than the individual (dyad) under study, to assess certain events/states (cell 11 of Table 13.1). A potential strength of this approach is its relative unobtrusiveness when compared with traditional experiential sampling. An inherent limitation is the lack of coordination between the request for information and the recording of that information.

Several other examples will help illustrate the use of Table 13.1 for identifying alternative measurement procedures. One procedure would ask the subject (source) to provide a verbal protocol (obtrusive) of decision rules to be used for a future decision (time) across a number of decision tasks (depth). This procedure would be classified in cell 3 of Table 13.1. Alternatively, the researcher could use an observer (source) to conduct in-depth interviews (depth) to determine what decision rules that subject will use to make future decisions (time). The relation of the observer to the respondent is likely to affect whether the assessment procedure is obtrusive. For instance, if the observer is a friend and the assessment is part of a "normal" conversation, then the procedure is likely to be relatively unobtrusive (cell 12 in Table 13.1). If the observer is unknown to the respondent, however, then the procedure is likely to be relatively obtrusive (cell 6 in Table 13.1). As a final example, a procedure that uses an observer (source) who casually records a respondent's current behavior (depth and time) and is undetected by the respondent would be in cell 23 of Table 13.1. For instance, an observer interested in "dating decisions" could sit at a bar and observe the behavior of a respondent.

The selection of an assessment procedure will depend on which aim(s) (e.g., precision, realism, or generalizability) the researcher wishes to emphasize and which weaknesses the researcher wishes to reduce. Each facet in Table 13.1 has several *potential* strengths and *inherent* limitations. Table 13.2 contains a brief summary of some strengths and weaknesses of each level of each facet specified in Table 13.1.

We have described the strengths as potential because the researcher can implement the assessment procedure in a way that reduces (or eliminates) the strength of that procedure. For instance, a strength of unobtrusive measurement is the nondisruption of naturally occurring events/processes. The researcher, however, might inadvertently make his/her presence known; thus, increasing the amount of disruption of the phenomenon. The weaknesses, however, are inherent. If the researcher selects a particular assessment procedure, then the limitations associated with that procedure can not be eliminated. For instance, an inherent weakness of obtrusive measurement is the interference (disruption) of the natural unfolding of the phenomenon. The researcher can not remain obtrusive (e.g., control setting, stimuli) and at the same time allow the phenomenon to occur without constraints. The inherent weaknesses and strengths described in Table 13.2 only highlight the types of factors that affect each facet. Our intent, here, is to be illustrative, and not exhaustive.

The entries presented in Table 13.2 may be found in the discussion of measurement issues in most standard research methods books (e.g., Kerlinger, 1973). A number of the entries concerning weaknesses focus on attributional biases in the recall or prediction of events/processes. Many of the strengths of these facets center on control and contextual richness. We have focused our presentation of the strength and weaknesses of those factors most likely to influence research on dyadic processes.

Table 13.2. Some strengths and weaknesses of time, source, obtrusiveness, and depth as facets for organizing empirical evidence.

Time-past	
Strength	Provides basis/baseline and historical context for interpreting events/processes.
Weakness	Misrepresentation of past information. Weak linkage between measures and concept.
Time-present	
Strength	Assessment of on-going events/processes. Few historical biases or information.
Weakness	Little historical/contextual perspective.
Time-future	
Strength	Allows prediction of events/processes.
Weakness	Unknown internal or external changes. Social desirability. Prediction biases.
Source-subject	
Strength	Access to own cognitive states. Ease of data collection.
Weakness	Biases in reporting states. Inability to access some processes. Subject role biases.
Source-observer	
Strength	Entry to states/processes inaccessible to subject. Less susceptible to attributional bias.
Weakness	Inability to observe cognitive states/processes. Deliberate filtering of information.
Obtrusive	
Strength	Controlled view of events/processes.
Weakness	Interference with natural unfolding of events.
Unobtrusive	
Strength	Allows events/states to occur without disruption. Access to private information.
Weakness	No control of timing/patterning of events/processes. Constrained view of phenomena.
Depth-Detail	
Strength	Rich description, scrutiny of states/processes. Careful monitoring of measurement.
Weakness	Overwhelming complexity of information. Difficulty in recognizing general patterns.
Depth-Cursory	
Strength	Allows broad perspective of events/patterns.
Weakness	Superficial examination of events/processes. Contextual richness is ignored.

Direct Observation of Dyadic Interaction

The transformation of direct observation of dyads into usable research information has a relatively short history in the social sciences. As noted earlier, Bales and his associates conducted the seminal work on the analysis of interaction processes in groups. These researchers developed an Interaction

Process Analysis (IPA) to study socioemotional and instrumental processes in small-group task performance. The emphasis in this research was the analysis of phase shifts—from socioemotional to instrumental—during task performance. Bales's theoretical perspective on group task performance helped to define the coding system. The strong link between the IPA coding system and Bales's theory of group task performance was both its strength and weakness. The major strength was the theoretical basis for the observation of task performance in groups (e.g., the occurrence of socioemotional or instrumental behaviors). The major weakness was the inability to use the IPA with other theoretical perspectives.

Additional coding schemes (e.g., conference process analysis (CPA) Rubin & Brown, 1975) have been developed to examine negotiation behavior. These systems focus on multiple codes per act. For example, the CPA coding system uses three dimensions (mode, resource, and referent) in coding each act. In contrast, IPA places an act in one and only one category.

Several coding systems have been developed in communication research. We have described two types of metacommunication coding systems in our discussion of prominent methods in relational communication (e.g., Ellis, Rogers-Farace). Additional coding systems have been developed for negotiation behavior (e.g., Donahue, 1981) and conflict resolution strategies (e.g., Sillars & Kalbflesch, this volume). Categories in these coding systems involve behaviors such as initiation, topic change, charge fault, offer, and concession (Donahue, 1981) or denial, topic management, noncommittal remarks, humor, and analytic remarks (Sillars & Kalbflesch, this volume). These systems differ on a number of dimensions such as the content of the categories, the level of inference required of the observer, and the unit of analysis (e.g., time, floor shifts, category units).

Coding systems also have been developed in the family relations area. Gottman (1979) has provided an extensive discussion of the development of the couple interaction scoring system. Briefly, this system uses eight mutually exclusive and exhaustive content codes (i.e., agreement, disagreement, communication talk, mind-reading, problem solving and information exchange, expressing feeling, summarizing self, and summarizing other) to code each behavioral unit. In addition to coding content, Gottman recommends that affect be coded concurrently. As a first approximation, Gottman uses voice tone (positive, neutral, or negative) as a indicant of affect. More refined measures might use voice as well as facial and body expressions in determining the level of affect in the interaction.

Criteria for Constructing Coding Systems

Five facets can be used to structure the development of an interaction coding system—unit of analysis, perspective of the system, single versus multiple codes, data versus theory-based codes, and the level of inference required of the observer. The unit of analysis may be viewed as a continuum of micro-level to macro-level analysis. A macro-level unit implies that numerous subprocesses exist within that unit. A micro-level analysis, however, implies that the unit represents the "basic building blocks" for the process of interest. We should note that any unit of analysis may be viewed as either micro or macro and will depend on the perspective of the researcher. For instance, facial expressions may be viewed as a micro-level analysis of emotion or macro-level analysis of muscle movement. From our point of view, the specification of micro- or macro-level units is an indicant of the researcher's orientation toward the processes of interest.

A second feature of this facet is the role of time in the coding of dyadic interactions. Two approaches have been proposed (e.g., Moore, 1986). One approach treats time as the unit of analysis and then codes all states/ behaviors that occur during that time interval. The second approach treats the state/behavior codes as the unit of analysis rather than time and does not allow multiple occurrences of codes for a single state/behavior.

A second facet is the perspective from which the observer codes the interaction. Three perspectives may be adopted—source, target, or context. The first perspective views the interaction in terms of the intent—either stated or implicit—of the information/feelings communicated to the other person in the relationship. The second perspective views the interaction in terms of the impact of the information/feelings communicated, that is, the perceived meaning of the message. The third perspective views the interaction process in terms of its effect on an outside agent (e.g., other family member) or the environment (e.g., the impact of strategic decisions to reduce environmental contaminants).

A third facet is whether the codes in the observational system are treated as mutually exclusive and exhaustive or whether multiple coding of an act is allowed. A strength of the former approach is its ability to organize the interaction into "neat" and definable segments. That ability, of course, also is its weakness, that is, the procrustean effect of a structured system. The strength of the latter approach is its ability to allow multiple meanings for each act. The weakness, however, is the increased complexity in the analysis and interpretation of the multiple meanings.

A fourth facet is whether the coding system is derived from a theoretical perspective or from an observational data base. The former approach provides a strong conceptual grounding, but constrains the researcher's ability to test theoretical propositions because the coding system imposes "meaning" on the interaction. The latter approach allows "patterns to emerge from the data" (e.g., Glaser & Strauss, 1967) by not imposing a priori (theoretical) structure. The weakness, however, is that "data-driven" systems result in a high dross rate (Webb, Campbell, Schwartz, & Sechrest, 1966); that is, patterns of data with little use and no apparent explanation.

The fifth facet is the level of inference on the part of observer. This facet may be viewed as the degree of observer interpretation necessary for the coding of a state/behavior. Some coding systems (e.g., CPA) require the observer to make attributions concerning the intent of the sender of the information (e.g., whether a statement is an offer/concession). Other coding systems [e.g., Couple Interaction Scoring System (CISS)] require much lower level attributions (e.g., does this statement indicate agreement/ disagreement). The higher level attributions provide more structure to the interaction but seem more prone to unreliability because of the "subjective" judgment of the observer. The lower level attributions are likely to lead to higher interjudge reliability but provide less structure to the observation.

Each of the five facets can be used to summarize a set of issues a researcher should consider when developing a coding system. We have presented a brief discussion of each facet to highlight how these facets affect the development of a coding system.

Part Summary

The wide variety of measures and methods to study dyadic decision making is substantial. As we have noted, each method and measure brings with it potential strengths and inherent weaknesses. We believe that no one method or measure provides a sufficient assessment of the interaction process. Thus, we view one aspect of future research activities as the coordination of these different approaches when assessing dyadic interaction.

Research Agenda for Dyadic Decision Making

The diversity of the chapters in this volume is one strong indicant of the need to examine dyadic decision making from multiple perspectives. We believe that research in this area must examine both individual and dyadic-level processes. In this section of our chapter, we will summarize a number of suggestions for future research that draws from both processes.

Individual-Level Processes

Several contributors to this volume (e.g., Anderson & Armstrong; Troutman & Shanteau; Jaccard, Brinberg, & Dittus) have described an approach for studying dyadic decision making by using individual processes as the focal point. In effect, these researchers (and others) have argued that the resources, perceptions, preferences, emotions, wants, needs, and values an individual brings to the dyad will influence the decision outcome. We can examine these issues from both theoretical and methodological perspectives.

Theoretical Perspective

Approaches such as image theory, subjective-expected utility (SEU) theory, information integration theory, and the behavioral alternatives model all have been described in this volume as a perspective from which to examine dyadic decision making. Questions that these theories are able to address include the integration rules used by individuals (and dyads) for combining information, the effect of perceptions and preferences on decision rules, and the role of schema on choice processes. Additional questions that arise but are not addressed directly by the traditional application of these theories to dyadic decision making are the effect of more abstract values, emotions, needs, wants, and desires (Hirschman & Holbrook, 1986) on what the individual brings to the dyad. For a more complete understanding of the dyadic decision process, we need a more thorough articulation and conceptual foundation for the complex array of facets brought into the dyad by each individual. Thus, one item for future research is a conceptual model of the decision process that incorporates individual difference factors (e.g., personality, values, emotions) with the set of factors that dominate current work in decision making (e.g., perceptions, preferences, and attitudes).

Further work also can focus on an individual's perception of the dyad and how his/her behavior in that dyad is likely to influence the decision process. One set of variables that has received considerable attention is the perceived role relations (Fitzpatrick, this volume). We suggest that future research focus on role relations in addition to context variables (Scanzoni, this volume) when examining dyadic decision making.

Methodological Perspective

In this chapter and others in this volume, both experimental and observational methods have been applied toward dyadic decision making. Neither method, alone, provides information that is sufficient for understanding the decision process. For the most part, the individual-level analysis involves the presentation of information to examine preferences, perceptions, and integration rules. Additional research should focus on the assessment of other factors an individual will bring to the dyad (e.g., emotional states, personality traits, and values). Jaccard et al. (this volume) suggest some personality orientations that may be relevant for decision processes. Fitzpatrick (this volume) describes the use of an instrument to measure role relations. A second agenda item for future research is the development of instruments and assessment procedures for the measurement of these "additional" variables. A secondary component of this agenda item is the specification and use of alternative assessment procedures in Table 13.1.

Dyadic Level Processes

Several contributors in the volume (e.g., Fitzpatrick, Poole & Billingsley, and Sillars & Kalbflesch) have described an approach toward dyadic decision process that makes use of dyadic- (rather than individual) level factors. Numerous theories have been proposed to explain dyadic processes (see the earlier discussion in this chapter). In the next two sections, we will discuss a set of theoretical and methodological issues that should be addressed in future research within this research tradition.

Theoretical Perspective

Current dyadic and small-group theories (e.g., exchange theory, role theory, game theory) are inadequate in their ability to incorporate the relative differences (and similarities) of each individual's resources, perceptions, preferences, and emotions when determining a dyad's decision. Moreover, the effect of resource inequality (in amount, type, and importance) or perceptual and preference incongruity on the dyadic decision process is poorly understood. Theoretical work on a dyadic level needs to include the individual factors described in the previous section of this chapter. In so doing, a more complete portrayal of the decision process may occur. Thus, a third item for future research on dyadic decision making is a more detailed articulation of current dyad (small-group) theories: (1) by including individual level factors, (2) by specifying the dyad level factors (e.g., interaction patterns) that will influence the decision process, and (3) by identifying variables exogenous to the dyad but that influence the process and final decision (e.g., social class, stage in the life cycle).

Methodological Perspective

As in the individual-level analysis, both experimental, survey, and observational methods are used to examine dyadic processes. The major methodological limitations in the dyadic-level perspective are two-fold: (1) individual-level variables are often not included in the analysis of dyadic processes—which result in an incomplete portrayal of the dyad, and (2) either observational or experimental methods *and not both* is used in a study. Thus, a fourth item for future research is to incorporate multiple methods to study the decision process of a dyad and to use individual-level factors to facilitate specific prediction of the dyad's decision.

In this chapter, we have provided a broad stroke portrait of factors that influence dyadic decision making. From our point of view, multiple perspectives are needed to better understand dyadic processes. The issues we have raised here highlight the breadth of these factors.

References

Adams, J. S. (1965). Inequity in social exchange. In L. Berkowitz (Ed). *Advances in experimental social psychology Vol. 2.* New York: Academic Press.

Allport, G. W. (1954). The historical background of modern social psychology. In G. Lindzey (Ed.), *Handbook of social psychology.* Cambridge, MA: Addison-Wesley.

Anderson, N. H., & Armstrong, M. A. (this volume). Cognitive theory and methodology for studying marital interaction. In D. Brinberg & J. Jaccard (Eds), *Dyadic decision making,* New York: Springer-Verlag.

Bales, R. F., and Cohen, S. P. (1979). *Symlog: A system for the multilevel observation of groups*. New York: Free Press.

Bateson, C. (1972) *Steps to an ecology of mind*. New York: Balantine Book.

Beach, L. R., & Morrison, D. (this volume). Expectancy theory and image theory in the description of decisions about childbearing. In D. Brinberg & J. Jaccard (Eds), *Dyadic decision making*. New York: Springer-Verlag.

Brinberg, D., & Castell, P. (1982). A resource exchange theory approach to interpersonal interaction. *Journal of Personality and Social Psychology, 43(8)*, 260–269.

Brinberg, D., & McGrath, J. E. (1985). *Validity and the research process*. Beverly Hills, CA: Sage Publications.

Brinberg, D., & Wood, R. (1983). A resource exchange theory analysis of consumer behavior. *Journal of Consumer Research, 10*, 330–338.

Brunswik, E. (1955). Representative design and probabilistic theory in a functional psychology. *Psychological Review, 62*, 193–217.

Burgoon, J. R., & Hale, J. L. (1984). The fundamental topoi of relational communication. *Communication Monographs, 51*, 193–214.

Burgoon, J. R., & Hale, J. L. (1987). Validation and measurement of the fundamental themes of relational communication. *Communication Monographs, 54*, 19–41.

Buss, W. C., & Schaninger, C. M. (in press). An overview of dyadic family behavior research: A summary of finding and an agenda for future research. In M. Houston (ed.) *Review of marketing*, Greenwich, CN: JAI Press.

Donahue, W. A. (1981). Development of a model of rule use in negotiation interaction. *Communication Monographs, 48*, 106–120.

Davis, J. H. (1969). *Group performance*. Reading, MA: Addison-Wesley.

Emery, D. (1982). Marital interaction: Perceptions and behavioral implications of control. *Communications yearbook*. New Brunswick, NJ: Transaction Books.

Epstein, N. B., & Bishop, D. (1982). McMaster model of family functioning: A view of the normal family . In F. Walsh (Ed.), *Normal family processes*. New York: Guilford Press.

Festinger, L. (1950). Informal social communication. *Psychological Review, 57*, 271–292.

Fiedler, F. E. (1967). *A theory of leadership effectiveness*. New York: McGraw-Hill.

Fitzpatrick, M. A. (this volume). After the decision: Compliance-gaining in marital interaction. In D. Brinberg & J. Jaccard (Eds), *Dyadic decision making*. New York: Springer-Verlag.

Foa, U. G. & Foa, E. (1974). *Societal structures of the mind*. Springfield, Ill: Charles C. Thomas.

Glaser, B. G., & Strauss, A. (1967). *The discovery of grounded theory: Strategies for qualitative research*. Chicage: Aldine.

Gottman, J. M. (1979). *Marital interactions: Experimental investigations*. New York: Academic Press.

Hammond, K. R., & Wascoe, N. E. (1980). *New directions for methodology of social and behavioral science: Realizations of Brunswik's representative design*. San Francisco: Jossey-Bass.

Hirschman, E. C., & Holbrook, M. B. (1986). Expanding the ontology and methodology of research on the consumption experience. In D. Brinberg & R. J. Lutz (Eds) *Perspectives on methodology in consumer research*. New York: Springer-Verlag.

Homans, G. C. (1961). *Social behavior: Its elementary form*. New York: Harcourt.

Jaccard, J., Brinberg, D., & Dittus, P. (this volume). Dyadic decision making: An individual and dyadic-level analysis. In D. Brinberg & J. Jaccard (Eds), *Dyadic decision making*. New York: Springer-Verlag.

Kenny, D. A., & Acitelli, L. K. (this volume). The role of the relationship in marital decision making. In D. Brinberg & J. Jaccard (Eds), *Dyadic decision making*, New York: Springer-Verlag.

Kerlinger, F. N. (1973). *Foundations of behavioral research*. New York: Holt, Rinehart, and Winston.

Komorita, S. S. (1976). A model of the N-person dilemma type game. *Journal of Experimental Social Psychology, 12*, 357–373.

Kumar, A., & Dillon, W. R. (this volume). Analyzing sequential categorical data on dyadic interaction, In D. Brinberg & J. Jaccard (Eds), *Dyadic decision making*, New York: Springer-Verlag.

Landesman, S., Jaccard, J., & Gunderson, V. (1988). The family as environment: The combined influence of family goals, strategies, resources, and individual characteristics on child development. In M. Lewis & S. Feinstein (Eds.), *Social influence*. New York: Praeger.

Lewin, K. (1951). *Field theory and social science*. New York: Harper.

Lewis, M. & Feiring, C. (1981). Direct and indirect interactions in social relationships. In L. Lipsitt (Ed.), *Advances in infancy research*. New York: Albex.

Locke, H. J. (1951). *Predicting adjustment in marriage: A comparison of a divorced and a happily married group*. New York: Holt and Co.

Luce, R. D., & Raiffa, H. (1957). *Games and decisions: Introduction and critical survey*. New York: Wiley.

McGrath, J. E. (1984). *Groups: Interaction and performance*. Englewood Cliffs, NJ: Prentice-Hall.

Miller, J. G. (1978). *Living systems*. New York: McGraw-Hill.

Millars, E. R. & Millars, F. E. (1979). Domineering and dominance: A transactional view. *Human Communications Research, 5*, 238–246.

Moore, D. L. (1986). Social interaction data: Procedural and analytic strategies. In D. Brinberg & R. J. Lutz (Eds), *Perspectives on methodology in consumer research*. New York: Springer-Verlag.

Olson, D. H. (1985). Commentary: Struggling with congruence across theoretical models and methods. *Family Process, 24* 203–207.

Olson, D. H., Sprenkle, D. H., & Russell, C. S. (1979). Circumplex model of marital and family systems: Cohesion and adaptability dimensions, family types, and clinical applications. *Family Process, 18*, 3–28.

Parks, M. R. (1977). Relational communication: Theory and research. *Human Communications Research, 4*, 372–381.

Patterson, G. R. (1978). A performance theory for coercive family interaction. In R. Cairns (Ed.), *Social interaction "Methods, analysis and illustration."* Society for Research in Child Development Monograph.

Poole, M. S., & Billingsley, J. (this volume). The structuring of dyadic decisions. In D. Brinberg & J. Jaccard (Eds), *Dyadic decision making*, New York: Springer-Verlag.

Pruitt, D. G., & Kimmel, M. J. (1977). Twenty years of experimental gaming: Critique, synthesis, and suggestions for the future. *Annual Review of Psychology, 28*, 363–392.

Pruitt, D. G., & Rubin, J. Z. (1986). *Social conflict*. Chicago: Random House.

Rubin, J. Z., & Brown, B. R. (1975). *The social psychology of bargaining and negotiation*. New York: Academic Press.

Runkel, P. J., & McGrath, J. E. (1972). *Research on human behavior: A systematic guide to method*. New York: Holt, Rinehart, and Winston.

Scanzoni J. (this volume). Joint decision making in the contemporary sexually primary relationship. In D. Brinberg & J. Jaccard (Eds), *Dyadic decision making*, New York: Springer-Verlag.

Sillars, A., & Kalblesch, P. J. (this volume). Implicit and explicit decision-making styles in couples. In D. Brinberg & J. Jaccard (Eds), *Dyadic decision making*, New York: Springer-Verlag.

Steiner, I. D. (1972). *Group process and productivity*, New York: Academic Press.

Terman, L. M., Buttenwieser, P., Ferguson, L. W., Johnson, W. B., & Wilson, D. P. (1938). *Psychological factors in marital happiness*. New York: McGraw-Hill.

Thibaut, J. W., & Kelley, H. H. (1959). *The social psychology of groups*. New York: Wiley.

Troutman, C. M., & Shanteau, J. (this volume). Consumer information integration in husband-wife decision making about health-care services. In D. Brinberg & J. Jaccard (Eds), *Dyadic decision making*, New York: Springer-Verlag.

Trujillo, N. O. (1981). Relational communication: A comparison of coding systems. *Communication Monographs, 48*, 91–105.

Von Neumann, J., & Morgenstern, O. (1947). *Theory of games and economic behavior*. Princeton, NJ: Princeton University Press.

Webb, E. J., Campbell, D. T., Schwartz, R. D., & Sechrest, L. (1966). *Unobtrusive measures: Non-reactive research in the social sciences*. Chicago: Rand-McNally.

Weiss, R., Birchler, G., and Vincent, J. (1974). Contractual models for negotiation training in marital dyads. *Journal of Marriage and the Family, 36*, 1–11.

Wilder, C. (1979). The Palo Alto group: Difficulties and directions of the interactional views of communication research. *Human Communications Research, 5*, 171–186.

Yin, R. K. (1984). *Case study research*. Beverly Hills, CA: Sage Publications.

Author Index

Subject Index

Lightning Source UK Ltd.
Milton Keynes UK
UKOW03f0841091013

218712UK00003B/60/P